First World War
and Army of Occupation
War Diary
France, Belgium and Germany

4 DIVISION
Headquarters, Branches and Services
General Staff
1 July 1916 - 31 July 1916

WO95/1445

The Naval & Military Press Ltd
www.nmarchive.com
Published in association with The National Archives

Published by

The Naval & Military Press Ltd

Unit 10 Ridgewood Industrial Park,

Uckfield, East Sussex,

TN22 5QE England

Tel: +44 (0) 1825 749494

www.naval-military-press.com

www.nmarchive.com

This diary has been reprinted in facsimile from the original. Any imperfections are inevitably reproduced and the quality may fall short of modern type and cartographic standards.

© Crown Copyright
Images reproduced by permission of The National Archives, London, England, 2015.

Contents

Document type	Place/Title	Date From	Date To
Heading	4th Division War Diaries. General Staff July 1916		
Heading	H.Q. General Staff 1916 July To 1916 Dec		
Heading	4th Division War General Staff November To December 1916		
Heading	General Staff 4th Division November 1916 Appendices Attached. Relief of French.		
Miscellaneous	Officer In Charge A. G's Office At Base	05/12/1916	05/12/1916
Miscellaneous	General Staff 4th Division.		
Miscellaneous	Preliminary Instructions Regarding The Relief Of Portion Of The 20th French Corps By The 4th Division	28/11/1916	28/11/1916
Miscellaneous	Appendix 'A'		
Miscellaneous			
Miscellaneous	Agreement		
Miscellaneous	Agreement Regarding The Relief Of The XXTH And Part Of The VI French Army Corps By The British	30/11/1916	30/11/1916
Heading	General Staff 4th Division December 1916		
War Diary	Oisemont	01/12/1916	09/12/1916
War Diary	Treux	04/12/1916	07/12/1916
War Diary	B. 4.c. 2.2. (P.C. Monnet).	08/12/1916	09/12/1916
War Diary	P.C.le Duc. (Maurepas)	10/12/1916	31/12/1916
War Diary	Chipilly	31/12/1916	31/12/1916
Operation(al) Order(s)	4th Division Operation Order No 83	03/12/1916	03/12/1916
Operation(al) Order(s)	4th Division Operation Order No 89	10/12/1916	10/12/1916
Operation(al) Order(s)	4th Division Operation Order No 90	14/12/1916	14/12/1916
Operation(al) Order(s)	4th Division Operation Order No 91	19/12/1916	19/12/1916
Operation(al) Order(s)	4th Division Operation Order No 92	21/12/1916	21/12/1916
Miscellaneous			
Miscellaneous	Area No.		
Miscellaneous	Casualties 4th Division For Period 1st To 31st Decr 1916		
Map	IVth Div. Trench Map. Scale 1:10,000		
Miscellaneous	Record Plex Map Which Were Made at Le Duc		
Heading	4th Division War December General Staff October 1916		
Heading	General Staff 4th Division October 1916		
War Diary	Corbie	01/10/1916	08/10/1916
War Diary	Citadel	08/10/1916	10/10/1916
War Diary	A10.b.3.8	10/10/1916	11/10/1916
War Diary	Briqueterie (Bernafay Wood) Somme.	12/10/1916	12/10/1916
War Diary	A.10.b.3.8	13/10/1916	13/10/1916
War Diary	Briqueterie (Bernafay Wood) Somme.	14/10/1916	14/10/1916
War Diary	A. 10.b. 3. 8	15/10/1916	25/10/1916
War Diary	Citadel (F. 21. b)	25/10/1916	27/10/1916
War Diary	Treux	27/10/1916	29/10/1916
War Diary	Treux Hallencourt.	30/10/1916	30/10/1916
Miscellaneous	Operation On 12 Oct Appendix A B C D E F G H & M		
Miscellaneous	Narrative	12/10/1916	12/10/1916
Map	Fourth Army Trench Map		
Miscellaneous	Appx B		
Operation(al) Order(s)	XIV Corps Operation Order No 70	09/10/1916	09/10/1916
Operation(al) Order(s)	Reference XIV Corps Operation Order No 70	10/10/1916	10/10/1916

Type	Description	Date	Date
Operation(al) Order(s)	4th Division Operation Order No. 67	10/10/1916	10/10/1916
Map	British Trenches In Red		
Map	App B		
Operation(al) Order(s)	Ref 4th Div Operation Order No 67 The Hour Of 300 Will Be 2.5 P.m	11/10/1916	11/10/1916
Operation(al) Order(s)	4th Divisional Artillery Operation Order No. 17	10/10/1916	10/10/1916
Miscellaneous	4th Division Warning Order	01/10/1916	01/10/1916
Miscellaneous	Reference 4th Division Warning Order Dated 1st October 1916	04/10/1916	04/10/1916
Operation(al) Order(s)	4th Division Operation Order No 65	06/10/1916	06/10/1916
Operation(al) Order(s)	4th Division Operation Order No 66	08/10/1916	08/10/1916
Operation(al) Order(s)	4th Divisional Artillery Operation Order No 18	10/10/1916	10/10/1916
Operation(al) Order(s)	4th Divisional Artillery (Right Artillery). Operation Order No 19	11/10/1916	11/10/1916
Operation(al) Order(s)	4th Divisional Artillery (Right Artillery) Operation Order No 20	11/10/1916	11/10/1916
Operation(al) Order(s)	4th Division Operation No 69	13/10/1916	13/10/1916
Miscellaneous	Operation Of 18 October		
War Diary	Briqueterie (Bernafay Wood) Somme.	18/10/1916	18/10/1916
Miscellaneous	XIV Corps Warning Order	15/10/1916	15/10/1916
Operation(al) Order(s)	XIV Corps Operation Order No 73	16/10/1916	16/10/1916
Miscellaneous	C Form (Duplicate). Messages And Signals		
Operation(al) Order(s)	Amendment To XIV Corps Operation Order No 73	17/10/1916	17/10/1916
Map	Fourth Army Trench Map C		
Miscellaneous	4th Division Warning Order		
Operation(al) Order(s)	4th Divisional Artillery (Right Artillery). Operation Order No. 23	17/10/1916	17/10/1916
Miscellaneous	Table Of Tasks For Right Artillery		
Operation(al) Order(s)	10th Infantry Brigade Operation Order No 78	14/10/1916	14/10/1916
Operation(al) Order(s)	4th Division Operation Order No 70	16/10/1916	16/10/1916
Operation(al) Order(s)	4th Division Operation Order No 71	16/10/1916	16/10/1916
Miscellaneous	10th Bde	17/10/1916	17/10/1916
Operation(al) Order(s)	4th Division Operation Order No 72	17/10/1916	17/10/1916
Operation(al) Order(s)	Reference 4th Division Operation No 72		
Operation(al) Order(s)	Supplementary Order to 4th Divn O.O. No 72	17/10/1916	17/10/1916
Operation(al) Order(s)	Amendment To 4th Division Operation Order No 72	17/10/1916	17/10/1916
Map	Approx. Situation Map Secret		
Miscellaneous			
Miscellaneous	Operation 23 Oct		
War Diary	Briqueterie (Bernafay Wood) Somme	23/10/1916	23/10/1916
Operation(al) Order(s)	XIV Corps Operation Order No 76	20/10/1916	20/10/1916
Operation(al) Order(s)	Note To Operation Order No 76	20/10/1916	20/10/1916
Map	XIV Corps Situation Map		
Operation(al) Order(s)	4th Division Warning Operation Order 74	21/10/1916	21/10/1916
Map	Appdx. Situation Map X.A.I. British Trenches Red.		
Operation(al) Order(s)	4th Divisional Artillery (Right Artillery). Operation Order No 26	21/10/1916	21/10/1916
Operation(al) Order(s)	4th Divisional Artillery (Right Artillery). Warning-Operation Order No. 27	21/10/1916	21/10/1916
Miscellaneous	Appendix To Warning Order		
Miscellaneous	Amendments And Addition	23/10/1916	23/10/1916
Miscellaneous	2nd Amendment	23/10/1916	23/10/1916
Miscellaneous	3rd. Amendment	23/10/1916	23/10/1916
Operation(al) Order(s)	4th Divisional Artillery (Right Artillery) Warning-Operation Order No 27	21/10/1916	21/10/1916

Type	Description	Date From	Date To
Operation(al) Order(s)	4th Divisional Artillery (Right Artillery) Operation Order No 28	22/10/1916	22/10/1916
Miscellaneous	Table Of Tasks for Right Artillery on 23rd. instant.	22/10/1916	22/10/1916
Operation(al) Order(s)	4th Division Operation Order No 73	18/10/1916	18/10/1916
Operation(al) Order(s)	4th Division Operation Order No 75	22/10/1916	22/10/1916
Map			
Operation(al) Order(s)	4th Division Operation Order No 76	22/10/1916	22/10/1916
Miscellaneous	XIV Corps No. S. 82/80	23/10/1916	23/10/1916
Operation(al) Order(s)	4th Division Operation Order No 77	24/10/1916	24/10/1916
Operation(al) Order(s)	Amendment To 4th Division Operation Order No 77	24/10/1916	24/10/1916
Operation(al) Order(s)	4th Division Operation Order No 78	26/10/1916	26/10/1916
Miscellaneous			
Operation(al) Order(s)	4th Division Operation Order No 79	28/10/1916	28/10/1916
Operation(al) Order(s)	Amendment to 4th Division Operation Order No. 78		
Miscellaneous	XIV Corps. 4th Army Long.	29/10/1916	29/10/1916
Miscellaneous	Casualties For Period 1st-31st October 1916	31/10/1916	31/10/1916
Map	No 9 Squadron		
Miscellaneous			
Map	Approx Situation Map		
Heading	4th Division War Diaries General Staff August September 1916		
Heading	General Staff 4th Division August 1916		
War Diary	Convent St Sixte	01/08/1916	02/08/1916
War Diary	St Sixte	02/08/1916	21/08/1916
War Diary	Poperinghe	21/08/1916	24/08/1916
War Diary	Reninghelst	24/08/1916	31/08/1916
Miscellaneous	Gas Attack Night 8/9th August	08/08/1916	08/08/1916
Miscellaneous	Notes On Report By 4th Division Of The Gas Attack On The Night Of August 8/9th 1916	08/08/1916	08/08/1916
Miscellaneous	Corps Commander's Remarks On Report By 4th Division Of The Gas Attack August 8/9th	08/08/1916	08/08/1916
Miscellaneous	4th Division No GGG 23/16	13/08/1916	13/08/1916
Miscellaneous	Report On Gas Attack On The 11th Infantry Brigade 8th August 1916	08/08/1916	08/08/1916
Miscellaneous	Notes On The Attack		
Miscellaneous	Notes On The Attack	12/08/1916	12/08/1916
Miscellaneous	Diary of Events Brigade Headquarters. Appendix "A".		
Miscellaneous	4th Division No GGG. 23/16	08/08/1916	08/08/1916
Miscellaneous	Report On Casualties In Gas Attack	12/08/1916	12/08/1916
Operation(al) Order(s)	4th Division Operation Order No 48	02/08/1916	02/08/1916
Operation(al) Order(s)	4th Division Operation Order No 49	09/08/1916	09/08/1916
Operation(al) Order(s)	4th Division Operation Order No 50	10/08/1916	10/08/1916
Miscellaneous	4th Division	15/08/1916	15/08/1916
Miscellaneous			
Miscellaneous	4th Div. No. GGG/66/3	16/08/1916	16/08/1916
Miscellaneous	10th Infantry Brigade	17/08/1916	17/08/1916
Miscellaneous	4th Div. No. GGG/66/3	17/08/1916	17/08/1916
Operation(al) Order(s)	4th Division Operation Order No 51	17/08/1916	17/08/1916
Operation(al) Order(s)	4th Divn Preliminary Operation Order No 52	19/08/1916	19/08/1916
Operation(al) Order(s)	Reference 4th Division Operation Order No. 52 And 53	19/08/1916	19/08/1916
Operation(al) Order(s)	4th Division Operation Order No 53	19/08/1916	19/08/1916
Operation(al) Order(s)	4th Division Operation Order No 54	20/08/1916	20/08/1916
Miscellaneous			
Miscellaneous	4th Division No GGG 23/7	27/08/1916	27/08/1916
Miscellaneous			
Operation(al) Order(s)	4th Division Operation Order No 55	28/08/1916	28/08/1916

Miscellaneous	Appendix "A"		
Miscellaneous	4th Div Q.R. 1297	29/08/1916	29/08/1916
Miscellaneous	Casualties 4th Division From 1st To 31st Aug/1916	31/08/1916	31/08/1916
Heading	General Staff 4th Division September 1916		
War Diary	Reninghelst	01/09/1916	10/09/1916
War Diary	Esquelbecq	10/09/1916	18/09/1916
War Diary	Villers Bocage	23/09/1916	25/09/1916
War Diary	Corbie	25/09/1916	30/09/1916
Operation(al) Order(s)	4th Division Operation Order No 53	01/09/1916	01/09/1916
Miscellaneous	Appendix "A"		
Operation(al) Order(s)	4th Division Operation Order No 57	06/09/1916	06/09/1916
Miscellaneous	Appendix		
Operation(al) Order(s)	4th Division Operation Order No 58	10/09/1916	10/09/1916
Miscellaneous			
Operation(al) Order(s)	4th Division Operation Order No 59	14/09/1916	14/09/1916
Miscellaneous	2nd Army G 259 10/9/16		
Miscellaneous	Programme of Move Of Infantry Brigade And Artillery Brigade To Dunkirk		
Miscellaneous	4th Division No GGG 101	15/09/1916	15/09/1916
Miscellaneous	4th Division "G"	14/09/1916	14/09/1916
Operation(al) Order(s)	4th Division Operation Order No 60	16/09/1916	16/09/1916
Miscellaneous	Programme Of Move Of 4th Division (Less Artillery) VIA Calais	16/09/1916	16/09/1916
Miscellaneous	Table "D". 4th Division (Less Artillery)	16/09/1916	16/09/1916
Miscellaneous	4th Div. No Q.R.1320	15/09/1916	15/09/1916
Miscellaneous	Move Of 4th Division		
Operation(al) Order(s)	4th Division Operation Order No 61	23/09/1916	23/09/1916
Operation(al) Order(s)	4th Division Operation Order No 62	24/09/1916	24/09/1916
Operation(al) Order(s)	4th Division Operation Order No 63	28/09/1916	28/09/1916
Operation(al) Order(s)	4th Division Operation Order No 64	29/09/1916	29/09/1916
Miscellaneous	10th Infantry Brigade	30/09/1916	30/09/1916
Miscellaneous	Casualties-4th Division-1st-30th September 1916	01/09/1916	01/09/1916
Heading	4th Division War Diaries General Staff July 1916		
Map	France		
Map	France Edition 2 B		
Miscellaneous	Glossary		
Miscellaneous	Trench Map.		
Map	Hebuterne		
Map			
Miscellaneous	Glossary		
Miscellaneous	Trench Map Hebuterne		
Miscellaneous	Glossary		
Miscellaneous	Trench Map		
Miscellaneous	Appendix "A"		
Map	France		
Miscellaneous	Glossary		
Miscellaneous	Trench Map		
Heading	4th Div. G.S. July 1916		
Heading	General Staff 4th Division July 1916		
Heading	Appendices Are Separate		
War Diary	Bertrancourt	01/07/1916	22/07/1916
War Diary	Beauval	22/07/1916	23/07/1916
War Diary	Chateau Couthove	23/07/1916	27/07/1916
War Diary	Sainte Sixte	27/07/1916	31/07/1916
Miscellaneous	Appendix "A"		
Miscellaneous	The Following Appendices Are Attached		

Type	Description	Date From	Date To
Miscellaneous	Operations On 1st July, 1916 Appendix "A"	01/07/1916	01/07/1916
Heading	G. L. 4th Division July 1916 Appendix "B" (1)		
Miscellaneous	Appendix "B" (1) 1st July 1916	01/07/1916	01/07/1916
Heading	4th Div. G. L July 1916 Appendix "D" (1)		
Miscellaneous	4th Divn Q.R. 1150/5		
Miscellaneous	Table Moves By Units		
Miscellaneous	Table Of Moves By Units		
Heading	G. L. 4th Division July 1916 Appendix "F".		
Map			
Miscellaneous	Appendix "D" (2)		
Miscellaneous	Trench Map		
Miscellaneous	12th Brigade During Advance		
Miscellaneous	10th Brigade		
Miscellaneous	11th Brigade 2nd Objective		
Miscellaneous	Appendix "F" 11th Brigade 1st Objective		
Heading	4th Division G.S. July 1916 Appendix "G"		
Miscellaneous	Appendix "G" 4th Div. Arty B. 17	18/07/1916	18/07/1916
Heading	G.S. 4th Division July 1916 Appendix "I"		
Miscellaneous	Communications during the action of July 1st '16	01/07/1916	01/07/1916
Heading	4th Division G.S. July 1916 Appendix "J"		
Map	Trench Map No. 6		
Miscellaneous	Reference		
Heading	G.S. 4th Division July 1916 Appendix "K"		
Miscellaneous	Casualties 1/7/16	01/07/1916	01/07/1916
Heading	4th Division G.S. July 1916 Appendix "L"		
Miscellaneous	Fourth Army	06/07/1916	06/07/1916
Miscellaneous	4th Division Q.	07/07/1916	07/07/1916
Miscellaneous	4th Division.	07/07/1916	07/07/1916
Miscellaneous	4th. Div. No. Q. C. 179	10/07/1916	10/07/1916
Miscellaneous	4th Division.	10/07/1916	10/07/1916
Miscellaneous	Small British Airship. Dirigeable Anglais Petit.		
Miscellaneous	Headquarters, 4th Division.	20/07/1916	20/07/1916
Miscellaneous	4th. Div. Q.C. 185	25/07/1916	25/07/1916
Miscellaneous	2nd Divn		
Miscellaneous	4th. Div. Q.C. 182	20/07/1916	20/07/1916
Miscellaneous	VIIIth. Corps, Q.S. 60	12/07/1916	12/07/1916
Miscellaneous	4th Division-Billeting List	24/07/1916	24/07/1916
Miscellaneous	XIV Corps No. Q.Z./101	24/07/1916	24/07/1916
Operation(al) Order(s)	Second Army Routine Order No. 310-Special Stores		
Miscellaneous	Held in reading for incoming division		
Miscellaneous	Required From New Area.		
Miscellaneous	A. A. Q. M. G. 4 Division.	26/07/1916	26/07/1916
Miscellaneous	4th Divn Q.R. 1150/5		
Miscellaneous	Table Showing allocation of units to trains and Horse of Departure	24/07/1916	24/07/1916
Miscellaneous	Table Showing allocation of units to trains and Horse of Departure		
Miscellaneous	Timetable Of Marches For 4th and 48th Divisions.		
Miscellaneous	4th Division.		
Miscellaneous	Table shewing allocation of units to trains and Hours of Departure.		
Miscellaneous			
Miscellaneous	4th Division.		
Miscellaneous	Timetable Marches For 4th And 48th Divisions.		
Miscellaneous	Instructions As Regards Transport, Roads, Rockets, Grenade Carriers, Packs, Tents, Very Lights, S. A. A.	21/06/1916	21/06/1916

Miscellaneous	Timetable Of Ammunition, Stores, etc.	13/06/1916	13/06/1916
Miscellaneous	4th Div. Q.C. /157	24/06/1916	24/06/1916
Miscellaneous	4th. Div. Q. C. 166/2	28/06/1916	28/06/1916
Miscellaneous	Water Supply Report VIII Corps.		
Miscellaneous	Forward Pumping Scheme	07/06/1916	07/06/1916
Miscellaneous	Water Supply Report. VIII Corps Area.	06/06/1916	06/06/1916
Heading	4th Division G.S. July 1916 Appendix "M"		
Miscellaneous	Casualties-4th Division-1st to 31st July 1916	01/07/1916	01/07/1916
Miscellaneous	G.S. 4th Division July 1916		
Miscellaneous	Alteration In Administrative Arrangements.	28/06/1916	28/06/1916
Operation(al) Order(s)	4th Division Operation Order No. 40	04/07/1916	04/07/1916
Operation(al) Order(s)	4th Division Operation Order No. 41	08/07/1916	08/07/1916
Operation(al) Order(s)	4th Division Operation Order No. 42	13/07/1916	13/07/1916
Operation(al) Order(s)	4th Division Operation Order No. 43	19/07/1916	19/07/1916
Operation(al) Order(s)	4th Division Operation Order No. 44	20/07/1916	20/07/1916
Operation(al) Order(s)	4th Division Operation Order No. 45	21/07/1916	21/07/1916
Operation(al) Order(s)	4th Division Operation Order No. 46	23/07/1916	23/07/1916
Operation(al) Order(s)	4th Division Operation Order No: 47	25/07/1916	25/07/1916
Miscellaneous	4th Division No. GGG/19/4	27/07/1916	27/07/1916

4th Division
War Diary
General Staff

July 1916

H.Q. GENERAL STAFF.
1916 JULY TO 1916 DEC.

1445

H.Q. GENERAL STAFF.
1916 JULY TO 1916 DEC

4th Division

War Diaries

General Staff

November + December

1915

GENERAL STAFF

4th DIVISION

NOVEMBER 1 9 1 6

Appendices attached :-   Relief of French.

Officer in Charge,
    A.G's Office at Base.

        Herewith War Diary, General Staff, 4th Division (with appendices) for November 1916.

                                            Major General,
5th December 1916.   Commanding 4th Division.

WAR DIARY - GENERAL STAFF, 4TH DIVISION.

1ST - 30TH NOVEMBER 1916.

Division at rest.

Units carrying out training etc,.

28TH NOVEMBER 1916.

Preliminary instructions issued regarding the relief of portions of XXth French Corps by 4th Division.

The front to be taken over by the XVth Corps extends from the BOUCHAVESNES - MOISLAINS Road exclusive to the Cross Roads at U.14.b.9.9.

This front will be taken over by the 33rd Division on the right and the 4th Division on the left.

The 4th Division front will be taken over by the 10th Brigade and 12th Brigade on the right and left respectively.

11th Brigade will be in Divisional Reserve.

12th Brigade will carry out their relief on the night 7/8th December and the 10th Brigade on the night 8/9th December.

SECRET -
****

Copy No: 17

Reference attached Map &
Sheet 3 N.W. Europe.

PRELIMINARY INSTRUCTIONS REGARDING THE RELIEF OF PORTION OF THE 20th FRENCH CORPS BY THE 4th DIVISION

28th November 1916

1. The front to be taken over by the XV Corps extends from the BOUCHAVESNES - MOISLAINS road exclusive to the cross roads at U.14.b.9.9. This front will be taken over by the 33rd Division on the right and by the 4th Division on the left.

    The attached map shows the XV Corps area and the dividing lines between 4th and 33rd Divisions in the front trenches.

2. The 4th Division front will be taken over by the 10th and 12th Infantry Brigades, the 10th Brigade on the right and the 12th Brigade on the left.

    The 11th Infantry Brigade will be in Divisional Reserve.

    The 12th Infantry Brigade will carry out their relief on the night 7/8th December.

    The 10th Infantry Brigade will carry out their relief on the night 8/9th December.

3. The fronts to be taken over by the 10th and 12th Infantry Brigades are each held at present by 3 French Battalions.

    2 Battalions in the front line and 1 in local reserve (as shown in circles on attached map).

    In addition, the French have one battalion about FREGICOURT in reserve.

4. The preliminary movements of Brigade Groups are shown in attached Appendix "A".

5. Field Artillery reliefs will commence on the night December 11/12th. Further details will be issued.

Issued at 6pm

Major.
General Staff., 4th Division.

Copies to :- 10th, 11th, 12th Inf. Bdes.   21st ___ rks.R.
     4th Div Arty.
     -:- Engineers.
     -:- Signal Coy.
     -:- "Q" (4 Copies)
    A.P.M.
    A.D.M.S.

APPENDIX 'A'.

Unit & date	From	To	Remarks
2nd December Transport { 10th Inf.Bde Group. / 12th Inf.Bde Group.	Present area	ARGOEUVRES / ST SAUVEUR.	By road.
3rd December Transport 11th Inf. Bde Group.	Present area.	ARGOEUVRES	By road
3rd December Transport { 10th Inf.Bde Group. / 12th Inf.Bde Group.	ARGOEUVRES / ST SAUVEUR.	XV Corps area.	By road.
3rd December Personnel { 10th Inf.Bde Group. / 12th Inf.Bde Group.	Present area	MORLANCOURT. / SAILLY-LE-SEC. VAUX.	By road.
4th December Transport 11th Inf.Bde Group.	ARGOEUVRES.	SAILLY-LE-SEC. VAUX.	By road.
4th December Personnel 11th Inf.Bde Group.	Present area.	SAILLY-LE-SEC. VAUX.	By train.

Unit and date	From	To	Remarks
4th December			
12th Inf. Bde Group.	MORLANCOURT	BRONFAY or vicinity.	By road.
4th December			
10th Inf. Bde Group.	SAILLY-LE-SEC. VAUX.	MORLANCOURT	By road.
6th December			
12th Inf. Bde Group.	BRONFAY	Forward area	}
10th Inf. Bde Group.	MORLANCOURT	BRONFAY or vicinity	} By road.
11th Inf. Bde Group.	SAILLY-LE-SEC. VAUX.	MORLANCOURT	}
7th December			
12th Inf. Bde.	Forward area.	Trenches.	}
10th Inf. Bde.	BRONFAY	Forward area	} By road.
11th Inf. Bde.	MORLANCOURT	BRONFAY or vicinity	}
8th December			
10th Inf. Bde.	Forward area.	Trenches	

Note: The attached document, 4th Division No.GGG/156, dated 30th November 1916, Agreement regarding the relief of the XXth and part of the VI French Army Corps by the British, is Appendix 50 to the War Diary of the C.R.E., 8th Division, for March 1918, and has been detached from the latter diary.

A.C.C.

Secret. C.R.E.

A G R E E M E N T
****

REGARDING THE RELIEF OF THE XXTH AND PART OF THE VI

FRENCH ARMY CORPS BY THE BRITISH.

****

Agreement regarding the relief of the
XXTH and part of the VI French Army Corps
by the BRITISH.
****

Reference Plan Directeur
1/20,000.

The XX French Corps and the 127th Division, VI French Corps will be relieved by a part of the XIV and the whole of the XV British Corps as follows :-

I. INFANTRY.

The XIV British Corps (Guard Division) after having relieved the right of the IX French Corps during the nights of the 2/3 and 3/4 December, will relieve during the night of the 6/7 with 2 battalions the 1st French Infantry Regiment which has 2 Bns. in the front line and one in support. This Regt. holds that part of the XX Corps Sector which lies between the present boundary between the IX and XX French Corps and the line Pt. 747 in the PFALZ Trench - fork of the roads at the Southern exit of SAILLY - MOUCHOIR Wood (exclusive) - cross roads at BOIS de la HAIE - COMBLES Cemetery - 60 c.m. trolley line in the COMBLES Ravine - SAVERNAKE Wood.

The relief will be completed by 6 a.m. 7th December (1) From that time :-

(i) The boundary between the XIV British Corps and the XX French Corps will be the line above mentioned, which will constitute from the 8th the boundary between the XIV and XV British Corps.

(ii) The XIV British Corps will take over the artillery barrages on the front of the sector thus handed over (2)

English
(1). The Headquarters of the/units of the XIV British Corps in the neighbourhood of the XX French Corps will be as follows. Headquarters of the Regt. near the BOIS du MOUCHOIR (not the same as that of the Brigade on the left of the XV Corps). The Headquarters of the Brigade at COMBLES. Headquarters of the Division at GUILLEMONT. (H.Qs.No.9)

(2). In the event of the state of the atmosphere not permitting the artillery of the XIV British Corps to carry out the necessary registration the G.O.C. Guards Division will arrange with the G.O.C. 39th French Division to take over during the necessary period the barrages with his artillery.

/The

The XV British Corps will relieve successively from left to right (N. to S.) the remainder of the XX French Corps and the 128th Div. of the VI French Corps during the 4 nights from the 7th to the 11th December. One Bde. of infantry (4 battalions etc.) will relieve as follows :- On each of the 4 nights a section of the front of these two Army Corps and of the troops billeted behind them.

A. <u>Night of the 7/8 December.</u>

One Brigade of the 4th British Division will relieve troops of the 39th Div. occupying the sector between the boundary South of the XIV British Corps and the actual boundary of the 39th and 11th Divs. that is to say, 4 Bns. of infantry (2 in the front line, 1 in support, and 1 in reserve) in addition to R.E.Coys. Headquarters of the Bde. BOIS de MOUCHOIR.

The command of the front thus relieved will be handed over by the G.O.C. 39th French Div. to the G.O.C. 4th British Div. on the 8th December in the morning at his Headquarters in the BOIS LOUAGE (P.C.MONNET).

B. <u>Night of the 8/9 December.</u>

One Brigade of the 4th British Div. will relieve troops of the 11th French Div. in the sector between the actual boundary of the 39th and 11th French Div. and the line Pt. 281 on the road from RANCOURT to SAILLY-SAILLISEL - LE PRIEZ Farm inclusive - cross roads East of MAUREPAS (that is to say 4 bns. of infantry, 2 in the front line, 1 in support and 1 in reserve) which will constitute provisionally the boundary between the 2 divisions (4th and 33rd) of the XV British Corps. Bde.H.Qrs. P.C.0066.

The G.O.C. of the French 11th Div. will hand over the front thus relieved to the G.O.C. 4th British Division on the 9th in the morning at his Headquarters in the BOIS LOUAGE (P.C.MONNET).

The necessary telephone communication between the H.Qrs of the Brigade at 0066 and that of the Division at the BOIS LOUAGE will be previously established by the XX French Army Corps.

C. **Night of the 9/10 December.**

One Brigade of the 33rd British Div. will relieve the troops occupying the sector situated between the provisional boundary mentioned above between the 4th and 33rd British Divisions and the present boundary between the XX and the VI French Corps, that is to say 4 Bns. of infantry (2 in the front line, 1 in support and 1 in reserve in the PETIT BOIS in the area of the 127th Div. which will have to be relieved the following night). Plus 2 R.E. Coys. Brigade Headquarters P.C.de la CRANIERE, near LE FOREST.

The G.O.C.11th Division (1) will hand over the command of the front to the G.O.C.33rd British Division on the morning of the 10th December at the present Headquarters of the VI French Army Corps 1200 metres S.W. of MAUREPAS (P.C.BONNET).

The telephonic communication between the H.Qrs. of the Bde and LE CRANIERE and that of the Div. (P.C.BONNET) will be established beforehand by the VI French Army Corps.

D. **Night of the 10/11 December.**

One Brigade of the 33rd British Div. will relieve the troops occupying the sector lying between the present boundary of the XX and VI French Corps and the new boundary of the XV British Corps and that of the VI French Corps, that is to say 4 Bns. of infantry (3 Bns. in the front line, 1 in support) plus 2 R.E. Coys. Bde H.Qrs. at P.C. du PETIT BOIS (actually P.C. of the 127th French Div.

The G.O.C.127th French Division acting for the G.O.C. VI French Corps will hand over the front thus relieved to the G.O.C. 33rd British Division at his H.Qrs. (P.C.Bonnet) on the morning of the 11th December.

---

(1). These H.Qrs. is at a point 800 metres S.W. of MAUREPAS (P.C.HUOT).

II. ARTILLERY.

I. Field Artillery.

The relief of the Field Artillery of the XX French Corps and the 127th Div. of the VI French Corps by that of the XV British Corps will be carried out between the 11th and 14th December.

A. On each of the nights 11/12th, 12/13th and 13/14th one battery of each group of the XX French Corps and of the 127th French Div. will be relieved by a Field ~~Artillery~~ battery of the XV British Corps.

B. The evening before the departure of each French battery half the battery's ammunition will be sent back to the depot of it's Corps. The remaining ammunition will be sent back next day, i.e. the day of departure of the battery.

C. British batteries which replace French batteries will bring down ammunition for 1 day's fire, the evening before relief and for one day on the day of relief.

D. The Field Artillery of the XV British Corps will attach from the 8th December 1 Officer to each Group Commander of French Artillery and one officer to each Commander of Divisional Artillery.

II. Heavy Artillery.

The relief of the French Heavy Artillery will take place from now on to the 13th December according to a programme which has been agreed upon between the Artillery Commanders concerned and which has been approved of by the superior authorities of the 2 Armies.

III. Artillery telephonic communication.

All telephone lines now laid will remain. Any further lines considered necessary for either Field or Heavy Artillery will be laid by the XV British Corps.

III. BILLETING AREAS AND MOVEMENTS OF TROOPS DURING RELIEF.

I. Billeting Areas.

The camps and billets belonging to the area of the XX French Corps will be placed at the disposal of the XV British Corps from the morning of the 4th December as follows :-

Ravin de la Halte de MAUREPAS. 120 tents (2 Bns.).

MARICOURT. Room for 500 men (Area of the XIX French Corps).

Camp 20 (1600 men) Near MARICOURT.

Camp 16 (1600 men) and 107 (2400 men) near Farm BRONFAY).
BRAY (2500 men).

Camp 117 (1600 men) to the West of BRAY.

Camp 14 (3400 men) In the BOIS GHESSAIRE.

The VI French Corps from the same date and the period of the relief will place room for 1300 men in Camp 17 near SUZANNE at the disposal of the XX French Corps.

The Camps and billets of the XX French Corps other than those mentioned above situated in the new area of the XV British Corps will be handed over to the authorities of this Corps for the purpose of the carrying out of the reliefs/up to and the latest the 16th December. Camp 21 near MARICOURT, Camp 12 in the BOIS de CELESTINE and the billet of CHIPILLY will be handed over last of all.

Tents (with the exception of 120 tents mentioned first of all) and the shelters in the Ravin of MAUREPAS between the Halte of MAUREPAS and the BOIS de L'ANGLE. (1). will remain as well as that part of the ravine at the exclusive disposal of the French troops detailed for the clearing/the battlefield during the whole period of their work.

---

(1) And of the shelters for 1 Coy. at COMBLES, 1 Coy. at FREGICOURT 1 Coy. at LE PREEZ Farm, 2 Coys. at LE FOREST, that is to say a total of 5 Coys. which will be provisionally employed in the clearing of the advanced sector of the XX French Corps area.

II. Movements in relief.

The evening before their entry into the sector British Infantry (about a Bde.) will be billeted partly in the ravine of the Halte of MAUREPAS, partly in MARICOURT and Camp 20.

British mounted troops will come into the area within any half way spot at the Halte of MAUREPAS.

Troops of the XX French Corps on relief will reform in the camps at their disposal in the area MARICOURT, SUZANNE, BRAY (Camp 21, 2800 men, Camp 17 1200 men, and the locality of BRAY) from which they will be immediately removed by motors to their final camps and billets. Mounted troops of the XX French Corps will reform in the same camps and billets and will remain there 24 hours before being sent to the rear. The movements of relief of the VI French Corps will be arranged by that Corps.

III. Routes during the relief.

During the relief that is to say commencing from the 5th Decr.

1. All movements towards the front will take place by the road BRAY passing that place by the North, BRONFAY Farm, MARICOURT, HARDECOURT, MAUREPAS.

2. All movements from front to rear by the road MAUREPAS - Ferme ROUGE - HILL 131 - MARICOURT - SUZANNE - BRAY.

A traffic control will be carried out by the VI and XX French Corps up to mid-day 11th December and after that time by the VI French Corps and the XV British Corps, in their own particular areas.

From the 5th December British police will be attached to French control posts for road patrol work.

IV. **Miscellaneous.**

Officers of the Staff of the XIV and XV British Corps can from today move about in the areas of the XX and VI French Corps and ask any information that would be useful for their future work from anybody qualified to give it.

Preliminary reconnaissances by units which should take place either two nights or the night before the entry into the sector should be arranged between the G.Os.C. of the Divisions concerned.

The Staff of the XV British Corps can quarter 10 officers at ETINEHEM from the 1st December and can quarter itself as a whole from the 7th December in this place without turning out any of the personnel of the Sixth French Army or of the XX French Corps who are there already.

IV. **HANDING OVER OF COMMAND.**

I. Commanders of French units - in the infantry from the Coy. to the Bde. - in the artillery from the batteries to groups - all Divisions and Corps will hand over to the O.Cs. units who replace them the command as soon as the last fraction of their unit has been relieved.

An officer of each French unit relieved will remain for 24 hours with the O.C. of the corresponding British unit.

II. The handing over command to Divisions will be carried out on the days mentioned in para.1. From the moment that a report has been received that the relief of the infantry has been completed which ought to be done each day by 6 a.m.

An officer of the General Staff of each of the 11th, 39th and 127th French Divs. will remain with the General Staff of the British Division concerned for 24 hours.

III. In the same manner the G.O.C. of the XX French Corps will hand over to the G.O.C. of the XV British Corps on the 10th December. The former immediately on handing over proceed to ETINEHEM to hand over any useful information he has.

The Chief of the Staff of the XX French Corps, the G.O.C., R.A. XX Corps and his Staff will remain at the Staff of the XV British Corps at ETINEHEM until the 16th December.

Signed.   30th Novr. 1916.

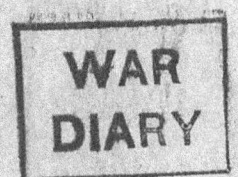

GENERAL STAFF

4th DIVISION

DECEMBER 1916

Appendices attached :-   Operation Orders.
                         Casualties for month.

A wad of messages under separate cover accompanies
this War Diary

WAR DIARY - GENERAL STAFF - 4th DIVISION.

OISEMONT.   1st December, 1916.

          Units of the Division carrying out training.

OISEMONT.   2nd December, 1916.

                    As for 1st Dec.

OISEMONT.   3rd December, 1916.

                    As for 1st Dec.

Operation Order 83 issued to all concerned. app. A

4th Division will relieve a portion of the French XXth Corps on the front approximately between U.25.b 5.5 and the SUNKEN Road (excl.) North of SAILLISEL at U.14.b 9.8.

10th Brigade will take over the Southern Sector of the front at present held by a Regt. of the 11th French Div. on the night 8/9th December.

12th Brigade will take over the Northern Sector of the front at present held by a Regt. of the 39th French Div. on the night 7/8th December.

11th Brigade will be in Divisional Reserve.

4th Divnl. H.Q. will move as follows :-

    OISEMONT to TREUX on 4th December.

    TREUX to present H.Q. French 39th Div. at B.4.c 2.2 on 7th December.

    To present French XXth Corps H.Q. MAUREPAS on 10th Dec.

Moves to carry out the above reliefs will take place as under.

6th December.   12th Brigade Group from Camps 16 and 107 (BRONFAY Area) to Camp 20, MAUREPAS and MARICOURT Camps.

                10th Brigade Group from Camps 111 and 112 to Camps 16 and 107.

                11th Brigade Group from present area to ARGOEUVES and LONGPRE.

7th December.   11th Brigade Group from ARGOEUVES and LONGPRE to MORLANCOURT and VAUX SUR SOMME.

                12th Brigade Group from Camp 20, MAUREPAS and MARICOURT Camps to Trenches, Left Sector.

                10th Brigade Group from Camps 16 and 107 to Camp 20, MAUREPAS and MARICOURT CAMPS.

8th December.   10th Brig. Group from Camp 20, MAUREPAS and MARICOURT Camps to Trenches Right Sector.

                11th Brigade Group from MORLANCOURT and VAUX to CAMPS 111 and 112 North of BRAY.

9th December.   11th Brigade Group from Camps 111 and 112 to Camps 16 and 107 BRONFAY Area.

TREUX.	**4th December, 1916.**

Divnl. H.Q. established at TREUX.

TREUX.	**6th December, 1916.**

Movements ordered to be carried out in Op.Order 83 completed.

Dispositions of Inf. Brigades.

12th Brigade Group in Camp 20, MAUREPAS & MARICOURT CAMPS.

10th Brigade Group in Camps 16 and 107.

11th Brigade Group in ARGOEUVES and LONGPRE.

TREUX.	**7th December, 1916.**

Divnl. H.Q. established at P.C. MONNET (B.4.c 2.2).

Moves completed in accordance with Op.Order 8e.

Dispositions of Inf. Brigades.

11th Brigade Group in MORLANCOURT and VAUX.

12th Brigade Group to Trenches, Left Sector.

10th Brigade Group in Camp 20, MAUREPAS & MARICOURT CAMPS.

B.4.c 2.2. (P.C.MONNET).	**8th December, 1916.**

8.30 a.m.	Corps informed relief of Regt. of 39th French Div. by 12th Brigade in Left Sector completed.
6 p.m.	Evening report - situation.

Moves in accordance with Op.Order 83 completed.

Dispositions.

10th Brigade Group to Trenches, Right Sector.

11th Brigade Group in Camps 111 and 112.

B.4.c 2.2. (P.C. MONNET.)	**9th December, 1916.**

6.20 a.m.	XV Corps informed relief of Regt. of 11th French Div. by 10th Brigade in Right Sector completed.
6.20 a.m.	Morning report - situation normal.
5 p.m.	Evening report - situation normal.

11th Brigade Group moved from Camps 111 and 112 to Camps 16 and 107 (BRONFAY Area.)

P.C. le DUC. (MAUREPAS).	**10th December, 1916.**

Divnl. H.Q. established at P.C. le DUC, MAUREPAS.

5.40 a.m.	Quiet night, situation unchanged.
5.45 p.m.	Evening report - some shelling in vicinity of PRIEZ Farm during the day, otherwise situation normal.

10th Dec.1916. (continued).

Op.Order 89 issued to all concerned. app. B

In order to equalise Divnl. Fronts, the 4th Division will take over a portion of the front at present held by the 33rd Division.

Readjustments of fronts will be carried out as follows :-

Night 10/11th December. 12th Brigade will take over the front now held by 10th Brigade as far as approximately U.20.b 3.3.

Night 11/12th December. 10th Brigade will take over front now held by the left battalion of 33rd Division.

On completion of the relief on night 11/12th December, the Southern boundary of the 4th Division will run due West from approximately U.26.c 8.3 and will join the old boundary at U.25.a 5.3.

P.C. le DUC. (MAUREPAS).	## 11th December, 1916.
	Readjustment of front ordered in Op.Order 89 took place last night.
5.23 a.m.	Morning report - quiet night, situation normal.
5.25 p.m.	Evening report - Increased artillery activity throughout the day, especially on support line.
P.C.le DUC. (MAUREPAS).	## 12th December, 1916.
4.30 a.m.	12th Brigade report readjustment of line ordered in Op. Order 89 successfully carried out last night. Southern boundary now runs as given in the Op.Order quoted.
5.30 a.m.	Quiet night - situation unchanged.
5.40 p.m.	Evening report. Right Sector, considerable shelling in neighbourhood of PRIEZ Farm. Left Sector, some increase in hostile shelling during afternoon.
P.C.l DUC. (MAUREPAS).	## 13th December, 1916.
5 a.m.	Quiet night - no change in situation.
5.16 p.m.	Evening report - Enemy shelling of area between front line and support line of Left Sector.
P.C.le DUC. (MAUREPAS).	## 14th December, 1916.
5.10 a.m.	Morning report - slight shelling of front line junction between subsectors Right Bde. Following reliefs in 10th Bde.Sector (Right) last night. Household Bn. relieved R.War.R. in left subsector. R.Ir.Fus. relieved Seaforths in right subsector.
5.10 p.m.	Evening report. Situation normal.
	Op.Order 90 issued. app. C.
	11th Bde. will relieve 10th Bde. in the Right Sector on night 15/16th December.
	10th Brigade on relief will move to Camps 16 and 107.

15th December 1916.

P.C. le DUC.
(MAUREPAS)

5 a.m.   Morning report - quiet night.

5.17 pm.   Evening report - Enemy artillery fairly active.

P.C. le DUC.
(MAUREPAS)

16th December 1916.

5.20 am.   Morning report - situation unchanged. Relief of 10th Brigade by 11th Brigade in Right Sector completed.

Disposition of 11th Brigade

     Somersets - Right Sub-sector.
     Hampshires - Left sub-sector.
     (less 2 Cos)
     2 Cos Hants-in Support.
     East Lancs- Brigade Reserve.

Battalion relief in Left Sector 12th Brigade.

     King's Own relieved Lancs Fusrs in left sub-sector.
     W.Ridings relieved Essex Regt in right sub-sector.

5.20 p.m.   Evening report - situation normal.

P.C le Duc.
(MAUREPAS)

17th December 1916

5.1 am.   Quiet night - situation unchanged.

5.5 pm.   Evening report - quiet day.

P.C. DUC.
(MAUREPAS)

18th December 1916

Quiet day - nothing of interest to record.

P.Cle DUC.
(MAUREPAS)

19th December 1916

4.40 am.   Morning report - quiet night.

5.6 pm.   Evening report - Front line of Left Sector (12th Bde) was shelled by field guns also support line of left battalion (Kings Own) with 5.9's during the day.

Operation Order No: 91 issued. *app D*

10th Bde will relieve 12th Bde in the Left Sector on night 23/24th December.

12th Bde on relief will move to Camps 16 and 107.

P.C. le DUC.
(MAUREPAS) 20th December 1916

5.10 am. Quiet night. Battalion relief in Left sector (12th Bde)

Lancs Fusrs relieved Kings Own in Left sub-sector.

Essex Regt relieved W.Ridings in Right sub-sector.

5.5 p.m. Evening report- Hostile artillery very active. FREGICOURT shelled heavily throughout the day. RANCOURT also shelled. Enemy aeroplanes active and flying very low.

P.C le DUC.
(MAUREPAS) 21st December 1916.

4.5 a.m. Morning report - situation unchanged.

4.50 pm. Evening report - Enemy shelled FREGICOURT and neighbourhood between 7 and 8 a.m. and again between 2 and 3 p.m. with shelled which had a delay action fuze and some gas shells. At 3 p.m. enemy also shelled hollow about U.19.c.5.5 with gas shells which did not appear to effect the eyes but were very irritating to the throat. Enemy's artillery very active all day.

Operation Order No: 92 issued. app. E.

4th Division (less Artillery) will be relieved in its present line by the 8th Division.

11th Brigade will be relieved by 23rd Brigade in Right Sector on night 29/30 December.

10th Brigade will be relieved by 25th Brigade in Left Sector on night 30/31st December.

G.O.C. 4th Division will hand over command of the line to G.O.C. 8th Division at 12 noon 31st December.

Following moves will take place :-

28th December 12th Bde from Camps 16 and 107 to Camp ½ 12 and 124 and SAILLY LAURETTE.

29th December 11th Brigade (on relief) will move to Camp 13 - ½ 12.

30th December 10th Brigade (on relief) will move to Camps 111 and 112.

31st December Divisional Headquarters from MAUREPAS to CHIPILLY.

P.C le DUC.
(MAUREPAS) 22nd December 1916

Quiet day. Nothing of interest to record.

P.C le DUC.
(MAUREPAS) 23rd December 1916

Inter-battalion relief Left Sector (12th Brigade) carried out last night.
King's Own relieved Lancs Fusrs in left sub-sector.
W.Ridings relieved Essex Regt in right sub-sector.

5.5 am.	Morning report – enemy shelled support line of right battalion Left sector (Essex Regt) with 5.9" Hows yesterday.
5.10 pm.	Evening report – quiet day. Situation normal.

P.C. le DUC.
(MAUREPAS)

24th December 1916

4.45 am. Morning report – situation normal. Following reliefs completed :-

Right Sector. East Lancs relieved Rif. Bde in right sub-sector
Somersets relieved Hamps in left sub-sector.
Rifle Bde to PRIEZ FARM (support)
Hamps Regt to MAUREPAS (Brigade reserve)

Left sector 10th Bde relieved 12th Brigade.

Dispositions- 10th Brigade Household Bn – Right sub-sector
Seaforths   – Left sub-sector.
Irish Fus.   – FREGICOURT
R.War.Rgt   – MAUREPAS.

12th Brigade to Camps 16 and 107.

4.55 p.m. Evening report – quiet day.

P.C le DUC.
(MAUREPAS)

25th December 1916

5 a.m. Morning report – BULLET Cross roads was fairly heavily shelled about 9 p.m. last night, otherwise situation normal.

5.10 pm. Evening report – situation unchanged. Enemy's retaliation to our bombardment reported to be feeble.

P.C le DUC.
(MAUREPAS)

26th December 1916

Situation normal. Nothing of interest to record.

P.C le DUC.
(MAUREPAS)

27th December 1916

Situation unchanged.

P.C le DUC.
(MAUREPAS)

28th December 1916

4.50 a.m. Morning report – situation normal.

Following reliefs completed night 27/28th December –

Right Sector Hamts relieved East Lancs in right sub-sector.
Rifle Bde relieved Somersets in left sub-sector
East Lancs to MAUREPAS. Somersets to PRIEZ FME.

Left Sector R.War.Rgt relieved Household Bn in right sub-sec
R.Irish Fusrs relieved Seaforths in left -:-
Household Bn to MAUREPAS. Seaforths to FREGICOUR

4.50 p.m. Evening report – situation unchanged.

Move of 12th Brigade from Camps 16 and 107 to Camp ½ 12

and 124 and SAILLY LAURETTE completed in accordance with Operation Order No: 92.

P.C le DUC.
(MAUREPAS)

29th December 1916

Quiet day. Nothing of interest to record.

P.C. le DUC.
(MAUREPAS)

30th December 1916

Relief of 11th Brigade by 23rd Brigade (8th Divn) completed.

11th Brigade moved to Camp 13 and ½ = 12.

4.55 a.m.	Morning report - situation unchanged.
5.8 p.m.	Evening report - enemy shelled BAPAUME Road with 15 cm Howitzers this morning.

31st December 1916

P.C le DUC.
(MAUREPAS)

Relief of 10th Brigade by 25th Brigade (8th Division? completed

10th Brigade moved to Camps 111 and 112.

CHIPILLY
12 noon.

G.O.C. 4th Division handed over command of the Left Sector of XV Corps front to G.O.C. 8th Division.

4th Division Headquarters established at CHIPILLY.

* SECRET *

COPY NO: 1

4TH DIVISION OPERATION ORDER NO. 83.

Ref: Maps
Sheets No.57.c., S.W., 62.c., N.W., 1/20,000.
Sheet ALBERT, 1/40,000.

3rd December, 1916.

1. The 4th Division will relieve a portion of the French XXth Corps on the front approximately between U.25.b.5.5. and the Sunken Road (exclusive) North of SAILLISEL at U.14.b.9.8.

2. The 10th Infantry Brigade will take over the Southern Sector of the front at present held by a regiment of the 11th French Division on the night 3/4th December.
    The 12th Infantry Brigade will take over the Northern sector of the front at present held by a regiment of the 39th French Division on the night 3/4th December.
    Details of relief will be arranged between G.Os.C.Brigades concerned.
    The 11th Infantry Brigade will be in Divisional reserve.

3. The Field Artillery reliefs will commence on the night Dec. 11/12th. and will be completed by 8 a.m. on December 15th. Further orders for the relief will be issued.

4. Movements to carry out this relief will take place in accordance with table attached to 4th Division Operation Order No.82 and with Appendix "A" attached to this order.
    Troops marching forward will use the road - BRAY - MARICOURT - HARDECOURT - MAUREPAS.

5. 4th Divisional Headquarters will move as follows :-
    OISEMONT to TREUX on 4th December.
    TREUX to present Headquarters French 39th Division at B.4.c.2.2. on 7th December.
    To present French XXth Corps H.Q. MAUREPAS on 10th Dec.

6. ACKNOWLEDGE.

Major,
General Staff, 4th Division.

Issued at 6.a.m.
Copies to :-
10th.11th.12th Inf.Bdes.
4th Div.Arty.
4th Div.Engineers.
4th Div.Sig.Coy.
4th Div."Q" (4copies).
A.D.M.S.4th Division.
A.P.M.4th Division.
Camp Commandant, 4th Divn.
21st W.Yorks (Pioneers) Bn.
XVth Corps (2copies).
XXth French Corps.
39th French Division. 11th French Division.
33rd Division.
War Diary.
File.

APPENDIX "A" to accompany 4th Divn.
Operation Order No.83.

Date and Unit.	From.	To.	Route.	Remarks.
4th December. TRANSPORT - 21st W.Yorks Regt. (Pioneers).	ARGOEUVES.	Camps 111 & 112	VECQUEMONT & CORBIE.	Under orders of 33rd Divn.
6th December. 12th Inf.Bde Group.	Camps 16 & 107 BRONFAY Area.	Camp 20 - MAUREPAS Camp MARICOURT Camp		Under orders of G:O:C: 12th Inf.Bde. To be clear of Camps 16 & 107 by 11 a.m.
6th December. 10th Inf.Bde Group.	Camps 111 & 112	Camps 16 & 107.	Via Road junction in L.15.b. just North of ERAY.	Under orders of G:O:C: 10th Inf.Bde; to be clear of Camps 111 & 112 by 11 a.m.
6th December. Transport - 11th Inf.Bde Group. viz :- 11th Inf.Bde. Durham Fd Coy. 11th Fd. Amb.	Present Area.	ARGOEUVES. LONGPRE.	AIRAINES PICQUIGNY	Under orders of G.O.C. 11th Inf.Bde.
7th December. Transport - 11th Inf.Bde Group.	ARGOEUVES LONGPRE	MORLANCOURT VAUX-sur-SOMME	VECQUEMONT - CORBIE - ERAY Road.	To be clear of AMIENS by 11 a.m.

Date and Unit.	From.	To.	Route.	Remarks.
7th December. 12th Inf.Bde Group.	Camp 20. MAUREPAS Camp. MARICOURT Camp.	Trenches Left Sector.		Under orders of G.O.C.12th Inf.Bde.
7th December. 10th Inf.Bde Group.	Camps 16 & 107.	Camp 20. MAUREPAS Camp. MARICOURT Camp.		Under orders of G.O.C.10th Inf.Bde.
7th December. 11th Inf.Bde Group Personnel.	Present Area.	MORLANCOURT. VAUX.	By train. Detrain at DERNANCOURT or MERICOURT and at CORBIE or MERICOURT.	Under orders of G.O.C. 11th Inf.Bde. Time table of trains & entraining stations (probably CISEMONT) will be issued later.
8th December. 10th Inf.Bde Group.	Camp 20. MAUREPAS Camp. MARICOURT Camp.	Trenches Right Sector.		Under orders of G.O.C. 10th Inf.Bde.
8th December. 11th Inf.Bde Group.	MORLANCOURT. VAUX.	Camps A11 & 112 North of FRAY.	Via FRAY	Under orders of G.O.C. 11th Inf.Bde.
9th December. 11th Inf.Bde.Group.	Camps 111 & 112	Camps 16 & 107 ERONFAY Area.		Under orders of G.O.C. 11th Inf.Bde.

- SECRET -

Copy No: _____

APP. B

4th DIVISION OPERATION ORDER NO: 82.

Reference Map 1/20,000
57.C. S.W.
62.C.N.W.

10th December 1916.

1. In order to equalise Divisional fronts, the 4th Division will take over a portion of the front at present held by the 33rd Division.

2. The re-adjustments of fronts will be carried out as follows :-

   (a) On the night 10/11th December, the 12th Inf. Bde will take over the front now held by the 10th Inf. Brigade as far as approximately U.20.b.3.3.
   All details of the relief will be made between G.Os.C. Brigades concerned.

   (b) On the night 11/12th December the 10th Inf. Bde will take over the front now held by the left battalion of the 33rd Division.
   All details of the relief will be made by G.Os.C. Brigades concerned.

3. On completion of the relief on the night 11/12th December, the southern boundary of the 4th Division will run due West from approximately U.26.c.8.5 and will join the old boundary at U.26.c.5.3.

4. Completion of reliefs will be reported to Divisional H.Qrs.

5. ACKNOWLEDGE.

Lieut:Colonel
General Staff., 4th Division.

Issued at 1 p.m.

Copies to :-
    10th.11th.12th Inf. Bde.
    4th Div Arty.
    -:- Engineers.
    -:- "Q"
    -:- Signal Coy.
    A.D.M.S.
    A.P.M.
    XV Corps. (2 Copies)
    33rd Division.

* S E C R E T *   Diary   COPY NO. 16

4TH DIVISION OPERATION ORDER NO.90.

APP. C

14th December 1916.

1.   The 11th Infantry Brigade will relieve the 10th Infantry Brigade in the right sector on the night of the 15/16th.

2.   The 11th Infantry Brigade will move up from its present Camps as follows :-

   Front line and support Battalions, T.M.Battery and M.G. Coy. by lorries as far as MAUREPAS.
   Surplus personnel of above units by march route to new transport lines.
   Reserve Battalion by march to new camp close to MAUREPAS HALTE.

3.   The 10th Infantry Brigade will move to Camps 16 and 107 on relief as follows :-

   As many men as possible by lorries which brought up 11th Infantry Brigade.
   Remainder march to new camp near MAUREPAS HALTE, and thence to Camps 16 and 107 on 16th inst.

4.   Times of marches will be arranged will be arranged by Brigadiers. Return journey of lorries will be organized by Major Kelly, attached Divisional H.Q., assisted by Staff Captain, 12th Infantry Brigade. Arrangements will be notified to the latter by Major Kelly.

5.   Orders re moves of transport will be communicated separately to Brigades.

6.   Details of relief will be arranged between Brigadiers.

7.   The relieved Brigade and battalions will hand over to the units relieving them all trench stores, maps, information, programmes of work, details of work in hand &c,.
   Receipts for trench stores will be sent to Div. 'Q'.

8.   All permanent parties employed under the Division or the C.R.E. by the 10th Infantry Brigade will be relieved by similar parties from the 11th Infantry Brigade. The former will furnish details to the latter.

9.   Command will pass on completion of the relief.

10. Completion of relief and passing of command will be reported to Divisional Headquarters by wire, using the code message 'Nominal rolls despatched'.

                                           [signature]
                                           Lieut:Colonel.

Issued at 10 a.m.   General Staff., 4th Division.

Copies to :-
         10th,11th,12th Inf. Bde.
         4th Divnl Arty.
         -:-   Engineers.
         -:-   'Q'
         -:-   Signal Coy.
         A.D.M.S.
         A.P.M.
         33rd Division.
         XV Corps.

Secret

Copy No. 15

4th DIVISION OPERATION ORDER NO. 91.   19th DECEMBER, 1916.

Ref. Map 1/40,000. Sheet ALBERT combined.

APP'D

1. The 10th Infantry Brigade will relieve the 12th Infantry Brigade in the left Sector of the line, on the night 23/24th December.

2. The 10th Infantry Brigade will move up from its present camps as follows :-
    Front line and support battalions, T.M.Battery, and M.G. Coy. by lorries as far as road junction B.14.a.9.5. First lorry to reach this point by 2 p.m. 23rd December. Surplus personnel of above units by march route to 10th Brigade Transport Lines.
    Reserve battalion by march to K Camp B.14.a.10.
    Relieving troops will not move east of the line FREGICOURT - FRITZ farm before 4.30 p.m. 23rd inst.

3. The 12th Infantry Brigade will move to Camps 16 & 107 on relief as follows :-
    Two companies of reserve battalion at Camp X by march route. Front line and support battalions and the two coys. reserve battalion at COMBLES by lorries which brought up 10th Infantry Brigade, enbussing at B.14.a.9.5.

4. Times of march will be arranged by Brigadiers. Return journeys of lorries will be organised by Major Kelly, attached Div.H.Q., assisted by Staff Captain 12th Brigade. Arrangements will be notified by Major Kelly.

5. First line Transport 12th Brigade will march to new lines near Camp 16, route by HAUREPAS - CURLU ROAD - Rd. junction A.30.b.8.5. - thence by main CLERY - CARNOY ROAD.

6. Details of relief will be arranged between Brigadiers.

7. The relieved Brigade and battalions will hand over to the units relieving them, all trench stores, maps, programmes of work, etc. Receipts for trench stores will be sent to Div. "Q". Gum Boots will not be handed over.

8. All permanent parties employed under the Division or the C.R.E. by the 12th Brigade will be relieved by similar parties of the 10th Brigade. The former will furnish details to the latter.

9. Command will pass on completion of relief.

10. Completion of relief and passing of command will be reported to Divisional Headquarters by wire, using the code message "Nominal rolls despatched".

11. Acknowledge.

Major,
General Staff, 4th Division.

Issued at 12 noon.
Copies to :-
10th. 11th. 12th Bdes.
4th Divisional Arty.   Major Kelly.
4th Div.Engineers.   Guards Division.
4th Div."Q".   XVth Corps.
4th Div.Signals.
A.D.M.S.
A.P.M.

SECRET.

Diary

Copy No. 21

APP. E

4th DIVISION - OPERATION ORDER NO. 92.

Reference - ALBERT Sheet 1/40,000.

21st December, 1916.

1. The 4th Division (less Artillery) will be relieved in its present line by the 8th Division.

2. The 11th Inf.Brig. will be relieved by the 23rd Inf.Brig. in the Right Sector on the night 29th/30th December.

   The 10th Inf.Brig. will be relieved by the 25th Inf.Brig. in the Left Sector on the night 30th/31st December.

3. The 9th Fd.Coy. R.E., Renfrew Fd. Coy.R.E., and 21st West Yorks.Regt. (Pioneers), will replace corresponding units of 40th Division at MAUREPAS and will work under the orders of the C.E. XV Corps.

4. On completion of the Infantry reliefs the 2 resting Brigades R.F.A. will each relieve a R.A. Brigade of their own Divnl.Arty. in the line. Reliefs will be by half batteries on nights Dec. 31st/Jan.1st and Jan.1st/2nd.

   C.R.A. 4th Division will hand over command of Field Arty. to C.R.A. 8th Division on completion of reliefs.

5. On relief the Division will move to the Middle Area in accordance with attached table and will be in Corps Reserve.

6. Details of relief will be made direct between C.R.A's, G.Os.C. Brigades, C.R.E's and A.Ds.M.S.

   Reliefs of all units not mentioned in this order will be arranged by 4th Div. Q.

7. Completion of all reliefs will be reported to Divnl.H.Q.

8. G.O.C. 4th Division will hand over command of the line to G.O.C. 8th Division at 12 noon on 31st December.

9. ACKNOWLEDGE.

Issued at 7 Am.

Major,
General Staff, 4th Division.

Copies to 10th, 11th, 12th Brigades.
          4th Div.Arty.
          4th Div.Engrs.
          4th Div. Q.
          A.D.M.S.
          A.P.M.
          21st W.Yorks.R. (Pioneers).
          4th Div. Signals.
          8th Division.
          33rd Division.
          Guards Division.
          15th Corps.
          40 DIVN.

Date	Unit	Location	Remarks
Dec. 27th	21st W.Yorks.R. (Pioneers).	SAVERNAKE Wood	MAUREPAS	To replace Pioneer Battn. 40th Div. for work under C.E. 15th Corps. Time to be arranged direct between C.O.C.Battns.
Dec. 28th	12th Inf. Brig. Durham Fd. Co.	Camps 16 and 107	Camp ? 12 and 124 and SAILLY LAURETTE.	(Durham Fd.Co. to concentrate in Camps 16 or 27th inst.) Under orders of G.O.C.12th Brig. Starting Point - BRONFAY Fm. 10 a.m.
Dec. 29th	11th Inf.Brig.	Trenches Right Sector Camp 13 - ? 12.	Relieved by 23rd Brig. 8th Division. Personnel by Lorry from MAUREPAS. Transport by road.
Dec. 29th	9th Fd. Coy. R.E.	Forward Area. Right Sector.	MAUREPAS.	To work under C.E. XV Corps.
Dec. 30th	Renfrew Fd.Co.	Forward Area. Left Sector.	MAUREPAS.	To work under C.E. XV Corps.
Dec. 30th	10th Inf.Brig.	Trenches Left Sector Camps 111 and 112	Relieved by 25th Brig. 8th Division. Personnel by Lorry from MAUREPAS. Transport by road via Fme.ROUGE - MARICOURT- SUZANNE - BRAY.
Dec. 31st	Divnl. Hd. Qrs.	MAUREPAS	CHIPILLY

Copy

Nature of accommodation.	Map ref: or No. of Camp	Accommodation available.				Accommodation occupied.				Occupied by	Water supply
		Offrs.	O.R.	Horses Shelter	No. of Horses under Shelter	Offrs.	O.R.	Horses Shelter	No. of Horses under Shelter		L = Latrines. C = Cookhouses A = Ablution Sheds. M = Messes.
Shelters and dug-outs (Tents given on a separate return)	Sector 1.	18.	710.	260.	280.	18.	710.	260.	280.	French Army	4 wells dotted along Ravine, [illeg] Well (Sector 3) one Sector 5. Water is pumped up by motor engine and stored in circular iron tanks. Pits outside from which water is carried. Please see remarks overleaf. Marked overleaf.
	2.	4.	460.	325.	325.	4.	460.	325.	325.	11th Brigade Transport Transport 21st Pioneers 140 Transport 12th Pioneers [illeg] Balloon Section	
	3.	27.	1966.	157.	157.	27.	1966.	157.	157.	12th Pioneers, 40th 224 S Fd. Coy. R.E. Sig. Dutham Fd. Coy. R.E. 21st Heavy Artillery Group Details French Army	
	4.	19.	610.	570.	570.	19.	610.	570.	570.	Transport 12 Brigade R.E. Parl Headqrs. Coy. R.E. 9th Field Coy. R.E. Artillery French Army	Bordering attention and confusion
	5.	39.	1390.	355.	355.	39.	1390.	355.	355.	33rd Division 15th Middx. etc. etc.	

20th December 1916.

Note. The above is necessarily and attached to this. Any staff living yet been supplied to check and supply area. The detail given, but present clerk strength [illeg] [illeg] only flourish but can supply the urgently required return.

N.B. Any remarks or suggestions on improvements required should be made on a separate sheet and attached to this.

H.S. Wm. Major
Area Commandant

App. F

Casualties 4th Division for period 1st to 31st Decr 1916.

	Killed	Wounded	Missing
Officers	4	6	-
Other Ranks	90	247	6
	94	253	6

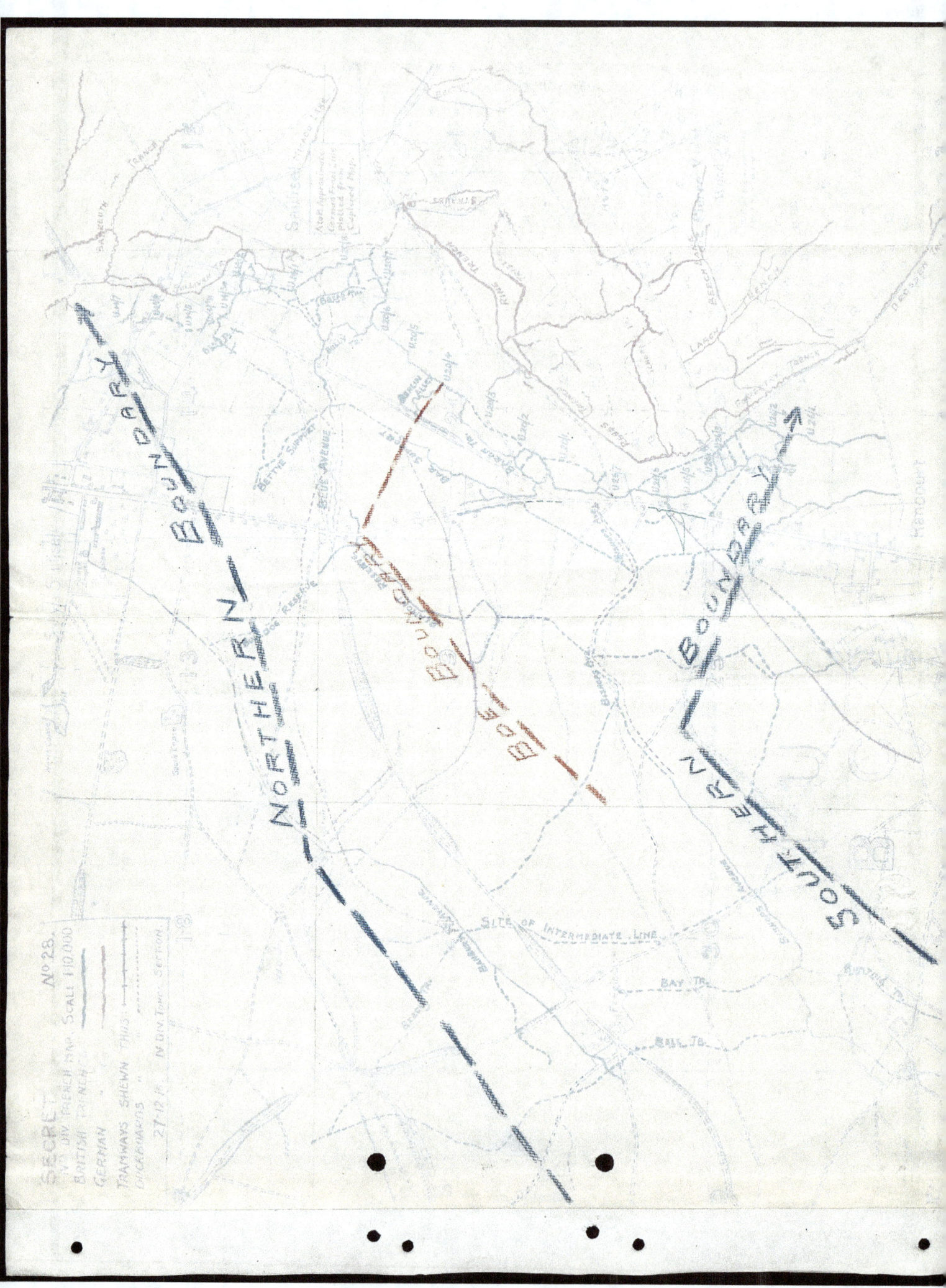

Record.

Plex Map which were made at LeDue

APP. 6

4th Division

War Diaries

General Staff

October 1916

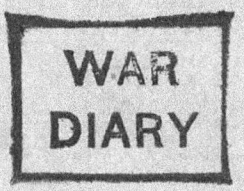

GENERAL STAFF

4th DIVISION

OCTOBER 1 9 1 6

Appendices attached:-   Operations 12th: 18th & 23rd
                        Casualties for month

A wad of messages under separate cover accompanies
this War Diary.

WAR DIARY - GENERAL STAFF - 4th DIVISION.

CORBIE. 1st October.

Fine day.

Battalion and Brigade training now being carried out.

Warning Order issued. (app F)
The Fourth Army will renew the attack on October 10th on the front LE TRANSLOY-THILLOY-WARLENCOURT-EAUCOURT. The objective of the XIV Corps is the line N.3.d.8.5 - N.16.a.9.3 (marked in blue on map attached, marked A) The attack of the XIV Corps will be made by the 4th Division on the right and the 6th Division on the left. Boundaries are as follows (see map A)
Between 4th Division and French.
N.36.d.8.3 - T.5.central - T.10.b.6.5 - T.10 central - T.15.central - Road junction in GUILLEMONT T.19.c.9.4.
Between 4th and 6th Divisions.
Road from N.29.b.2.8 to N.28.d.9.9 (inclusive to 4th Division) - N.34.a.1.8 - T.3.a.0.0 - T.8.central - Road junction in GINCHY T.13.d.9.5 - GUILLEMONT Station.
The attack by the 4th Division will be made by the 10th Brigade on the right and the 11th Brigade on the left.
10th Brigade objective.
N.36.d.8.7 - Road at N.30.c.1.4 (exclusive)
11th Brigade objective.
Road at N.30.c.1.4 (inclusive) - Road at N.29.b.2.8 (incl.)
12th Brigade and Renfrew Field Coy. will be in reserve.
Dividing line between 10th and 11th Brigades (inclusive to 11th Brigade) is as follows:-
Road from Pt. 209 (N.34.d.9.8) past LE TRANSLOY Church road junction at N.30.b.9.5.
The 4th Division will take over the line from which it will attack about 7th October and the Brigades in the line will push forward before the attack to the general line - first L in LE TRANSLOY - N.35 central - T.6a.4.9.
Divisional Headquarters will be at the Briqueterie A.4.b.5.5.

CORBIE. 6th October

Fine day - very high wind. (app G)

Operation order No. 65 issued.
4th Division will be prepared to relieve the 56th Division in the line on the night 9/10th October.
Following moves will take place on 7th and 8th October, when Brigade training period will end.
7th October.
11th Brigade (less 1st E. Lancs. Regt.) and 10th Fd. Ambulance will move from CORBIE to SANDPITS (E.18.c.)
10th Brigade and 11th Field Ambulance will move from DOUARS and LA NEUVILLE respectively to MEAULTE.
12th Brigade H.Q. and 2nd Essex Regt. will move from LA NEUVILLE TO CORBIE.
8th October.
11th Brigade (less 1st E. Lancs. Regt.) and 10th Fd. Ambulance will move from Sandpits (E.18.c.) to CITADEL Camp (F.21.b.)
10th Brigade and 11th Field Ambulance will move from MEAULTE to MANSEL Camp (F.17.b.)
12th Brigade, 1/1 Renfrew Fd. Coy. and 12th Fd. Ambulance will move from CORBIE to CITADEL Camp (F.21.b.)
4th Divisional H.Q. will move from CORBIE to CITADEL.

CORBIE 7th October.

Fine

Moves took place in accordance with Operation Order No. 65.

CORBIE.
CITADEL.

8th October, 1916.
Dull wet day

Moves took place in accordance with Operation Order No. 65.

12 noon — Divisional Headquarters established at CITADEL.

Operation Order No. 66 issued. *(app H)*
4th Division will relieve the 56th Division on night 9/10th October.
10th and 12th Brigades will take over sectors of 56th Division front as under -
10th Brigade - right sector from 168th Bde.
H.Q. at T.19.c.2.3 (QUARRY - GUILLEMONT)
12th Brigade - Left sector from 167th Bde. H.Q. at T.19.a.2.4.
Artillery distribution.
Right sector covered by 56th Div. Arty. (Southern group)
Left sector covered by 4th Div. Arty. (Northern group)
~~Preparation~~ Preparatory moves as under will take place on 9th October.
10th Bde. to be clear of MANSEL Camp area (F.17.b.) by 8.30 am. 2 Bns. moving to area T.9.d. and T.19.b. and 2 Bns. to area between TRONES WOOD and GUILLEMONT.
12th Brigade to march at 8.15 am. to destinations as under -
2 Bns. to area T.8.d and T.9.c. and 2 Bns. to area between BERNAFAY and TRONES Wood.
11th Bde. to start at 10.15 am. to Camps in A.8.b and A.3.b. Bde. H.Q. will be established at Briqueterie.
11th Bde. will be prepared to take over at short notice a portion of the front from 10th and 12th Brigades.
G.O.C. will take over command of the line on the 10th inst. at 10 a.m. at which hour Advanced H.Q. will open at A.10.b.3.8 and Rear H.Q. at A.3.c.1.6.

CITADEL.

9th October.
Still raining

Preparatory moves ordered in Operation Order No. 66 completed.

CITADEL.
A10.b.3.8.

10th October. *Fine day*

Reliefs of 168th and 167th Brigades (56th Division) by 10th and 12th Brigades completed.

10 a.m. — G.O.C. 4th Division assumed command of the line. Divnl. H.Q. established at A.10.b.3.8.
Evening report - situation normal.
Operation order No. 67 issued.
On October 12th the Fourth Army will renew the attack on the Brown line as shown in Map A (marked Appendix B) simultaneously with an attack by the French on the 4th Division front.
The task of the XIV Corps will be carried out in two stages, 4th Division attacking on the right and the 6th Division on the left.
The first objective of the 4th Division includes the portion of SPECTRUM Trench which is not in our possession, DEWDROP and HAZY Trenches and the establishment of a line along the Western ~~crest~~ of the ridge from SPECTRUM to HAZY Trench up to ~~and~~ the boundary with the French (shown as a dotted line in App.B)
The second objective of the 4th Division is to establish a line on the general line running from N.28.b.8.1 where junction will be obtained with the 6th Division through N.35.a. 7.8 - N.35.d.4.8 - T.6.a.5.8 where junction will be obtained with the French 18th Division. The object of the attack is to obtain a line from which the TRANSLOY line can be seen and assaulted at a later date.
10th Brigade will attack on the right and 12th Brigade on the left, boundary between Brigades a line drawn from N.34.d.0.0 to junction of road and tracks at N.34.d.6.6 and thence along the LESBOEUFS-TRANSLOY Road, inclusive to the 12th Brigade.

October 10th continued.

Strong points will be established as under -

By 10th Bde.	By 12th Bde.
T.5.central	N.35.a.5.4
T.5.b.9.9	N.35.a.4.9
N.35.c.5.5	N.28.d.8.8

A.10.b.3.8

11th October.

5.30 am. Morning report - situation normal, enemy artillery very active on and about SUNKEN Road.

5.10 pm. Evening report - retaliation ordinary, situation normal.

5.50 pm. 6th Division (on right of 4th Div.) reports that during the Chinese attack which took place during the afternoon Germans put up a heavy barrage along whole front. 16th Bde. reports that the enemy barrage started one minute after our bombardment commenced and became very intense after 3 minutes and gradually advanced towards NEEDLE Trench. Enemy sent up many white lights from their lines and occasionally a red one.

Operation Order No. 68 issued.
11th Brigade will be in Divisional Reserve tomorrow, 12th instant, and from zero hour onwards the Brigade will be in readiness to move at short notice from Camps now occupied.

WAR DIARY - GENERAL STAFF - 4th DIVISION.

12th Oct 16

BRIQUETERIE
  (BERNAFAY WOOD)
    SOMME.

        The action of the 4th Division in the attack on October 12th is described in the following appendices which are attached in separate parcel.

- A. Narrative of operations on October 12th 1916.
- B. Copy of telegrams received and despatched.
- C. XIV Corps Operation order No. 70.
- D. Division Operation Order No. 67.
- E. 4th Divisional Artillery Operation Orders Nos. 17, 18, 19, 20

13TH OCTOBER 1916.

Weather bright

A.10.b.3.8.

5 a.m. — Morning report - quiet night.
LES BOEUFS and front line system of right sector shelled during the night.

5 p.m. — Evening report - situation normal.

5.30 p.m. — 6th Division (on left of Division) reports quiet day but RAINBOW Trench heavily shelled at intervals. Heavy but intermittent shelling on valley in N.27.c. and d.

7.30 p.m. — R.F.C. observer states that his machine was fired on from MUGGY and FOGGY trenches this afternoon and that he saw German troops in them. 10th Brigade were asked to investigate this and they reported that no aeroplane was fired upon from either of these trenches and further that there were no Germans in MUGGY or FOGGY. Probably the shots came from shell holes which were occupied by the enemy.

11 p.m. — Situation report 10 p.m. 10th Brigade reports Warwick's are making a strong point about T.5.d.2.9. to T.5.c.8.9. rest of battalion being in FOGGY and TWENTY-FIVE Trenches. Irish Fusiliers are in FOGGY, BURNABY and SHAMROCK. Dublin's in support. Seaforth's in reserve. 12th Brigade reports West Riding's hold SPECTRUM from SUNKEN ROAD at N.34.d.8.6. to N.34.b.7.5. with probably some men in ZENITH. Lancs.Fus. in shell holes between SPECTRUM and ZENITH from N.34.b.7.5. to junction with 6th Division. Essex in support. King's Own in reserve. Points gained are being strengthened.

WAR DIARY - GENERAL STAFF - 4th DIVISION.

BRIQUETERIE   14th October, 1916.
  (BERNAFAY WOOD)
    SOMME.

        An unsuccessful attempt to capture the GUNPITS in T.5.a. and RAINY and DEWDROP Trenches by surprise and without any preliminary bombardment either before or at zero hour was made by the 2nd R. Dublin Fusiliers and the 2nd Seaforth Highrs. on October 14th at 6.30 pm.

        One company of the Seaforths reached the Northern Gunpits and RAINY Trench was also occupied, but the troops in the Gunpits were unable to maintain themselves when counterattacked by the enemy.

        The night was very dark and it appears that the rear lines of the Seaforth Highlanders lost direction and did not arrive in time to repulse the counter-attack madeby the enemy on the GUNPITS.

        RAINY Trench was abandoned as its occupation would have made it impossible to bombard DEWDROP Trench.

        The attack of the Dublin Fusiliers on the Southern GUNPITS also failed.

        Appendix F - 10th Bde. Operation Order No. 78.
        M - 4 Div. Op. Order 69

15TH OCTOBER.

A.10.b.3.8.

5.50 a.m. Morning report - 10th Brigade report heavy shelling of front line, support line and LES BOEUFS during the attack last night by the Dublin's and Seaforth's. 12th Brigade reports situation unchanged. King's Own found no sign of Seaforth's in DEWDROP.

1 p.m. Corps informed that in attack last night Seaforth's got to within 120 yards of GUNPITS before being discovered and leading wave entered pits but were bombed out by Germans from trenches or dugouts East of and connected to the GUNPITS. Supporting waves were cut off by very heavy barrage. The GUNPITS appear to be open in rear and to be commanded by the trenches to the East and were very strongly held. No information at present regarding platoons which attacked DEWDROP but the trench is reported to be now wired.

5.10 p.m. Evening report. 10th Brigade reports intermittent shelling of front and rear lines of right battalion; between 1 and 3 p.m. about twenty 4.2" shell fell fell in T.9.d. otherwise situation quiet.
12th Brigade reports intermittent shelling all day.

A.10.b.3.8.   16TH OCTOBER 1916.
   5.10 a.m.   Quiet night. Bombing attack by 12th Brigade
                      on DEWDROP did not progress.

   5 p.m.   Evening report. Intermittent shelling, on front
                      and rear trenches throughout the day.

                      Operation Order No.70 issued to all concerned. (App.K)
                      1st Rifle Brigade and 1st E.Lancs.Regt. (11th
                      Brigade) will relieve the 1st.R.Irish Fus.
                      and 1st.R.Warwick.Regt. (10th Brigade) in
                      support and reserve respectively to right
                      sector on night 16/17th October.
                      On completion of relief -
                      (a) 1st Rifle Brigade and 1st E.Lancs.R.
                           will come under the command of G.O.C.
                           10th Infantry Brigade.
                      (b) 1st R.Irish Fus. and 1st R.Warwick.R.
                           will come under the command of the G.O.C.
                           11th Infantry Brigade.

                      Operation Order No.71 issued. (App.L)
                      11th Brigade will relieve the 10th Brigade
                      in the right sector of the 4th Division front
                      line on night 17/18th October.
                      On completion of relief 10th Brigade will be
                      in Divisional Reserve and will be located in
                      area A.9.a.& C.,A.3.c.,A.4.d.,Brigade H.Q.A.4.d.

A.10.b.3.8.   17th October.

   5 a.m.   Morning report - situation unchanged. THISTLE
                      trench heavily shelled by 5.9's between 4 p.m.
                      and 6 p.m. yesterday.
                      Between midnight and 2 a.m. several tear shell
                      burst in vicinity of left battalion H.Q.

   5.25 p.m.   Evening report. Between 11 a.m. and 1 p.m.
                      SHAMROCK and THISTLE trenches were heavily
                      shelled by 5.9's. The northern end of SHAMROCK
                      trench for about 300 yards was very badly blown
                      in and made practically impassable in daylight.
                      Our artillery bombardment appeared to be very
                      effective.

                      Operation Order No.72 issued.
                      The attack will be resumed by the 4th Army
                      on October 18th.
                      The 6th French Army will attack on the same day.
                      The objectives of the Division will be :-
                      HAZY TRENCH, FROSTY TRENCH, GUNPITS in T.5.a.,
                      DEWDROP TRENCH and any portion of SPECTRUM
                      TRENCH which is not in our hands.

                      The 11th Brigade will attack on the right from
                      our junction with 18th French Division to the
                      LES BOEUFS and LE TRANSLOY Road.
                      Objectives :- Trench from T.5.b.5.1.(point of
                      junction with 18th French Division) to T.5.b.3.3.
                      HAZY TRENCH (T.5.d.4.8. - T.5.b.2.0. - T.5.a.9.9.);
                      FROSTY TRENCH; GUNPITS and Strong Points in T.5.a.;
                      RAINY TRENCH; DEWDROP TRENCH.

                          The line HAZY TRENCH - DEWDROP will be
                      consolidated and posts will be pushed out in front
                      of this line. A strong point will be established
                      at T.5.a.9½.6½.
                          The 12th Brigade (on the left) will capture
                      any portion SPECTRUM still held by the enemy as
                      far South as the LES BOEUFS - LE TRANSLOY Road
                      (inclusive).

OCTOBER.

A.10.b.3.8.   17TH ~~NOVEMBER~~ (Continued).

Dividing line between 11th and 12th Brigades
is a line drawn from N.34.d.0.0. to junction of
the LES BOEUFS - LE TRANSLOY Road with the
track at N.34.d.6.6.
10th Brigade will be in Divisional Reserve.
A "Tank" will assist in the operations moving
from GINCHY at 5.45 p.m. on 17th inst. and
taking up a position to be selected in LES
BOEUFS.
Role. To assist the infantry in the capture
of the strong point (T.5.a.) and to destroy
the enemy's machine gun emplacements.

18TH OCTOBER.

Dull wet day greatly hampering operations

The attack of the 4th Division in the attaack
of October 18th is described in the following
appendices which are attached :- *Separate for assal*

A(2)   Narrative of operations on Oct.18th.
B(2)   Copy of telegrams received and despatched.
C(2)   XV Corps Operation Order No.73.
D(2)   Division Operation Order No.72.
E(2)   4th Divisional Artillery Operation Order
       No.23.

Operation Order 73 issued. (App.IV.)
On night 19/20th the 12th Brigade will take over
from 11th Brigade that portion of the front
which lies between the present left of the 11th
Brigade and Point T.4.b.7.6. in BURNABY Trench.
On night 20/21st the 23rd Brigade (8th Division)
will take over from 12th Brigade (4th Division)
that portion of front which lies between present
4th Division front and the South end of SPECTRUM
Trench - N.34.b.7.2. inclusive.
The Northern boundary of the 4th Division after
the relief will then be as follows :-
N.34.b.7.2. - N.34.Central - WINDMILL -
N.33.d.6½.4½. (exclusive) - Cross roads T.5.a.8½.8.
- T.3.a.0.0. and thence as old boundary.
G.O.C.8th Division will take over command of the
sector from G.O.C.4th Division at 9 a.m. on
21st October.

A.10.b.3.8.   19TH OCTOBER.

5.10 a.m.   Quiet night - situation normal.

9 a.m.   Message to Corps to the effect that as the result
               of operations on 18th.inst. we now hold FROSTY
               Trench and it is being joined up with ANTELOPE.
               HAZY is held by the enemy.

5 p.m.   Evening report - situation unchanged.

A.10.b.3.8.   20TH OCTOBER.

5 a.m.   Morning report. 12th Brigade (left sector) reports
               an enemy's dump at N.24.d.3.0. Parties of
               Germans seen moving backwards and forwards there
               yesterday and to-day. Also report that new
               trench about 70 yards long in front of SPECTRUM
               near N.34.b.7.5. We established 6 posts between
               50 and 100 yards in front of SPECTRUM.

20TH OCTOBER (Continued).

New earthworks appear to have been dug along the high ground in O19.a. Enemy working parties were dispersed by Lewis gun fire which also silenced a German machine gun. 11th Brigade (right sector) reports no change in situation.

5.15 p.m. Evening report - situation normal.

Relief ordered in Operation Order No.73 of 18th. inst completed.

A.10.b.3.8.
21ST OCTOBER.

5.10 a.m. Quiet night. Relief ordered in Operation Order 73 of 18th October completed.

5 p.m. Evening report - no change in situation. Operation Order No.74 issued to all concerned. Fourth Army will renew the attack on October 23rd in combination with the French Army on the left. The task of the 14th Corps will be carried out in two stages shown respectively by a Brown and Green line (on Map "A" attached to Operation Order No.74).

The object of the operation by the XIV Corps on this date is to establish itself in such a position that MOON Trench, LE TRANSLOY CEMETERY, LE TRANSLOY and also SUN TRENCH can be attacked from the S.W. at a later date.
The 4th Division with one Brigade 33rd Division attached will attack on the right and the 8th Division on the left.

The first objective of the 4th Division (Brown Line) includes the portions of BORITSKA and MIRAGE Trenches which lie within the 4th Division boundary, HAZY Trench, GUNPITS in T.5.a. and DEWDROP Trench and the establishment of a line through T.5.b.7.3. (junction with French) - N.35.c.9.4. - SUNKEN ROAD at N.35.a.5.5.

The second objective of the Division (Green Line) includes HAIL Trench, SLEET trench, the trenches between SLEET Trench and ORION (ORION inclusive to 4th Division) and the establishment of a line through N.36.c.6.0. (junction with French) - N.36.c.6.5. - N.36.a.0.3. - N.35.b.6.6. - N.35.a. 9.8.(junction with 8th Division).

The 11th Brigade will attack on the right and 12th Brigade on the left, boundary between Brigades the GINCHY - LES BOEUFS Road - Junction of SHAMROCK and THISTLE Trenches - SOUTHERN end of DEWDROP - Northern end of SLEET - junction of track with HAIL Trench at N.35.b. 7.0. (Marked on Map"A" in Blue).

Both objectives will be consolidated immediately after capture and strong points constructed as below :-

By 11th Brigade.
About T.5.b.½.7.
Point of junction with French.
SLEET Trench.

By 12th Brigade.
HAIL Trench.
About N.35.b.2.7.
About N.35.a.3.2.

21ST OCTOBER (Continued).

One "Tank" is allotted to each Brigade.

Objectives - 11th Bde Tank - Gunpits in T.5.a.
12th Bde Tank - To clear LES BOEUFS-TRANSLOY Sunken Road as far East as N.35.a.5.5.

(Operation Order No.75 issued on 22nd October cancelled the above portion of the Operation Order No.74 with reference to the "Tanks".)

A.10.b.3.8.
22ND OCTOBER.

5.15 a.m. Morning report - situation unchanged. *fine*

5.14 p.m. Evening report - hostile artillery more active than usual.
Operation Order No.76 issued. (app. P.)
The 4th Division (less Artillery) will be relieved on the night 23/24th October by the 33rd Division.
On relief Brigade groups will be accommodated as follows :-
    10th Brigade group in the SANDPITS (E.18.d.)
    11th Brigade group in MANSEL CAMP.(F.17.b.)
    12th Brigade group in CITADEL (F.21.b.)
Divisional Headquarters will move to the CITADEL.
Command of the Divisional front will pass from G.O.C.4th Division to G.O.C.33rd Division when the relief is complete.

23RD OCTOBER.

Very foggy morning - clearing up slightly during the afternoon

The action of the 4th Division in the attack on October 23rd is described in the following appendices which are attached *in separate parcel*.

A (3) Narrative of operations on October 23rd.
B (3) Copy of telegrams received and despatched.
C (3) XIV Corps Operation Order No.76.
D (3) Divisional Operation Order No.74.
E (3) 4th Divnl.Arty.Operation Order Nos 26 & 27.

A.10.b.3.8.
24TH OCTOBER.

Rain still falling

Quiet day - situation unchanged.

Operation Order 77 issued to all concerned. (app. Q.)
4th Division Operation Order No.76 is cancelled.
Reliefs of Brigades in front line will be carried out night 24/25th October as under :-
    11th Brigade by 19th Brigade.
    12th Brigade by 98th Brigade.

Destinations of Brigades on 25th inst. will be :-
    10th Bde group. No move.
    11th -do- MANSEL CAMP.
    12th -do- CITADEL.
Divisional H.Q. will move to CITADEL on 25th October. G.O.C.4th Division handing over command of the line to G.O.C.33rd Division at 10 a.m. on that date.

A.10.b.3.8.
CITADEL (F.21.b.) 25TH OCTOBER.
5.15 a.m.
Morning report - situation unchanged.
Relief in accordance with Operation Order No.77
still in progress.

6.10 a.m. Reliefs completed.

10 a.m. Command of the line passed to G.O.C. 33rd Division.
H.Q. established at the CITADEL (F.21.b).

CITADEL (F.21.b.) 26TH OCTOBER. (app.2)

Operation Order No.78 issued to all concerned.
The 4th Division (less Artillery, 12th Field Ambce.
and one Coy.Pioneers 21st.W.Yorks Regt.) will march
from present area to area MEAULTE - VILLE - TREUX -
MERICOURT - CORBIE on 27th inst.
10th Brigade (less Dublin's and Warwick's) will
move from SANDPITS to CORBIE.
12th Brigade will move from CITADEL to VILLE.
11th Brigade (less East Lancs.) will move from
MANSEL CAMP to CORBIE MEAULTE.
Dublin's and Warwick's will move from MANSEL CAMP
to CORBIE.
East Lancs.R. will move from SANDPITS to MEAULTE.
Divisional H.Q. will close at CITADEL at 4 pm.
and re-open at the same hour at TREUX.

CITADEL (F.21.b.) 27TH OCTOBER.
TREUX.

Moves in accordance with Operation Order No.78
completed.

4 p.m. Divisional H.Q. established at TREUX.

TREUX. 28TH OCTOBER. (app 3)

Operation Order No.79 issued to all concerned.
4th Division (less Artillery, 1 Coy.21st.W.Yorks.
Regt(Pioneers) and 12th Field Ambce.)will move from
present area to area No.5 in the neighbourhood of
ABBEVILLE on 29th and 30th October.
Divisional H.Q. will close at 2 p.m. 30th inst.
at TREUX and reopen at HALLENCOURT at the same
hour.

TREUX. 29TH OCTOBER.

Moves of 4th Division in accordance with Operation
Order No.79 in progress.

TREUX. 30TH OCTOBER.
HALLENCOURT.
2 p.m. Divisional H.Q. established at HALLENCOURT.

Operation on 12 Oct

Appendices

A
B
C
D
E
F
G
H & M

OCTOBER 12th, 1916.

NARRATIVE.

The objectives assigned to the Division which attacked in combination with the French on the right and the remainder of the XIV Corps were as shown in map attached to Operation Order No. 67.

The attack which took place on October 12th was preceded on October 10th and 11th by a bombardment which became intense for a short time on the 11th October when artillery barrages were placed on the objectives to be attacked the next day (vide XIV Corps Operation Order No. 70.)

The enemy's artillery fire all day on the 10th and 11th was heavy and the troops of the 10th and 12th Infantry Brigades which had taken over the line on the night 9/10th October suffered considerably and some of the front line trenches were badly knocked about.

The 10th Infantry Brigade on the right attacked with 2 battalions (1st R. Warwickshire Regt. on the right and the 1st R. Irish Fusiliers on the left).

The 12th Infantry Brigade on the left attacked with 2 battalions (2nd West Ridings on the right and the 2nd Lancashire Fusiliers on the left).

Both brigades attacked at zero hour (2.5 pm.) and the 1st R. Warwickshire Regt. on the right got forward some 500 yards to the line T.5.d.1.7 - T.5.c.7.9 (vide map attached to operation order) where they at once entrenched themselves with their flanks thrown back. The left of the Warwickshire Regt. was met by heavy machine gun fire and failed to reach their first objective, the GUNPITS in T.5.a.

The 1st R. Irish Fusiliers on the left of the 10th Infantry Brigade were also met by heavy machine gun fire from the Strong Point East of the GUNPITS and failed to capture DEWDROP Trench. The G.O.C. 10th Infantry Brigade who had already moved forward 2 companies of the Dublin Fusiliers in support to FOGGY and BURNABY Trenches from their assembly trenches South of LES BOEUFS ordered the battalion to renew the attack on the GUNPITS but this attack also failed.

Meanwhile, the Duke of Wellington's Regt. on the right of the 12th Brigade which also attacked at zero hour had advanced from WINDY and THISTLE Trenches, crossed SPECTRUM Trench, and is reported to have pushed on towards the final objective leaving a party to clear and hold SPECTRUM Trench.

It is estimated that 2 companies from this battalion moved on towards the final objective but could not make good the ground gained and were compelled to withdraw. A considerable proportion of these two companies were cut off by the enemy and did not return to our lines.

The 2nd Lancashire Fusiliers on the left of the 12th Infantry Brigade were timed to start from their assembly trench at zero hour plus 20 minutes, but were caught by heavy machine gun fire from the front and the advance was held up.

About 5.40 pm. the enemy counter-attacked the 1st R. Warwicks which had established themselves on the line T.5.d.1.7 - T.5.c.7.9 but the attack was driven back by rifle and machine gun fire.

During the night of the 12/13th October the ground gained by this battalion was further consolidated and joined up with the French on our right who had made no material progress.

Such reports as were received by Brigade and Battalion commanders made it appear possible that portions of both Brigades had reached their objectives, and it was impossible to verify the situation in time to bring back the Artillery barrage before nightfall.

Approximate casualties 32 officers, 1414 other ranks.

SECRET

Copy No ...14... C

XIV CORPS OPERATION ORDER NO. 70.

Reference Map: 57c, S.W. 1:10,000. 9th October, 1916.

1. XIV Corps Operation Order No. 69 will be cancelled and the following substituted.

2. On October the 12th, at an hour zero, to be notified later, the Fourth Army will renew the attack on the Brown line, as shown on the attached map, simultaneously with an attack by the VIth French Army on our right.

3. The exact scope of this attack cannot be definitely settled until photographic confirmation of the trenches mentioned in this office G.526 has been received, but should the trench reported from N.28.b.6.9 to N.35.a.3.6 exist as stated, and be occupied by Germans, it will be included in the day's objectives.

4. The attack will be made in two stages.

   At zero, the Infantry will advance to the attack of those portions of SPECTRUM TRENCH which are not in our possession, of DEWDROP TRENCH and HAZY TRENCH.

   At zero plus twenty minutes, they will advance to the attack of the other objectives contained within the Brown line.

   At zero and zero plus twenty minutes, respectively, a standing barrage will be placed on the objectives to be attacked, and a creeping barrage will be opened in front of the attacking infantry, which barrage will advance at the rate of fifty yards per minute.

   Details of these barrages will be settled by the Divisions concerned.

- 2 -

5. Once the Brown line is reached, every opportunity will be taken of advancing and straightening out our line preparatory for the assault of the LE TRANSLOY line.

6. A bombardment of the objectives to be attacked will be carried out from 7 a.m. to 5 p.m. on the 11th October, and will be continued from 7 a.m. to zero on the 12th October.

The rate of fire of the heavy howitzers will be maintained at a reduced rate during the night 11th/12th October.

There will be no period of intense fire prior to zero.

7. Active night firing will be continued up to the hour of attack.

8. Owing to the difficulties of bombarding that portion of SPECTRUM TRENCH held by the Germans on the immediate flank of RAINBOW TRENCH, the 4th Division should establish Stokes Mortars to carry out this bombardment.

9. In order to inflict losses on the enemy by inducing him to man his trenches, and at the same time check the accuracy and intensity of our barrage, a Chinese attack will be carried out at 3.15 p.m. on 11th October all along the line.

At this hour the barrage will commence and the heavy artillery lift off the first objectives.

The barrage will continue on the enemy's trenches until 3.20 p.m., when it will creep slowly back till 3.25 p.m.

At 3.25 p.m. both the barrage and heavy artillery will be brought back on to the first objectives and kept there till 3.35 p.m.

- 3 -

At 3.35 p.m. the barrage will cease and the normal bombardment be continued.

Our trenches will be kept as clear of troops as possible during the Chinese attack.

On the front of the 6th Division where the Brown line has already been reached, a suitable objective for the Chinese attack will be selected by the G.O.C., 6th Division so that the enemy may get no indication as to what are to be our objectives for the attack on the 12th October.

10. A contact aeroplane will be in the air from zero till dark.

Flares will be lit on reaching each objective, and at 5 p.m.

11. Watches will be synchronized from Corps Headquarters by telephone at 6 p.m. on October 11th, and again at 8 a.m. on October 12th.

12. ACKNOWLEDGE by wire.

F. Gathorne Hardy
Brigadier-General.
General Staff, XIV Corps.

Issued at 8.15 pm

Copies to :-

Corps Commander	Copy No. 1.	
B.G.G.S.	" " 2.	
I.G.	" " 3.	
D.A.&Q.M.G.	" " 4.	
G.O.C., R.A.	" " 5.	
C.E.	" " 6.	
A.D.A.S.	" " 7.	
D.D.M.S.	" " 8.	
A.P.M.	" " 9.	
Fourth Army.	" " 10,11.	
XV Corps.	" " 12.	
1st French Corps	" " 13.	
4th Division.	" " 14.	
6th Division	Copy No. 15.	
20th Division.	" " 16.	
56th Division.	" " 17.	
XIV Corps H.A.	" " 18.	
9th Sqdn. R.F.C.	" " 19.	
Lieut. Tassart.	" " 20.	
Major Baillie.	" " 21.	
XIV Corps Cav. Regt.	" " 22.	
2nd Cav. Divn.	" " 23.	
Record.	24.	
	25, 26.	

SECRET

XIV Corps No. S.82/41.

Copy No ...14...

ADDENDA TO XIV CORPS OPERATION ORDER NO. 70.

10th October, 1916.

1. Air photographs have been taken to-day of the whole of the Corps front, and the results of these reconnaissances have been communicated to all concerned.

2. The objectives for the attack on the 12th October will be as follows :-

   4th DIVISION.

   At zero.

   HAZY TRENCH, the unnamed trenches between HAZY and DEWDROP TRENCHES, DEWDROP TRENCH and RAINY TRENCH, and that portion of SPECTRUM TRENCH which is not at present in our possession.

   At zero plus twenty.

   That portion of the new trench running from N.28.Central through N.28.d.10.0 to N.35.a.$\frac{1}{2}$.5$\frac{1}{2}$ which lies within the 4th Divisional boundary.

   The 4th Division will, at zero plus twenty, also establish a line of posts from about T.6.a.5.7 to about N.28.b.8$\frac{1}{2}$.0, which will be formed into a continuous trench under cover of darkness.

   6th DIVISION.

   At zero.

   That portion of RAINBOW TRENCH within the Corps zone which is not at present in our possession.

   At zero plus twenty.

   That portion of the trench running south-east from N.28.Central which lies within the 6th Divisional boundary.
   CLOUDY TRENCH from our present left up to N.21.c.6.7.
   The new German trench from N.21.d.7$\frac{1}{2}$.5 to N.21.d.3$\frac{1}{2}$.6, and thence to N.21.d.$\frac{1}{2}$.3.
   Also the trench from N.21.d.2.4 to N.21.d.$\frac{1}{2}$.6, and thence to N.21.c.9$\frac{1}{2}$.5.

   The 6th Division will, at zero plus twenty, also establish a chain of posts from N.28.a.9$\frac{1}{2}$.8 to about N.28.b.8$\frac{1}{2}$.0, which will be formed into a continuous line under cover of darkness.

- 2 -

The exact line to be taken up by the posts of the 4th and 6th Divisions is left to the discretion of Divisional Commanders on the understanding that observation On the LE TRANSLOY line must be obtained, and also our line should be advanced as early as possible to within assaulting distance of the main LE TRANSLOY system.

3. The XV Corps attack is also being made in two stages.

At zero, the Infantry will advance to the line - RAINBOW TRENCH - BAYONET TRENCH.

At zero plus twenty, BACON TRENCH will be occupied and a chain of posts established, thence to join up with our left.

4. In view of the fact that a small portion of the objectives assigned to the 6th Division lie properly within the XV Corps zone, careful co-operation must be made between the 6th and 12th Divisions, as regards the artillery fire on these objectives.

5. ACKNOWLEDGE by wire.

F. Gathorne Hardy
Brigadier-General.
General Staff, XIV Corps.

Issued at 8.20 p.m.

Distribution as for O.O.No. 70.

SECRET

Copy No. 6

XIV Corps No. S.82/45.

11th October, 1916.

1. Reference XIV Corps Operation Order No. 70, the hour of ZERO will be 2.5. p.m.

2. This hour is only to be communicated to those whom it immediately concerns, and in no case should it be communicated by telephone.

3. ACKNOWLEDGE by wire.

J E Hume Maj.
for Brigadier-General.
General Staff, XIV Corps.

Issued at 4.25 p.m.

Copies to :-
Corps Commander	Copy No. 1.
D.A.Q.M.G.	" " 2.
G.O.C., R.A.	" " 3.
C.E.	" " 4.
9th French Corps	" " 5.
4th Division	" " 6.
6th Division	" " 7.
20th Division	" " 8.
XIV Corps H.A.	" " 9.
No. 9 Sqdn R.F.C.	" " 10.

1/20,000 Map 57.c., S.W. & Map A.

SECRET   COPY NO. 21

4TH DIVISION OPERATION ORDER NO. 67.

1. (a). On October 12th the Fourth Army will renew the attack on the Brown Line as shewn on "Map A" simultaneously with an attack by the French on the 4th Division right. Zero hour will be communicated later.

   (b). Boundaries of the XIVth Corps Objective are marked in Red.

2. The task of the XIVth Corps will be carried out in two stages, shewn respectively by a Green and Brown Line. The 4th Division will attack on the right and the 6th Division on the left - boundary between 4th and 6th Divisions is marked in Yellow.

3. The first objective of the 4th Division includes the portion of SPECTRUM TRENCH which is not in our possession, DEWDROP TRENCH and HAZY TRENCH and the establishment of a line along the Western crest of the ridge from SPECTRUM to HAZY TRENCH up to the boundary with the French.

   The Second Objective of the 4th Division is to establish a line on the general line running from N.28.b.8.1. where junction will be obtained with the 6th Division through N.35.a.7.8. - N.35.d.4.8. - T.6.a.5.8. where junction will be obtained with the 18th French Division. The object of the attack is to obtain a line from which the TRANSLOY Line can be seen and assaulted at a later date.

4. (a). The 10th Infantry Brigade will attack on the right and 12th Infantry Brigade on the left, boundary between Brigades - a line drawn from N.34.d.0.0. to junction of Road and tracks at N.34.d.6.6. and thence along the LES BOEUFS - TRANSLOY Road inclusive to 12th Infantry Brigade.

   (b). The 9th Field Company R.E. and 1/1st Durham Field Company R.E. will be attached respectively to the 10th and 12th Infantry Brigades.

   These units will be allotted definite tasks but will not leave their positions of assembly before the objectives are definitely captured.

5. The infantry will advance to the attack on the First Objective at Zero. At Zero plus twenty minutes they will advance to the attack of the Second Objective.

   At Zero and Zero plus twenty minutes respectively a standing barrage will be placed on the objectives to be attacked and a creeping barrage will be opened in front of the attacking infantry which barrage will advance at the rate of 50 yards per minute.

   Details of barrages will be communicated later.

6. Bombardment of the objectives to be attacked will be carried out from 7 am. to 5 pm. on October 11th and will be continued from 7 am. to Zero. on the 12th inst. There will be no period of intense fire prior to Zero.

   As there may be difficulty in bombarding SPECTRUM TRENCH near the point at which the German and English lines meet, preparation must be made by the 12th Infantry Brigade to bombard the Northern portion of this trench with Stokes Mortars.

7.   Strong Points will be established as under :-

By the 10th Infantry Brigade.
{ T.5. Central.
T.5.b.9.9.
N.35.c.5.5.

By the 12th Infantry Brigade.
{ N.35.a.5.4.
N.35.a.4.9.
N.28.d.8.8.

8.   A contact patrol will be in the air from Zero till dark, flares will be lit on reaching each objective and at 5 pm.

9.   An Officer from Divisional Headquarters will synchronise watches at 10th Infantry Brigade Headquarters at 7 pm. on October 11th. and again at 9 am. on October 12th. Representatives from 10th and 12th Infantry Brigades and R.F.A. Groups will attend at 10th Infantry Brigade Headquarters at these hours.

10.   A C K N O W L E D G E.

W H Bartholomew

Issued at 7 pm.
10th October 1916.

Lieut-Colonel,
General Staff, 4th Division.

Copies to :- 10th 11th & 12th Inf.Bdes. 14th Corps "G".
4th Div.Arty.   14th Corps "Q".
4th Div.Engineers.   6th Division.
A.L.M.S.   French Liaison Officer.
4th Division "Q".   56th Division.
A.P.M.
21st W.Yorks.Regt.
4th Div.Signal Coy.

SECRET.

Copy.

~~[scribbled out]~~

GGG/122

Ref 4th Div. Operation order no. 67 the hour of zero will be

2.5 p.m.

This hour is only to be communicated to those whom it immediately concerns and in no case should it be communicated by telephone.

Acknowledge.

F. Hunton
Capt GS.
4 Div.

11/10/16

To 10th & 12th Bdes

4th Divisional Artillery

OPERATION ORDER NO.17

10th October, 1916.

1. In order to inflict losses on the enemy by inducing him to man his trenches and also to check the accuracy and intensity of our barrage, a Chinese bombardment will be carried out by the RIGHT ARTILLERY at 3.15 pm. on 11th October.

2. Barrages will be exactly as laid down in 4th D.A. Warning Order issued to-day, with the exception that the valley in N.36.d. and T.6.b. will not be fired on and no lethal or lachrymatory shell will be used.

3. Time Table will be as under :-

CREEPING BARRAGE

- 3.15   Barrage will be put down.
- 3.16   It will commence creeping at usual rate (50 yards per minute at increases of 25 yards), till it reaches the first standing point.
- 3.20   It will commence creeping backwards at rate as before until it reaches its starting point.
- 3.35   Cease Fire.

STANDING BARRAGE

- 3.15   Barrage will be put down.
- 3.16   Change to "E" Line.
- 3.20   Change to "F" Line.
- 3.25   Change back to "E" Line.
- 3.30   Change back to starting line.
- 3.35   Cease Fire.

4. RATES OF FIRE

    | 3.15 - 3.17 | ... | ... | ... | ... | Intense. |
    | 3.17 - 3.30 | ... | ... | ... | ... | Ordinary. |
    | 3.30 - 3.32 | ... | ... | ... | ... | Intense. |
    | 3.32 - 3.35 | ... | ... | ... | ... | Ordinary. |

5. Group Commanders should arrange for F.O.O's to watch this barrage, and should, if possible, do so themselves with such Battery Commanders as can be spared, with a view to rectifying any mistakes.

Copies to :-
4th Div. "G"	10th Inf.Bde.	D.C.SPENCER-SMITH.
Arty. XIVth Corps	11th " "	Major.
RIGHT Group 4th D.A.	12th " "	Brigade Major R.A.
LEFT " "	H.A.Liaison Officer	4th Division.
29th Brigade.	French " "	
56th D.A.		
20th D.A.		

SECRET.   Copy No. ../....

4th DIVISION WARNING ORDER.

Reference - 1/20000 Map 57 c S.W.   1st October, 1916.
            Map A.

1. The Fourth Army will renew the attack on October 10th on the front LE TRANSLOY - THILLOY - WARLENCOURT - EAUCOURT.

2. The objective of the XIV Corps is the line N.36.d 8.8 - N.16.a 9.3 marked in blue on Map A.

The attack of the XIV Corps will be made by the 4th Division on the right and the 6th Division on the left.

Boundaries which are shown on the attached map are as follows :-

Between 4th Division and French.

N.36.d 8.8 - T.5 central - T.10.b 6.5 - T.10 central - T.15 central - Road junction in GUILLEMONT T.19.c 9.4.

Between 4th and 6th Divisions.

Road from F.29.b 2.8 to N.28.d 9.9 (inclusive to 4th Div.) - N.34.a 1.8 - F.3.a 0.0 - T.8 central - Road junction in GINCHY T.13.d 9.5 - GUILLEMONT STATION.

The 50th Division on the right and the 20th Division on the left now holding the line will establish themselves on the line of the brown line shown on the attached map by 5th October.

3. The attack by the 4th Division will be made by the 10th Infantry Brigade on the right and the 11th Infantry Brigade on the left.

10th Brigade Objective.

N.36.d 8.7 - Road at N.30.c 1.4 (exclusive).

11th Brigade Objective.

Road at N.30.c 1.4 (inclusive) - Road at N.29.b 2.8 (incl.)

12th Infantry Brigade and Renfrew Field Coy. will be in Reserve.

4. The dividing line between 10th and 11th Infantry Brigades (inclusive to 11th Infantry Brigade) is as follows :-
Road from Pt.209 (N.34.d 9.8) past LE TRANSLOY Church road junction at N.30.b 9.5.

5. The 4th Division will take over the line from which it will attack about 7th October and the brigades in the line will push forward before the attack to the general line - first L in LE TRANSLOY - N.35 central - T.6.a 4.9.

6. 9th Field Coy. R.E. and 1/1 Durham Field Coy. R.E. will be at the disposal of G.Os.C. 10th and 11th Infantry Brigades respectively but will not leave their positions of assembly before the objective has been definitely secured.

21st W. Yorks. R. (Pioneers) will act under orders to be issued by the C.R.E.

7. Reports to Divisional Head Quarters at the BRIQUETERIE, A.4.b 5.5.

W. H. Bartholomew
Lieut.Colonel,
General Staff, 4th Division.

Issued at 12 noon.

Copies to 10th, 11th, 12th Brigades.
  5 4th Div. Arty.
  6 4th Div. Engrs.
  7 4th Div. Q.
  8 4th Div. Signals.
  9 21st W. Yorks. R. (Pioneers).
 10 A.D.M.S.
 11 A.P.M.
 12 14th Corps G.
 13 14th Corps Q.
 14 6th Division.
 15 20th Division.
 16 56th Division.
 17 56th (French) Division.

* S E C R E T *

COPY NO. 14

Reference :- 1/20,000.Map 57.C.,S.W.

4th October 1916.

Reference 4th Division Warning Order dated 1st October 1916 :-

1. The Brown Line on which the 56th Division and 20th Division will establish themselves by 5th October will now run as follows:-
From N.21.d.5.9. (where junction will be obtained with the XVth Corps) to N.22.c.9½.½. thence to N.28.d.9.9. - thence to N.35.a.4.9. - thence to N.35.d.7.½. thence a defensive flank to T.5.b.3.0. where touch will be obtained with the French First Corps.

2. Strong Points will be established as follows :-
    56TH DIVISION.
        N.35.d.7.½.
        N.35.a.5.4.
        N.35.a.4.9.

    20TH DIVISION.
        N.21.d.6.7.

3. ACKNOWLEDGE.

Major,
General Staff, 4th Division.

Issued at 12 noon.

Copies to :-   10th.11th.12th Inf.Bdes.
                4th Divl.Artillery.
                4th Div.Engineers.
                4th Div."Q".
                4th Div.Signals.
                A.D.M.S.4th Division.
                A.P.M.4th Division.
                21st. W.Yorks (Pioneers).

SECRET   Copy No. 21

4th DIVISION - OPERATION ORDER No. 65.

Reference - Sheet 17 - AMIENS 1/100,000.   6 - OCT 1916
            Sheet ALBERT 1/40,000

1. Moves in accordance with the attached table will take place on 7th and 8th October.

2. All movements will be by cross country tracks as far as possible, unless weather is wet, in which case available roads may be used.

3. (a) Troops moving by road must keep the following distances -
       200 yards between companies
       1,000 "   "   battalions

   (b) Troops moving by cross country tracks will keep a distance of 500 yards between battalions.

   (c) Transport will follow units at a distance of 500 yards.

4. (a) Orders for moves of 1st Battalion East Lancashire Regiment, 21st Battn. W. Yorks Regt. (Pioneers), 9th Field Company and Durham Field Company will be issued later.

   (b) Moves of units of 4th Division not mentioned in this order will be as ordered by 4th Division "Q".

5. The Division will be prepared to relieve the 56th Division in the line on the night 9th/10th October.

6.   ACKNOWLEDGE.

                                        Lieut.-Colonel,
                                General Staff, 4th Division.

Issued at 2 pm.

Copies to
    10th, 11th & 12th Inf. Bdes.   21st Bn. W. Yorks Regt.
    4th Divnl. Artillery   XIV Corps "G"
    4th Div. "Q" (3 copies)   XIV Corps "Q"
    C. R. E.   56th Division
    A. D. M. S.   20th Division
    A. P. M.   29th Division
    4th Signal Coy.   6th Division.

MARCH TABLE to accompany ●●n Division Operation Order No. 6●.

Date	Unit	From	To	Remarks
7th Oct.	11th Inf. Bde. (less 1st Bn. E. Lancs. R.) } 10th Fd. Amb. }	CORBIE	SANDPITS (E.13.c.)	Under orders of B.G.C. 11th Bde. Route. HERICOURT L'ABBE – TREUX – VILLE–sur–ANCRE – MEAULTE. Rear of Group to be clear of CORBIE by 11 a.m. No unit to enter MEAULTE before 12 noon
7th Oct.	10th Inf. Bde. } 11th Fd. Amb. }	DAOURS LA NEUVILLE	MEAULTE	Under orders of B.G.C. 10th Inf. Bde. Route. CORBIE–HERICOURT L'ABBE–TREUX–VILLE–sur–SOMME ANCRE Head of Group to enter CORBIE at 11 am.
7th Oct.	12th Inf. Bde. } E.Q. } 2nd Essex Regt. } 12th M.G. Coy. } 12th T.M. Bty. }	LA NEUVILLE	CORBIE	Under orders of B.G.C. 12th Inf. Bde. No unit to move before 12.30 p.m.
8th Oct.	11th Inf. Bde. (less 1st Bn. E. Lancs. R.) } 10th Fd. Amb. }	SANDPITS (E.13.c.)	CITADEL Camp (F.21.b.)	Under orders of B.G.C. 11th Inf. Bde. Route. – By Cross country roads Not to enter CITADEL before 12 noon

Date	Unit	From	To	Remarks
8th Oct.	10th Inf. Bde. 11th Fd. Amb.	MEAULTE	MANSEL ~~MAMETZ~~ CAMP (F.17.b.)	Under orders of B.G.C. 10th Inf. Bde. Route. LA HARGAILLOT Cross roads - Cross roads F.8.a.5.0. - Main ALBERT -MAMETZ COURT Road. Head of Group to enter MANSEL Camp at 12.30 P.M.
8th Oct.	12th Inf. Bde. Renfrew Field Coy. 12th Fd. Amb.	CORBIE	CITADEL CAMP (F.21.b.)	Under orders of B.G.C. 12th Inf. Bde. Route. BRAY - CORBIE Road as far as cross roads J.18.c. - MORLANCOURT - Cross country roads (BRAY-CORBIE Road East of the cross roads K.8.16.0. must NOT be used) Head of Group to march at 8.30 a.m.
8th Oct.	4th Division Headquarters	CORBIE	CITADEL	Route - as for 12th Inf. Bde. group Hour of start will be issued later.

SECRET.   COPY NO. 21

4TH DIVISION OPERATION ORDER NO. 66.

Reference :- 1/40,000 Map - Albert Sheet, &
            1/20,000 Sheet 57.C., S.W.

1. 4th Division will relieve 56th Division night 9/10th October.

2. Infantry Brigades will take over sectors of 56th Division front as below :-

   10th Inf. Bde.   Right Sector from 168th Infantry Brigade.
   12th "   "   Left Sector   "   167th   "   "

   H.Q. 168th Inf. Bde at T.19.c.2.3. (Quarry - GUILLEMONT).
   H.Q. 167th "   " at T.19.a.2.4.

3. Arrangements for relief will be made between G.Os.C. concerned. G.Os.C. 4th Division Brigades will take over command on completion of relief. Completion of all reliefs will be reported to 56th Division.

4. ARTILLERY DISTRIBUTION.

   Right Sector covered by 56th Divisional Artillery (Southern Group).
   Left Sector covered by 4th Divisional Artillery (Northern Group).
   C.R.A. - Brigadier-General Prescott Decie.

5. Preparatory moves on roads to carry out this relief will be as follows :-

(a) 10th Infantry Brigade.- to be clear of MANSEL Camp Area (F.17.b) by 8.30 am. and march as under.

   2 Bns. to area T.9.d. and T.19.b, advance parties to report to 168th Brigade Headquarters for exact localities to be used.

   2 Bns to area between TRONES WOOD and GUILLEMONT. Advance parties report to Town Major, BERNAFAY Wood (Office at S.E. Corner of Wood).

Route :- By cross country tracks or via MAMETZ - MONTAUBAN Road.

(b) 12th Infantry Brigade to march at 8.15 am. to destinations as under. Rear of column to be clear of Citadel Area by 9.45 am.

   2 Bns to area T.8.d. and T.9.c., advance parties report to 167th Brigade Headquarters for exact location.

   2 Bns to area between BERNAFAY and TRONES Woods, advance parties report to Town Major, BERNAFAY Wood.

Route :- By cross country tracks South of CARNOY and thence via TALUS BOISE VALLEY or via MAMETZ - MONTAUBAN Road.

2.

(c) 11th Infantry Brigade to start at 10.15 am. and clear CITADEL Area by 12 noon.

Destination :- Camps in A.8.b. and A.3.b. Advance parties to report to Town Major, at 56th Division Rear H.Q. at A.3.c.2.6. at 9 am.

    Brigade H.Q. to BRIQUETERIE.

Route :- By cross country tracks South of CARNOY and thence by TALUS BOISE VALLEY.

(d) On arrival at destination in forward area 4th Division Brigades will come under the command of 56th Division and will report arrival to 56th Division.

6. (i) Troops moving by road must keep following distances :-

    200 yards between Companies.
  1,000   "   "   Battalions.

Troops moving by cross country tracks will keep a distance of 500 yards between Battalions.

(ii) East of BERNAFAY WOOD Troops must move in small detachments

7. (i) Relief of Field Companies and Pioneer Battalion 56th Divn. will be arranged direct between C.R.Es. 4th and 56th Divisions.

(ii) Relief of medical units will be arranged direct between A.Ds.M.S. 4th and 56th Divisions.

8. A Staff Officer 4th Division will be at 56th Division H.Q. from 10 am. 9th inst.

9. 11th Infantry Brigade will be prepared to take over at short notice a portion of the front from 10th and 12th Infantry Brigades.

10. G.O.C. 4th Division will take over command of the line on the 10th inst. at 10 am. at which hour Advanced Divisional Headquarters will open at A.10.b.3.8. and Rear Headquarters at A.3.c.1.6.

                              W. H. Barthtolm
                                    Lieut-Colonel,
8th October 1916.   General Staff, 4th Division.
Issued at 3 pm.

Copies to :- 10th 11th & 12th Inf.Bdes.   4th Div. 'Q'.
           4th Divisional Artillery.   21st W.Yorks Regt.
           4th Divisional Engineers.   XIV Corps 'G'.
           A.D.M.S. 4th Division.   XIV Corps 'Q'.
           A.P.M. 4th Division.   56th Division.
           4th Div. Signal Coy.   20th Division.
                                            29th Division.
                                            6th Division.

56 French Div.

SECRET.   Copy No. 25

4th. Divisional Artillery.
Operation Order No. 18.

From 7a.m. onwards until 5p.m. on 11th. instant, 4.5"
Howitzer Batteries of Right Artillery will bombard deliberately
any enemy trenches within their Zones.

Care must be taken not to unterfere with the shooting of
Heavy Batteries by firing on trenches simultaneously with them.

Trenches on which direct observation can be obtained should
be selected.

100 rounds per gun will be expended.

This bombardment will be repeated on the 12th. instant and
the 100 rounds expended prior to Zero hour.

    Issued at 8p.m.   D.C. Spencer-Smith Major
    10/October/1916.   Brigade Major 4th. Div. Artillery.

Issued to:-

    Arty. 14th. Corps   No. 1
    56th. Div. Arty.   Nos.2 to 6
    Left Group   " 7 to 15
    Right Group   " 15 to 23
    29th. Arty. Brig.   " 24
    4th. Div. G.   " 25 - 26
    10th. Inf. Brig.   " 27
    11th. Inf. Brig.   " 28
    12th. Inf. Brig.   " 29
    H.A. Liaison Officer " 30
    French Liaison Officer " 31
    4th. Div. Am. Col.   " 32
    20th. Div. Arty.   " 33 - 37

SECRET.   Copy No. 26

4th. Divisional Artillery (Right Artillery).

Operation Order No. 19.

The following arrangements have been made for Barrage on extreme Right about Junction with French.

Zero - + 1'.   Barrage on T.5.a.6.0.---T.5.d.2.8½.

At + 1'.   This will start creeping up to the line
              T.5.b.3.5.---T.5.b.6½.1½. where it will
              stand until -

+ 10'   when the fire will be concentrated on line
              T.5.b.3.5.---T.5.b.4½.3¼. until -

+ 11'   when it will creep along this belt up to the
              line N.36.c.2.2.---N.36.c.4.0., where it will
              open out on to the boundary line with the
              French and creep on until it reaches the line
              N.36.d.0.3.---N.36.c.3.6., where it will
              stand until further orders.

The French have undertaken to barrage the area T.5.b.8.3.---T.5.b.7.4.---N.36.c.3.2.---T.6.a.6.9. in addition during their advance.

           ACKNOWLEDGE

Issued at 6.30p.m.   D.C. Spencer-Smith Major

11/October/1916.   Brigade Major 4th. Divisional Artillery

Issued to:-

    Arty. 14th. Corps   No. 1
    56th. Div. Arty.   Nos. 2 to 6
    Left Group   "   7 to 15
    Right Group   "   16 to 23
    29th. Arty. Brig.   "   24
    4th. Div. G.   "   25 - 26
    10th. Inf. Brig.   "   27
    11th. Inf. Brig.   "   28
    12th. Inf. Brig.   "   29
    H.A. Liaison Officer   "   30
    French Liaison Officer "   31
    4th. Div. Am. Col.   "   32
    20th. Div. Arty.   "   33 - 37

SECRET.   Copy No. 26

4th. Divisional Artillery (Right Artillery)

Operation Order No. 20.

1. The attack will be resumed on 12th. instant, with Objective the BROWN Line at a Zero hour to be notified later.

2. For the purposes of this order certain lines will be lettered as follows:-

   Line A.1.   :- N.28.d.2½.7½.---N.28.d.6½.3.---N.28.a.7½.1.---
                  N.28.d.9½.0.---N.35.a.1.8.---N.35.a.1.6½.---
                  N.35.a.0.5.---N.35.a.½.4.

   Line A.   :- N.34.d.2½.6½.---N.34.d.8.1.---T.5.a.2.5.---
                  T.5.a.6.0.---T.5.d.2.8½.

   Line B.   :- N.35.a.½.4.---N.35.a.1.3.---N.35.a.0.0.---
                  N.35.c.2½.5½.---N.35.c.9.2.---T.5.b.3.5.---
                  T.5.b.6½.1½.

   Line C.   :- N.29.a.4½.3½.---N.29.a.6½.1.---N.29.c.7½.8½.---
                  N.29.c.8.5.---N.29.c.9.2.---N.29.d.1.0.---
                  N.35.b.6.1.---N.35.d.8½.7½.---N.36.c.3.6.---
                  N.36.d.0.3.

   Line D.   :- (i) N.34.b.6.0.---N.34.d.7½.5½.---T.5.a.1½.8½.
                  (ii) N.34.d.9½.4.---N.35.c.½.5.
                  (iii) N.35.c.1.1½.---T.5.a.2½.8.
                  (iv) FROSTY TRENCH.
                  (v) HAZY TRENCH.

   Line E.   :- (i) N.28.d.3½.9.---N.35.a.5.6.
                  (ii) SUNKEN Road N.35.a.2½.1½.---N.35.a.4½.4½.
                  (iii) N.35.a.2½.1½.---N.35.b.0.0.
                  (iv) N.35.b.0.0.---along SUNKT Tr.---T.5.b.9.9.

   Line F.   :- TRANSLOY Line including CEMETERY and HIGH
                  GROUND in O.25.c.

3. Boundaries between 4th. Division and flank divisions will be as heretofore but for the purposes of these operations the boundary between 4th. Div. Arty. and 56th. Div. Arty. will be a line N.34.d.6.0.---N.35.b.0.0.---N.30.c.3.0. Boundary between Right and Left Groups 4th. Div. Arty. will then be the line N.34.d.0.8.---N.30.a.1.0.

4. CREEPING BARRAGE.
   At Zero Hour - The Creeping Barrage will be put down on Line A. and A.1.

   On Line A. this will commence moving at + 1' and will creep by increases of 25 yards at a rate of 50 yards a minute till it reaches Line B., where it will stand till + 20'.
   On Line A.1. this barrage will remain stationary until + 20'. At + 21' the whole creeping barrage along A.1. and B. will move forward at rate as before until it reaches line C. where it will stand until further orders.

5.

5. **STANDING BARRAGE.**

At Zero Hour - The first Standing Barrage will be put down on Line D.
It will be found by 4th. Div. Arty. as far South as T.5.a.1½.9., and Left Group will provide one Battery towards this - arrangements being made between Group Commanders direct.
At + 1' this barrage will lift to Line E. -
and Left Group Battery lent will return to Left Group Area -
and at + 21' it will creep forward at 50 yards a minute till it reaches Line F., where it will stand until further orders.

6. **4.5" Howitzers.**

   56th. Div. Arty. .. .. .. 4 Batteries.

Zero - + 10'.
 2 Batteries on -
  (i) SLEET TRENCH (N.35.d.5½.6½.---N.35.d.6.0.)
  (ii) Gun Pits and short trenches about
   N.35.d.2½.6½.---N.35.d.1½.8½.---
   N.35.d.2½.9½. and T.5.b.9½.9½.

At + 10'.
 These two batteries will lift and fire lethal and lachrymatory shell into the Valley in N.36.b. and N.36.d., N. of the line N.36.d.3.2.---N.36.d.9.7., until + 50' or as otherwise ordered.
 56th. Div. Arty. will also arrange to sweep this Valley occasionally with shrapnel fire from + 10' onwards, using one of their standing barrage batteries, and will watch the exit of this Valley about T.6.a. and T.5.b. to check any hostile advance immediately.

Zero - + 20'.
 2 Batteries on -

  HAIL TRENCH (N.35.b.5½.1½.---N.35.d.8.8.).

At + 20'.
 These two batteries will lift on to the TRANSLOY line and remain there until further orders.

   4th. Div. Arty. .. .. .. 4 Batteries.

Zero - onwards.
 2 Batteries Right Group on the CEMETERY, TRANSLOY, throughout.

Zero - + 20'.
 2 Batteries Left Group on gun pits and small trenches about N.29.a.6½.1½., N.29.c.8.8., N.29.c.8.3½., N.29.c.8.1., N.29.d.½.½., N.35.b.½.6.

At + 20'.
 The two last named batteries will lift on to the front houses of TRANSLOY, N. of the CEMETERY, where they will stand until further orders, firing a proportion of lethal shell in bursts.

3.

7. Allotment of guns to Standing and Creeping barrage will be 50% to each.

8. **Liaison.**

56th. Div. Arty. will detail a Field Officer to act as Liaison Officer with 10th. Inf. Brig. and 4th. Div. Arty. with 12th. Inf. Brig.
Lieut. Col. C.O. Head (29th. Bde. R.F.A.) is detailed for the latter Brigade, to whom he should report early on 12th. instant.

9. Group Commanders will send a F.O.O. to each Battalion in the Front Line. This F.O.O. must be provided with means to open visual as well as telephonic communication and should not go beyond battalion H.Q., until our line is definitely established on our Objective.
He should then move forward to a point where observation can be obtained between the BROWN Line and TRANSLOY Line.
If on forward slope the best chance to obtain communication may be by telephone back to SPECTRUM, or other similar trench, and thence by visual.
This F.O.O. should send back any possible information throughout. He is primarily for Artillery and Observation purposes and not merely for Liaison.

10. Group Commanders must arrange to establish visual receiving station, through which messages may be sent back to Group H.Q. from F.O.O.

11. Watches will be synchronized at 10th. Inf. Brig. H.Q. at 9a.m. on October 12th.
Representatives of Field Arty. Groups will attend there at that hour.
The greatest care must be taken to secure accurate timing.

12. **Rates of Fire.**

```
Zero - +10'     ..  ..  ..   Intense.
+10' - +20'     ..  ..  ..   Ordinary.
+20' - +30'     ..  ..  ..   Intense.
+30' - +40'     ..  ..  ..   Ordinary.
+40' - Onwards  ..  ..       Slow or as situation
                             demands.
```

13. These orders are to be read in conjunction with 4th. Div. Arty. (Right Artillery) Operation Order No. 19.

14. Zero hour will be at   p.m.

15. ACKNOWLEDGE.

Issued at 10p.m.   D.C. Spencer-Smith Major

11/October/1916.   Brigade Major 4th. Divisional Artillery

Issued to:-

Arty. 14th. Corps	No. 1	11th. Inf. Brig.	28
56th. Div. Arty.	Nos. 2 - 6	12th. Inf. Brig.	29
Left Group	" 7 -15	H.A. Liaison Officer	30
Right Group	" 16- 23	French Liaison Officer	31-32
29th. Arty. Brig.	" 24	4th. Div. Am. Col.	33
4th. Div. G.	" 25- 26	20th. Div. Arty.	34-38
10th. Inf. Brig.	" 27		

SECRET.   Copy No. 20

App. M

4th DIVISION OPERATION NO. 69.

Reference - 1/20000 Sheet 57 c S.W.   13th October, 1916.

1. On October 14th 10th Infantry Brigade will attack and capture

    (i) Gun pits lying between T.5.a 4.2 and T.5.a 3.7,

    (ii) Such portions of RAINY TRENCH and DEWDROP TRENCH as are not in our hands.

Hour of ZERO will be notified later.

2. After the capture of the objectives, T.5.a 4.2 will be connected with TWENTY FIVE TRENCH, and DEWDROP TRENCH will be joined to the Gun pit at T.5.a 3.7.

(3). The infantry will attack at ZERO hour; details of any barrage required will be communicated later.

There will be no preliminary bombardment of DEWDROP TRENCH and no intense fire on any of the objectives before ZERO.

A slow and deliberate bombardment of the Gun pits between T.5.a 4.4 and T.5.a 3.7 will take place on October 14th lasting till the hour of ZERO.

4. Instructions for medical arrangements will be issued separately.

5. Prisoners of war will be disposed of as directed in para. 2 of Operation Order No. 68 dated October 11th.

6. Watches will be synchronised by General Staff, 4th Division at 1 p.m. on October 14th at 10th Brigade Hd.Qrs.

7. ACKNOWLEDGE.

W. H. Bartholomew

Lieut.Colonel,

Issued at 11.45 p.m.   General Staff, 4th Division.

Copies to 10th, 11th, 12th Brigades.   12 21st W.Yorks. R.
    5,6 4th Div. Arty.   13 14th Corps G.
    7 4th Div. Engrs.   14 14th Corps Q.
    8 4th Div. Q.   15 6th Division.
    9 4th Div. Sig. Co.   16,17 French Liaison Officer.
    10 A.D.M.S.   18 14th Corps H.A.
    11 A.P.M.   19 No. 9 Sqdn. R.F.C.
       20 War Diary

SECRET.

The following addition will be made to 4th Division Operation Order No. 69.

1. The hour of ZERO will be 6 p.m. on 14th October.

2. There will be no artillery barrage to accompany the attack.

3. A contact aeroplane will be in the air at 7.30 a.m. on 15th instant. The most forward troops of the 10th and 12th Infantry Brigades will light flares at the above hour.

[signature]

14th October, 1916.

Lieut.Colonel,
General Staff, 4th Division.

Issued at 2.30 p.m. to all recipients of Op.Order No. 69.

Operations
of
18th October
———

A ②
B ②
C ②
D ②
E ②

WAR DIARY - GENERAL STAFF - 4th DIVISION.

BRIQUETERIE
(BERNAFAY WOOD)
SOMME.   18th October, 1916.

1.   Definite orders preceded by a warning order received
on the night of the 15/16th October were issued on October 16th
by the XIV Corps for the renewal of the attack on the 18th Oct.

            The 11th Infantry Brigade was ordered to capture FROSTY,
HAZY, RAINY and DEWDROP Trenches as well as the Northern and
Southern Gunpits and Strong Point in T.5.a.   The 12th Inf.
Brigade was to capture any portions of SPECTRUM trench, North of
LESBOEUFS-TRANSLOY Road which was still in the hands of the enemy
and to assist st the attack of the 11th Brigade by a flank attack
on DEWDROP.

2.   Zero hour was at 3.40 a.m. and was the same on the whole
front of the attack carried out by the Fourth Army.

            The 11th Infantry Brigade attacked with the 1st Rifle Bde.
and 1 Company Somerset L.I. on the right and 1st E. Lancs. Regt.
on the left.   The Rifle Brigade assembled on the frontage
BURNABY Trench from T.4.b.8.6 to GERMAN Trench inclusive and the
1st E. Lancs. Regt. on the frontage of the Northern portion of
BURNABY Trench.   Battalions attacked in 4 waves.

            The 12th Inf. Brigade attacked with the 1st King's Own
R. Lanc. Regt. from SPECTRUM Trench and UNION Trench.

3.   The assembly trenches for the 11th Brigade were badly
damaged by shell fire and were not very suitably sited to accommodated the different waves which in some cases were in
shell holes in the open.

            The alignment and direction of the advance were laid
out by tapes and most of the companies started in the correct
direction although many of the men were not well acquainted with the trenches
The night was very dark and heavy rain fell before the attack.

            The attack was met by a heavy German barrage and machine
gun fire and neither battalion gained its objective although
the E. Lancs. Regt. is believed to have got as far as DEWDROP

Trench. None of the officers and senior N.C.Os of the companies of this battalion have returned and it is impossible to say what happened. The men stated that the greater part of the hostile machine gun fire came from beyond DEWDROP Trench and not from the trench itself.

The King's Own R. Lanc. Regt. gained and held some 70 yards of SPECTRUM Trench North of the LESBOEUFS Road but their attack on the SUNKEN Road failed.

The cause of failure was undoubtedly primarily due to the state of the ground after the rain and to the darkness of the night, which made some portions of the attack lose their direction.

Approximate casualties - 16 officers
500 other ranks.

GOC

SECRET

XIV Corps No. S.82/54

XIV CORPS WARNING ORDER.

15th October, 1916.

1. Written orders have not yet been received from the Army, but it is understood that the following will be the objectives for the 18th October.

2. **4th DIVISION.**

   FROSTY TRENCH, HAZY TRENCH. GUNPITS in T.5.a. and DEWDROP TRENCH up to its junction with SPECTRUM TRENCH.

   6th DIVISION.

   CLOUDY TRENCH up to its junction with MILD TRENCH.
   MILD TRENCH from that junction down to T.21.d.½.3, and
   The continuation of SHINE TRENCH up to T.21.c.½.5.

   T 21 c 9½ c ←

3. A Tank is placed at the disposal of each of the 4th and 6th Divisions, who will arrange direct with the Officers commanding these Tanks for their move forward and for their action on the 18th instant.

4. Four Stokes Mortars for the firing of gas shells are placed at the disposal of each of the 4th and 6th Divisions, who will arrange direct with the O.C. No. 4 Special Coy., R.E. for their employment.

5. The objectives of the attack will be completely destroyed previous to the day of attack, by the Heavy Artillery under orders to be issued separately by the G.O.C., R.A. XIV Corps.

6. ACKNOWLEDGE by wire.

   Issued at 10 pm

   F. Gathorne Hardy
   Brigadier-General,
   General Staff, XIV Corps.

   Copies to : 4th Division. ✓
   6th Division.
   G.O.C., XIV Corps H.A.
   G.O.C., R.A.

SECRET

Copy No. 14

XIV CORPS OPERATION ORDER NO. 73.

16th Oct. 1916.

Ref. Map: Sheet 57c S.W. 1:10,000.
and Special map attached.

1. The attack will be renewed by the Fourth Army on the 18th October at an hour zero to be notified later.

   The 6th French Army will attack on the same day.

2. The objectives to be captured are shown in Green, and the boundaries between Corps in Red, on the attached map.

3. The 4th Division will capture FROSTY TRENCH, HAZY TRENCH, gun pits in T.5.a. RAINY TRENCH and DEWDROP TRENCH.

   The 6th Division will capture CLOUDY TRENCH from our present line up to N.21.d.5½.9½, those portions of MILD TRENCH not at present in our possession, up to the Corps Boundary and the continuation of SHINE TRENCH as far as N.21.c.9½.5, obtaining touch with the XV Corps on the Green line.

4. For this operation one Tank has been allotted to each of the 4th and 6th Divisions.

5. The Infantry will leave their trenches and advance to the attack at zero, at which hour a standing barrage will be placed on the objectives to be attacked, and a creeping barrage will commence to creep forward from the objectives to a distance of 500 yards in rear, advancing at the rate of 100 yards a minute. Subsequently the field artillery will be at the disposal of Divisional Commanders. The creeping barrage will cover the whole of the Corps front.

   The attack will be preceded by a bombardment of heavy artillery, which has already commenced.

- 2 -

6. Strong points will be established by the 4th Division at

T.5.a.9½.6½.

by the 6th Division at -

N.21.d.7½.5.
N.21.d.5½.9½.
N.21.d.3.6.

7. A contact aeroplane will be in the air from zero till 12 noon, and later as may be subsequently ordered.

Yellow flares will be lit on reaching the objective at zero plus 1 hour, and at 12 noon.

8. Watches will be synchronized from Corps Headquarters by telephone at 6 p.m. on October 17th.

9. ACKNOWLEDGE by wire.

Brigadier-General.
General Staff, XIV Corps.

Issued at 6.5 p.m.

Copies to -

Corps Commander	Copy No. 1.	6th Division Copy No. 15.
B.G.G.S.	" " 2.	8th Division " " 16.
I.G.	" " 3.	20th Division " " 17.
D.A.&Q.M.G.	" " 4.	XIV Corps H.A. " " 18.
G.O.C., R.A.	" " 5.	9th Sqdn R.F.C. " " 19.
C.E.	" " 6.	"O" and "Q" Sections
A.D.A.S.	" " 7.	No. 4 Spec. Coy.R.E. 20.
D.D.M.S.	" " 8.	Lieut. Tassart " " 21.
A.P.M.	" " 9.	Major Baillie " " 22.
Fourth Army	" " 10,11.	XIV Corps Cav Regt. " " 23.
XV Corps	" " 12.	2nd Cav. Division " " 24.
9th French Corps	" " 13.	Record 25.
4th Division	" " 14.	26, 27.

"C" Form (Duplicate). Army Form C. 2123.
MESSAGES AND SIGNALS. (In books of 50's in duplicate.)
No. of Message

| Charges to Pay. | Office Stamp. |
| £   s. | Y 16 X 16 OR |

Service Instructions.

Handed in at .... Office .... m. Received .... m.

TO

| Sender's Number | Day of Month | In reply to Number | A A A |

With reference to Para 2
14 Corps warning order
(282/54) of 15th October
our reference T 21 C ½ . 5
unless 6th Divn should be
amended to read T 21 C 7½ . 5
aaa added 4th and 6th Divns
14 Corps IA

11.30"

FROM
PLACE & TIME   Fourteenth Corps
11.55

Wt. 432—M437 500,000 Pads. HWV 5/16 Forms/C.2123.

Copy No 14

AMENDMENT TO XIV CORPS OPERATION ORDER NO. 73.

17th October, 1916.

Para. 7.

Delete and substitute.

A contact aeroplane will be in the air from 6.30 a.m. to 12 noon, and later as may be subsequently ordered.

Red flares will be lit at 7 a.m., 9 a.m., and 12 noon.

ACKNOWLEDGE.

Issued at 10.15am

Brigadier-General.
General Staff, XIV Corps.

Distribution as for O.O. 73

SECRET

Copy No. 3

XIV Corps No. S.82/60

17th October, 1916.

1. With reference to XIV Corps Operation Order No. 73 of 16/10/16, para. 1.

2. The hour of Zero will be 3.40 a.m. on the 18th October.

This hour is only to be communicated to those whom it immediately concerns. In no case should it be communicated by telephone.

3. The importance of obtaining good observation for the future should be impressed on all Commanders. This refers more particularly to the 6th Division area, in whose zone it is important to get observation from some place in N.21 on to BARLEY TRENCH.

If the exact objectives given to units do not obtain the necessary observation, they should at once advance their line to a position from which the necessary observation can be obtained.

4. ACKNOWLEDGE by wire.

Acknowledged 12.20p

F. Gathorne Hardy

Brigadier-General.

Issued at 10.10am

General Staff, XIV Corps.

Copies to :-

```
G.O.C., R.A.        Copy No. 1.    XIV Corps H.A. Copy No. 5.
9th French Corps     "    "  2.    No. 9 Sqdn R.F.C.     "   6.
4th Division         "    "  3.    "O" and "Q" Sects.
6th Division .       "    "  4.    No.4 Spec.Coy.R.E.    "   7.
```

4th Divisional Artillery
10th)
11th) Infantry Brigade
12th)
4th Division "Q"
A. D. M. S.

SECRET

D(2)

4th DIVISION WARNING ORDER

1. The 4th and 6th Divisions will renew the attack on the 18th instant.

2. Objectives of 4th Division FROSTY TRENCH, HAZY TRENCH, Gun Pits about T.5.a.4.2 - A...a.3.7, RAINY TRENCH, DEWDROP TRENCH and such portions of SPECTRUM TRENCH as are not in our possession.

3. The 11th and 12th Brigades will carry out this attack, 11th Brigade on the right, 12th Brigade on the left.

   Dividing line between Brigades:-

   A line drawn from N.34.d.0.0 to junction of track and TRANSLOY - LES BOEUFS Road at N.34.d.5.6 (Road inclusive to 12th Brigade.)

4. ACKNOWLEDGE.

16/10/16.

Lieut.-Colonel,
General Staff, 4th Division

SECRET.   Copy No. 25

4th. Divisional Artillery (Right Artillery).

Operation Order No. 23.

1. The 4th. and 6th. Divisions will renew the attack on 18th. instant, at Zero hour to be notified later.

2. The Objectives of 4th. Division will be:-

   FROSTY TR., HAZY TR., Gun-pits about T.5.a.3.7. and T.5.a.4.3., RAINY TR., DEWDROP TR., and portions of SPECTRUM TR. not yet in our possession.

3. 11th. and 12th. Inf. Brigs. will make the attack, 11th. Inf. Brig. on the Right and 12th. on the Left.

   Boundary between brigades N.34.d.0.0.---N.34.d.6.6.

4. For these operations 38th. Brig. R.F.A. will be attached to Right Group 4th. Div. Arty., which latter must establish communication forthwith. 20th. Div. Arty. is lending one battery of 74th. Brig. to assist Left Group 4th. Div. Arty, who will arrange for communication.
   38th. Brig. R.F.A. will come under orders of Right Group from 6p.m. 17th. instant.

5. Boundaries between 4th. D.A. Groups will be as at present. Between 4th. D.A. and 55th. D.A. the boundary will be the line N.35.c.0.0.---N.36.a.0.4., but for these operations only.

6. Right Group 4th. Div. Arty. will be covering part of 11th. and part of 12th. Inf. Brig. and must therefore arrange for communication with both.
   Lieut. Colonel HEAD R.F.A. will act as Liaison Officer with 12th. Inf. Brig. and Lt. Col. POTTINGER R.F.A. with 11th. Inf. Brig. These Officers should report at respective Brig. Hd. Qrs. not later than 6p.m. to-night.

7. Group Commanders will send a F.O.O. to each Battalion in the Front Line.
   This F.O.O. must be provided with means to open visual and telephonic communication and should not go beyond Battalion Hd. Qrs. until our line is definitely established on our Objective, when he should move to a point where best forward observation can be obtained.
   He should send back any possible information throughout and is primarily for Artillery and Observation purposes.

8. Group Commanders must arrange for visual signalling back from this F.O.O.

9. Tasks of Right Artillery will be as laid down in Table of Tasks attached.
   18 pounder guns will be employed -
         50% on Creeping, and
         50% on Standing Barrage.

10. Watches will be synchronised by an Officer from 4th. Div. H.Q. at 10th. Inf. Brig. Hd. Qrs. at 7p.m. to-night, when representatives from Groups will attend.

11. Rates of Fire.

    Rates of Fire - Zero - plus 2' - Super-intense.
                  Plus 2'- plus 10'- Intense.
                  Plus 10' onwards - Ordinary or as situation demands.

    Note:- Super-intense = 6 rounds per gun per minute.
           Intense = 4 " " " " "

12. Particular attention must be paid to the big drop in temperature, especially at night, and proper allowance made.

13. ACKNOWLEDGE.

    Issued at 2p.m.   D.C. Spencer-Smith Major

    17/October/1916.   Brigade Major 4th. Divisional Artillery

Copies to:-

    Arty. 14th. Corps   No. 1
    56th. Div. Arty.   Nos. 2 - 6
    Left Group   " 7 -15
    Right Group   " 16 -23
    4th. Div. G.   " 24 -25
    14th. Corps H.A.   " 26
    10th. Inf. Brig.   " 27
    11th. Inf. Brig.   " 28
    12th. Inf. Brig.   " 29
    French Liaison Offr." 30 -31
    H.A. Liaison Officer " 32
    20th. Div. Arty.   " 33 -37
    4th. Div. Am. Col. " 38
    29th. Arty. Brig.   " 39

Table of Tasks for Right Artillery.

18 Pounders.   50% for Standing and 50% for Creeping Barrage.

Standing Barrage. to be put down at Zero Hour.

Left Group 4th D.A.   (less 38th F.A.Bde.) and 1 Battery 20th D.A. on -

(i) ZENITH TRENCH between N.35.a.1.9. and N.34.b.9.5½.
(ii) Small trench about N.29.c.3.0.
(iii) Dug-outs about N.35.a.3.6.
(iv) Dug-out at N.35.a.0½.8½. and trenches immediately N.E. of this point.

This Barrage will remain on these points throughout, searching and sweeping over objectives until further orders.

Right Group 4th D.A.   (Plus 38th Bde.) on -

(i) RAINY TRENCH.
(ii) DEWDROP TRENCH and trench immediately E.of it as far S. as T.5.a.3.8.
(iii) Sunken Road N.35.a.2½.1½. --- N.35.a.4.4.

   To Lift off

(i) at Plus 2'.
(ii) at Plus 3½'.

   On to

Gun Pits about N.35.a.8½.3½.
Gun Pits about N.35.d.2½.9½.
CEMETERY - TRANSLOY (2 Batteries)., where they will remain searching and sweeping until further orders.
   To remain on (iii) throughout searching and sweeping as before.

56th Div.Arty.
On -   (i) Gun Pits T.5.a.2.7.
(ii) Gun Pits T.5.a.4.3
(iii) Small trench T.5.a.6½.6½. --- T.5.a.5.5.
(iv) FROSTY TRENCH.
(v) HAZY TRENCH and continuation to T.5.d.3.9½.
(vi) Trench T.5.b.2½.2½. --- T.5.b.5.1.

To Lift off (i) & (ii) at Plus 2½' and reinforce Barrage on (iii),(iv),(v) & (vi).

(iii) & (iv) at Plus 6½'.
(v) & (vi) From T.5.a.8½.6½. to T.5.d.3.9½. at Plus 6½'.
Remainder of HAZY Trench at Plus 14½'.

On to -
HAIL TRENCH.
SLEET TRENCH.
Gun-pits and small trenches about N.35.d.1½.6., N.35.d.1½.8½., T.5.b.9½.9½. where they will remain searching and sweeping over their objective until further orders.

Tasks (continued).

Creeping Barrage.

18 pounders - Remaining 50%.

Line A. :-

N.28.d.2.8.---N.35.a.4.2.

To be found by Left Group 4th. Div. Arty. and part of Right Group 4th. Div. Arty. within respective Zones.

Line B. :-

N.34.d.8.8.---T.5.d.3.9$\frac{1}{2}$.

To be found by remainder of Right Group 4th. Div. Arty. and 56th. Div. Arty. within respective zones.

Both Line A. and Line B. will be put down at Zero.

At plus 1' Line B. will commence to creep at 50 yards a minute by increases of 25 yards and at plus 9' - when both Line A. and B. are level - the whole line will creep on as before until the line -

N.29.a.5$\frac{1}{2}$.6$\frac{1}{2}$.---N.29.d.5.4.---N.36.a.0.8.---N.36.d.0.5. -

is reached, when it will reverse and creep backwards at the increased rate of 100 yards a minute by decreases of 50 yards until the line -

N.28.d.2.8.---N.35.a.4.2.---N.35.d.0.5.---T.5.b.6$\frac{1}{2}$.5.---

is reached, where it will stand as a defensive barrage until further orders.

4.5" Howitzers.

One battery of 56th. Div. Arty. will fire on High Ground in O.25.c. throughout.
Two batteries of 56th. Div. Arty. will fire on HAZY and FROSTY from Zero till Plus 4', and at that hour (plus 4') to lift on to SLEET, HAIL, Gun Pits and small trenches within their zone.
All other Howitzer batteries will fire lethal shell from Zero - plus 5' on to the CEMETERY CIRCLE between the Sunken Road and N.35.b.9$\frac{1}{2}$.9. during which period these batteries will fire at maximum rate that they can maintain with accuracy.
B.C's must watch the wind carefully and place their shell accordingly to obtain best possible effect.
At plus 5' 1 Battery Left Group 4th. Div. Arty. will lift back on to the elbow of ZENITH TRENCH about N.35.a.$\frac{1}{2}$.0$\frac{1}{2}$. and stand there until further orders.
1 Battery Right Group will continue on the CEMETERY until further orders.
Remaining How. Batteries will lift on to gun pits and small trenches within their respective Zones.
Lethal shell will not be employed after first 5 minutes.

SECRET.   Copy No. 7

10TH INFANTRY BRIGADE OPERATION ORDER NO: 78.
****

Reference - 1/20,000 Sheet 57c S.W.
and PLEX MAP "A".   14/10/16.

1. On October 14th the 10th Inf. Bde will attack and capture

    (i) Gun pits lying between T.5.a.4.2 and T.5.a.3.7.

    (ii) Such portions of RAINY TRENCH and DEWDROP TRENCH as are not in our hands.

   Hour of ZERO will be notified later.

2. The attack will be carried out by the 2nd Seaforth Highrs on the left and the 2nd R.Dublin Fusrs on the right.
   The 2nd Seaforth Highrs will attack, capture and consolidate RAINY and DEWDROP Trenches, and the NORTH GUNPITS, the 2nd R.Dublin Fusrs will attack, capture and consolidate the SOUTH GUNPITS in accordance with instructions already issued.
   After the attack the 2nd Seaforth Highrs will connect up DEWDROP TR with the NORTH GUNPITS and the 2nd R.Dublin Fusrs will connect up the WARWICKSHIRE TRENCH with the SOUTH GUNPITS.

3. The 21st West Yorks will dig a communication trench from FOGGY TRENCH to the centre of the NORTH GUNPITS immediately after the Gun Pits have been captured.

4. O.C. Machine Gun Company will arrange to have two Machine guns in Warwickshire Trench previous to ZERO hour with a view to stopping a counter-attack from the direction of FROSTY and HAZY Trenches.
   He will also send forward behind the attacking troops two gun teams with one gun only to take up position in the NORTH GUN PITS, and will give orders to the officer sent forward with the gun to make full use of any German machine guns which may be captured and in workable condition.

5. A slow and deliberate bombardment on HAZY and FROSTY trenches and the Gun Pits between T.5.a.4.4. and T.5.a.3.7. will take place on October 14th lasting till the hour of ZERO.

6. There will be no preliminary bombardment of DEWDROP TRENCH and no intense fire on any of the objectives before ZERO.

7. Instructions for medical arrangements will be issued later.

8. Prisoners of War will be handed over to Captain TROUSDELL (attached Hd Qrs, 10th Inf. Bde.) at junction of OX Trench and GINCHY-LES BOEUFS road at T.3.d.40.15, who will dispose of them in accordance with instructions already issued.

9. Watches will be synchronised by Brigade Signalling Officer at Brigade Hd Qrs at 1.15p.m.

10. "P" Bombs, Very Lights, grenades, rockets, flares, sandbags and tools will be issued to the assaulting troops previous to ZERO Hour.

11. Reports to be sent to Brigade Hd Qrs in QUARRY, GUILLEMONT.

12. O.C. 9th Field Coy, R.E. will report at Brigade Hd Qrs at a time to be notified later and will await orders.

13. ACKNOWLEDGE.

                                                                    Captain, B.M.
Issued at... 12. NOON   10th Infantry Brigade.

Copy No. 1 to 2nd Seaforth Highrs.
         2   2nd R.Dublin Fusrs.
         3   1st R.Irish Fusrs.
         4   1st R.Warwick Regt.
         5   Machine Gun Company.
         6   Trench Mortar Battery.
         7   4th Division "G".
         8.   Staff Captain.
         9   Capt. Trousdell.
        10   Brigade Signalling Officer.
        11   9th Field Coy, R.E.
        12   Artillery Liaison Officer.
        13   12th Infantry Brigade.
        14   35th French Inf. Bde.
        15   War Diary.
        16   -do-
        17   File.

****

- SECRET -   Copy No: 19

4th DIVISION OPERATION ORDER NO: 70.

16th October 1915.

1. 1st Bn Rifle Bde and 1st Bn E.Lancashire Regt (11th Inf. Bde) will relieve the 1st R.Irish Fusrs and 1st R.Warwickshire Regt (10th Inf.Bde) in support and reserve respectively to right sector on night 16/17th instant.

2. All details for the relief will be arranged between G.Os.C. 10th and 11th Inf. Bde. Completion of reliefs will be reported to Divisional H.Qrs.

3. On completion of relief -

(a) 1st Bn Rifle Bde and 1st Bn E.Lancashire Regt will come under command of G.O.C. 10th Inf. Bde.

(b) 1st R.Irish Fusrs and 1st Bn R.Warwickshire Regt will come under command of G.O.C. 11th Inf. Bde.

4. ACKNOWLEDGE.

Lieut:Colonel.
General Staff., 4th Division.

Issued at 6 a.m.

Copies to :-

10th.11th.12th Inf.Bde.
4th Div Arty.
-:- "Q"
C.R.E.
4th Div Signal Coy.
A.P.M. 4th Divn.
A.D.M.S.
14th Corps "G"
14th Corps "Q"
6th Division.
Capt Boillot. 2 Copies.

SECRET.   Copy No. ......

4th DIVISION OPERATION ORDER NO. 71.

16th October, 1916.

1.   11th Infantry Brigade will relieve the 10th Infantry Brigade in the right sector of the 4th Division line on the night 17/18th October.

All details of the relief will be arranged between G.Os.C. 10th and 11th Infantry Brigades direct. Completion of relief will be reported to Divnl. Head Quarters.

2.   On completion of relief 10th Infantry Brigade will be in Divisional Reserve and will be located in area A.9.a and c, A.3.c, A.4.d.

Brigade Head Quarters - A.4.d.

3.   ACKNOWLEDGE.

Lieut.Colonel,
General Staff, 4th Division.

Issued at 7. p.m.

Copies to 10th, 11th, 12th Inf. Brigs.
   4th Div. Arty.
   4th Div. Engrs.
   A.D.M.S.
   A.P.M.
   4th Div. Q.
   21st W.Yorks. R.
   4th Div. Sig.Co.
   6th Division.
   14th Corps G.
   14th Corps Q.
   French Liaison Officer.
   14th Corps H.A.
   9th Squadron R.F.C.
   War Diary

(B 1)

10th
11th } Bdes
12th

GOC RA

Q

1. Reference 4th Divn War Operation Order
No 72 the hour of zero will
be 3.40 a.m on the 18th October

This hour is only to be communicated
to those whom it immediately concerns.
In no case should it be communicated
by telephone

Q will inform ADMS and APM please

2. Acknowledge by wire

W H Barthtland
Oct 17th   Lt Col GS

S E C R E T.   Copy No. ....21..

4th DIVISION OPERATION ORDER NO. 72.

Reference - 1/20,000 Map Sheet 57 c S.W.
           and Map A.   17th October, 1916.

1.   The attack will be resumed by the 4th Army on October 18th at an hour ZERO to be notified later.

   The 6th French Army will attack on the same day.

2.   The objectives of the XIV Corps are as follows :-

<u>4th DIVISION.</u> HAZY TRENCH, FROSTY TRENCH, Gunpits in T.5.a, DEWDROP TRENCH and any portion of SPECTRUM TRENCH which is not in our hands.

<u>6th DIVISION,</u> will capture CLOUDY TRENCH from our present line up to N.21.d 5½.9¼, those portions of MILD TRENCH not in our possession, up to the Corps Boundary and the continuation of SHINE TRENCH as far as N.21.c 9½.5 obtaining touch with the XV Corps.

   Boundaries between 4th and 6th Divisions and between 4th Division and 18th French Division are shown on Map A in red.

3. (a)   The 11th Infantry Brigade will attack on the right from our junction with 18th French Division to the LES BOEUFS -TRANSLOY Road.

<u>Objectives.</u> Trench from T.5.b 5.1 (point of junction with 18th French Division) to T.5.b 3.3.
   HAZY TRENCH (T.5.d 4.8 - T.5.b 2.0 - T.5.a 9.9) ;
   FROSTY TRENCH ; Gunpits and Strong Points in T.5.a ; RAINY TRENCH ; DEWDROP TRENCH.
   The line HAZY TRENCH - DEWDROP will be consolidated and posts will be pushed out in front of this line.
A strong point will be established at T.5.a.9½.6½.

(b)   The 12th Infantry Brigade will capture any portion of SPECTRUM still held by the enemy as far South as the LES BOEUFS - TRANSLOY Road (inclusive).

   Dividing line between 11th and 12th Infantry Brigades is a line drawn from N.34.d 0.0 to junction of the LES BOEUFS - TRANSLOY Road with the track at N.34.d 6.6.

4.   The 9th Fd. Co. R.E. and 1/1st Durham Fd. Co. R.E. will be attached respectively to the 11th and 12th Infantry Brigades.

These units will be allotted definite tasks but will not leave their positions of assembly before the objectives are definitely captured.

5. The infantry will leave their trenches and advance to the attack at ZERO at which hour a standing barrage will be placed on the objectives to be attacked, and a creeping barrage will commence to creep forward from the objectives to a distance of 500 yards in rear, advancing at the rate of 100 yards a minute. This creeping barrage will cover the whole Divisional front. Details of barrages will be communicated separately.

The attack will be proceded by a bombardment of Heavy Artillery which has already commenced.

6. A 'TANK' (O.C. Lieut. TULL) will be stationed in the vicinity of LES BOEUFS and will advance at ZERO; objective Gunpits at T.5.a 3.7.

The 'TANK' will follow in rear of the infantry and will be used to attack any portion of the "Gunpit" Strong Point which holds out. The infantry will move independently of the 'TANK' and will NOT wait for it to advance.

Orders for the move of the 'TANK' prior to ZERO will be issued separately.

7. The 10th Infantry Brigade will be in Divisional Reserve.

8. A contact aeroplane will be in the air from ZERO till 12 noon and later as may be subsequently ordered. Red flares will be lit on reaching the objective, at Zero plus 1 hour and at 12 noon. Every effort must be made to mark the position of troops at the hours named.

9. Instructions as to medical arrangements will be issued separately

10. Prisoners of War will be dealt with as ordered in Operation Order No. 68 of 11th October.

11. An Officer from Divnl. Head Quarters will synchronise watches at 11th Inf. Brig. H.Q. at 7 p.m. on October 17th. Representatives from 11th and 12th Inf. Brigades and R.F.A. Groups will attend at 11th Inf. Brig. H.Q. at that hour.

12. ACKNOWLEDGE.

Issued at 8 a.m.

Lieut.Colonel,
General Staff, 4th Division.

Copies to 10th, 11th, 12th Inf.Brigs.
          4th Div. Arty.
          4th Div. Engrs.
          4th Div. Q.
          4th Div. Sig. Co.
          A.D.M.S.
          A.P.M.
          21st W.Yorks R. (Pioneers).
          14th Corps G.
          14th Corps Q.
          14th Corps H.A.
          6th Division.
          9th Squadron, R.F.C.
          French Liaison Officer.
          Lieut.TULL, O.C. TANK.

SECRET.

REFERENCE 4th DIVISION OPERATION NO. 72.

1. A 'TANK' commanded by Lieutenant TULL will assist in the operations on the 18th instant.

2. The 'TANK' will move from GINCHY at 5.45 p.m. on 17th instant and will take up a position to be selected by Lieut. Tull in LES BOEUFS.

ROUTE. GINCHY - LES BEOUFS Road, thence across country to T.10.b 5.5 to road running through T.4.d 5.5.

3. The 10th Infantry Brigade will detail an officer of M.G. Coy. with 2 guns to take up a position in a trench East of LES BOEUFS from 6 p.m. on 17th instant until arrival of 'TANK' in its position in the village.

The officer will listen for any sound of the 'TANK' moving, and if heard will at once open fire with his machine guns to drown the noise.

4. At ZERO hour on 18th instant the 'TANK' will move from its position of departure to its objective, the Gunpits in T.5.a 3.5.

ROLE. To assist the infantry in the capture of the strong point and to destroy the enemy's M.G. Emplacements.

When the objective has been gained the 'TANK' will withdraw.

- SECRET -
　　　　　　　　　　　　　　　　　　　　　　　　　　　　Copy No: 1

SUPPLEMENTARY ORDER to 4th DIVN O.O. No: 72.

17th Oct. 1916.

1. The French are carrying out an attack to-morrow on the right of the 4th Division. The G.O.C 11th Inf. Bde will arrange to support the left flank of the French attack, will keep in touch with it and will join up the right of the 11th Inf. Bde with the left of the French by a series of posts strongly held.

　　　The objectives of the French attack are as given in copy of 18th French Division Orders (Map attached) sent to G.O.C. 11th Inf. Bde.

　　　The advance of the 11th Inf. Bde must conform to the movements of the left of the 18th French Division in order to protect its left flank.

　　　G.O.C, R.A, 4th Division will arrange a barrage in conjunction with the Artillery Commander of the 18th French Division.

2. The hour of zero for the 18th French Division (which will not coincide with the zero of this Division) will be notified as soon as possible.

3. Acknowledge.

　　　　　　　　　　　　　　　　　　　　　　W. H. Barkthes
　　　　　　　　　　　　　　　　　　　　　　　　Lieut:Colonel.
Issued at 7 p.m.　　　　　　　　　　　General Staff., 4th Division.

Copies to :-
2　French Liaison.
3　XIVth Corps.
4　11th Inf. Bde.
5　10th Inf. Bde.
6　12th Inf. Bde.
　　File.
9　War Diary.
7　G.O.C., R.A.
8　Gale.

AMENDMENT TO 4TH DIVISION OPERATION ORDER NO.72.

Para.8.

Delete and substitute.

A contact aeroplane will be in the air from 6.30 am. to 12 noon, and later as may be subsequently ordered.

Red flares will be lit at 7 am. 9 am. and 12 noon. *Every effort must be made by troops to show their positions*

ACKNOWLEDGE.

[signature]
Lieut-Colonel,
General Staff, 4th Division.

17th October 1916.
Issued at :- *1.30 pm*

Copies to recipients of O.O.72.

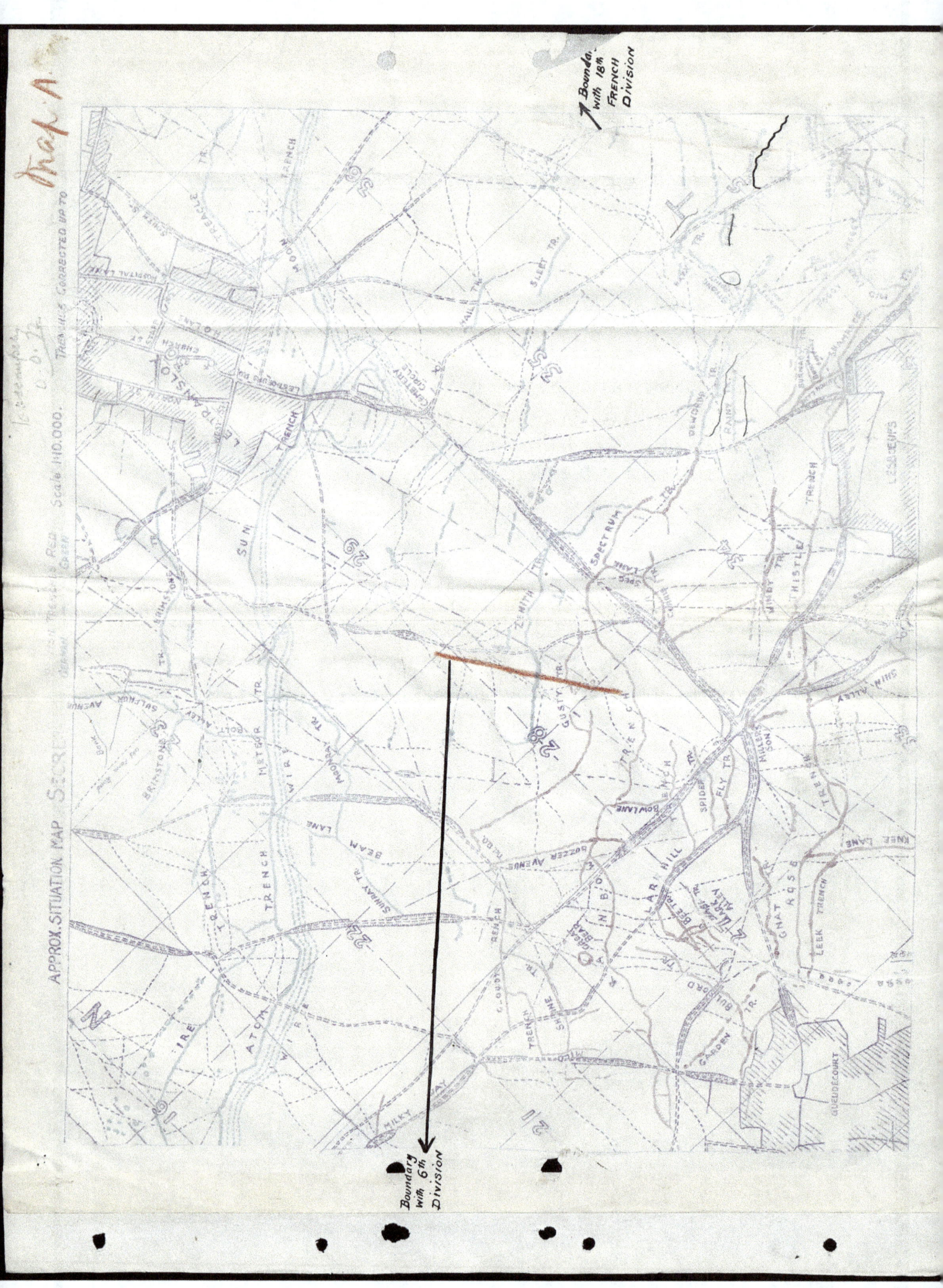

Operations

23 Oct

A ③
B ③
C ③
D ③
E ③

WAR DIARY - GENERAL STAFF - 4th DIVISION.

BRIQUETERIE,   NARRATIVE - 23rd October, 1916.
(BERNAFAY WOOD)
SOMME.

      Between the 18th and 23rd October preparations were made for a renewal of the attack on the enemy's positions and definite orders for the attack on the 23rd October were issued by the XIV Corps on the 20th instant.

      The French Army on the right of the 4th Division were also ordered to attack at the same date and at the same hour.

      The objectives allotted to the division are shown on the map attached to 4th Division Operation order No. 74.

      The attack was preceded by a continuous bombardment lasting several days. Zero hour which had originally been fixed for 11.30 a.m. was postponed till 2.30 p.m. on account of the dense fog which prevailed. The fog lifted before the attack began but visibility was never good.

      Objectives and dividing lines are shown on the map attached to 4th Division Operation Order.

      The 11th Infantry Brigade (less 1st E. Lancs. Regt.) and reinforced by the 1st R. Warwick Regt. and 2nd R. Dublin Fusiliers attacked on the right and the 12th Infantry Brigade (with the 2nd Seaforths) attached) on the left.

      The 10th Infantry Brigade (less 1st R. Warwicks and 2nd R. Dublin Fusiliers and 2nd Seaforths) with the 1st E. Lancs. was in Divisional Reserve.

      The 11th Infantry Brigade attacked with the 1st Hants. Regt. on the Right and the 2nd R. Dublin Fusiliers on the left in the first line supported respectively by the 1st Rifle Brigade and the 1st R. Warwick Regt.

      <u>Assembly Trenches for the 11th Inf. Bde.</u>

      1st Hants. Regmt.   FROSTY-ANTELOPE-ANDREWE'S POST-
                                   Half new trench from ANDREWE'S POST
                                   to FOGGY-FOGGY and part of THUNDER
                                   Trench.

1st Rifle Bde.	GERMAN TRENCH-MUGGY-SHAMROCK S.E. of FLANK AVENUE.
2nd R. Dub. Fus.	BURNABY-FOGGY-Half new trench to ANDREWE'S POST.
1st R. Warwicks	SHAMROCK and FLUFF Trenches
1st Somerset L.I. (Bde. Res.)	OX Trench

The 12th Inf. Brigade attacked with the 2nd Essex on the right, 2nd Lancs. Fus. in the centre, 1st King's Own on the left, and the 2nd Seaforths in support. ~~Dukes=~~ 2nd Duke of Wellington's in ~~reerv~~ reserve.

ASSEMBLY TRENCHES for 12th Brigade.

The 12th Inf. Brigade assembled in new trench from WINDY to BURNABY (constructed on night 22/23rd Oct.), WINDY Trench, THISTLE Trench and SPECTRUM Trench.

The 2nd Seaforths assembled in COW Trench.

Both Brigades advanced at zero hour and escaped the greater part of the enemy's barrage which was chiefly concentrated on the line of trenches just East of LESBOEUFS.

The right of the 11th Infantry Brigade (1st Hants Regt.) and the French left was almost immediately stopped by rifle and machine gun fire from BORITSKA Trench and from machine guns outside and beyond the trench, but a few ~~were~~ men occupied the end of BORITSKA Trench nearest to FROSTY.

The 1st Hants Regt were reinforced by the 1st Rifle Brigade. All attempts to advance on the right failed owing to machine gun fire but the left of the Hampshires with some of the Rifle Brigade eventually established a line East of FROSTY Trench. This party joined hands during the night with the 2nd R. Dublin Fusiliers in the Gunpits.

The left of the 11th Infantry Brigade (2nd R. Dublin Fusiliers) was stopped by machine gun fire within 30 yards of the gunpits but fired by the example of Sergt. Downie who charged a German machine gun the battalion again advanced and cleared a part of the Gunpits and the Strong point to the

Eastward destroying several machine guns.

The 1st R. Warwick Regt. started to advance through the Dublin Fusiliers but became involved in the hand to hand fighting at the Gunpits and the two battalions became completely mixed. Part of this force attempted to continue the advance but as both flanks were in the air and the men were under heavy machine gun fire from both DEWDROP, where the attack of the 12th Inf. Brigade had failed, and from BORITSKE Trench, no progress could be made.

The 12th Infantry Brigade did not succeed in capturing DEWDROP Trench although a few men of the Essex Regt. are believed to have reached the trench and to have moved on to the first objective.

Reports on this point are conflicting as few of the men, if any, who got beyond DEWDROP Trench returned.

The failure of the 12th Infantry Brigade to attain their objective appears to have been due entirely to machine gun fire which was very heavy and appeared to come from positions on the right front as well as from the front. DEWDROP Trench was found to be full of the enemy.

The 1st King's Own Regt. on the left after several attempts succeeded in gaining some 60 yards of SPECTRUM Trench but were unable to reach the SUNKEN Road at N.34.d.8.7.

The delay caused by the heavy fighting all along the Divisional front prevented our troops from closely following the Artillery barrage. As it was impossible to obtain accurate information of the whereabouts of the leading troops the artillery were unable to shorten their range and re-bombard the first objectives against which the attack had failed.

At the conclusion of the operations the Southern Gunpits, half the Northern Gunpits, the Strong Point, and some 60 yards of SPECTRUM Trench remained in our hands.

During the night trenches were dug connecting TWENTY FIVE Trench with the Southern GUNPITS, the STRONG POINT with FROSTY TRENCH.

Approximate casualties - 51 Officers.
1139 Other ranks.

SECRET

Copy No. 14

XIV CORPS OPERATION ORDER NO.76.

C(3)

Ref. Map: SHEET 57c. S.W. 1/10,000.
Special map attached.   20th October, 1916.

1. XIV Corps Warning Order No. S.82/67 of the 19th instant is cancelled.

2. The XIV Corps will renew the attack on the 23rd of October in conjunction with an attack by the 6th French Army, at an hour zero to be communicated later.

3. The object of the operation by the XIV Corps on October the 23rd is to establish itself in such a position that MOON TRENCH, LE TRANSLOY CEMETERY, LE TRANSLOY and also SUNRAY TRENCH can be attacked from the S.W. at a later date.

It is essential that the attack should be pushed with the utmost determination, and the Corps front advanced to within assaulting distance of the LE TRANSLOY line.

4. The attack will be carried out by the 4th Division, reinforced by one Infantry Brigade of the 33rd Division, on the right, and by the 8th Division on the left.

5. The line to be reached will be the line - N.36.c.6.0 - N.36.c.6.4 - N.35.b.7.3 - N.35.b.0.6 - N.35.a. 5.9½ - N.28.b. 4½.2½ - N.28.a.8½.9, and that portion of MILD TRENCH and CLOUDY TRENCH which is not at present in our possession.

6. The attack will be carried out in two bounds.

The objectives to be reached at each bound, the dividing line between Corps and the dividing line between Divisions are shown on the attached map.

7. At zero, the Infantry will leave their trenches and advance to the attack of the first objective, at which hour a standing barrage will be placed on the objectives to be attacked, and a creeping barrage will commence in front of

- 2 -

the Infantry, and creep forward at the rate of 50 yards a minute.

At zero plus 30 minutes, the barrage will again become intensive and the Infantry will advance to the attack of the second objective.

The attack will be preceded by a bombardment of heavy artillery, which has now already commenced.

The ground between the objectives to be captured, and the LE TRANSLOY system, will be systematically swept by 18-pounder shrapnel and H.E., especially the latter, and 4.5" Howitzers, throughout the period of bombardment.

8. Certain Tanks will be placed at the disposal of Divisions, details of which will be communicated later.

9. Strong points will be established as follows :-

    4th DIVISION.   T.5.b.$\frac{1}{2}$.7.
                               Point of contact with the French.
                               SLEET TRENCH.
                               HAIL TRENCH.

    8th DIVISION.   ORION,
                               N.21.d.7$\frac{1}{2}$.5.

10. A contact aeroplane will be in the air from zero plus three minutes till dark, and will not show in the neighbourhood of our lines previous to the hour of zero.

Red flares will be lit on obtaining each objective and at 4 p.m.

11. Watches will be synchronized by telephone from Corps Headquarters at 6 p.m. on October the 22nd.

12. ACKNOWLEDGE by wire

F. Gathorne Hardy

Issued at ....6 p.m.......

Brigadier-General.
General Staff, XIV Corps.

DISTRIBUTION.

Copies to :-

Corps Commander	Copy No. 1.
B.G.G.S.	" " 2.
I.G.	" " 3.
D.A.&Q.M.G.	" " 4.
G.O.C., R.A.	" " 5.
C.E.	" " 6.
A.D.A.S.	" " 7.
D.D.M.S.	" " 8.
A.P.M.	" " 9.
Fourth Army	" " 10, 11.
XV Corps	" " 12.
9th French Corps	" " 13.
4th Division	" " 14.
6th Division	" " 15.
8th Division	" " 16.
33rd Division	" " 17.
XIV Corps H.A.	" " 18.
9th Sqdn R.F.C.	" " 19.
"O" and "Q" Sect.	
No. 4 Spec. Coy. R.E.	" 20.
Lieut. Tassart	" 21.
Major Baillie	" 22.
XIV Corps Cavalry Reg.	" 23.
2nd Cavalry Division	" 24.
Record	" 25.
	26. 27.

SECRET

NOTE TO OPERATION ORDER NO. 76.

The interval between the first bound and the second bound is still under discussion, and the time of zero plus 30 minutes, given in para.7, is subject to alteration.

The final decision will be communicated to-morrow.

F. Gathorne Hardy
Brigadier-General,
General Staff, XIV Corps.

20th Oct. 1916.
Issued with O.O. No. 76.

XIV CORPS SITUATION MAP   SCALE — 1:20,000.   No. Y.17.
SITUATION 9 A.M. 19-10-16.   BRITISH FRONT LINE
NEW TRENCHES FROM PHOTOS 16-10-16

Issued with XIV Corps.
O.O. 76 dated 20/10/16.

Key.
Corps Boundy. —
Division Boundy. —
1st Objective. —
2nd Objective. —

SECRET.
~~CONFIDENTIAL.~~

Copy No. 25

Reference:- Sheet 57.c.S.W.1/20,000.
and Map A attached..

D(3)

4TH DIVISION WARNING OPERATION ORDER. 74.

~~20~~th October 1916.

1. The Fourth Army will renew the attack on the 23rd. October in combination with the French Army on the right.

Zero hour will be communicated later.

2. The task of the XIV Corps will be carried out in two stages, shown respectively by a BROWN and GREEN Line.

The object of the operation by the XIV Corps on October 23rd. is to establish itself in such a position that LOOP TRENCH, LE TRANSLOY CEMETERY, LE TRANSLOY and also SUNRAY TRENCH can be attacked from the S.W. at a later date.

The 4th Division with one brigade 33rd Division attached will attack on the right and the 8th Division on the left. XIV Corps boundaries are shown in RED, boundary between 4th and 8th Divisions in YELLOW.

(3. (a) The first objective of the 4th Division (BROWN Line) includes the portions of BORITSKA and MIRAGE Trenches which lie within the 4th Division boundary, HAZY TRENCH, GUNPITS in T.5.a. and DEWDROP TRENCH, and the establishment of a line through T.5.b.7.3.(junction with French) - N.35.c.9.4. - SUNKEN Road at N.35.a.5.5. The creeping barrage will halt to indicate this line.

(b) The second objective of the 4th Division (GREEN Line) includes HAIL TRENCH, SLEET TRENCH, the trenches between SLEET TRENCH and ORION (ORION exclusive to 4th Division), and the establishment of a line through N.36.c.6.0. (junction with French) - N.36.c.6.5. - N.36.a.0.3. - N.35.b.6.6. - N.35.a.9.8. (junction with 8th Division).

4. (a) The 11th Infantry Brigade will attack on the right and 12th Infantry Brigade on the left, boundary between Brigades the GINCHY - LES BOEUFS Road - junction of SHAMROCK

and THISTLE TRENCHES - Southern end of DEWDROP - Northern end of SLEET - junction of track with HAIL TRENCH at N.35.b.7.0. (Marked on attached map in BLUE).

(b) The 9th Fd.Coy.R.E. and 1/1st Durham Fd.Coy R.E. will be attached respectively to the 11th and 12th Infantry Brigades. These units will be allotted definite tasks and will only be employed to consolidate objectives which have been definitely secured.

(c) The 1/1st Renfrew Fd.Coy.R.E., 10th Infantry Brigade, one Infantry Brigade of the 33rd Division and 21st W.Yorks.R. (Pioneers) will be in Divisional Reserve.

5. Troops will be assembled as under :-

<u>11th and 12th Inf. Brigs.</u>

East of the line T.9.d.9.0. - T.9.Central - T.3.a.0.0. by 4.30 a.m. on October 23rd.

<u>10th Infantry Brigade.</u>

2 Battalions in T.8.d. and T.9.c. by 4.30 a.m. Oct.23rd.
2 Battalions in GUILLEMONT.

<u>Inf.Brigade 33rd Division.</u>

TRONES WOOD Area by Zero hour on October 23rd.

6. At Zero hour the infantry will leave their trenches and advance to attack the first objective (BROWN Line), at which hour a standing barrage will be placed on the objectives to be attacked, and a creeping barrage will commence in front of the infantry and creep forward at the rate of 50 yards a minute. At Zero <u>plus</u> 30 minutes the barrage will again become intense and the infantry will advance to attack the second objective (GREEN Line).

Artillery barrages in detail will be notified later.

As soon as the leading battalions of the 11th and 12th Infantry Brigades have left their assembly trenches for the attack of the first objective the remaining battalions of these

/Brigades

Subject to alteration

Brigades will move forward to occupy the departure trenches of the leading battalions.

It is essential that the Divisional front should be advanced to within assaulting distance of LE TRANSLOY and the attack will be pushed with the utmost resolution all along the line.

7. Both objectives will be consolidated immediately after capture and strong points constructed as below :-

<u>By 11th Infantry Brigade.</u>

About T.5.b.?.7.

Point of junction with the French.

SLEET TRENCH.

<u>By 12th Infantry Brigade.</u>

HAIL TRENCH.

About N.35.b.2.7.

About N.35.a.3.2.

8. The preliminary bombardment has already begun and will continue up to the hour of Zero on October 23rd.

9. One 'TANK' is allotted to each Brigade.

<u>Objectives.</u>

11th Inf.Brig. 'TANK' - GUNPITS in T.5.a.

12th Inf.Brig. 'TANK' - To clear LES BOEUFS - TRANSLOY SUNKEN ROAD as far East as N.35.a.5.5.

Tanks will leave their positions of assembly in LES BOEUFS at Zero hour. Orders for move to position of assembly and routes after Zero will be issued separately.

10. A contact aeroplane will be in the air from Zero plus 3 minutes till dark.

Red flares will be lit on attaining each objective and at 4 p.m.

11. Watches will be synchronised at 11th Brigade H.Q. at 7 p.m. on October 22nd.

12. A C K N O W L E D G E.

Issued at ~~11.15 p.m~~ 1.15am

[signature]
Lieut-Colonel,
General Staff, 4th Division.

Copies to :-

10th, 11th, 12th Inf.Brigs.
4th Div.Arty.
4th Div.Engineers.
4th Div.Signal Coy.
A.D.M.S.4th Division.
A.P.M.4th Division.
4th Division "Q".
Pioneers(21st W.Yorks Regt.)
14th Corps "G".
14th Corps "Q".
14th Corps H.A.
8th Division.
33rd Division.
9th Squadron R.F.C.
French Liaison Officer.
Officer i/c Tanks.

APPROX. SITUATION MAP. X.A1.   BRITISH TRENCHES. RED.   GERMAN TRENCHES. GREEN.   SECRET

SCALE 1:10,000.   20-10-1916.

SECRET.   Copy No. 17

4th. Divisional Artillery (Right Artillery).

Operation Order No. 26.

1. Right Artillery will put down the following barrages to-night (21/22nd.).
   Group Commanders will take that portion of the line within their own zones. 4th. Div. Arty. will overlap 25 yards in 56th. Div. Arty. and vice versa.

2. **7p.m. (Zero).**

   All 18 pdrs.

   Line N.35.a.2.4½.---N.35.a.1.0.---T.5.a.7½.7½.---T.5.b.3½.1⅓.

   All 4.5" Hows.

   Same line with exception that those belonging to 56th. Div. Arty. will start 50 yards E. of this line.

   At plus 1' the whole barrage will move and creep at usual rate until the line N.35.a.9.8.---N.35.d.7.5.---T.6.a.1½.8. is reached when barrage will cease and batteries resume ordinary night firing.

   5a.m. (Zero).

   All 18 pdrs. & 4.5" Hows.

   Line N.30.c.6.5¼.---N.36.b.6½.0.

   At plus 1' the whole barrage will move and creep backwards at same rate as before until the line N.35.a.6.6½.---T.6.a.0.5. is reached when barrage will cease and batteries resume tasks as before.

3. 50% H.E. and 50% Shrapnel to be used in each case.

4. Apart from above tasks 18 pounders will fire 25 rounds per gun during the night.

5. Watches will be synchronised at 5p.m. tonight from this Office.

6. Rate of Fire:- 18 pounders 2 rounds per gun per minute.
                  4.5" Hows. 1 round per gun per minute.

7. Acknowledge.

   Issued at 11a.m.   D.C. Spencer-Smith Major

   21/October/1916.   Brigade Major 4th. Divisional Artillery

Copies to:-

Arty. 14th. Corps	No. 1	French Liaison Officer	No.	22-23
56th. Div. Arty.	Nos. 2-6	H.A. Liaison Officer	"	24
4th. Div. Arty.	" 7-15	Left Artillery	"	25-29
4th. Div. G.	" 16-17	14th. F.A. Brig.	"	30
14th. Corps H.A.	" 18	29th. F.A. Brig.	"	31
10th. Inf. Brig.	" 19	4th. Div. An. Col.	"	32
11th. Inf. Brig.	" 20			
12th. Inf. Brig.	" 21			

SECRET.   Copy No. __16__

4th. Divisional Artillery (Right Artillery).
Warning - Operation Order No. 27.

1. 4th. Army will renew the attack on October 23rd. in conjunction with the French, at a Zero hour to be notified later.
   The task of 14th. Corps will be carried out in two stages - objective in each case being called the BROWN and GREEN Line respectively.

2. 4th. Division will attack on the right, with 8th. Division on its left.
   11th. Inf. Brig. will attack on the right and 12th. Inf. Brig. on the Left.

3. Boundaries:-

   Between 4th. Division and French - as now.

   Between 4th. and 8th. Division - the line N.34.b.7.2.---N.35.a.5.5.---N.35.a.9.8.---road N. of CEMETERY.

   Between 11th. Inf. Brig. and 12th. Inf. Brig. the line T.4.b.4.3.---T.5.a.2½.8½.---N.35.c.9.3½.---N.36.a.0.2.

   Between 4th. Div. Arty. and 56th. Div. Arty. as now except when otherwise ordered.

4. BROWN LINE will be -

   T.5.b.7.3.---N.35.c.9.4.---N.35.a.5.5.

   GREEN LINE will be -

   N.36.c.6.0.---N.36.c.6.5.---N.36.a.0.3.---N.35.b.6.6.---N.36.a.9.8.

   In case of each advance the creeping barrage will halt 150 yards E. of BROWN and GREEN LINE respectively to mark the line for the infantry.

5. 4th. Div. Arty. will provide Liaison Officer (Lieut. Col. HEAD) with 12th. Inf. Brig. and 56th. Div. Arty. with 11th. Inf. Brig.
   F.O.O's with Battalions in the front line will be provided as in previous operations.

6. Tasks of Right Artillery are outlined in Appendix attached.

7. Watches will be synchronised at 11th. Inf. Brig. Hd. Qrs. at 7p.m. on October 22nd., when representatives of Groups will attend.
   They will be synchronised every day in future from this Office at same hour.

8. Acknowledge.

   Issued at 6p.m.   D.C. Spencer-Smith Major
   21/October/1916.   Brigade Major 4th. Divisional Artillery

Copies to:-
   Arty. 14 Corps   No. 1   12th. Inf. Brig.   No. 21
   56th. Div. Arty.   Nos. 2-6   French Liaison Officer   " 22-23
   4th. Div. Arty.   "   7-15   H.A. Liaison Officer   " 24
   4th. Div. G.   "   16-17   Left Artillery   " 25-29
   14th. Corps H.A.   "   18   14th. F.A. Brig.   " 30
   10th. Inf. Brig.   "   19   29th. F.A. Brig.   " 31
   11th. Inf. Brig.   "   20   4th Div Am. Col.   " 32

Reference Map Y.16 A.

APPENDIX to WARNING ORDER.

General Idea of Tasks for Right Artillery on 23rd. instant.

1. Three Roving Sections will be detailed. One from 4th. Div. Arty. and two from 56th. Div. Arty.
   Officers in charge of these will watch for special or fleeting opportunities and act on their own initiative to assist our advance in every possible way.

2. Two barrages will be formed - Creeping and Standing - 50% of 18 pounders on each, with 4.5" Hows. added to Standing Barrage.

CREEPING BARRAGE.

(A) On line - T.5.b.3.0.---T.5.a.7.8.
    This is subject to modification for safety reasons.

(B) 100 yards in front of the jumping off line of our Infantry - between points T.5.a.4.2. and N.34.d.5.2. (approx.).

Special care must be taken by guns forming (B) to avoid SPECTRUM and FROSTY trenches.

The "Creeper" will move at plus 1' and creep at usual rate to a line 150 yards E. of the BROWN Line where it will stand until further orders, -

(A) moving to the line T.5.b.9.5½.---N.35.d.4.4½. and
(B) to the line N.35.d.4.4½.---N.35.a.7.6½.

4th. Div. Arty. will form (B) Creeper, owing to difficulties of crest for 56th. Div. Arty., and guns must be registered accordingly in good time.

STANDING BARRAGE.

On (i) SUNKEN Road N.34.d.9½.9.---N.35.a.4½.4½.
   (ii) A line 25 yards W. of DEWDROP and Gun Pits in T.5.a. as far as FROSTY TR. admits with safety.
  (iii) Northern portion of HAZY.
   (iv) MIRAGE TR. within 4th. Div. Zone.

At plus ½' this barrage would move and creep at the rate of 100 yards a minute by increases of 50 yards to the line SLEET TR---TRENCH N.35.a.8½.3½., where it will remain for 10 minutes - sweeping and searching 100 yards on either side of that line.
At conclusion of these 10 minutes it will again advance at previous rate up to the TRANSLOY Line, on reaching which it will jump back on to the following:-

CEMETERY.
HAIL Tr.
SLEET TR.
Gun Pits N.35.d.9½.0.

It will remain here sweeping and searching as before until 5 minutes before 2nd advance of the Infantry when all guns

of Standing Barrage will jump on to the line T.6.a.3½.7½.---
N.35.b.1.8. and creep forward as before as far as the TRANSLOY
support line N.36.b.9½.5.---N.30 Central and then continue
creeping backwards and forwards between TRANSLOY front and
support lines until further orders.

All Standing Barrage will be found by 56th. Div. Arty.
In addition to the above the two roving sections of 56th. Div.
Arty. will fire H.E. at intense rate on to gun pits at
T.5.a.2.7. ~~for first 10 minutes after Zero.~~
From zero to plus 1'.

4.5" Howitzers.

4th. Div. Arty.

One Battery will commence on the SUNKEN Road N.35.a.0.9.---
N.35.a.4½.4½. and lift -

First on to Gun Pits and small trenches in N.35.a. & b. and
Subsequently on CEMETERY CIRCLE between N.35.b.9.9.---
N.29.d.9½.0.---N.29.d.9.1½.

One Battery on SUNKEN Road N. of CEMETERY and CEMETERY CIRCLE
N.29.d.6½.0.---N.35.b.9.9. - throughout.

56th. Div. Arty.

One Battery on N. end of HAZY, lifting -

First on to HAIL TR. and
Subsequently on to front house of TRANSLOY S. of LES BOEUFS Road.

One Battery on SLEET TR, Small trenches in N.35.d. and Gun Pits
N.35.d.9½.0. lifting subsequently on to front houses of
TRANSLOY S. of LES BOEUFS Road.

One Battery on any high houses in LE TRANSLOY with occasional
salvoes on to the High Ground in O.25.c.

One Battery on the SUNKEN Road N.36.a.6.0.---N.30.c.8.0.

RATES of FIRE.

1st. Advance.

    Zero - plus 10'   Intense.
    Plus 10' - plus 15'   Ordinary.
    Plus 15' - plus 20'   Intense.
    Plus 20' -   Ordinary (1 round per gun per min)
                           until next advance, unless S.O.S.
                           is sent up.

2nd. Advance.

As in 1st.

No definite times can be given for lifts at present.

SECRET

Amendments and Additions

to

Table of Tasks for Right Artillery on 23rd October, 1916.
_____

Page 1. Para.2. line 5. after "T.5.a.8.8." add "Found by 56th D.A."

Para.2. line 8. after "N.34.d.4½.3½." add "Found by 4th D.A."

line 9. after 'travel' strike out "up the SUNKEN ROAD" and

insert "along a line 50 yards South of, and parallel to the SUNKEN ROAD".

line 12. Strike out "plus 1'" and substitute "plus ½'".

line 19. For "N.36.b.1.3." read "N.36.d.1.3."

line 22. After "Barrage" add "Found by 56th D.A."

line 25. Strike out and substitute -
"To move at Plus 3' and jump into place on the standing barrage line -
T.6.a.0.5½. --- SLEET TRENCH --- N.35.a.6.6."

line 27. Strike out and substitute -
"To move at Plus 4' and jump to standing barrage line as above".

line 29. Strike out and substitute -
"To move at Plus 5' and jump to standing barrage as above".

NOTE:- These times of Lifts have still to be confirmed.

lines 31 & 32. Strike out sub-paras:(iii) & (iv) and substitute -
"(iii) N.of HAZY TRENCH to S.End of MIRAGE TRENCH within British Zone".

Page 2. line 2. Strike out -
"picking up section as detailed in (ii)"

line 4. Strike out - and substitute -
"T.6.a.0.5½. --- SLEET TRENCH --- N.35.a.6.6. and add
"Keeping 50 yards South of and parallel to SUNKEN Road - N.35.c.0.9. --- N.35.a.4½.4½."

line 16. After 'support' - Strike out -
"and front line until further orders"
and substitute -
"line and a line N.36.d.2.6. --- N.29.d.8.0.

22/October/1916.

D.C.Spencer-Smith.Major.RA.
Brigade Major, 4th Divisional Arty.

Copies to:-
   Arty.14th Corps.   French Liaison Officer.
   56th Div.Arty.   H.A.Liaison Officer.
   4th Div.Arty.   Left Artillery.
   4th Div.G.   14th F.A.Bde.
   14th Corps H.A.   29th F.A.Bde.
   10th Inf.Bde.   4th Div.Am.Col.
   11th Inf.Bde.
   12th Inf.Bde.

2nd Amendment
to

Table of Tasks for Right Artillery on 23rd October 1916.

Para.2.
Creeping Barrage. Line A.

Line A will now be put down in 2 sections -
Northern Section -
T.5.b.$\frac{1}{2}$.3. --- T.5.a.8.8.
Southern Section -
T.5.d.1$\frac{1}{2}$.0$\frac{1}{2}$. --- T.5.a.9$\frac{1}{2}$.2.
Of these Sections -
The Northern Section will start creeping at Plus 1$\frac{1}{2}$'
and not at Plus $\frac{1}{2}$' as before ordered.
The Southern Section will start creeping at Plus $\frac{1}{2}$' as already ordered.

56th D.A. must arrange to register the Southern Section early on 23rd instant.

STANDING BARRAGE.

Reference sub-section (ii) and amendments thereto -
The lines given in the amendments for Lifts are cancelled and the sections will lift as follows:-

First Section at Plus   1'
Second Section at Plus   2'.
Third Section at Plus   4'.

4.5" Howitzers.

4th D.A.
Times given in Table of Tasks for Lifts of First Battery are cancelled, and the following substituted:-

(A) Section will lift off SUNKEN ROAD at Plus 1'.
(B) Section will lift off SUNKEN ROAD at Plus 3'.

Page 2. Line 22.
For "HAZY down to T.5.a.0.6." read "HAZY down to T.5.b.0.6".

Page 3. Line 3.
For "T.5.a.0.6."   read "T.5.b.0.6."

Page 1. Para.2.
Lines 13 and 15 and in Amendments and additions to Page 2.
For "N.35.a.6.6." substitute "N.35.a.7.7."

Appendix issued with "Warning Operation Order" No.27.
is cancelled and "Table of Tasks for Right Artillery on 23rd instant" issued with Operation Order No.28. substituted for it.
Acknowledge.

22/10/1916.   D.C.Spencer-Smith.Major,R.A.
                        Brigade Major, 4th Divisional Artillery.
Copies to:-
    As for Operation Order.

SECRET.

3rd. Amendment

to

Right Artillery Table of Tasks for 23rd. instant.

Page 3.

Strike out lines 10 and 11 and insert -

"One Battery -
One Section on MOON TRENCH between N.36.b.6.0. and N.36.a.7½.8.

One Section on TRANSLOY support line between O.31.a.⅓.5. and N.30.d.1.1.

throughout".

Rates of Fire.

At end of para. - add:-

18 pounders.

"During intense rate on each occasion - First Two minutes will be at 6 rounds per gun per minute, - Next Eight minutes at 4 rounds per gun per minute - Next Ten minutes at 3 rounds per gun per minute."

ACKNOWLEDGE.

Issued at 6a.m.   D.C.Spencer-Smith Major

22/10/16.   Brigade Major 4th. Divisional Artillery

Copies to:-

As for Operation Order No. 28.

SECRET.   Copy No. 17

4th. Divisional Artillery (Right Artillery).

Warning - Operation Order No. 27.

1. 4th. Army will renew the attack on October 23rd. in conjunction with the French, at a Zero hour to be notified later.
   The task of 14th. Corps will be carried out in two stages - objective in each case being called the BROWN and GREEN Line respectively.

2. 4th. Division will attack on the right, with 8th. Division on its left.
   11th. Inf. Brig. will attack on the right and 12th. Inf. Brig. on the Left.

3. Boundaries:-

   Between 4th. Division and French - as now.

   Between 4th. and 8th. Division - the line N.34.b.7.2.---N.35.a.5.5.---N.35.a.9.8.---road N. of CEMETERY.

   Between 11th. Inf. Brig. and 12th. Inf. Brig. the line T.4.b.4.3.---T.5.a.2½.8½.---N.35.c.9.3½.---N.36.a.0.2.

   Between 4th. Div. Arty. and 56th. Div. Arty. as now except when otherwise ordered.

4. BROWN LINE will be -

   T.5.b.7.3.---N.35.c.9.4.---N.35.a.5.5.

   GREEN LINE will be -

   N.36.c.6.0.---N.36.c.6.5.---N.36.a.0.3.---N.35.b.6.6.---N.36.a.9.8.

   In case of each advance the creeping barrage will halt 150 yards E. of BROWN and GREEN LINE respectively to mark the line for the infantry.

5. 4th. Div. Arty. will provide Liaison Officer (Lieut. Col. HEAD) with 12th. Inf. Brig. and 56th. Div. Arty. with 11th. Inf. Brig.
   F.O.O's with Battalions in the front line will be provided as in previous operations.

6. Tasks of Right Artillery are outlined in Appendix attached.

7. Watches will be synchronised at 11th. Inf. Brig. Hd. Qrs. at 7p.m. on October 22nd., when representatives of Groups will attend.
   They will be synchronised every day in future from this Office at same hour.

8. Acknowledge.

   Issued at 6p.m.   D.C. Spencer-Smith Major
   21/October/1916.   Brigade Major 4th. Divisional Artillery

Copies to:-
Arty. 14 Corps	No. 1	12th. Inf. Brig.	No. 21
56th. Div. Arty.	Nos. 2-6	French Liaison Officer	" 22-23
4th. Div. Arty.	" 7-15	H.A. Liaison Officer	" 24
4th. Div. G.	" 16-17	Left Artillery	" 25-29
14th. Corps H.A.	" 18	14th. F.A. Brig.	" 30
10th. Inf. Brig.	" 19	29th. F.A. Brig.	" 31
11th. Inf. Brig.	" 20	4th. Div Am. Col.	" 32

SECRET.   Copy No ___17___

4th Divisional Artillery (Right Artillery).

Operation Order No. 28.
---------oOo---------

1.   4th D.A. Warning Operation Order No.27. is confirmed with following additions and amendments.

2.   Reference Para.4. Barrages will halt on lines laid down in Table of Tasks attached.

3.   25% H.E. and 75% Shrapnel will be used throughout.

4.   Group Commanders will send an F.O.O. to each Battalion on the Front Line.
     This F.O.O. must be provided with means to open visual and telephonic communication and should not go beyond Battalion H.Q. until objective is reached and our line definitely established in each case, when he should move to wherever best forward observation can be obtained.
     He should send back any possible information throughout and is primarily for Artillery and Observation purposes.

5.   Group Commanders must arrange for visual signalling back from these F.O.O's.

6.   ACKNOWLEDGE.

Issued at 2 p.m.
22/10/1916.   D.C.Spencer-Smith.Major.RA.
                           Brigade Major 4th Divisional Artillery.

Copies to:-

    Arty. 14th Corps.   No.1.
    56th Div.Arty.   Nos.2-6
    4th Div.Arty.   " 7-15.
    4th Div.G.   " 16-17.
    14th Corps H.A.   No.18.
    10th Inf.Bde.   " 19.
    11th Inf.Bde.   " 20.
    12th Inf.Bde.   " 21.
    French Liaison Officer. Nos.22-23.
    H.A.Liaison Officer.   No.24.
    Left Artillery.   " 25-29.
    14th F.A.Bde.   " 30.
    29th F.A.Bde.   " 31.
    4th Div.Am.Col.   " 32.

SECRET.   Reference Map X.A.2
                                                       attached.

Table of Tasks
for
Night Artillery on 23rd. instant.

1. Three roving Sections will be detailed -
   One from 4th. Div. Arty. and two from 56th. Div. Arty.
   Officers in charge of these will watch for special fleeting
   opportunities and act on their own initiative, except when
   otherwise ordered, and assist the Infantry in every possible
   way.

2. Two barrages will be formed - "Creeping" and "Standing" -
   50% of remaining 18 pounders on each, with 4.5" Hows. added
   to the "Standing" Barrage.

CREEPING BARRAGE.

(A)   On line T.5.b.3.0.---T.5.a.8.8.

(B)   100 yards in front of the jumping off line of our
      Infantry - approximately the line T.5.a.5.1½.---
      N.34.d.4½.3½.

The left gun of this barrage is to travel up the SUNKEN Road
N.34.d.7½.7.---N.35.a.4½.4½. keeping along the northern edge
as far as possible.

The "Creeper" (both (A) & (B)) will move at plus 1' and
creep at rate of 50 yards a minute by increases of 25 yards
on to a line T.6.a.0.5½.---N.35.d.4.4½.---N.35.a.6.6.

(A) moving to T.6.a.0.5½.---N.35.d.4.4½.
(B) moving to N.35.d.4.4½.---N.35.a.6.6.

where it will stand until plus 31', when it will again move
on at rate as before until the line -

N.36.b.1.5.---N.36.a.5.0.---N.36.a.0.5.---N.35.b.4.8.---
N.35.b.0.9.---

is reached, when it will stand until further orders.

STANDING BARRAGE.

On (i)   Line T.5.a.5.1½.---N.34.d.6½.6½.
   (ii) One Section on SUNKEN Road at N.34.d.8½.7½.
         To move forward at plus 1½'.

         One Section on SUNKEN Road at N.35.c.½.9½.
         To move forward at plus 2½'.

         One Section on SUNKEN Road at N.35.a.3.2.
         To move forward at plus 4½'.

         These Sections must not fire N. of this road.

   (iii) N. portion of HAZY down to T.5.b.0.6.
   (iv) MIRAGE TR. within British Zone.

2.

At plus ½' this barrage will move and creep forward at 100 yards a minute, (picking up section as detailed in (ii)), by increases of 50 yards until the line -

N.35.d.8.0.---SHEET TR.---TRENCH N.35.a.8.3½.---

is reached when it will remain sweeping and searching 100 yards on either side of this line until plus 11'. At which hour it will again move on at rate as before until the line

N.36.d.5½.9.---N.30.c.3.5½.---

is reached (at plus 21'), when it will creep backwards at same rate to the line -

T.6.a.3.8.---N.35.b.4½.0.---N.35.a.8.9.---

is reached (at plus 29'), where it will stand until plus 31'.

This barrage must on no account come W. of the last named line.

At plus 31' it will move forward again at rate as before until the TRANSLOY support line viz N.36.b.9½.5.---N.30 Central is reached, when it will continue creeping backwards and forwards between TRANSLOY support and front line until further orders.

All barrage called "Standing Barrage" to be found by 56th. D.A.

In addition to the above -

The two Roving Sections of 56th. D.A. will fire H.E. on to Gun Pits at T.5.a.2.7. from Zero to plus 1', when they will lift on to N. portion of HAZY down to T.5.a.0.6. and remain rolling over this (with H.E. and Shrapnel) until plus 7½', when they will become "Rovers" as laid down in para. 1 "Table of Tasks".
Roving Section of 4th. D.A. will ROVE from Zero hour onwards.

4.5" Howitzers.

4th. Div. Arty.

From Zero hour - One Battery will fire on to the SUNKEN Road
N.35.c.0.9.---N.35.a.4½.4½.
One Section (A) between N.35.c.0.9.---
N.35.a.3.2. and
One Section (B) between N.35.a.3.2.---
N.35.a.4½.4½.

(A) will lift at plus 2') On to SUNKEN Road N.
) of CEMETERY & CEMETERY
) CIRCLE N.29.d.7.1.---
) N.35.b.9.9. and remain
(B) will lift at plus 4') there throughout.

One battery will fire on to trench and gun pits about N.35.a.8½.3. and Small Trench about N.35.d.1½.9½. lifting at plus 6' on to CEMETERY CIRCLE between -

N.35.b.9.9.---N.29.d.9½.0.---N.29.d.9.1½.---

and remain there throughout.

3.

56th. Div. Arty.

From Zero Hour — One Battery on N. portion of HAZY down to T.5.a.0.6. lifting -

    at Plus 6' on to HAIL TR., and

    at Plus 30' on to Front House of TRANSLOY S. of LES BOEUFS Road.

One Battery on SLEET TR. lifting -

    at plus 6' on to Front House of TRANSLOY S. of LES BOEUFS Road.

One Battery on any high houses in TRANSLOY with occasional salvoes on to high ground in O.25.c.

One Battery on SUNKEN Road N.36.a.6.0.---N.30.c.8.0. throughout.

RATES of FIRE.

Zero - plus 20'   .. .. Intense.
Plus 20' - plus 30' .. .. .. Ordinary.
Plus 30' - plus 50' .. .. .. Intense.
Plus 50' - Onwards .. .. .. Ordinary, or as situation demands.

Note:- Guns must be watched during Intense period and fire slacked off, if necessary.

22/October/1916.

App IV

SECRET　　　　　　　　　　　　　　　　　COPY NO. 1

4TH DIVISION OPERATION ORDER NO.73.

Ref:- 1/20,000. 57c. S.W.　　　　　　　　　　　　16th October 1916.

1. On night 19/20th October the 12th Infantry Brigade will take over from 11th Infantry Brigade that portion of the front which lies between the present left of the 11th Infantry Brigade and Point T.4.b.7.8. in BURNABY Trench.

    The boundary between Brigades will then be as shewn on attached map.

    All arrangements for the relief will be made between B.Gs.C. 11th and 12th Infantry Brigades direct.

    Completion of relief will be reported to Divisional H.Q.

2. On night 20/21st October the 23rd Infantry Brigade, 8th Division will take over from the 12th Infantry Brigade, 4th Division that portion of front which lies between present 4th Division left and the South end of SPECTRUM Trench - N.34.b.7.2. inclusive.

    The Northern boundary of the 4th Division will then be as follows :-

    N.34.b.7.2. - N.34.Central - Windmill - N.33.d.6½.4½. (exclusive) - Cross Roads T.3.a.8½.8. - T.3.a.0.0. and thence as old boundary.

    All arrangements for the relief will be made between B.Gs.C. 12th and 23rd Infantry Brigades direct.

    G.O.C.8th Division will take over command of the sector from G.O.C.4th Division at 9 a.m. on the 21st October.

3. ACKNOWLEDGE.

　　　　　　　　　　　　　　　　　　　　　　[signature]
　　　　　　　　　　　　　　　　　　　　　　Lieut-Colonel,
　　　　　　　　　　　　　　　　　　　General Staff, 4th Division.

Issued at 9-30pm
Copies to :-
- 10th, 11th, 12th Inf. Bdes.
- 4th Div. Arty.
- 4th Div. Engineers.
- 4th Div. "Q".
- 4th Div. Signals.
- A.D.M.S. 4th Division.
- A.P.M. 4th Division.
- Liaison Officer.
- 6th Division.
- 48th Division.
- 14th Corps "G".
- 14th Corps "Q".
- 14th Corps H.A.
- 9th Squadron R.F.C.

SECRET
****

Copy No. 26

4TH DIVISION OPERATION ORDER NO. 75.

1. The following additions and amendments are made to 4th Division Warning Operation Order No. 74.

2. For the operation on the 23rd October:

(a) 2nd Royal Dublin Fusiliers and 1st Royal Warwickshire Regt. are placed under command of G.O.C. 11th Infantry Brigade.

(b) 2nd Seaforth Highlanders are placed under command of G.O.C. 12th Infantry Brigade.

(c) 1st East Lancashire Regt. will be placed under command of G.O.C. 10th Infantry Brigade.

3. Para. 5 is cancelled.
Troops will be assembled as under :-

<u>11th and 12th Infantry Brigades.</u>
East of the line T.9.d.9.0. - T.9.Central - T.3.a.0.0. by 5 a.m. on October 23rd.

<u>10th Infantry Brigade.</u>
1st Royal Irish Fusiliers and 1st East Lancashire Regt. in HOG'S BACK TRENCH and BODMIN TRENCH - by 5 a.m. on October 23rd.

<u>19th Infantry Brigade (33rd Division).</u>
2 Battalions in SERPENTINE TRENCH and STRAIGHT TRENCH by 7 a.m. October 23rd. (Troops will march in bodies not larger than 1 platoon.)
2 Battalions in GUILLEMONT Area by 7 a.m. October 23rd.

4. Brigade Headquarters will be established as follows :-

10th and 11th Infantry Brigades - GUILLEMONT QUARRIES.
12th Infantry Brigade - GUILLEMONT Station.
19th Infantry Brigade - BRIQUETERIE (A.10.b.)

5. Para. 9 is cancelled.
Tanks will not be employed.

6. All prisoners of war will be taken under Brigade arrangements to the Advanced Divisional Compound at T.8.d.6.8. where they will be handed over to an escort of XIV Corps Cyclists attached to the Division. These cyclists, who are under the orders of the A.P.M. 4th Division will be responsible for providing the necessary escorts to conduct batches of prisoners to the Intermediate Divisional Cage at South end of BERNAFAY WOOD.
From the Intermediate Divisional Cage prisoners will be sent in batches to the Advanced Corps Cage at A.8.c.6.8. on the MONTAUBAN - CARNOY Road under arrangements to be made by the A.P.M. who will superintend the arrival and departure of batches.

/7.

7. Instructions as to Medical arrangements are being issued by "Q" branch of the Staff.

8. Acknowledge.

Issued at 6 a.m.
October 22nd 1916.

Major,
for Lieut-Colonel,
General Staff, 4th Division.

Copies to :-

10th, 11th and 12th Inf. Bdes.
4th Divisional Artillery.
4th Divisional Engineers.
4th Divisional Signal Company.
A.D.M.S. 4th Division.
A.P.M. 4th Division.
4th Division "Q".
Pioneers (21st W. Yorks Regt.)
14th Corps "G".
14th Corps "Q".
14th Corps H.A.
8th Division.
33rd Division.
9th Squadron R.F.C,
French Liaison Officer.
19th Infantry Brigade.

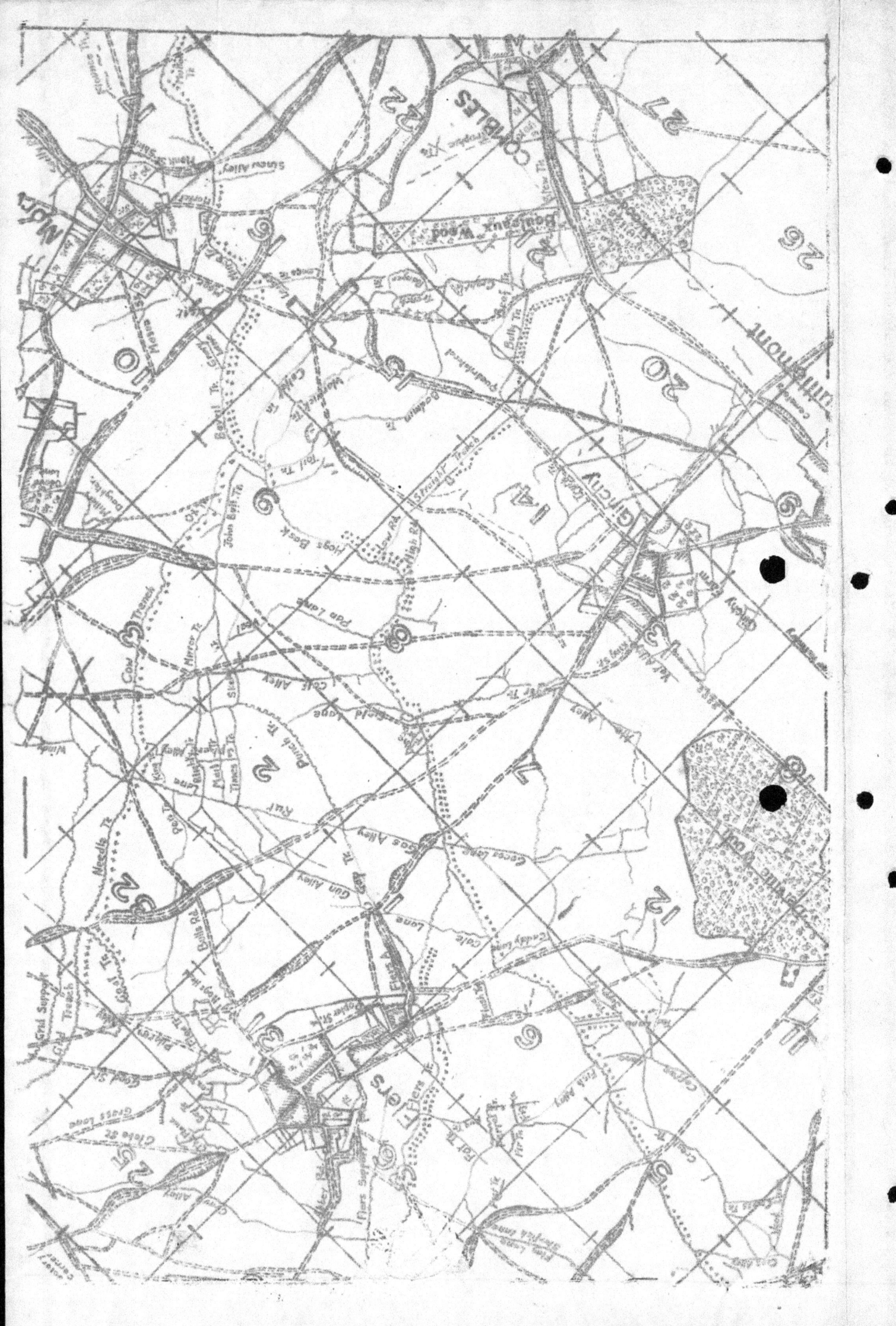

SECRET
****

Copy No. 24

4TH DIVISION OPERATION ORDER NO. 76.

app P

Ref:- Sheet ALBERT 1/40,000.   22nd October 1916.

1. The 4th Division (less Artillery) will be relieved on the night 23/24th October by the 33rd Division.

2. Two Brigades of the 33rd Division will take over the line from the 11th and 12th Infantry Brigades.
Further details will be issued later.

3. On relief the Brigade Groups will be accommodated as follows:

   10th Inf.Bde. Group in the SANDPITS. (E.18.d.)
   11th Inf.Bde.Group in MANSEL CAMP. (F.17.b.)
   12th Inf.Bde.Group in CITADEL (F.21.b.)

   Divisional Headquarters will move to CITADEL.
   Battalions temporarily attached for the operation on the 23rd October will move under the orders of the Brigade Head-Quarters to which they are attached.

4. Details of relief of the R.E.Companies and Pioneer Battalion will be arranged direct between C.R.E.4th and 33rd Divisions.

5. Details of relief of R.A.M.C.Units will be arranged by the A.Ds.M.S.4th and 33rd Divisions direct.

6. The relief of all units not mentioned in this Order will be arranged by "Q".

7. (a) All movements will be by cross-country tracks unless the weather is wet in which case units will move by the MONTAUBAN - CARNOY Road and thence units for the CITADEL and SANDPITS Areas will move by cross-country tracks.

   (b) Troops moving by road must keep following distances -
      200 yards between Companies.
      500 ~~1000~~ yards between Battalions.

   (c) Troops moving by cross-country tracks will keep a distance of 500 yards between Battalions.

   (d) A distance of 500 yards will be maintained between units and their transports.

8. Command of the Divisional front will pass from G.O.C. 4th Division to G.O.C.33rd Division when the relief is complete.

9. ACKNOWLEDGE.

Issued at 6 a.m.

Major for Lt-Col,
General Staff, 4th Division.

Copies to:-
10th,11th,& 12th Inf.Bdes.
4th Div.Arty.
56th Div.Arty.
4th Div."Q".
C.R.E.4th Divn.
4th Div.Signals.
A.P.M.4th Division.
21st.W.Yorks Regt.

A.D.H.S.4th Division.
14th Corps "G".
14th Corps "Q".
14th Corps H.A.
8th Division.
33rd Division.
French Liaison Officer.
No.9 Squadron R.F.C.
19th Infantry Brigade.

SECRET

Copy No... 4

XIV Corps No. S.82/80.

In confirmation of telephone message, owing to the fog, zero hour will be 2.30 p.m. instead of 11.30 a.m. as previously ordered.

[signature]
Brigadier-General,
General Staff, XIV Corps.

23rd Oct. 1916.
Issued at 8.45 a.m.

Distribution -

Fourth Army	Copy	No.1.
XV Corps	"	" 2.
9th French Corps	"	" 3.
4th Division	"	" 4.
8th Division	"	" 5.
33rd Division	"	" 6.
XIV Corps H.A.	"	" 7.
9th Sqdn. R.F.C.	"	" 8.
G.O.C., R.A.	"	" 9.
Record		10.
		11,12.

SECRET

COPY NO. 2

4TH DIVISION OPERATION ORDER NO. 77.

Reference Sheet ALBERT 1/40,000.   24th October 1916.

1. 4th Division Operation Order No.76 is cancelled.

2. (a) 10th Brigade Group consisting of 1/East Lancs.R. 1/R.Irish Fusiliers and 2/Seaforth Highlanders and 10th Bde M.G.Coy. will march to-day to SANDPITS Camp. Instructions as to roads which may be used where cross-country tracks are impossible will be issued by 4th Division "Q".

    (b) Reliefs of Brigades in front line will be carried out to-night 24/25th October as under :-

    11th Inf. Bde. by 19th Inf. Bde.
    12th Inf. Bde. by 98th Inf. Bde.

    Details of relief will be arranged direct between Brigadiers concerned.
    G.Os.C. 11th and 12th Infantry Brigades will hand over command of line on completion of relief.
    On relief tonight (24/25th Oct.) 11th Infantry Brigade will move to TRONES WOOD Area and 12th Infantry Brigade to BRIQUETERIE Area. A representative from each Brigade to report to Town Major, BERNAFAY WOOD as soon as possible.

    (c) March table for moves on 25th inst. will be issued as soon as possible but Brigades will probably move as under :-

    10th Bde Group on 25th from SANDPITS to MEAULTE.
    11th Bde Group on 25th to MANSEL CAMP.
    12th Bde Group on 25th to SANDPITS.

    (d) Instructions as to future moves of R.E. and Pioneers will be issued later.

3. Divisional H.Q. will move to TREUX on 25th inst. G.O.C. handing over command of line to G.O.C. 33rd Division at 10 a.m. on that date.

4. A C K N O W L E D G E.

Issued at 9 a.m.

Lieut-Colonel,
General Staff, 4th Division.

Copies to :-
10th, 11th, 12th Inf.Bdes.
4th Div."Q".
19th Inf.Bde.
98th Inf.Bde.
33rd Division.
14th. Corps "G".
14th. Corps "Q".

SECRET.

AMENDMENT TO 4th DIVISION OPERATION ORDER 77.

24th October, 1916.

1. Paragraph 2 (c) of 4th Division Operation Order 77 is cancelled. Destinations of Brigades on 25th instant will be as under :-

        10th Brig. Group - No move.
        11th Brig. Group - MANSEL CAMP.
        12th Brig. Group - CITADEL.

2. Divisional Head Quarters will now move to CITADEL on 25th instant.

                                      Lieut.Colonel,
                              General Staff, 4th Division.

Issued at 10.30 a.m. to all recipients
        of Op.Order 77.

App. R

* S E C R E T *

Copy No. 20

4TH DIVISION OPERATION ORDER NO.78.

Reference :- Map ALBERT)
              1/40,000.)
                                       26th October 1916.

1. The 4th Division (less Artillery, 12th Field Ambulance and one Company Pioneers) will march from present area to area MEAULTE - VILLE - TREUX - MERICOURT - CORBIE on 27th inst.

2. Marches will be carried out as per attached march table - tracks alongside road being used where possible.

3. Distance of 200 yards between Companies and 500 yards between Battalions will always be kept. Transport will accompany Battalions at a distance of 300 yards.

4. Divisional Headquarters will move to TREUX.
Hour will be notified later.

5. A C K N O W L E D G E.

                                       Lieut-Colonel,

Issued at 12 noon.   General Staff, 4th Division.

Copies to :-
10th, 11th, 12th Inf.Bdes.
4th Divisional Artillery.
4th Divisional Engineers.
4th Div.Signal Coy.
A.D.M.S.4th Division.
A.P.M.4th Division.
4th Division "Q".
21st W.Yorks Regt.
XIV Corps "G"
XIV Corps "Q".

TO ACCOMPANY ...TH DIVISION OPERATION ORDER ...

Unit.	From.	To.	Route.	Remarks.
10th Infantry Brigade (less 2/R.Dublin Fus. and 1/R.Warwick.R) 9th Field Co.R.E. 10th Field Ambce.	SANDPITS.	CORBIE.	MEAULTE - VILLE - TREUX - MERICOURT.	Under orders to be issued by G.O.C. 10th Inf.Bde. Head of column to leave SANDPITS at 1 p.m.
1/E.Lancs.R. Renfrew Field Co.R.E. 11th Field Ambce.	SANDPITS.	MEAULTE.		To follow 10th Inf.Bde.Group under orders of G.O.C.10th Inf.Bde. Will rejoin 11th Bde Group on arrival.
12th Infantry Brigade. 21st F.Yorks (Pioneers). (Less 1 Coy.) Durham Field Co.R.E.	CITADEL.	VILLE. TREUX. MERICOURT.	To MEAULTE by cross-country tracks if fine - if wet by CEMETERY - F.9.a. - CARCAILLOT FARM - thence via main road.	Not to enter MEAULTE before 3 p.m.
11th Infantry Brigade (less 1/E.Lancs R.)	MANSEL CAMP.	MEAULTE.	HALTE - road bend F.4.c. - CARCAILLOT FARM.	Head to leave MANSEL CAMP 3.15 p.m.
2/R.Dublin Fus. 1/R.Warwick.R.	MANSEL CAMP.	CORBIE.	Personnel by cross country tracks to PLATEAU (A.20.a.) thence by train leaving 12.30 p.m. Transport by road via MEAULTE to follow 11th Inf.Bde.	Orders to be issued by G.O.C.11th Inf.Bde. Bns.will rejoin 10th Inf.Bde on arrival in CORBIE.

SECRET

   Reference 4th Division Operation Order No. 78 - 4th Divisional Headquarters will close at the CITADEL at 4 p.m. on the 27th October and will re-open at TREUX at the same hour.

                  Major,

26/10/16.   General Staff, 4th Division.

SECRET   COPY NO. 17

app. 5

4TH DIVISION OPERATION ORDER NO. 79.

28th October 1916.

1. The 4th Division (less Artillery, 1 Coy. 21st W.Yorks.R. (Pioneers) and 12th Field Ambulance) will move from present area to Area No.5 in neighbourhood of ABBEVILLE on 29th and 30th October.

2. Dismounted personnel will move by train in accordance with the attached table.

All transport will move by road under instructions to be issued by 4th Division "Q".

3. 12th Infantry Brigade will detail a working party of 1 Officer and 100 other ranks to remain behind at MERICOURT at the disposal of the XIVth Corps till further orders.

4. A C K N O W L E D G E.

                                                              Lieut-Colonel,

Issued at 12 noon.   General Staff, 4th Division.

Copies to :-
10th, 11th, 12th Bdes.
4th Division "Q" (4).
4th Divisional Artillery.
C.R.E.
A.D.M.S.
4th Div.Signal Coy.
21st W.Yorks.R.(Pioneers).
A.P.M.4th Division.
14th Corps "G".
14th Corps "Q".

TO ACCOMPANY 4TH DIVISION OPERATION ORDER NO.79.
****

Unit and date.	From.	To.	Route.	Remarks.
29TH OCTOBER. 12th Inf.Bde. Durham Field Coy.R.E. 21st W.Yorks.R.(Pioneers) (less 1 Coy). 1 Section 10th Fd.Ambce.	MERICOURT Area.	DETRAINING STATION IN ALL CASES - AIRAINES.	By train from MERICOURT.	Under orders of G.O.C. 12th Infantry Brigade.
30TH OCTOBER. 11th Inf.Bde. Renfrew Fd.Coy.R.E. 11th Fd.Ambce. (less 1 Section).	MEAULTE.		By train from MERICOURT	Under orders of G.O.C. 11th Infantry Brigade.
30TH OCTOBER. Divisional H.Q.	TREUX.		By train from MERICOURT.	
30TH OCTOBER. 10th Inf.Bde. 9th Field Coy.R.E. 10th Fd.Ambce.	CORBIE.		By train from CORBIE.	Under orders of G.O.C. 10th Infantry Brigade.

SECRET

AMENDMENT to 4th Division OPERATION ORDER No. 78

10th Infantry Brigade and other units of the 4th Division at present at SANDPITS will march on 27th October at 10.45 a.m. from that place instead of at 1 p.m.

Major,
General Staff, 4th Division.

To all recipients
of O.O. 78.

XIV Corps.

4th Army LONG.

      Headquarters 4th Division will close tomorrow 30th inst at TREUX at 2 p.m. and reopen at HALLENCOURT at the same hour.

                                                        Sgd. W. B. Somerville.

                                                              Major-General,

29th October, 1918.   Commanding 4th Division.

CASUALTIES FOR PERIOD 1ST - 31ST OCTOBER 1916.

	KILLED.	WOUNDED.	MISSING.
Officers.	39	99	31
Other ranks.	554	2437	1033

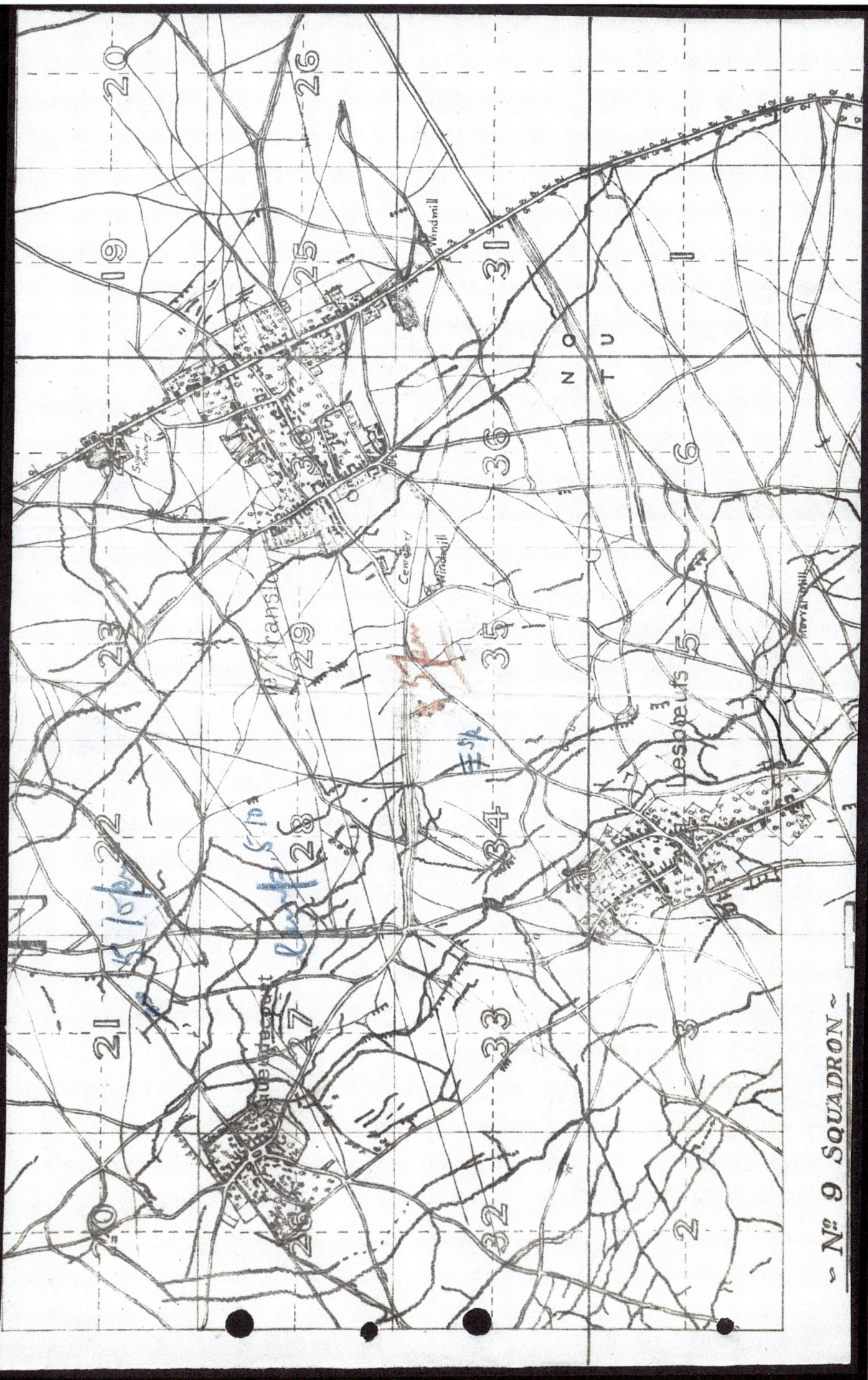

.. = flares (red)
≡ = white Very lights.
o o = double red Very lights.

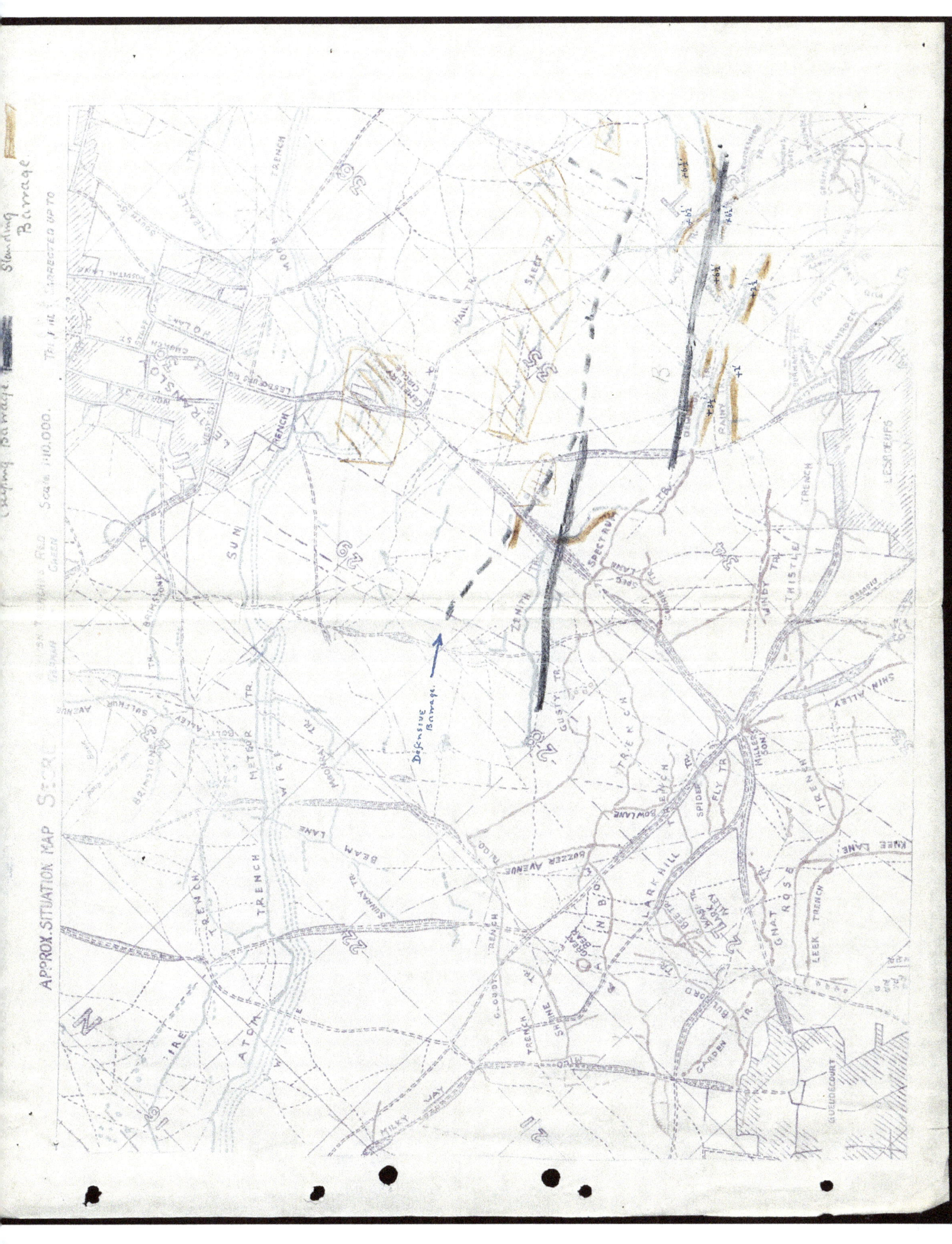

4th Division

War Diary

General Staff

August + September

1916

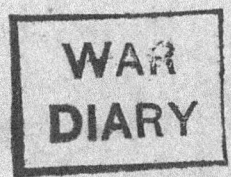

GENERAL STAFF

4th DIVISION

AUGUST 1 9 1 6

@ppendices attached:=

    Reports on the GAS ATTACK 8/9th August 1916.

    Operation Orders 48-55.

    Notes on Trenches.

    Casualties for the month.

A wad of messages under separate cover accompanies this War Diary.

WAR DIARY - GENERAL STAFF, 4th DIVISION.

CONVENT
ST SIXTE.
1st AUGUST 1916.

Situation unchanged - nothing of interest to record.

2nd AUGUST 1916.

ST SIXTE.

5 a.m.   Morning report. situation normal.

12.10 pm.   Mid-day report.   - ditto -

3.45 pm.   Left sector reports British aeroplane shot down by hostile machine and is lying at C.7.c.9.4.

4.40 pm.   Evening report. Quiet day.

Operation Order No: 48 issued.

12th Inf. Bde will relieve 10th Inf.Bde in the right sector of the Divnl Line on nights 3/4th, 4/5th August.

Relief will be carried out as follows :-

Night 3/4th

2 Bns 12th Bde will move from A.30 to CANAL BANK
2 Bns 10th Bde   "   "   " CANAL BANK to A.30.
12th Bde M.G.Coy will relieve 10th Bde M.G.Coy in trenches.

Night 4/5th

2 Bns 12th Bde will move from CANAL BANK to trenches.
2 Bns 12th Bde   "   "   " A.30 to CANAL BANK
2 Bns 10th Bde   "   "   " Trenches to A.30.
12th Bde T.M.Bty will relieve 10th Bde T.M.Bty.

G.O.C 12th Brigade will take over command of the line on completion of relief on night 4/5th August.

ST SIXTE
3rd AUGUST 1916.

Situation unchanged.

ST SIXTE
4th AUGUST 1916.

Nothing of interest to record.

Reliefs carried out in accordance with Operation Order 48.

ST SIXTE
5th AUGUST 1916

3.35 a.m.   Relief of 10th Bde by 12th Bde in Right sector completed 3.5 a.m. 8th Corps informed.

5.20 a.m.   Morning report - quiet night.

12.5 p.m.   Mid-day report - situation unchanged.

12.40 p.m.   29th Division (on our right) report some artillery and trench mortar activity south of WIELTJE.

4.55 p.m.   Evening report - no change in situation.

6th AUGUST 1916.

ST SIXTE.

Situation unchanged.

7th AUGUST 1916.

ST SIXTE.

Situation unchanged.

8th AUGUST 1916.

ST SIXTE.

4.40 a.m.   Quiet night reported.

12.5 p.m.   Midday report - Situation normal.

5. p.m.   Evening report - no change.

Full report on gas attack which took place about 10.15 p.m. is attached marked A.

9th AUGUST 1916.

ST SIXTE.

5. a.m.   Morning report - since midnight the situation has been normal. Considerable damage was done to our trenches by the hostile bombardment. It is believed the enemy did not enter any part of our trenches. Casualties estimated about 200.

5.55 a.m.   29th Division (on right of 4th Division) report gas was discharged by enemy from about the MOUND and that then trenches opposite were shelled from 10 p.m. to 12.30 a.m. Estimated total casualties under 100. As far as can be ascertained enemy did not penetrate the line.

12 noon.   Midday report - no change.

5. p.m.   Evening report - situation unchanged.

Operation Order 49 issued.

10th Brigade will relieve 11th Brigade on the Left Sector of the Divisional line on nights 11th/12th, 12th/13th August.

Relief will be carried out as folows.

Night 11th/12th August.
2 Battalions 10th Brigade will move from reserve billets to CANAL BANK and L Defences.

2 Battalions 11th Brigade will move from CANAL BANK and L Defences to reserve billets.

10th M.G. Company will relieve 11th M.G. Company in the trenches.

Night 12th/13th August.
2 Battalions 10th Brigade will move from CANAL BANK and L Defences to trenches.

2 Battalions.........

9th AUGUST (continued).

2 Battalions 10th Brigade will move from reserve billets to CANAL BANK and L Defences.

2 Battalions 11th Brigade will move from trenches to reserve billets.

10th T.M. Battery will relieve 11th T.M. Battery.

G.O.C. 10th Brigade will take over Command of the Left Sector on completion of relief on night 12th/13th August.

10th AUGUST 1916.

ST SIXTE.

Situation unchanged.

Operation Order 49 of 9th August cancelled.

Operation Order 50 issued.

Relief of 11th Brigade will be carried out as follows :-

Night 10/11 Aug.
2 Battalions 10th Brigade will relieve 2 battalions 11th Brigade in the left sub-sector of the Brigade front. (1 Battalion 10th Bde to trenches, 1 Bn. 10th Bde. to CANAL BANK.)

Night 11/12 Aug.
2 Battns. 10th Bde will relieve 2 Battns. 11th Bde. in the right sub-sector of the Bde front (1 Battn. 10th Bde to trenches, 1 Battn. 10th Bde to CANAL BANK or ELVERDINGHE.

G.O.C. will take over command of the line on completion of relief on night 11/12 August.

ST. SIXTE

11th August, 1916.

Situation unchanged

Relief of Rifle Brigade by Seaforth Highrs and Somerset L.I. by R. Irish Fus. in accordance with Op. Order 50 completed.

ST. SIXTE

12th August, 1916.

3.40 am. Relief of E. Lanc. R. by R. War. R. and Hants. R. by R. Dublin Fus. in accordance with Op. order 50 completed.

5.15 am. Quiet night.

12 noon Midday report - no change.

5 pm. Evening report - situation normal.

ST. SIXTE.

13th August, 1916.

Situation unchanged.

14th August, 1916.

ST. SIXTE Situation unchanged.

ST. SIXTE.

15th August, 1916.

2.15 am. Relief of Seaforths by R. Irish Fus. in left sub-sector of left sector of Divisional front completed.

Situation unchanged.

ST. SIXTE.   16th August, 1916.

5 am.   Quiet night. Relief of R. Dublin Fus. by R. War. R. in
             right sub-sector of Left sector completed.

11.50 am.   Midday report - no change.

5 pm.   Evening report - situation normal.

ST. SIXTE.   17th August, 1916.

             Situation normal - nothing of interest to record.

             Op. Order No. 51 issued.

             11th Bde. will relieve 12th Bde. in the right sector on nights
             19/20 and 20/21 Aug.

ST. SIXTE.   18th August, 1916.

             Quiet night - following reliefs in Left sector completed
             during the night.
             W. Riding R. relieved Essex in right sub-sector
             R. Lanc. R. relieved Lancs. Fus in left sub-sector.

ST. SIXTE.   19th August, 1916.

             Situation unchanged. Nothing of interest to record.

             Op. Order 52 issued at 10 am.
             38th Division will relieve 4th Division in the line on
             nights 19/20 and 20/21 August.
             12th Bde will be relieved night 19/20 August by 115th Bde and will
             be billeted in POPERINGHE.
             10th Bde. will be relieved night 20/21 August by 113th Bde. and
             on relief will billet in Camps K, L and M.
             4th Division putting 3 brigades into the line will relieve
             3rd Canadian Division in the line from the right of the 29th
             Division to the YPRES-COMINES Canal. Reliefs of Canadian
             Division Brigades will take place on nights 22/23rd, 23/24th,
             24/25th August respectively, 11th Bde. to take over its section
             on the first night.
             4th Divisional Artillery will relieve 3rd Canadian Division
             on nights 24/25th, 25/26th August.
             Op. Order 53 issued at 2 pm.
             Reliefs of 10th and 12th Bdes ordered in Op. Order 52 will
             be arranged direct between Brigadiers of 4th and 38th Divisions
             12th M.G.Coy. will be relieved night 20/21st August.
             Artillery personnel of 4th Division will be relieved by 38th
             Divisional Artillery on nights 21/22, 22/23rd August.
             G.O.C. 4th Division will hand over command of the line to G.O.C.
             38th Division at 10 am. 21st August at which hour 4th Div.
             H.Q. will close at ST. SIXTE and reopen at POPERINGHE.

ST. SIXTE.   20th August, 1916.

4.40 am.   Relief of 12th Bde. by 115th Bde. (38th Division) completed.
             H.Q. 12th Bde. established at 63 Rue d'Ypres, POPERINGHE.

             Situation unchanged.

             Op. Order 54 issued.
             4th Division will take over the line at present held by 3rd
             Canadian Division as follows:-

20th August Contd.

10th Bde. will relieve 9th Canadian Bde. in the centre sector on night 24/25th Aug.
11th Bde. will relieve 7th Can. Bde in the left sector on night 22/23rd Aug.
12th Bde. will relieve 8th Can. Bde. in the right sector on night 23/24th Aug.
Command of Artillery on present 3rd Can. Div. front will pass to the G.O.C., R.A. 4th Division on completion of Artillery reliefs on night 25/26th August.
G.O.C. 4th Division will take over command of the line at 5 am. 25th August, at which hour Divisional H.Q. will be established at RENINGHELST.

ST. SIXTE
POPERINGHE.
21st August, 1916.

Relief of 10th Bde. by 113th Bde. (38th Divz) completed. 10th Bde move to billets in Camps K, L and M.

10 am. G.O.C. 4th Division handed over command of the line to G.O.C. 38th Division.
H.Q. 4th Division established at Town Hall, POPERINGHE.

POPERINGHE.
22nd August, 1916.

Moves took place in accordance with Op. Order No. 54.

23rd August, 1916.

POPERINGHE.

Relief of 7th Canadian Brigade by 11th Brigade in Left Sector of Canadian Division front completed.

POPERINGHE
RENINGHELST
24th August, 1916.

12th Bde. relieved 8th Canadian Divisie Brigade in right sector of Div Canadian Division front.
H.Q. 4th Division moved from POPERINGHE to RENINGHELST.

RENINGHELST.
25th August, 1916.

12.50 am. Relief of 9th Can. Bde. by 10th Bde in centre sector of Can. Div. front completed.

5 am. G.O.C. 4th Div. took over command of line from G.O.C. 3rd Can. Division.

5.40 am. Morning report - quiet night.

11.55 am. Midday report - situation normal.

12.55 pm. Somerset L.I. report that British aeroplane was brought down behind German lines N.E. of HOOGE, apparently landing intact.

5 pm. Evening report - no change in situation.

For tactical purposes 4th Division will be temporarily transferred from VIII Corps to Canadian Corps.

RENINGHELST.
26th August, 1916.

Quiet day - nothing of interest to record.

27th August, 1916.

RENINGHELST.

Rifle Brigade relieved Somerset L.I. in left sub-sector

	in left sub-sector of of left sector of Divisional front.
5 am.	Quiet night.
12 noon	Midday report - situation normal
4.45 pm.	Evening report - quiet day.

28th August, 1916.

RENINGHELST.

Following reliefs took place last night.
<u>Left Sector.</u> E. Lancs. relieved Hants. in right sub-sector.
<u>Right sector.</u> W. Riding R. relieved Essex R. in right sub-sector.

Op. order No. 55 issued.
1st Australian Division will relieve the portion of 4th Divn. in the line YPRES-COMINES Canal to Trench 55 (both inclusive) by September 2nd.
2nd Aus. Bde. will relieve 12th Bde. in right sector
1st Aus. Bde. will relieve 10th Bde. in centre sector.
Command of this portion of the ~~Divisional~~ line will pass to G.O.C. 1st Australian Division on completion of reliefs on night 1/2nd September.

RENINGHELST.   29th August, 1916.

5.30 a.n.	Quiet night.
11.45 am.	Midday report - all quiet.
5 pm.	Evening report - enemy shelled Right sector with 5.9" Hows. and trench mortars at 3 pm.

Following reliefs took place last night.
<u>Right Sector.</u> 1st R. Lanc. R. relieved Lancs. Fus in left sub-sector.
<u>Centre sector.</u> Seaforth Highrs. relieved 2nd R. Irish Fus. in left sub-sector.

RENINGHELST.   30th August, 1916.

Quiet day - nothing to report.

Last night R. Dublin Fus. relieved R. War. R. in right sub-sector of Centre sector.

RENINGHELST.   31st August, 1916.

Quiet day.

Reliefs in accordance with Op. Order No. 55 took place last night.
7th Aus. Bde. relieved W. Riding R. in right sub-sector of Right sector.
6th Aus. Bde. relieved Essex R. in Bde. Reserve.

GAS ATTACK NIGHT 8/9th AUGUST

Notes on the report by 4th Division.

Report by 4th Division.

Report by 11th Infantry Brigade. with notes.

Report by 12th Infantry Brigade.

Report by A.D.M.S.

NOTES ON REPORT BY 4th DIVISION OF THE GAS ATTACK ON
THE NIGHT OF AUGUST 8/9th, 1916.

※※※※※※※※※※

Brigadier General Rees stated that at 10-20 pm he was at the head of Huddersfield and heard the tinkling of the gas gongs. The gas cloud was moving in the direction of point 98. He distinctly heard the hissing from the gas cylinders 200 yds west of the Pilkem road to point 98. The wind was blowing E-S-E, and he was 450 yards away. It was a very still night.

Two whole battalions were moving up and two whole battalions moving back with different intervals.

At E 28 the relief was actually in progress there being a double garrison at the time. All the men had their packs on and there was a total of 4 platoons in that neighbourhood, which was a distance of 40 yards from the enemy. The gas came straight on top of them and there are very few survivors.

The platoons coming up were not seriously affected. They got satisfactory warning and had time to put their helmets on.

It is reported the gas was released from the sap that comes S-W from Mill Cot or from Fortin 17 just to the West.

The officer of the extreme left flank Company reports that the gas came over in two clouds with an interval of about 5 minutes. The gas was moving so slowly that one was able to walk ahead of it.

The enemy attempted to get out of their trenches opposite our E 25. General Rees put a heavy barrage of artillery fire from point 98 westward as the gas cloud was driven in that direction, and there did not appear to be much danger of an attack to the east. The Germans however turned a heavy bombardment on to our trenches east of Point 98. When General Rees saw this he turned his guns on to the trenches from point 98 to the eastward with the French and Belgian guns continuing to fire on the German trenches west of point 98.

The alarm appears to have been satisfactory with the exception of E 28 where the people were practically wiped out immediately. West of E 28 the gas alarm was not satisfactory owing to it being drowned by heavy rifle and machine gun fire and to the noise made by the men walking on the trench boards.

The necessity for much louder means of alarm was raised and it is strongly recommended that the number of Strombos horns be considerably increased.

The sentries in the front line trenches in this part were able to see the gas cloud coming and to warn their men in time to enable the men in the Yorkshire and White Trench to put on their helmets in time. The casualties, therefore, in this part were not heavy.

There are roughly 450 casualties in the 4th Division. 2 Company Commanders and 7 other Officers in the Rifle Brigade and One Company Officer and 11 other Officers in the Somerset L.I. Roughly 20 Officers and 450 men. Of the other battalions there are 5 and 7 officers respectively.

In the vicinity of E 28 there were at least 200 cases that were immediately fatal. All other fatal cases were due to Officers and N.C.O's who were more concerned about the men putting on their helmets than their own. A party halted whilst the gas cloud had passed, and finding that the air was quite clear they took off their helmets and moved on again, and moved suddenly into a hollow full of gas.

It is said that an order had been passed by somebody to remove helmets, and some men took off their helmets before the gas had sufficiently cleared. Some men owing to the burning of their foreheads shuffled the helmets about or took them off owing to their eyes hurting.

A small party of men got gassed owing to their

clothes being saturated with gas, and going into a small dugout.

Orderlies and other people who had a lot of moving about to do suffered from the after effects.

A case was quoted of two Company Commanders who after fixing up their companies reported at the Battalion Headquarters and then went back, returning later to the Battalion Headquarters. At that time they were quite alright. Now they are dead.

The 4th Division do not favour the idea of the order for the taking off of the gas helmets being left to the Battalion Commander. They say the Battalion Commander is not in a position to know when the gas cloud has passed and therefore they suggest it be left to the Company Commanders. The Corps Commander stated a point should be made of instructing the younger Company Commanders what to do.

It was pointed out that vermoral sprayers were no earthly use against Phosgene. They have no effect whatever on this gas. As regards the use of flappers the exertion of the men using these must not be lost sight of.

It was stated the telephones were situated in the dug-out next to the Company Commander Commander's.

General Rees said he did not see a single rocket discharged. He was asked to enquire whether the rockets went off, and if not, why not.

It was reported the Artillery heard the strombos horns at 10-25 and opened fire at 10-32pm.

CORPS COMMANDER'S REMARKS ON REPORT BY 4TH DIVISION
OF THE GAS ATTACK AUGUST 8/9th.
****

Is it possible that the cylinders were in the enemy's main front line and that the gas was conducted from the cylinders up the saps in a pipe and discharged with a nozzle at the south west end ?

At what time did the alarm and the gas/reach respectively the different points. By what means was the alarm passed and was it satisfactory.

The sentries of the garrison must not be affected by the relieving troops. They and the garrison must be ready for immediate action.

Particular precautions to be taken in particular parts of the line for the carrying of helmets. The particular precautions to be left to the Brigadiers concerned.

In relieving too many men not to be jammed up in one place.

Experiment to be made as to whether the clothes can be so saturated with gas as to be dangerous to health or life.

Advisable that men who have been gassed should not be carried back. No good to themselves and dangerous to the men who carry them. Bterr leave them outside the trenches until fresh men come up to carry them away.

Telephones to be placed in the Company Commander's dug-out, and suitable notice posted as shewn in notes re 29th Division.

Is it wise for Commanders to send up an S.O.S. signal which means infantry attacking.

Rockets to be in water tight boxes and fired by automatic lighter.

Strombos horns to be tested periodically by the Brigade Staff only.

Necessity for relief of battalions or Companies who have been exposed to the gas.

SECRET   4th Division No. GGG 23/16.

VIII Corps.
----

1.   I forward the reports of G.Os C. 11th and 12th Infantry
Brigades on the gas attack of the night 8th August, together with
a report from the A.D.M.S.

   The gas appears to have been discharged on a front of 500
yards from C.14.a.7.1 to C.13.b.8.8

   There is a report that a further discharge was made from
either the sap leading S.W. from KIEL COTTAGE or from the Salient
E. of FORTIN 17, but this I have been unable to verify though it
is probably correct.

   The gas cloud took a West-North-Westerly direction striking
E.27 and E.28, but the wind was very light and an eddy appears to
have taken a portion of the cloud down COLNE VALLEY to the CANAL,
the other portion passing to the East and North of WHITE TRENCH
striking S.32 and moving towards BOESINGHE.

2.   The alarm was given at about 10.20 p.m., all gas appliances
being used; the Strombos Horns were effective and plainly heard,
the gas gongs, owing to the musketry and machine gun fire and the
tramping of the men on the trench boards, were not so effective.

   With the exception of 4 platoons which were on the point of
relieving at E.27 and E.28 to opposite Point 98 inclusive, all troops
received warning in ample time to adjust the gas helmets.

   Of the 4 platoons above mentioned at least two were
within 50 to 100 yards of the discharge which was probably
carried by the pressure from the cylinders at a very rapid
pace straight into our trenches from opposite Pt. 98 and the centre
of E.28.   The men in these trenches were unable to adjust
their helmets before the gas cloud was on them and the majority were
gassed, in most cases fatally.

   Both Artillery Groups plainly heard the Strombos
Horns, and batteries were all warned about 10.25 p.m.

3. ACTION TAKEN.

The report of the G.O.C. 11th Infantry Brigade gives full details ; the artillery co-operation was most satisfactory, fire was opened at 10.32 p.m. the French and Belgian batteries on our left co-operating and rendering good service. The attempted attack by the enemy was immediately checked by the Artillery fire and by heavy machine gun and rifle fire given by the troops holding the line in the threatened sector.

4. CASUALTIES.

A list, Appendix 'A' is attached.

I attribute the heavy losses to the following -

(i) That a relief was taking place and that a double garrison was in the front line at the actual moment of the discharge.

(ii) That the men of these platoons were hampered by wearing full equipment and by rations and other trench stores which were being carried up. This caused delay in putting on the helmets, and the gas cloud was on them before they could be adjusted.

I have not been able to ascertain whether notice of the gas was given by the sentries on duty, but from what evidence is obtainable I am inclined to think that the hissing noise of the discharge was the first intimation received. Under ordinary circumstances, there should have been time to put on the gas helmet.

The casualties due to delayed action I attribute to the following causes -

(a) Helmets being taken off too soon.

(b) To the gas hanging about in dug-outs and shell holes owing to insufficiency of wind to dissipate the gas.

(c) To fumes from the clothes of the men who had been in the centre of the gas attack, and who afterwards occupied the dug-outs.

- (d) To the vermorel sprayer being of little use is dissipating gas other than chlorine.

- (e) To excessive fatigue causing violent exertion while wearing gas helmets.

5. SUGGESTIONS

- (i) That Strombus Horns be supplied in place of the shell cartridges and steel rails now in use.

- (ii) That after a gas attack men who have been in the cloud should not use dug-outs for at least 24 hours. From the evidence given me personally I think there is little doubt that clothes impregnated with gas are liable to cause poisoning. I suggest experiments in this direction.

- (iii) That all men who have been in the gas cloud should be kept as quiet as possible and that working and carrying parties should be detailed from units who have remained clear of the gas. Though orders already exist providing for this, it is difficult to carry them out where, as in the present case, a relief was in progress. The delayed gas action is, however, so serious that this is a most important point.

Steps are being taken to put these suggestions into immediate action in the Division.

6. The existing orders and precautions against gas appear to be quite effective, and the helmet to afford complete protection, the chief difficulties being to know when helmets should be removed, and how long dug-outs and hollows remain infected.

The heavy casualties among Officers and N.C.O's were due to the fact that these ranks looked after the men under their charge before thinking of their own safety.

7. There is no doubt that the fact that the gas alarm was taken off contributed to delay in getting on helmets quickly, and that General Rees committed an error in judgement in taking it off. The wind at the time was, however, so slight and variable that I consider he had good reasons to think that the conditions were unfavourable

to a gas attack.

sgd W Lambton.
Major-General.
Commanding 4th Division.

13th August 1916.

REPORT ON GAS ATTACK ON THE 11th INFANTRY BRIGADE - 8th August 1916.

1. The enemy discharged Gas on a frontage C.14.a.7.1. to C.13.b.8.8. There was practically no wind below the crest of ridge, but such as there was appears to have been slightly S. of E. and took the cloud in the direction of BOESINGHE.

2. The Gas was discharged at the moment, when a relief was taking place. The 1st Rifle Brigade was relieving the 1st Somerset Light Infantry in the left sub-sector, and the 1st East Lancashire Regiment were relieving the 1st Hampshire Regiment in the right sub-sector. The latter relief had not actually commenced. The leading platoons of the 1st East Lancashire Regiment being in the communication trenches between 300 and 400 yards from the front line. The former relief was in progress, and there was a double garrison in the trenches of E.28 at the moment when the Gas was discharged. It was here that most of the casualties occurred, about 200 men being immediately gassed. Owing to the proximity of the German trenches, the crowded state of trenches and the men wearing full marching order, helmets were not put on quickly enough. The 1st Hampshire Regiment also suffered a number of casualties in E.27 and E.26. No great quantity of Gas appears to have crossed our line in E.25, whilst South and East of the junction of E.24 and E.25 there was no gas.

3. The gas cloud, after release, appears to have divided into two. One cloud moving down COLNE VALLEY, the second cloud crossing our trenches just S.E. of S.32 and passing over our trenches N.W. of this point. The gas was not very strong between S.32 and BARNSLEY ROAD.

4. A certain number of Gas Shells were fired into COLNE VALLEY and two or three were reported in the neighbourhood of F.35 - the latter report being un-confirmed.

5. The enemy attempted to advance against our trenches in the neighbourhood of the junction of E.25 and E.24 - some 30 or 40 men were seen, and were driven back by rifle and machine gun fire; the enemy did not enter our trenches at any point.

6. The enemy did not open Artillery bombardment until about

- 2 -

a quarter of an hour after the first release of Gas. The bombardment was particularly severe on the front line, combined with the fire of Trench Mortars and rifle grenades, between D.21 and E.28. In the neighbourhood of F.35 there was also a bombardment.

In rear of the front line, the junction of HOLME VALLEY and BARNSLEY ROAD, received a good deal of attention. The hostile barrage, - chiefly shrapnel, was put up about 50 yards in rear of the support line, - both Banks of the CANAL were heavily shelled with both Shrapnel and High Explosives. This bombardment slackened off about 11-30.p.m.

Brigadier-General.
Commanding 11th Infantry Brigade.

12.8.1916.

(11th Bde Report)

NOTES ON THE ATTACK.

1. **Spreading of the Alarm.** Spreading of the Alarm by means of empty Shell cases and Iron rails was not found satisfactory. The best method appears to be by Strombus Horns, which can be heard above the noise of the firing. The number of Strombus Horns require to be greatly increased. When the Gas was first let off, the night was very still and the enemy did not fire heavily during the first few minutes. In spite of this, the sound of the Gas Gongs was heard in the support line but not more than just enough to attract attention. The Centre Company of the Left Sub-sector, heard no sounds of Gongs at all owing to the trampling of men on the foot-boards, and Machine Gun fire until warned by hearing Strombus Horns let off at Battalion Headquarters. The Company on the extreme left received their warning

   The initial velocity of the gas when first discharged appears to have been high. It was when this ceased that the cloud travelled slowly. The wind at the time was very light.

   it appears to have reached in about 20 seconds from the moment of discharge. No reliable information is obtainable regarding the time at which these companies received the warning, and the arrival of the Gas cloud.

2. **Gas Cloud.** The extreme Left Coy. on the CANAL BANK reports that there appeared to be two Gas clouds - the first being almost invisible and the second dense - this was not reported from anywhere else and might possibly have been caused by the separation of the Gas after travelling a little distance. The Gas appears to have been of an extremely powerful kind and killed a number of men in E.28 almost immediately. About 40 or 50 men, many of whom when found, had got their helmets on and properly adjusted walked down as far as SKIPTON POST a matter of some 200 yards, and died there. A further number appeared to have reached the CANAL BANK. - Any exact details are impossible to obtain as all officers and N.C.O's who were on the spot were gassed.

3. **Delayed Cases.** About 150 cases occurred during the day following the Gas attack and cases are still reporting sick today. Some of the chief caused contributing to these cases appear to be as follows

(11th Bde Report)

NOTES ON THE ATTACK.

1. <u>Spreading of the Alarm.</u> Spreading of the Alarm by means of empty Shell cases and Iron rails was not found satisfactory. The best method appears to be by Strombus Horns, which can be heard above the noise of the firing. The number of Strombus Horns require to be greatly increased. When the Gas was first let off, the night was very still and the enemy did not fire heavily during the first few minutes. In spite of this, the sound of the Gas Gongs was heard in the support line but not more than just enough to attract attention. The Centre Company of the Left Sub-sector, heard no sounds of Gongs at all owing to the trampling of men on the foot-boards, and Machine Gun fire until warned by hearing Strombus Horns let off at Battalion Headquarters. The Company on the extreme left received their warning from the Centre Company - both these Companies had time to put their helmets on before the arrival of the cloud. The movement of the Gas cloud was extremely slow, and its speed does not appear to have been faster than two miles an hour, after passing our front line, which it appears to have reached in about 20 seconds from the moment of discharge. No reliable information is obtainable regarding the time at which these companies received the warning, and the arrival of the Gas cloud.

2. <u>Gas Cloud.</u> The extreme Left Coy. on the CANAL BANK reports that there appeared to be two Gas clouds - the first being almost invisible and the second dense - this was not reported from anywhere else and might possibly have been caused by the separation of the Gas after travelling a little distance. The Gas appears to have been of an extremely powerful kind and killed a number of men in E.28 almost immediately. About 40 or 50 men, many of whom when found, had got their helmets on and properly adjusted walked down as far as SKIPTON POST a matter of some 200 yards, and died there. A further number appeared to have reached the CANAL BANK. - Any exact details are impossible to obtain as all officers and N.C.O's who were on the spot were gassed.

3. <u>Delayed Cases.</u> About 150 cases occurred during the day following the Gas attack and cases are still reporting sick today. Some of the chief caused contributing to these cases appear to be as follows

"2".

I. Men being slow in putting on their helmets.

II. Men shifting the helmet about, because they found the helmet burnt their foreheads, where pressed by the steel-helmet.

III. Men taking violent physical exercise, and so exhausting the helmet, or by their movements allowing a small amount of gas to enter occasionally.

IV. Removal of helmet too early.

V. Men moving along the communication trench after removing their helmets, suddenly walking into a belt of gas hanging about in a hollow.

VI. Men being gassed in dug-outs, after the dug-outs had been cleared by Vermoral Sprayers, on account of the men's clothes being saturated with gas sufficiently to effect the men in a confined space.

VII. Men employed in examining the kits and packs of men gassed.

The following instance provided considerable support to the theory that gas can be carried in men's clothes in sufficient quantity as to be dangerous :

On the day following the attack, three Headquarter Orderlies of the Somerset Light Infantry were employed in the examination of packs and effects of men who had been gassed the night before. They do not appear to have been seriously exposed to the gas the previous night. These men were all effected during the course of the evening. Further, an Officer of the Somerset Light Infantry states that he put his pipe, full of tobacco, in his haversack, just before the attack, and that 30 hours afterwards he put his pipe in his mouth, and got a sufficiently strong whiff from it to make him feel uncomfortable for some little time.

VIII. Men exerting themselves unduly within 24 hours after being through a Gas cloud.

4. <u>Clearing the Battle-field.</u> It is essential to remove, as early as possible, wounded and gassed men from the trenches, and also for repairs to trenches to be carried out, caused by the bombardment. This work should, whenever possible, be carried out by men who have not been through the gas cloud. Fresh men employed on this work should have their gas helmets pinned on inside their coats, so as to be instantly ready to put them on in case gas is found in the communication trenches.

"3".

5. <u>Removal of Gas Helmets.</u>   Gas Helmets were removed by order of Coy. Commanders in the Centre Company, Left Sub-sector at 11-15.p.m.,- in the Left Company at 1.a.m. and from the Right Company no information is available. At midnight the remains of this Company were wearing their Helmets rolled up on their heads.

    The Companies of the Somerset Light Infantry marched back after relief with their Gas Helmets on. I consider that the Company Comdrs should order Helmets to be taken off - it is impossible for a higher commander to know the conditions sufficiently to be able to judge whether it is safe to be without them. It is however difficult to know when Helmets can be taken off, and the only method at present available is for an Officer to raise his Helmet and estimate the conditions.

6.   The Gas was discharged through some form of jet - the hissing noise was audible for a considerable distance. I happened to be standing at the time and at the junction of HUDDERSFIELD & THE NILE and could distinctly hear it from this point - a matter of about 450 yards from where the Gas was being released. Theer is no information to show that pipes were laid out into NO MAN'S LAND from Cylinders in the enemy's lines.

7.   Two RED rockets were sent up - more were not sent up partly owing to the rockets being damp and partly to the difficulty of firing the rockets when men had their Gas Helmets on. The Rocket Signal is unsatisfactory - Strombus Horns could take its place. If Rockets are considered necessary, all Rockets should be provided with an automatic lighter,

8.   Any accuracies as regards times of events during the actual attack is impossible. One Officer states that he could not read his watch with the help of an Electric Torch.

9.   The O.C., Machine Gun Company reports that the Box Respirator were most unsatisfactory as the pipe caught in everything. Battalion Commanders report that they were satisfactory. Only men who need not move at all need be issued with them.

10.   Both P.H. and P.H.G.Helmets are reported on as satisfactory. The P.H.G. takes longer to adjust on account of the Elastic band. The

"4".

chief fault found with the P.H.G. Helmet is the difficulty of seeing through it as the sponges press on the eye and obscure the view. This matter is serious and requires attention.

11. <u>Preliminary Precautions.</u> Gas "Alert" had been in force for about 24 hours ending 3.p.m. on the day of the attack, at which hour on account of a strong wind blowing from S.S.E., I withdrew the order and sent out instructions that the "Alert" was to be put on again by order of Battn Commanders, should they consider the conditions favoured Gas. The "Alert" was not in force at the time of the attack, and owing to the stillness of the night, and variableness of what wind there was, I did not consider a Gas attack at all probable.

12. <u>Vermoral Sprayers.</u> The question of efficiency of Vermoral Sprayers require scientific examination. The O.C., 1st Hampshire Regiment considers that many men of his men were gassed in dug-outs and trenches which had been thoroughly sprayed.

13. Attached Appendix "A" gives a brief Diary of times noted at Brigade Headquarters.

JHCRees

Brigadier-General.

12.8.1916. Commanding 11th Infantry Brigade.

Appendix "A".

DIARY OF EVENTS → BRIGADE HEADQUARTERS.

10-20.p.m.   Gas discharged.

10-30.p.m.   Enemy attempted to leave his trenches and advance against E.25, but driven back.

10-32.p.m.   Our Artillery opened fire.

10-35.p.m. (a). Hostile bombardment of front line from E.28 to D.21, also heavy shelling of CANAL and communication trenches. There is some reason to believe that the hostile barrage in rear of the front line commenced some distance short of the CANAL and worked down to it.

(b). Order issued for one platoon 1st Rifle Brigade to move along West Bank of CANAL to ROTHERHAM ROAD to cover left flank of Brigade.

(c). Report received that barrage called for by Centre Coy, 1st Rifle Brigade, at 10-30.p.m.

10-40.p.m.   G.O.C. returned to Brigade Headquarters from trenches. Barrage by both Divisional, French, and Belgium Artillery asked for on frontage of left sub-sector.

11- 5.p.m.   Report from Centre Company, left sub-sector, of hostile attack, subsequently cancelled.

11-15.p.m.   O.C., left group Artillery informed by G.O.C. that danger point was frontage of right sub-sector, and asking for fire on that frontage.

11-30.p.m.   Hostile Bombardment slackened.

11-50.p.m.   Our Artillery slackened - demand of G.O.C.

12-15.a.m.   All quiet. G.O.C. asked O.C., Left Group to lay guns of Divisional Artillery on frontage Right Sub-sector.

1-30.a.m.   Relief completed Left sub-sector.

2-30.a.m.   Relief completed Right Sub-sector.

12th Infantry Bde Report

4th Division No. GGG. 23/16.

Report on the Gas attack on the night of the 8/9th August 1916.

The 12th Infantry Brigade H.Qrs first received the Gas alarm at 10 p.m. from the Staff Captain of the 12th Infantry Brigade. He came up from the direction of the 11th Brigade and reported that 11th Inf. Brigade were sounding the Gas alarm and putting on their Gas helmets. Nothing however had been reported by the units, although "GAS ALERT" had been on since 2 p.m.

At 10 p.m. Germans put a very heavy barrage on and behind our front line with Trench Mortars and Guns.
At 10.15 p.m. LANCASHIRE FUSILIERS reported Gas Alarm.
At 10.25 p.m. LANCASHIRE FUSILIERS reported Gas alarm was false.
Nothing at all from the ESSEX.
At 11.35 p.m. ESSEX reported all quiet.
At 11.40 p.m. LANCASHIRE FUSILIERS reported all quiet.

Report from LANCASHIRE FUSILIERS, Left battalion of the right sector.
10 p.m. the Battalion stood to on account of the German bombardment. At 10.10 p.m. the Gas alarm was heard on their right and was also received from the Gunners (SOUTH GROUP) whose signals are near Battn H.Qrs Immediately Brigade H.Qrs was warned, gas helmets put on, and STROMBUS HORN was sounded. At 10.20 p.m. a message was received from the companies in the front line that there was no gas and never had been any. Gas helmets were immediately taken off by the support companies. The companies in the front line did not put their helmets on, nor did they beat the gongs as there had been no gas.
There had also been no Gas alarm heard from the left (11th Brigade).

Effect of the STROMBUS HORN.
The noise made by the horn was very bad, where it was heard, but it was confined to a very small space and was not heard by men in the support and front line trenches.
Suggested the HORN be put up on the parapet when sounded.

Report from ESSEX Regiment, right battalion of the right sector.
The Gas alarm was heard very plainly from the right (29th Division) both horns and gongs being easily heard. There was no alarm on the left. It is thought that the gas alarm was originally started by horns which were heard in the German lines prior to the bombardment which began at 10 p.m. These horns were evidently a signal either for the enemy working parties to withdraw or else because the gas had escaped. When the bombardment began at 10 p.m. the Battalion stood to. As no gas was reported from the front line companies, gas helmets were not put on, nor were gongs beaten.
It was suspected that there was gas on the right, but the Battalion had no idea that there was gas on the left Brigade front. This is probably due to the fact that the wind was blowing from the right and prevented the noise of the alarm reaching them from the left.
The Battalion ceased standing to when the bombardment stopped, and reported all quiet to Brigade at 11.35 pm.

Report from DUKE OF WELLINGTON'S.
At 10.15 p.m. the Battalion was advancing to relieve the ESSEX and had crossed the CANAL when the alarm was heard from the 29th Division front (Gas Horns and Gongs) at the same time heavy shelling was going on at IRISH FARM and along our front. Gas Helmets were put on and some
/difficulty

difficulty was experienced in finding the way.
The Officers report that they had difficulty in getting at their
helmet which was in the Alert Position on the chest, owing to
the fact that they had some straps across their chest.

It is suggested that more STROMBOS HORNS be provided in the line.

                                      Sd.J.D.Crosbie.
                                               Brigadier General,
12th August 1916.   Commanding 12th Infantry Brigade.

REPORT ON CASUALTIES IN GAS ATTACK. by ADMS. 4th Div

From midnight, 8/9th, to 9 am. 10th instant 21 officers suffering from gas were admitted to Field Ambulances, and of these 2 died in Field Ambulance. All officers except one were admitted to 11th Field Ambulance, the remaining one was admitted to 10th Field Ambulance and was a very slight case.

297 O. R. were admitted during the same period suffering from gas to the 11th Field Ambulance and of these 48 died.

During the period 9 am. on 10th to 9 am. 11th instant, 27 O. R. were admitted to 11th Field Ambulances. 4th Division "Q" furnished me with the information that 89 deaths had occurred from gas in the trenches before the cases could be brought to the regimental Aid Posts or Advanced Dressing Stations.

The onset and character of the symptoms in these cases varied considerably, and have therefore been classified as "Immediate" and "Delayed."

(a) 11 Officers and 194 O. R. suffered from the immediate effect, and the large majority of these exhibited the following common symptoms: very severe constricting pain in chest and throat, severe spasmodic cough, cyanosis, dyspnoea, nausea, vomiting, and later profuse watery, frothy and even blood stained expectoration. These cases had at first a fairly strong and regular pulse which rapidly deteriorated especially in fatal cases.

All deaths occurred in this group.

It appears that most of the men affected had inhaled the gas for a few seconds before putting the helmet on, others inhaled it after taking them off.

(b) 10 Officers and 130 O. R. suffered from delayed action. In these cases the preliminary symptoms were not, as a rule, so prominent. The majority complained of pains in the head and chest, vomiting and faintness. Others complained of severe abdominal pains. The colour was not as a rule affected. A few were flushed, others were abnormally pallid, but cyanosis was generally absent.

(2)

The onset of symptoms varied greatly, ranging between 9 and 48 hours. An officer of the 1st Somerset L. I. went to sleep in the M.O's dugout after the gas attack was over, and after sleeping for 12 hours he developed very serious symptoms of gas poisoning. No deaths from this variety occurred in the Field Ambulances.

All gas cases were treated by rest and inhalations of ammonia. Oxygen was tried in the worst cases with no appreciable benefit. Atropine was injected in cases where exudation was very great but without success. Vomiting gave great relief, and hot drinks, etc. were given to encourage it. All patients were kept in the open air as much as possible.

In cases of delayed action, rest in the prone position gave relief, which in some cases was absolute.

All cases with a few exceptions were evacuated to No..3 and No. 10 Casualty Clearing Stations by Motor Ambulances.

26 cases died at the Advanced Dressing Stations, and 22 at the main Dressing Station of No. 11 Field Ambulance, making up the 48 deaths shown in my return.

There seems to be no doubt that a large number of men were gassed some time after the attack was over, and after the helmets were ordered off. In my opinion, there can be only one solution of the problem, and that is, that gas, either in the form of the original compound or some part of it, still remains in the hollows, dugouts, between sandbags, round dead bodies, etc. We know that the Vermorel Sprayer does away with the Chlorine, but I think it is generally admitted that it does not affect the phosgene. If this is true, then we can account for the symptoms shown in the "delayed" cases being different from those produced in the "Immediate" ones, which, as a rule, are those of chlorine poisoning. We can also presume that men going back to dugouts become poisoned by phosgene gas which still hangs about or is brought in by the men in their clothes. The same thing would apply to moving dead bodies and equipment in the trenches, thereby liberating volumes of gas that fill the various spaces.

H.Q. 4th Division   (Sd) J. Grech, Colonel,
12th August, 1916.   A.D.M.S. 4th Division.

P.S.   From 9 am. 11th to 9 am. 12th instant, 2 O.R. have been admitted to 11th Field Ambulance, suffering from gas, Delayed Action.

(Sd) J. G.

SECRET   COPY No. 13

4th DIVISION - OPERATION ORDER No. 48.

2nd August 16

1. 12th Infantry Brigade will relieve 10th Infantry Brigade in the right sector of the Divisional line on nights 3/4, 4/5. 5/6th August, 1916.

2. The relief will be carried out as follows -

(a) Night 3/4th August.

    2 Battns. 12th Inf. Brigade will move from A.30 to CANAL BANK

    2 Battns. 10th Inf. Brigade will move from CANAL BANK to A.30.

    12th M.G.Coy. will relieve 10th M.G.Coy. in trenches.

(b) Night 4/5th August.

    2 Battns. 12th Inf. Brigade will move from CANAL BANK to Trenches.

    2 Battns. 12th Inf. Brigade will move from A.30 to CANAL BANK

    2 Battns. 10th Inf. Brigade will move from Trenches to A.30.

    12th Bde. T.M.Batteries will relieve 10th Bde. T.M. Batteries.

(c) All further details will be arranged direct between G.Os C. Brigades.

3. G.O.C. 12th Infantry Brigade will take over command of the line on completion of relief on night 5/6th August.

Completion of relief will be reported to Div. H.Q.

4. ACKNOWLEDGE.

W. H. Bartholomew
Lieut.-Colonel,
General Staff, 4th Division.

Issued at

Copies to:-
10th, 11th, 12th Inf. Bdes.
4th Divisional Artillery
4th Divisional Engineers
4th Division "Q"
A.D.M.S.
Signal Coy.
A.P.M.
29th Division
VIII Corps.

War Diary

-SECRET-

Copy No: 1

4th DIVISION OPERATION ORDER NO: 49.

August 9th 1916.

1. 10th Inf. Bde will relieve 11th Inf. Bde in the left sector of the Divisional line on nights 11/12th, 12/13th August.

2. The relief will be carried out as follows :-

   (a) <u>Night 11/12th August.</u>

   2 Battns 10th Inf.Bde will move from reserve billets to CANAL BANK and L Defences.

   2 Battns 11th Inf.Bde will move from CANAL BANK and L Defences to reserve billets.

   10th Inf.Bde M.G.Company will relieve 11th Inf.Bde M.G. Company. in the trenches.

   (b) <u>Night 12/13th August.</u>

   2 Battns 10th Inf.Bde will move from CANAL BANK and L Defences to Trenches.

   2 Battns 10th Bde will move from reserve billets to CANAL BANK and L Defences.

   2 Battns 11th Inf.Bde will move from Trenches to reserve billets.

   10th Inf.Bde T.M.Batteries will relieve 11th Inf.Bde T.M. Batteries.

   All further details will be arranged direct between G.O's.C. Brigades.

3. G.O.C. 10th Inf.Bde will take over command of the line on completion of relief on night 12/13th August, completion of relief will be reported to Divnl Headquarters.

4. ACKNOWLEDGE.

<u>Issued at 6 a.m.</u>

Lieut:Colonel.

Copies to :-
General Staff., 4th Division.
10th.11th.12th Inf.Bde.
4th Div Arty.
-:- Engrs.
-:- " Q "
A.P.M.
A.D.M.S.
8th Corps.
29th Divn.

- SECRET -

Copy No: 12

4th DIVISION OPERATION ORDER NO: 50

August 10th, 1916.

1. 4th Division Operation Order No: 49 is cancelled.

2. The relief of the 11th Inf.Bde will be carried out as follows:-

   Night 10/11th August

   2 Battns 10th Bde will relieve 2 Battns 11th Bde in the left sub-sector of the Brigade front (1 Battn 10th Bde to Trenches 1 Battn 10th Bde to CANAL BANK).

   Night 11/12th August.

   2 Battns 10th Bde will relieve the 2 Battns 11th Bde in the right sub-sector of the Brigade front. (1 Battn 10th Bde to Trenches, one Battn 10th Bde to CANAL BANK & ELVERDINGHE.

   Arrangements for relief to be made direct between G.O's.C. Brigades.

3. Arrangements are being made to provide busses for the move of the 11th Brigade to-night, time and place of rendezvous will be notified.

Issued at 7½ a.m.

Copies to :-

Lieut:Colonel.
General Staff., 4th Divn.

10th.11th.12th Inf.Bde.	2 3 4
4th Div Arty.	5
-:- Engrs.	6
-:- " Q "	7
-:- Signal Coy.	8
A.D.M.S.	9
A.P.M.	10
8th Corps.	11
Diary	12
File	1

4TH DIVISION   VIII CORPS

                                                              G.2602.

An Officer of the Corps Staff visited the Left portion of your Front yesterday and made the following notes :-

1.   The wire in front of E.28 is in a very poor condition and requires to be considerably thickened.

2.   The new trench from E.28 to the junction of WHITE TRENCH and YORKSHIRE TRENCH is not traversed at present. The Corps Commander wishes to know whether this trench was intentionally dug without traverses, and wished me to point out the great difficulty of adding traverses to a trench after it has once been dug.

   He hopes that work will be pushed forward on this new trench as quickly as possible, as he understands that the portion nearest WHITE TRENCH has not yet been dug.

3.   This trench is crossed at right angles by HUDDERSFIELD ROAD (Box Drain) and two other old trenches running North and South. These trenches are not protected with wire within bombing distance of the new trench.

4.   BARNSLEY ROAD from the point where it crosses WHITE TRENCH at C.13.b,0.5 to junction of the new trench about C.13.b,3.8 is deep, but wet and derelict. Is it intended to reclaim this portion, as it would seem to be an important piece of trench which should be made tenable.

                                                W. Ruthven
                                                          B.G., G.S.,
15/8/16.   VIII CORPS.

4th Div. No. GGG/66/3.

VIII Corps.

With reference to 8th Corps G.2602 of the 15th inst. the points mentioned are all receiving attention.

The new trench from E.28 to the junction of WHITE and YORKSHIRE Trenches followed in part an old and disused trench. The officer in charge of the work was instructed to traverse it but found difficulty in getting the alignment and decided on the spot to put the traverses in later. The difficulty of adding traverses to a trench is realised and the matter had already been noted and brought to the notice of the officer concerned.

It is intended eventually if time and labour permit to reclaim BARNSLEY Road between WHITE Trench and Point C.13.b 3.8 but as communication will be assured at both ends of the new trench and by the box drain along HUDDLESTON Road this has been deferred till the whole trench is well wired and in good fighting condition throughout.

Sgd W Lambton
Major General,
Commanding 4th Division.

16th August, 1916.

4th Div. No. GGG/66/3.

10th Infantry Brigade.

The following notes on the new trench from E.28 to junction of WHITE and YORKSHIRE trenches are brought to your notice.

1. The wire in front of E.28 is in a very poor condition and requires to be considerably thickened.

2. The new trench from E.28 to junction of WHITE and YORKSHIRE trenches should be traversed. The Divisional Commander hopes the trench will be completed and wired throughout as soon as possible.

3. The old trenches (including the HUDDLESTON ROAD Box Drain) which run into the trench from NO MAN'S LAND must be wired to keep any parties from creeping up to within bombing distance of the new trench

4. Will you please let me know, whether the white new trench is occupied by day

[signature]
Lieut-Colonel,
17th August 1916.   General Staff, 4th Division.

Keep

4th Div. No. GGG/66/3.

11th Brigade.

The attached letters are forwarded for your information.

Lt.Colonel,
17th August, 1916.   Gen.Staff, 4th Div.

- SECRET - Copy No: 2

4th DIVISION OPERATION ORDER NO: 51

Reference Map 1/20,000 Sheet 28. 17th August 1916.

1. The 11th Infantry Brigade will relieve the 12th Infantry Brigade in the right sector of the line on the nights 19/20, 20/21st August.

2. The relief will be carried out as follows :-

   (a) <u>Night 19/20th August</u>

   2 Battns 11th Inf.Bde will move from reserve billets to CANAL BANK and L Defences.

   2 Battns 12th Inf. Bde will move from CANAL BANK and L Defences to reserve billets.

   11th Inf. Bde M.G.Coy will relieve 12th Inf.Bde M.G.Coy in the trenches.

   (b) <u>Night 20/21st August</u>

   2 Battns 11th Inf.Bde will move from CANAL BANK and L Defences to trenches.

   2 Battns 11th Inf. Bde will move from Reserve billets to CANAL BANK and L Defences.

   2 Battns 12th Inf. Bde will move from trenches to reserve billets.

   11th Inf. Bde T.M.Bty will relieve 12th Inf.Bde T.M.Bty.

   All further details will be arranged direct between G.Os.C. Brigades.

3. G.O.C. 11th Inf. Bde will take over command of the line on completion of relief on night 20/21st August. Completion of relief will be reported to Divisional Headquarters.

4. ACKNOWLEDGE.

Lieut:Colonel.
General Staff., 4th Division.

Issued at 6 a.m.

Copies to :- 10th.11th.12th Inf.Bde.
4th Div Arty.
-:-   Engrs.
-:-   " Q "
-:-   Signal Coy.
A.P.M.
A.D.M.S.
8th Corps
29th Divn

-SECRET-

Copy No: 2

War Diary

4th DIVN PRELIMINARY OPERATION ORDER NO: 52.

19th AUGUST 1916.

1. The 38th Division will relieve 4th Division in the line on nights 19/20th and 20/21st August.

   12th Brigade will be relieved night 19/20th August by 115th Brigade.

   10th Brigade will be relieved night 20/21st August by 113th Brigade.

2. On relief 12th Brigade will be billeted in POPERINGHE and 10th Brigade in Camps K. L. M.

3. 4th Division putting 3 Brigades into the line will relieve 3rd Canadian Division in the line from the right of the 29th Division to the YPRES - COMMINES CANAL.

   Reliefs of Canadian Division brigades will take place on nights 22/23rd, 23/24th, 24/25th August respectively, 11th Brigade to take over its section on the first night.

4. The Artillery of the 4th Division will relieve that of the 3rd Canadian Division on nights 24/25th and 25/26th the Canadian guns being left in position and taken over by the personnel of the 4th Division.

   Personnel of the 3rd Canadian Divisional Artillery will take over guns of 38th Division.

5. The 19th Welsh (Pioneer Battn) and 124th & 151st Field Coys of 38th Divn will revert to command of the 38th Division.

W. H. Bartholomew.
Lieut:Colonel.

Issued at 10 a.m.   General Staff., 4th Division.

Copies to :-   10th,11th,12th Inf. Bde.
              4th Div Arty.
              -:-   Engrs.
              -:-   " Q "
              -:-   Signal Coy.
              A.D.M.S.
              A.P.M.
              8th Corps.
              29th Division.
              38 Divn
              5 Divn

10th Infantry Brigade.

Reference 4th Division operation order No. 52 and 53

1. The following amendments (arrangements) for trains have been made to convey units of your Brigade from the ASYLUM on the night 20/21st

Train leaves ASYLUM 2.30 am. proceeds to POPERINGHE
"   "   "   3 am.   "   "   "
"   "   "   3.30 am.   "   "   "
"   "   "   4.30 am.   "   "   L.5.c.

2. Each train can carry 750 men, but as many men as possible should be sent by first two trains as some of the accommodation in the last two trains will probably be taken up by returning working parties.

                          Major,

19/8/16.   General Staff, 4th Division.

SECRET   COPY No. 16

4th DIVISION - OPERATION ORDER No. 53

1. (a) Reliefs of 10th and 12th Infantry Brigades ordered in 4th Division preliminary Operation Order No. 52, will be arranged direct between Brigadiers 4th Division and 38th Division concerned.

   (b) After relief personnel of 12th Infantry Brigade will move from ASYLUM H.12.b.6.0 to POPERINGHE in two trains each carrying 1100 passengers.

   First train to start from ASYLUM at 2 a.m. 20th August, second train will be at ASYLUM from 2.15 a.m. onwards and will start at time required but not later than 4.30 a.m. 20th August.

   (c) 12th Brigade M. G. Coy. will be relieved night 20/21st August.

2. Artillery personnel of 4th Division will be relieved by 38th Divisional Artillery on nights 21/22nd and 22/23rd August, guns of 4th Division being taken over by personnel of 38th Division. All details to be arranged direct between G.Os C. R.A. concerned.

3. 21st W. Yorks. Regt. (Pioneers) will concentrate at H Camp night 20/21st August. Detachments from TROIS TOURS and PELISSIER FARM not to start before 8.15 p.m. August 20th.

4. 4th Division Field Companies will be relieved by 38th Division Companies as under:-

   Three sections 9th Fd. Coy. on CANAL BANK, night 20/21st August
   Three sections 1/1 Durham Fd. Coy. on CANAL BANK, night 21/22 Aug.
   Two sections 1/1 Renfrew Fd. Coy. at BRIELEN, night 21,22 August.
   Companies to concentrate as ordered by C. R. E. after relief.

5. Reliefs of Field Ambulances will be arranged by A.D.M.S. 4th and 38th Division.

(2)

6. Caretakers in P and G works will be relieved by parties from 114th Infantry Brigade at 4 p.m. tomorrow. 4th Division parties to rejoin their brigades after relief.

7. G.O.C. 4th Division will hand over command of the line to G.O.C. 38th Division at 10 a.m. on 21st August.

   Completion of reliefs will be reported by Infantry Brigades both of 4th Division and 38th Division to 4th Division H.Q.

8. H.Q. 4th Division will close at ST. SIXTE at 10 a.m. on 21st August, and reopen at same hour at POPERINGHE.

W. H. Bartholomew
Lieut.-Colonel,
General Staff, 4th Division.

Issued at 2 p.m. 19th August, 1916.

Copies to 10th, 11th, 12th Inf. Brigades
    4th Divisional Artillery
    4th Divisional Engineers
    4th Division "Q"
    A. D. M. S.
    4th Division Signal Coy.
    A. P. M.
    VIII Corps
    29th Division
    38th Division
    5th Division (Belgian)

SECRET.   Copy No...... 2

4TH DIVISION OPERATION ORDER NO.54.

Reference Map 1/20,000 - Sheet 28.

20TH AUGUST 1918.

1. The 4th Division will take over the line at present held by the 3rd Canadian Division as follows :-

   10th Infantry Brigade will relieve 9th Canadian Infantry Brigade in the centre sector.

   11th Infantry Brigade will relieve 7th Canadian Infantry Brigade in the left sector.

   12th Infantry Brigade will relieve 8th Canadian Infantry Brigade in the right sector.

2. Infantry Brigade reliefs will be carried out in accordance with attached table. All details will be arranged direct between the Brigades concerned.

3. Relief of artillery will be arranged between G.Os.C.,R.A. of 4th Division and 3rd Canadian Division and will take place on nights 24/25th and 25/26th.
   Command of the artillery on the present 3rd Canadian Division front will pass to the G.O.C.,R.A. 4th Division after completion of reliefs on night 25/26th.

4. Reliefs of Field Companies R.E. and Pioneer Battalions of 3rd Canadian Division will take place on nights 23/24th 24/25th and 25/26th August and will be arranged between C.R.E.,4th Division and C.R.E. 3rd Canadian Division.

5. Reliefs of Field Ambulances will be arranged between A.D.M.S.4th Division and 3rd Canadian Division.

6. Arrangements for reliefs of other units will be made between Administrative Staffs of 4th and 3rd Canadian Divisions.

7. Brigades will take over Defence Schemes and Secret Maps from 3rd Canadian Division.

8. All trench stores, dumped S.A.A. and grenades will be taken over by relieving units.

9. G.O.C.,4th Division will take over command of the line at 5 am. on 25th August.
   Completion of all reliefs will be reported to Canadian Divisional Headquarters.

10. ACKNOWLEDGE.

Lieut-Colonel,
General Staff, 4th Division.

Issued at ......
Copies to:-
10th,11th & 12th Inf.Bdes.   A.P.M.   38th Divn.
4th Div.Arty.   Signal Coy.R.E.   5th Belgian
C.R.E.   21/W.Yorks.(Pioneers).   Divn.
4th Div."Q".   VIII Corps.
A.D.M.S.   29th Division.   3rd Canadian Divn.

Date.	Unit.	From.	To.	Remarks.
Night 21/22nd.	"A" Bn. 11th Inf.Bde.	J Camp.	Trenches of Left Sub-Sector of Left Sector.	Personnel by train to ASYLUM from BRANDHOEK.
"	"B" Bn. " "	A.30 Camps.	Bde. support Left Sector.	Personnel by train to ASYLUM from BRANDHOEK.
"	1/2 - 11th Bde M.G.Coy. 1/2 - 11th Bde T.M.Battery	A.30 Camps.	Trenches Left Sub-sector - Left Sector.	Personnel by train to ASYLUM from BRANDHOEK.
Night 22/23rd.	"B" Bn. 11th Inf.Bde.	Bde.support Left Sector.	Trenches Right Sub-Sector of Left Sector.	
"	"C" Bn. 11th Inf.Bde.	A.30 Camps.	Bde.support Left Sector.	Route to be arranged.
"	"D" Bn. 11th Inf.Bde.	P.Camp.	Camp F (MONTREAL) H.19.b. 5.6.	By march route.
"	1/2 - 11th Bde M.G.Coy. 1/2 - 11th Bde T.M.Bty.	A.32 Camp.	Trenches Right Sub-Sector of Left Sector.	Personnel by train to ASYLUM from BRANDHOEK.
"	H.Q. 11th Inf.Bde.	A.30 Camp.	H.Q.Left Sector YPRES Ramparts.	Personnel by train to ASYLUM from BRANDHOEK. Command of Left Sector will pass to G.O.C.11th Inf.Bde. on completion of relief.
"	"A" Bn. 12th Inf.Bde.	POPERINGHE.	Trenches Right Sub-Sector of Right Sector.	Personnel by train to ASYLUM.
"	"B" Bn. 12th Inf. Bde.	"	Bde. support Right Sector.	Personnel by train to ASYLUM.

Date.	Unit.	From.	To.	Remarks.
Night 22/23rd.	½ - 12th Bde.M.G.Coy. ½ - 12th Bde T.M.Batty.	POPERINGHE.	Trenches Right Sub-Sector of Right Sector.	Personnel by train to ASYLUM.
Night 23/24th.	"B" Bn. 12th Inf.Bde.	Brigade support Right Sector.	Trenches Left Sub-sector Right Sector.	Personnel by train to ASYLUM.
" "	"C" Bn. 12th Inf.Bde.	POPERINGHE.	Brigade Support Right Sector.	Personnel by train to ASYLUM.
" "	"D" Bn. 12th Inf.Bde.	"	Camp D (OTTAWA) G.24.d.2.2.	By march route.
" "	½ - 12th Bde M.G.Coy. ½ - 12th Bde T.M.Bty.	"	Trenches Left Sub-sector of Right Sector.	Personnel by train to ASYLUM.
" "	H.Q. 12th Inf.Bde.	"	H.Q.Right Sector - BEDFORD HOUSE - I.26.A.	Command of Right Sector will pass to G.O.C.12th Inf.Bde. on completion of relief.
" "	"A" Bn. 10th Inf.Bde.	K.L.M.Camps.	Trenches Left Sub-sector Centre sector.	Personnel by train to ASYLUM.
" "	"B" Bn. 10th Inf.Bde.	"	Brigade support Centre Sector.	Personnel by train to ASYLUM.
" "	½ - 10th Bde M.G.Coy. ½ - 10th Bde T.M.Bty.	"	Trenches Left Sub-sector Centre Sector.	Personnel by train to ASYLUM.
Night 24/25th.	"B" Bn. 10th Inf.Bde.	Bde.support Centre Sector.	Trenches Right Sub-sector Centre Sector.	Personnel by train to ASYLUM.
" "	"C" Bn. 10th Inf.Bde.	K.L.M.Camps.	Bde.support Centre Sector.	Personnel by train to ASYLUM.
" "	"D" Bn. 10th Inf.Bde.	"	"E" Camp (WINNIPEG) H.19.a. 8.4.	By march route.

Date.	Unit.	From.	To.	Remarks.
Night 24/25th.	10th Bde M.G.Coy. 10th Bde T.M.Bty.	K.L.N.Camps.	Trenches Right Sub-sector Centre Sector.	Personnel by train to ASYLUM.
	H.Q.10th Inf.Bde.	" "	H.Q.Centre Sector, RAILWAY DUG-OUTS – I.31.c.	Command of Centre Sector will pass to G.O.C.10th Inf.Bde. on completion of relief.

4th Division No. GGG 23/7

Second Army.

        Recent gas attacks have emphasised the importance of the role of Divisional Gas Officers and it is anticipated that, with the issue of the Small Box Respirators referred to in my O.B.215 of 25th instant, their duties will be further increased.

2.   In order to standardise the work of these officers throughout the British Expeditionary Force, the following points regarding their duties are brought to your notice:-

(a) <u>TRAINING</u>. The Divisional Gas Officer is in charge of the Divisional Anti-Gas School and is responsible for the training in anti-gas measures of selected officers and men from the units of the Division and for all demonstrations in anti-gas precautions or kindred matters that may be necessary.

(b) <u>INSPECTING AND ADVISATORY</u>.
While Officers Commanding units are directly responsible that the precautions laid down in the various pamphlets and instructions on anti-gas precautions are taken, the Divisional Gas Officer must place his special knowledge at the disposal of Commanding Officers and advise them on all questions of defence against gas attacks, bringing to their notice any defects in anti-gas equipment, training or organisation that come under his observation. To enable him to do this effectually, he must be in close and frequent touch with troops in the line. He will advise the General Staff of the Division on the Anti-gas protective measures to be taken and will bring to notice any alterations or improvements that he considers necessary. He will investigate all gas attacks made on the Divisional front and will report on them to the Divisional Commander, at the same time forwarding copies of all such reports to the Army Chemical Adviser.

3.   Letter O.B. 492 of 30/7/16 indicates duties to which more time can be devoted when, owing to active operations the Divisional Gas School has to be closed down, but which should also be carried out as far as other work will allow, at all times.

4.   The work of Divisional Gas Officers should be facilitated by permitting them to make use of the means of transport at the disposal of Divisions.

                        (Sd) J. Burnett Stuart,
                             Brig.-General
G.H.Q.   for Lieutenant-General
25/8/16.   C.G.S.

(2)

4th Division "Q"
Divisional Anti-Gas Officer

        For information.
        Letter No. O.B. 492 of 30/7/16 was forwarded to you under this office No. GGG 23/7 of 2nd instant.

27/8/16.   Major,
                           General Staff, 4th Division.

SECRET.   Copy No. 13

4th DIVISION - OPERATION ORDER No. 55.

Reference - Sheet 28 S.W.   28th August, 1916.
            (1/20000).

1.   The 1st Australian Division will relieve the portion of
4th Division in the line YPRES - COMINES Canal to Trench 55
(both inclusive) by September 2nd.

   The 2nd Australian Brig. will relieve the 12th Brig.
   The 1st Australian Brig. will relieve the 10th Brig.

   The 3rd Australian Brig. will move into Divisional Reserve
in Camps ~~TORONTO~~ DEVONSHIRE, DOMINION, OTTAWA and ~~WINNIPEG~~ SCOTTISH LINES.

2.   The relief of Infantry Brigades will be carried out in
accordance with attached table - Appendix A.   All other details
will be arranged directly between brigades concerned.
   On completion of the relief 10th Brig. will be located at
Camps ST.LAWRENCE, ERIE, ~~DEVONSHIRE~~, ~~SCOTTISH LINES~~ TORONTO SCOTTISH LIN
12th Brig. will be located at POPERINGHE.

3.   Artillery reliefs will be carried out subsequently to the
relief of the Infantry in each sector under arrangements to be
made between G.Os.C. R.A. 4th Division and 1st Australian Divn.
   Reliefs to be completed by night 2/3rd September.

4.   Reliefs of Field Cos. and Pioneer Battalions will be
arranged direct between C.R.E's 4th Division and 1st Australian
Division.
   Reliefs to be completed by night 1/2nd September.

5.   Details of relief of the Field Ambulances will be arranged
directly between A.D.M.S. 4th Division and A.D.M.S. 1st
Australian Division.

6.   The command of this portion of the line will pass from
G.O.C. 4th Division to G.O.C. 1st Australian Division on
completion of the Infantry reliefs on the night 1/2nd September.
   Completion of all reliefs will be reported to 4th Division
Head Quarters which will remain at REWINGHELST.

                                         W.R.Somerville Major
                                              for G.S.
Issued at 6 p.m.   Lieut.Colonel,
                                         General Staff, 4th Divn.

Copies to 10th, 11th, 12th Inf.Brigs.
          Div. Arty.
          Div. Engrs.
          4th Div. Q.
          A.D.M.S.
          A.P.M.
          4th Div. Signals.
          1st Australian Division.
          4th Canadian Division.
          Canadian Corps.

APPENDIX "A".

DATE.	UNIT.	FROM	TO.	REMARKS.
Night 30/31 August.	12TH INFANTRY BDE.			
	2/Duke of Wellington's Regt.	Trenches Right Sub-sector Right Sector.	POPERINGHE.	By train from ASYLUM.
	2/Essex Regt.	Trenches Bde support Right sector.	POPERINGHE.	By train from ASYLUM.
	M.G.Coy.) T.M.Battery.)	Trenches Right Sector.	POPERINGHE.	Personnel by train from ASYLUM.
Night 31/Aug. /1 Sept.	2/Lancs.Fus.	OTTAWA CAMP.	POPERINGHE.	By march route.
	1/King's Own.	Trenches Left Sub-sector, Right Sector.	POPERINGHE.	By train from ASYLUM.
	M.G.Coy.) T.M.Battery.)	Trenches Right Sector.	POPERINGHE.	Personnel by train from ASYLUM.
	Brigade Hd-qrs.	BEDFORD HOUSE.	POPERINGHE.	
Night 31 Aug./ 1 Sept.	10TH INFANTRY BDE.			
	2/Seaforth Hrs.	Trenches Left Sub-sector Centre Sector.	Camp ST LAWRENCE area.	By train from ASYLUM to BRANDHOEK.
	1/R.Ir.Fusiliers.	Trenches Bde support Centre Sector.	Camp ST LAW-RENCE area.	By train from ASYLUM to BRANDHOEK.
	M.G.Coy.) T.M.Battery.)	Trenches Centre Sector.	Camp ST LAW-RENCE area.	Personnel by train from ASYLUM to BRANDHOEK.

DATE.	UNIT.	FROM.	TO.	REMARKS.
	10TH INFANTRY BRIGADE.			
Night 1/2 Sept.	1/R.Warwick Regt.	WINNIPEG CAMP.	Camp ST LAWRENCE area.	By march route.
	2/R.Dublin Fus.	Trenches Right Sub-Sector Centre Sector.	Camp ST LAWRENCE area.	By train from ASYLUM to BRANDHOEK.
	¼ M.G.Coy. } ¼ T.M.Battery.}	Trenches Centre Sector.	Camp ST LAWRENCE area.	Personnel by train from ASYLUM to BRANDHOEK.
	Brigade Hd-qrs.	RAILWAY DUG-OUTS.	ST LAWRENCE CAMP.	

Draft

4th Div Q.R.1297.

Reference 4th DIVISION OPERATION ORDER 55 of 28th August.

Reference Sheet 28 S.W. $\frac{1}{20,000}$.

1. The attached Table shews moves of 1st Line Transport and M.G. Companies.

2. The Train and Field Companies remain in present billets until they move into the VIII Corps Reserve or 38th Division Areas.

3. The moves of the Field Ambulances will be notified later.

4. Railhead will change to PROVEN on the 5th September.

5. The A.P.M. will arrange reliefs for Traffic and Control Posts with the A.P.M., 1st Australian Division. 6. Petrol tins will be handed over to relieving units.

Continue Field Companies on relief will concentrate in their billeting area, Headquarters R.E. will remain at RENINGHELST.

7. Billeting parties of the 2/Duke of Wellington's and 2/Essex Regiment will report to the Town Major, POPERINGHE at 2 p.m. on 30th and those of the 2/Lancashire Fusiliers and 1st Kings Own at 2 p.m. on 31st.

W.P.H.HILL, Lieut-Colonel.,
29th August 1916.   A.A. & Q.M.G., 4th Division.

19/
Fair copy
on Q arcs
file

CASUALTIES - 4th DIVISION

From 1st to 31st Aug/1916

	Officers	Other Ranks
Killed	12	173
Wounded	35	631
Missing	-	12
Total	47	816

4th Division.

WAR DIARY

GENERAL STAFF

4th DIVISION

SEPTEMBER 1916

Appendices attached:- Operation Orders.

Casualties for month.

A wad of messages under separate cover accompanies this War Diary.

WAR DIARY - 4TH DIVISION GENERAL STAFF.

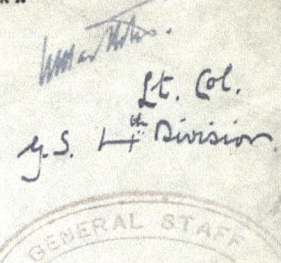

RENINGHELST.   **1ST SEPTEMBER.**

Situation unchanged.

Following relief in accordance with Operation Order No.55 of 28th August completed.
King's Own relieved by 8th Bn. 2nd Australian Brigade, 1st Australian Division in Left Sub-Sector, Right Sector.
King's Own moved to POPERINGHE.

Operation Order No.56 issued:-
On 4th September 10th Brigade H.Q. and three battalions will move from Camps ST LAWRENCE Area to PROVEN and K.L.M. Camps. 1 Battalion will move to POPERINGHE.

Following moves of 12th Brigade will take place on 4th September.
Brigade H.Q. and 2nd W.Riding Regt. from Canadian Corps area POPERINGHE to VIII Corps area POPERINGHE.
Lancs.Fus.(less 2 Coys) from POPERINGHE to ELVERDINGHE. 2 Companies Lancs.Fus.from POPERINGHE to BRANDHOEK.
King's Own (less 2 coys) from POPERINGHE to BRANDHOEK. 2 Coys. King's Own from POPERINGHE to 'L' Works.
Essex Regt. from POPERINGHE to P. Camp.

RENINGHELST.   **2ND SEPTEMBER.**

Situation unchanged.

Command of line from YPRE - COMINES Canal to TRENCH 55 inclusive passed to G.O.C. 1st Australian Division in accordance with Operation Order No.55 of 28th August.
Seaforth's and Irish Fusiliers moved to Camp ST LAWRENCE area.
Relief of Right and Centre Groups 4th. Divisional Artillery by 1st Australian Divisional Artillery completed.
Warwick's moved from WINNIPEG Camp to Camp ST LAWRENCE Area.
Dublin's on relief in Right Sub-Sector, Centre Sector, by battalion 1st Australian Brigade moved to Camp ST LAWRENCE Area.

RENINGHELST.   **3RD SEPTEMBER.**

Situation unchanged.

RENINGHELST.   **4TH SEPTEMBER.**

Situation unchanged.

Following moves took place in accordance with Operation Order No.56 of 1st. September.
Warwick's from WINNIPEG to Camp M.
Irish Fus.from TORONTO to Camp L.
Seaforth's from ST LAWRENCE to Camp K.

RENINGHELST.	**4TH SEPTEMBER (Continued).**	

Dublin's from ERIE to POPERINGHE.
10th Bde H.Q. from ST LAWRENCE to PROVEN.

Relief of 114th Brigade (38th Division) by 12th Brigade in ELVERDINGHE - BRANDHOEK Area completed.

RENINGHELST.   **5TH SEPTEMBER.**

Situation unchanged.

6TH SEPTEMBER.

RENINGHELST.   Situation unchanged.

Operation Order No.57 issued.
The 2nd Australian Division will take over the line at present held by the 4th Division from TRENCH 55 (exclusive) to the YPRES - MENIN Road (ibclusive).
11th Brigade will be relieved by 5th Australian Brigade on nights 8/9th and 9/10th September.
After the relief has taken place, 11th Brigade will be billeted in POPERINGHE and will move to BOLLEZEELE Area on 11th inst.
G.O.C.4th Division will hand over command of the line to G.O.C. 2nd Australian Divn. at 10 am. on 10th September at which hour 4th Div.H.Q. will close at RENINGHELST and re-open at ESQUELBEC.

7TH SEPTEMBER.

RENINGHELST.   Situation unchanged.

RENINGHELST.   **8TH SEPTEMBER.**

Situation unchanged.

RENINGHELST.   **9TH SEPTEMBER.**

Situation unchanged.

Relief of E.Lancs. in Right Sub-Sector, and Som.L.I. in Brigade support by units of 5th Australian Brigade completed.
E.Lancs. and Som.L.I. moved to POPERINGHE.

RENINGHELST.
ESQUELBEC.   **10TH SEPTEMBER.**

Relief of Rifle Bde. in Left Sub-Sector completed.
Hamps.R. moved from MONTREAL Camp to POPERINGHE.
Rifle Bde moved to POPERINGHE.

10 a.m.   Command of the line from TRENCH 55 (excl.) to the YPRES - MENIN Road (incl.) passed to G.O.C. 2nd Australian Division.
H.Q.4th Division established at ESQUELBEC.

Operation Order No.58 issued.

ESQUELBEC.	**10TH SEPTEMBER (Continued).**

In accordance with orders received from Second Army the following units of 4th. Division will march on 11th September to billets near DUNKERQUE.
      11TH INF.BDE.
      29TH F.A.BDE.
      12TH FIELD AMBCE.
      No.3 COY, DIV.TRAIN.

Full report as to reason for this move is attached marked "A".

ESQUELBEC.   **11TH - 13TH SEPTEMBER.**

Division at rest.

ESQUELBEC.   **14TH SEPTEMBER.**

Division at rest.

Operation Order No.59 issued.
The units of the 4th Division which are at present in the DUNKERQUE Area will return to the Second Army area on 15th inst. as under.
      11th Brigade to BOLLEZEELE Area.
      29th F.A.Bde to HOUTKERQUE Area.
      12th Field Ambce. to WATOU Area.

The move will be carried out under orders to be issued by Gen. Rees Commdg.11th Brigade.

ESQUELBEC.   **15TH SEPTEMBER.**

Move of units specified in Operation Order No.59 completed.

ESQUELBEC.   **16TH SEPTEMBER.**

Operation Order No.60 issued.

4th Division with S.A.A. and Grenade Portion of the Divisional Ammunition Column - less Divisional Artillery, Medium and Heavy Trench Mortars and Motor Vehicles will begin to entrain night 16/17th September for the South and will be replaced in VIII Corps by the 7th Division.
Entrainment orders etc,. for the move are attached.

17TH SEPTEMBER.

Move of 4th Division in accordance with Operation Order No.60 in progress.

18TH SEPTEMBER.

Entrainment completed.

Disposition of Division :-
Divisional H.Q. established at VILLERS BOCAGE.

10th Infantry Brigade.

Brigade H.Q.	Chateau COISY.
R.War.R.	COISY.
Seaforth Hrs.	RAINNEVILLE.
R.Irish Fus.	COISY.
Dublin Fus.	On move from ST.OMER to RAINNEVILLE.
M.G.Coy. & T.M.Bty.	RAINNEVILLE.

11th Infantry Brigade.

Brigade H.Q.	CARDONETTE.
Somerset L.I.	-:-
Hamps.R.	-:-
Rifle Bde.	ALLONVILLE.
E.Lancs.R.	-:-
M.G.Coy.	-:-
T.M.Bty.	-:-

12th Infantry Brigade.

Brigade H.Q.	Rue L'Ecole, BERTANGLES.
King's Own.	POULAINVILLE.
Lancs.Fus.	COISY.
W.Riding.R.	BERTANGLES.
Essex Regt.) H.Q. & 2 Coys.)	-:-
2 Coys.	VAUX.
M.G.Coy.	RAINNEVILLE.
T.M.Bty.	ALLONVILLE.

Divisional Engineers.

H.Q.	VILLERS BOCAGE.
9th Field Coy.	BERTRICOURT.
Durham Field Coy.	ALLONVILLE.
Renfrew Field Coy.	LONGPRE.

21st W.Yorks Regt. (Pioneers).   VILLERS BOCAGE.

4th Division now form part of X Corps.

VILLERS BOCAGE.

19TH -20TH SEPTEMBER.

Division at rest.

VILLERS BOCAGE.

21st SEPTEMBER.

4th Divisional Artillery completed its move to new area and disposed in the area BELLOY - ST SAUVEUR - PICQUIGNY - CHAUSSEE - BREILLY.

VILLERS BOCAGE.   23RD SEPTEMBER.

Orders received to the effect that
4th Division is transferred to 14th
Corps from midnight 24/25th September.
The Division (less Artillery) will
remain in G.H.Q. Reserve and will not be
moved from the CORBIE Area without
reference to A.H.Q.

Operation Order No.61 issued.
Following moves will take place on the
24th September :-
4th Divisional Artillery will march from
present area to BOIS des TAILLES.
10th Brigade, Durham Field Coy. 11th
Field Ambce. will march from present
area to billets about CORBIE.
9th Field Coy. and Renfrew Field Coy.
will march from present area to
ALLONVILLE.

VILLERS BOCAGE.
                        24TH SEPTEMBER.

Moves carried out in accordance with
Operation Order No.61 of 23rd September.

Operation Order No.62 issued:-
Following moves will take place on 25th
and 26th September :-
25th September.
10th Brigade. - from CORBIE Area to SAILLY-
LE-SEC - MERICOURT.
Durham Field Coy.) from CORBIE to SAILLY-
11th Field Ambce.) LE-SEC.

11th Brigade. - from CARDONETTE - ALLON-
VILLE AREA to CORBIE and VAUX-sur-SOMME.
9th Field Coy. from ALLONVILLE to
VAUX-sur-SOMME.
12th Field Ambce. from VAUX-en-AMIENOIS
to VAUX-sur-SOMME.

21st W.Yorks (Pioneers) from VILLERS
BOCAGE to CORBIE.

12th Brigade. - from BERTANGLES Area to
CARDONETTE and ALLONVILLE.

                        26TH SEPTEMBER.
12th Brigade. - from CARDONETTE - ALLONVILLE
Area to LA NEUVILLE and CORBIE.

Divisional H.Q. will close at VILLERS
BOCAGE at 2 pm. 25th inst. and re-open
at same hour at CORBIE.

VILLERS BOCAGE.   25TH SEPTEMBER.
CORBIE.

Moves took place in accordance with
Operation Order No.62.
Divisional H.Q. established at CORBIE.
From midnight 24/25th September 4th Divn.
is transferred to 14th Corps.

CORBIE.   26TH SEPTEMBER.

Moves completed in accordance with
Operation Order No.62.

Disposition of Units :-

10th Infantry Brigade.

Brigade H.Q.	MERICOURT L'ABBE.
R.Irish Fus.	-:-
R.War.R.	-:-
Seaforth Hrs.	MEAULTE.
R.Dub.Fus.	SAILLY-LE-SEC.
M.G.Coy.	-:-
T.M.Bty.	-:-

11th Infantry Brigade.

Brigade H.Q.	CORBIE.
Som.L.I.	-:-
Hamps.R.	-:-
Rif.Bde.	VAUX-sur-SOMME.
E.Lancs.R.	-:-
M.G.Coy.	-:-
T.M.Bty.	-:-

12th Infantry Brigade.

Brigade H.Q.	LA NEUVILLE.
Essex Regt.	-:-
W.Riding Regt.	-:-
M.G.Coy.	-:-
T.M.Bty.	-:-
King's Own.	CORBIE.
Lancs.Fus.	-:-

Divisional Artillery.

H.Q.	FORKTREE CAMP.
14th F.A.Bde.)	
29th F.A.Bde.)	BOIS des TAILLES.
32nd F.A.Bde.)	

Divisional Engineers.

H.Q.	CORBIE.
9th Field Coy.	MEAULTE.
Durham Field Coy.	-:-
Renfrew Field Coy.	CORBIE.

CORBIE.   28TH SEPTEMBER.

Operation Order No.63 issued.
Following moves will take place on the
29th September :-
R.Dublin Fus. 10th M.G.Coy. 10th T.M.Bty,
and section 11th Field Ambce. will
march from SAILLY-LE-SEC to DAOURS.
Renfrew Field Coy. from CORBIE to Camp
on CORBIE - VAUX-sur-SOMME Road.
1 battalion 11th Infantry Brigade from
VAUX-sur-SOMME to CORBIE.

CORBIE.   29TH SEPTEMBER.

Moves ordered to take place in Operation
Order No.63 completed.

Operation Order No.64 ~~completed~~ issued.

CORBIE.   29TH SEPTEMBER (Continued.)

On 30th September :-
10th Bde H.Q., R.Warwick Regt., and R.
Irish Fusiliers will move from MERICOURT
L'ABBE to DAOURS.

On October 1st :-
1st.E.Lancs R. will move from VAUX-sur-
SOMME to MEAULTE and Seaforth Highrs.
will move from MEAULTE to LA NEUVILLE.

CORBIE.   30TH SEPTEMBER.

Moves took place in accordance with
Operation Order No.64.

※※※※※※※※※※※※※※※※※※※※※※※※※※

-SECRET-

Copy No: 1

4th DIVISION OPERATION ORDER NO: 53

1st September 1916

1. In accordance with orders received from the 8th Corps, the following moves will take place.

    10th Inf. Bde will move from Camps in ST LAWRENCE area to Camps K L M and POPERINGHE.
    Bde H.Qrs - PROVEN.

    12th Inf. Bde will relieve 114th Inf. Bde (38th Divn).

    9th Field Coy will move to ELVERDINGHE.

    Renfrew Field Coy will move to 29th Division area for attachment to that Division.

    Durham Field Coy will move to 38th Division area for attachment to that Division.

    H.Qrs & 2 Coys 21st W.Yorks Regt (Pioneers) will move to 38th Division area.

    2 Coys 21st W.Yorks Regt (Pioneers) will move to 29th Division area.

2. Moves will be carried out in accordance with the attached table, Appendix A. Completion of all moves to be reported to Divisional Headquarters.

3. ACKNOWLEDGE.

[signature]

Major.

Issued at 6 p.m.   General Staff., 4th Division.

Copies to :-
    10th.11th.12th Inf. Bde.
    4th Divnl Arty.
    -:- Engineers.
    -:- " Q "
    -:- Signal Coy.
    21st W.Yorks Rgt. (Pioneers)
    A.P.M.
    A.D.M.S.
    38th Division.
    29th Division.
    Canadian Corps.
    8th Corps.

APPENDIX "A"

Date	Unit	From	To	Remarks
4th SEPTR	10th Infy. Bde. Bde H.Qrs	Camps ST LAWRENCE area	PROVEN	Move will take place in the morning under Brigade arrangements.
"	3 Battalions. Bde M.G.Coy. T.M.Batteries.	-:-	K L M Camps	
"	1 Battalion	-:-	POPERINGHE	
4th SEPTR	12th Infy. Bde. Bde H.Qrs.	POPERINGHE (Canadian Corps area)	POPERINGHE (6th Corps area)	
	2/Lancs Fusrs (less 2 Coys)	POPERINGHE	ELVERDINGHE	March to be carried out in small bodies to arrive by 9 a.m.
	2 Coys 2/Lancs Fusrs.	POPERINGHE	BRANDHOEK	To arrive by 11.30 am.
	1/King's Own Rgt. (less 2 Coys)	POPERINGHE	BRANDHOEK	To arrive by 11.30 am.
	2 Coys 1/King's Own Regt.	POPERINGHE	Work L.2 - 2Platoons & 1 Lewis Gun. " L.3 - 2 - ditto - " L.4 - 2 - ditto - " L.8 - 2 - ditto -	To arrive VLAMERTINGHE 8-30 p.m.
	2/Duke of Wellington's	-:- (Can.Corps area)	POPERINGHE (6th Corps area)	
	Bde M.G.Coy(less 2 Sections)	POPERINGHE (Can:Corps area)	- ditto -	
	2 Sections B.M.G.Coy	POPERINGHE	ELVERDINGHE	To arrive by 9 a.m.
	2nd Essex Regt.	POPERINGHE	P Camp.	To arrive by 11.30 am.

NIGHT 4/5th SEPTR.	Renfrew Fd Coy.	Present billets.	Billets in YPRES (29th Divn area)
7th SEPTR.	9th Field Coy.	Present billets	ELVERDINGHE.
NIGHT 7/8th SEPTR	Durham Field Coy.	Present billets	CANAL BANK (38th Divn area)
NIGHT 7/8th SEPTR	21st W.Yorks Rgt (Pioneers.) H.Qrs & 2 Coys 2 Coys.	Present billets - ditto -	L.8 Work. YPRES (29th Divn area)

SECRET. Copy No. ...1...

29/c

4th DIVISION - OPERATION ORDER No. 57.

Reference - Sheet 28 S.W. 6th September, 1916
(1/20000).

1. The 2nd Australian Division will take over the line at present held by the 4th Division from Trench 55 (exclusive) to the YPRES - MENIN Road (inclusive).

2. (a) The 5th Australian Brigade will relieve the 11th Brigade in the line; the relief will be carried out in accordance with the attached table - Appendix A.
     All other details will be arranged between G.Os.C. of these Brigades direct.

   (b) The 11th Brigade after relief will be billeted in POPERINGHE and will move to BOLLEZEELE area on 11th inst. by train.

3. Artillery reliefs will be carried out subsequently to the relief of the infantry under arrangements to be made between G.Os.C. R.A. 4th Division and 2nd Australian Division.

4. Relief of R.E. and Pioneer Battalions will be arranged between C.R.E. 4th Division and C.R.E. 2nd Australian Division.

5. Relief of Field Ambulances will be arranged between A.D.M.S. 4th Division and A.D.M.S. 2nd Australian Division direct.

6. All dumped S.A.A., Grenades, Stoke Mortar Ammn., trench stores, Secret and 1/10000 maps and aerial photos will be handed over to relieving units.

7. Completion of all reliefs will be reported to 4th Division Head Quarters.

8. G.O.C. 4th Division will hand over command of the line to G.O.C. 2nd Australian Division at 10 a.m. on 10th September.

9. 4th Div. H.Q. will close at RENINGHELST at 10 a.m. 10th instant and will reopen at ESQUELBEC at the same hour.

10. ACKNOWLEDGE.

Issued at 10 a.m.

Major,
General Staff, 4th Div.

Copies to 10th, 11th, 12th Inf.Brigs.
4th Div. Arty.
4th Div. Engrs.
4th Div. Q.
4th Div.Sig.Co.
A.D.M.S. 4th Div.
21st W.Yorks.R. (Pioneers).
A.P.M. 4th Div.

I Anzac Corps.
6th Corps.
2nd Australian Div.
1st Australian Div.
29th Division.
War Diary
file

APPENDIX

DATE.	UNIT.	FROM.	TO.	REMARKS.
Night 8/9th Sept.	11th Inf. Brig. 1st E.Lanc. R.	Trenches Right Sub-sector.	POPERINGHE.	Relieved by units 5th Australian Brigade.
	1st Som. L.I.	Trenches Brigade Support.	POPERINGHE.	Personnel by train from ASYLUM.
	11th M.G.Coy.	Trenches.	POPERINGHE.	
Night 9/10th Sept.	11th Inf. Brig. 1st Hamps. R.	MONTREAL Camp.	POPERINGHE.	By March Route.
	1st Rif.Brig.	Trenches Left Sub-sector.	POPERINGHE.	Relieved by units 5th Australian Brigade.
	11th T.M.Bty.	Trenches.	POPERINGHE.	Personnel by train from ASYLUM.
	Brig. H.Q.	YPRES Ramparts.	POPERINGHE.	G.O.C. 11th Inf.Brig. will hand over command of the line to G.O.C. 5th Australian Brig. on completion of the relief.

292c

- S E C R E T -
****

Copy No: 11

4th DIVISION OPERATION ORDER NO: 58
****

10th Septr 1916.
****

1. In accordance with orders received from Second Army, the following units of the 4th Division will march on 11th September to billets near DUNKIRK.

    (a) 11th Infantry Brigade.

    (b) 29th Artillery Brigade.

    (c) 12th Field Ambulance.

    (d) No: 3 Coy, Divnl Train and attached units of H.Qrs Coy.

2. Above units will march in accordance with attached table at such an hour so as to enable them to arrive in their billets by 2 p.m. 11th September.

3. On arrival they will report to Brig-Genl Rees.D.S.O. Comdg 11th Infantry Brigade and will remain under his orders.

4. Above units will move rationed for the 12th instant.

5. ACKNOWLEDGE.

Major.

Issued at 10.30 p.m.   General Staff., 4th Division.

Copies to :-

11th Brigade
29 F.A. Bde
No. 3. Coy Train
12 Fd. Amb ce.
4 Div D
8 Corps
ADMS
4 Div Arty
4 Div Signals
APM

UNIT	FROM	TO	ROUTE
4th Inf. Bde.	BOLLEZEELE	COUDKERQUE – TETEGHM – ARMBOUTS CAPPEL – CAPPELLE. Bde H.Qrs Admiralty Office, DUNKIRK (near Docks)	ZEGGERS CAPPEL – BERGUES. Billeting parties to report to Mayors of villages.
29th F.A.Bde.	BUSSEBOOM	B.Hqrs & 1 Bty – SPYCKER. 3 Batteries – BROUCKERQUE.	POPERINGHE – HOUTKERQUE – ZEGGERS CAPPEL – PITGAM. Billeting parties to report to Mayors of villages.
14th Field Amb.	WORMHOUDT	COUDKERQUE	BERGUES
No: 3 Coy. Div Train.	BOLLEZEELE	COUDKERQUE	BERGUES

S E C R E T   COPY No. 8

4th DIVISION - OPERATION ORDER No. 59.

14th September, 1916

1. The units of the 4th Division which are at present in the DUNKIRK area will return to the Second Army area on the 15th instant as under:-

    11th Infantry Brigade to BOLLEZEELE Area.
    29th F. A. Bde. to HOUTKERQUE Area.
    12th Field Ambulance to WATOU Area.

2. The move will be carried out under orders to be issued by Brig.-General Rees, D.S.O. Commanding 11th Infantry Brigade.

3. ACKNOWLEDGE.

Major, Lt Colonel
General Staff, 4th Division.

Issued at 2 pm.

Copies to 11th Inf. Bde.
    4th Div. "Q"
    4th Signal Coy.
    A.D.M.S.
    VIII Corps
    4th Div. Arty.

SECRET.   2nd Army G 259 10/9/16.

4th Division.
----

1.   A Force, composed as under, will march on 11th September to DUNKIRK, and carry out the attached programmes under instructions from Admiral Bacon, Commodore, DOVER Patrol.

       11th Infantry Brigade)
       1 Fld. Artillery Bde.) Under Brig.-Gen. H.C. Rees, D.S.O.
       1 Fld. Ambulance   ) Commanding 11th Inf. Brigade.
       1 Coy. Div. Train.   )

2.   Billeting arrangements - the force will billet in the area shown on attached map.

A billeting scheme has been handed to A.A.& Q.M.G. 4th Division.

An Officer will report at 8 a.m. on 11th September at the office of the Governor, Rue de Sud, DUNKIRK, to arrange billets.

3.   Supply arrangements -

The force will move rationed to 12th inclusive. During the stay at DUNKIRK supplies will be drawn as usual from PROVEN, and sent to DUNKIRK by lorry.

4.   On 15th September the Force will return to the 2nd Army area and will rejoin the 4th Division.

                         (Sd) C.H.Harington, M.G.G.S.
                                Second Army.

Programme of Move of Infantry Brigade and Artillery

Brigade to DUNKIRK.

11th Sept.   11th Infantry Brigade   )
                 Field Artillery Bde.,   ) Under Brig.-Gen. Rees,
                     4th Division.   ) Commanding 11th Infantry
                 1 Field Ambulance   ) Brigade
                 1 Coy. Divnl. Train   )

will march to billeting area, South of DUNKIRK, arriving about 2 pm.

The G.O.C. will report to Admiral Bacon, at Commodore's office at the Docks, on arrival.

Arrangements to be made to connect by telephone Brigade Headquarters in DUNKIRK with Commodore's office.

12th Sept.   Infantry Battalions and Artillery Brigade will march, with first line transport only, through principal streets of DUNKIRK to the Docks, arriving about 8 am.

Arrangements will be made by Commodore's Staff for about 600 - 800 Infantry only to embark in 6 or 7 drifters in the harbour : the drifters will not leave the harbour.

Guns and limbers only of Field Artillery Brigade will be loaded on the deck of a monitor, if available. No horses nor vehicles will be embarked.

The Infantry will disembark and the guns unloaded during the afternoon.

About 5 pm. infantry and artillery will return by companies and batteries to the billeting area by different routes to those followed in the morning.

13th Sept.   Repetition of programme for 12th September.

14th Sept.   Repetition of programme, but troops may leave the Docks at 12 noon and return to the billeting area.

15th Sept.   The Force will return to Second Army area, and rejoin the 4th Division.

SECRET.   4th Division No. GGG 101.

Headquarters,

    VIII Corps.

        Forwarded.

        Owing to the number of civilians frequenting the Docks and neighbourhood, I think the return of the troops without sailing must have been noticed.

        There is no doubt that the movement of the Brigade caused considerable discussion, and I have reason to believe that the fact that the brigade was moving to DUNKERQUE was known to civilians and others in POPERINGHE as early as Monday 11th.   How these rumours got about I do not know but I am making enquiries.

                              (Sd) W. Lambton, Major-General,
15/9/16.   Commanding 4th Division.

SECRET   B.M. 17/530

4th Division "G"

The following is the programme I carried out on the 12th, 13th and 14th September.

12th September.   With a view to looking as large a force as possible, I marched all available troops through the main street of DUNKIRK on one road.   The head of the column passed the starting point, Cross Roads H.28.b.9.8 at 7 a.m.

Order of March.

        1st Hampshire Regiment
        1st E. Lancashire Regt.
        1 Rifle Brigade
        1st Somerset L.I.
        11th M.G. Company
        29th Brigade R.F.A.
        12th Field Ambulance.

On arrival at the Docks, the 1st Hants. Regt. was embarked on eight trawlers, under the orders of the Naval Authorities, the 1st line Transport being parked nearly opposite the point from which they embarked.

The three other battalions, and the Machine Gun Company marched straight on through the Docks to the Dunes in B.20.b.

The 29th Brigade R.F.A. loaded the whole of the guns and limbers on the monitor "GENERAL WOLF."

The=29 12th Field Ambulance moved into the open space vacated by the Artillery as they loaded their guns and wagons.

The return march was made by companies and batteries; the leading company and battery moving off at 5 p.m.   This was carried out by the Infantry moving westward to the Aviation ground, thence by road which brought them on to the DUNKIRK-CALAIS Road at H.2.d.0.3, crossing the CANAL at the Bridge at G.12.d.9.4 - the artillery crossing at the Bridge G.12.a.7.9 - thence by most direct road to their billets.   The whole force moved by these roads with the exception of the 1st Somerset L.I.

and the 12th Field Ambulance, who returned to their billets via unfrequented streets in the North Eastern part of DUNKIRK.

13th September. Units marched into DUNKIRK independently, moving as far as possible by different roads to the one used the previous day. The Somerset L.I. marched through the main street of MALO-LES-BAINS thence to B.28.

The 1st Rifle Bde. from COUDEKERQUE, entered the town at the South-East end, and thence to the Docks.

The 1st Hants. Regt. 1st E. Lancs. Regt. 11th Machine Gun Coy. and the 29th Brigade R.F.A. marched as far as possible by different roads to the same point. Both the 1st Som. L.I. and the 1st Rifle Bde. were put on transports; the guns and limbers being put on to the "LORD CLIVE." Units returned to their billets by the roads by which they returned the previous day.

On the 14th, the same programme was repeated as on the 13th, with the exception that troops returned to their billets, companies and batteries moving off at 12 noon.

Remarks. There has been a good deal of discussion among the inhabitants, as to the reasons for this movement, in DUNKIRK itself. We were said to be going to SALONICA; about to make a landing on the Coast; and practising embarkation for some future operation. The last one appears to be the most generally accepted. It was freely said in one village outside the town that 10,000 men had embarked, and gone off. No unauthorised persons are supposed to enter the docks, but the docks were full of loafers of all sorts all day. It was somewhat difficult, in a place where one has no control of the movements of the civilian population, to make any secret moves; for instance, my interpreter heard a French boy relate his experiences from which it appeared that he had gone round the country side, on a bicycle, and located the position of nearly every unit.

(Sd) H.C. Rees, Brig.-General,

14/9/16.

Commanding 11th Inf. Bde.

SECRET   COPY No. 19

4th DIVISION - OPERATION ORDER No. 60.

1.   4th Division will begin to entrain tonight for the South and will be replaced in VIII Corps by the 7th Division.
        Entrainment stations and time tables will be issued separately.

2.   Units of the 4th Division at present attached to the 29th and 38th Divisions will be concentrated as under by 10 a.m. 17th September.

        2nd Essex Regiment   -   POPERINGHE
        2nd Lancs. Fus.   POPERINGHE
        1st K.O. Regiment   BRANDHOEK
        2nd West Riding Regt.   POPERINGHE
        21st West Yorks R. (Pioneers)   "J" Camp.

        Orders for these moves will be issued by 29th and 38th Divisions.

3.   2nd Lancashire Fusiliers will leave one officer and 3 other ranks in charge of ELVERDINGHE Defences.
        1st King's Own Regt. will leave 2 other ranks in charge of each of the following works:- L 4, L 8, L 3, L 2, under the command of an officer.
        The above officer and other ranks must be acquainted with the scheme of work. They will rejoin their units when relieved by the 7th Division under instructions which will be issued by VIII Corps.

4.   ROYAL ENGINEERS.
        1/1st Renfrew and 1/1st Durham Field Companies (less sections at ST. JAN TER BIEZEN) will concentrate at their Transport lines by 10 a.m. 17th instant.
        Sections now at ST. JAN TER BIEZEN will rejoin their units at entraining station.
        The 9th Field Company will be prepared to march to the entraining station at one hour's notice. The detached section at BOLLEZEELE will proceed by rail with the 11th Infantry Brigade. 9th Field Company will leave one officer and 3 other ranks at ELVERDINGHE to hand over work to 7th Division.

5.   ROYAL ARTILLERY
        Relief of 4th Divisional Artillery by 29th Divisional Artillery will continue under present arrangements.
        Orders for move of the artillery to new area will be issued later.

6.   Reserve Brigade of 29th Division will become Corps Reserve from 10 a.m. on 17th instant.

7.   ATTACHMENTS.

    (a) Officers and O.R. attached to 177th Tunnelling Company will rejoin brigades as follows:-

(2)

        10th Brigade details by 10 a.m. 17th
        12th Brigade details   do.
    11th Brigade details will join 12th Brigade by 10 a.m. 17th. and will accompany 12th Brigade to new area.

(b)   Men under instruction at Corps Signalling School will be returned to units:

        10th Brigade details to 10th Brigade 16th September.
        12th Brigade details to 12th Brigade 16th September.
        11th Brigade details will join 12th Brigade and will accompany 12th Brigade to new area.

8.   Instructions for caretakers of camps, stores and Horse standings will be issued by "Q" branch.

W. H. Bartholomew

16th September, 1916.   Lieut.-Colonel,

Issued at 3 p.m.   General Staff, 4th Division.

Copies to 10th)
          11th)Infantry Brigade
          12th)
          4th Divisional Artillery
          4th Divisional Engineers
          4th Signal Company
          4th Division "Q"
          A. D. M. S.
          O.C. 21st W. Yorks Regt.
          A. P. M.
          Train
          Supply Column.
          A.D.V.S.
          D.A.D.O.S.
          29th Division
          38th Division
          VIII Corps

PROGRAMME OF MOVE OF 4TH DIVISION (LESS ARTILLERY)

VIA CALAIS.

From Second Army
  ENTRAINING STATIONS
  A = ESQUELBECQ
  B = PROVEN
  C = HOPOUTRE

16.9.16 - 17.9.16

To Fourth Army.
  DETRAINING STATIONS
  A = LONGUEAU
  B = LONGUEAU
  C = SALEUX

Train No. from stations.			Serial No.	Time of dep. from Ent'g Station.	Date	Marche	Time of arr. at Det. Stn.	Date
A	B	C						
1	2	3	4	5	6	7	8	9
1			420,25,26,27	0.30	17.9	HT	4	
	2		410,25,26,27	22.54	16.9	"	5	
		3	430,35,36,37	1.30	17.9	"	6	
4			421	3.30	"	"	7	
	5		411	2.08	"	"	8	
		6	431	4.30	"	"	9	
7			422	6.20	"	"	10	
	8		412	4.54	"	"	11	
		9	432	7.15	"	"	12	
10			401,05,07,08,83	9.30	"	"	13	
	11		413	8.30	"	"	14	
		12	433	10.44	"	"	15	
13			423	12.30	"	"	16	
	14		492,88	11.30	"	"	17	
		15	491,90	13.36	"	"	18	
16			424	15.30	"	"	19	
	17		485	14.06	"	"	20	
		18	484,½409	16.36	"	"	21	
19			493,89	18.30	"	"	22	
	20		404	16.54	"	"	23	
		21	486	19.46	"	"	24	
			414	23.03	"	"	1	
	23		404a,87,94,95,½409	20.12	"	"	2	
		24	434	22.44	"		3	

SUMMARY.

    ESQUELBECQ (A) = 8 T.C's.
    PROVEN   (B) = 9 T.C's.
    HOPOUTRE   (C) = 9 T.C's.

* Train 22 will go from ST OMER

J.C. Owen
                         Captain. R.E.,
                 for Lieut. Colonel.
HAZEBROUCK.
                         A.D.R.T. II
16. 9. 16

TABLE "D". 4TH DIVISION (LESS ARTILLERY)

UNIT	Serial No.	DESCRIPTION.
Divisional Units.	401	Divisional Headquarters.
	404	Pioneer Battn less 04a
	404a	1 Company, 4 G.S.Wgns & teams.
	405	H.Q. & H.Q.Section Div. Signals.
	407	Corps Cable Section.
	408	Band.
	409	Reserve & Salvage Cos.
10th Infantry Brigade.	410	Brigade Headquarters.
	411	A Battalion.
	412	B "
	413	C "
	414	D "
	415	Signal Section.
	416	B.M.G.Co.
	417	Light T.M.Bty.
11th Infantry Brigade.	420	Brigade Headquarters.
	421	A Battalion.
	422	B "
	423	C "
	424	D "
	425	Signal Section.
	426	B.M.G.Co.
	427	Light T.M.Bty.
12th Infantry Brigade.	430	Brigade Headquarters.
	431	A Battalion.
	432	B "
	433	C "
	434	D "
	435	Signal Section.
	436	B.M.G.Co.
	437	Light T.M.Bty.
~~Divisional Ammunition Column.~~	~~479~~	~~S.A.A.Waggons. No.1 Section.~~
	~~480~~	~~do. No.2 "~~
	~~481~~	~~do. No.3 "~~
Divisional Engineers.	483	Headquarters.
	484	9th Field Co. R.E.
	485	1st Durham Field Co. R.E.
	486	1st Renfrew Field Co. R.E.
Divisional Train.	487	Headquarters.
	488	No. 2 Company.
	489	No. 3 "
	490	No. 4 "
Medical Units.	491	10th Field Ambulance.
	492	11th " "
	493	12th " "
	494	Sanitary Section.
	495	Mobile Veterinary Section.

16. 9. 16

SECRET.   4th Div. No. Q.R.1320.

1.   The 4th Division with S.A.A. and Grenade Portion of the Divl. Ammn. Col. less the R.A. – Medium and Heavy Trench Mortar Batteries and motor vehicles, will entrain tomorrow at the following stations.:-

   The Time Table will be issued later. The first train leaves at 6 p.m.

ESQUELBECQ.   Divisional Head Quarters.
                   4th Divl. Signal Coy. and Band.
                   11th Inf. Bde., M.G. Co. and T.M. Battery.
                   2nd Bn. Royal Dublin Fus.
                   12th Field Ambulance.
                   No. 3 Co. of 4th Div. Train.

HOUTPOUTRE.   12th Inf.Bde., M.G. Co. and T.M. Battery.
L.17.b.   10th Field Ambulance.
                   9th Field Coy. R.E.
                   2 Coys. 21st Bn. West Yorks Regt.
                   No. 4 Co. of 4th Div. Train.
                   1/1st Renfrew Fld. Co. R.E.

PROVEN.   10th Inf.Bde. M.G. Co. and T.M. Battery.
                   4th Div. Reserve Coy.
                   11th Field Ambulance.
                   No. 2 Co. of 4th Div. Train.
                   21st West Yorks Rgt. and Transport.
                   1/1st Durham Fld. Co. R.E.

   In the case of the Pioneer Battalion and Field Companies, these arrangements are open to alteration.

2.   Train and Baggage wagons will move with units.

3.   Marche indicates the official train number.

4.   Date.   Hour of departure.
     16/9.   18/10.   = 6.10 p.m. 16th July.

5.   The Divisional Artillery will move in accordance with instructions that will be issued later.

6.   Motor vehicles except cars with Staff Officers will move as convoys on 17th September – route will be issued later.

7.   The D.A.A. & Q.M.G. with Lieut. Edwards will proceed to the detraining area forthwith.

8.   The C.R.A. will detail one officer with experience in entraining troops and transport to report to the R.T.O. at each of the stations named in minute 1. 3½ hours before the time that the 1st Train from each station is due to leave. These Officers will remain on duty and supervise the loading of the trains until the completion of the move.

9. Infantry Brigades will detail 2 Officers and 100 Other Ranks to report to the R.T.O. at the respective entraining stations 3½ hours before the first train is due to leave. These parties will assist in loading the trains under the direction of the Entraining Officers and they will leave by the last train leaving their station.

10. Rendezvous for troops at Entraining Stations.

    HOUTPOUTRE.   HOUTPOUTRE Station.
    PROVEN.   H.14.c.8.6.
    ESQUELBECQ.   About B.6.c.

All units will send forward an officer to reconnoitre the roads.

11. All transport will reach the Entraining Points 3 clear hours and the personnel of units 1½ clear hours before the train is due to leave.

12. Infantry Brigades will detail their Brigade Transport Officer to superintend the detraining of units at their detraining stations. These Officers should proceed by the first trains.

13. <u>Supplies.</u> All units will entrain with the current rations for the 17th inst. on the men and cookers, supply wagons loaded with rations for the 18th.

14. Water carts and water bottles will be filled before starting.

15. Units will provide head ropes for all trucks carrying horses.

16. The O.C. Signal Co. will detail one motorcyclist for duty at each entraining station under the orders of the Entraining Officer. They will move on the last trains with the Entraining parties.

17. The C.R.A. will detail a party of 3 N.C.O's and 6 men to take over K. L. and M. Camps and the horse standings. This party will report to the Staff Captain, 10th Brigade at 2 p.m. for instructions.

18. Billeting parties from units moving by the first three trains from each Entraining Station will proceed on the 1st train, those of units leaving by the 4th train on the 2nd train, those by the 5th train on the 3rd train and so on.

15th September 1916.   W.P.H.HILL, Lt.Colonel.
                                  A.A. & Q.M.G., 4th Division.

UNITS ENTRAINING
HOPOUTRE.

MOVE OF 4th DIVISION.

Unit	Serial No.	Entraining Station	Hour of Departure	Date	Marche	Detraining Station	Hour of Arrival	Remarks.
12th Bde.H.Q.	430	HOPOUTRE	1.30	17th	6	SALEUX		
Signal Section	435	"	1.30	"	6	"		
Bde.M.G.Co.	436	"	1.30	"	6	"		
Light T.M.Battery	437	"	1.30	"	6	"		
Duke of Wellington's	431	"	4.30	"	9	"		
King's Own	432	"	7.15	"	12	"		
Lancs.Fus.	433	"	10.44	"	15	"		
10th Field Amb.	490	"	13.36	"	18	"		
No. 4 Co. Train	491	"	13.36	"	18	"		
9th Field Co. R.E.	485	"	16.36	"	21	"		
Renfrew Field Co.	486	"	19.46	"	24	"		
Essex Regt.	434	"	22.44	"	3	"		

MOVE OF 4th DIVISION.

UNITS ENTRAINING PROVEN.

Unit.	Serial No.	Entraining Station	Hour of Departure	Date	Marche	Detraining Station	Hour of Arrival	Remarks.
10th Bde.H.Q.	410	PROVEN	22.54	16th	5	LONGUEAU		
Signal Section	425	"	22.54	"	5	"		
Bde.M.G.Company	426	"	22.54	"	5	"		
Light T.M.Batty.	427	"	22.54	"	5	"		
R.Warwick Regt. Reserve Co.	411) 409)	"	2.08	17th	8	"		
Seaforth Hldrs.	412	"	4.54	"	11	"		
R.Irish Fus.	413	"	8.30	"	14	"		
11th Field Amb.	492	"	11.30	"	17	"		
No. 2 Co. Train	488	"	11.30	"	17	"		
Durham Field Co.	485	"	14.06	"	20	"		
21st W.Yorks Pioneers less 1 Co. & 4 wagons and teams	404	"	16.54	"	23	"		
1 Co.21st W.Yorks, and 4 wagons & teams	404a	"	20.12	"	2	"		
H.Q.,Div.Train	487	"	20.12	"	2	"		
Sanitary Section	494	"	20.12	"	2	"		
Mobile Vet.Section	495	"	20.12	"	3	"		

4th Div.Q.R.1320/2.

MOVE OF 4th DIVISION.

UNITS ENTRAINING ESQUELBECQ.

Unit.	Serial No.	Entraining Station.	Hour of Departure	Date.	Marche	Detraining Station	Hour of Arrival	Remarks.
11th Bde.H.Q.	420	ESQUELBECQ	0.30	17th	H.T. 4	LONGUEAU		Approx.10 hours later Billeting parties can obtain exact hour of detraining from R.S.O. LONGUEAU.
Somerset L.I.	421	"	3.30	"	7	"		
Rifle Brigade.	422	"	6.20	"	10	"		
Div.H.Q.	401	"	9.30	"	13	"		
H.Q.Sig.Coy.	405	"	9.30	"	13	"		
Cable Section	407	"	9.30	"	13	"		
Band	408	"	9.30	"	13	"		
Div.R.E.H.Q.	483	"	9.30	"	13	"		
Hants.Regt.	423	"	12.30	"	16	"		
E.Lancs.Regt.	424	"	15.30	"	19	"		
12th Field Amb.	493	"	18.30	"	22	"		
No.3 Co.Train	489	"	18.30	"	22	"		
2nd R.Dub.Fus.	414	ST.OMER	23.03	"	1	"		

W.P.H.HILL, Lieut.Colonel,
A.A. & Q.M.G., 4th Division.

September 16th, 1916.

-SECRET-

Copy No: 10

4th DIVISION OPERATION ORDER NO:61

Reference Sheet 17 AMIENS $\frac{1}{100,000}$.

23rd September 1916.

1. The following moves will take place on 24th September.

   (a) 4th Divisional Artillery will march from present area to BOIS des TAILLES.

   Route AMIENS - VECQUEMONT - LA NEUVILLE - BRAY road.
   Head of column to reach VECQUEMONT at 11 a.m.

   (b) 10th Infantry Brigade, Durham Field Company, 11th Field Ambulance will march from present area to billets about CORBIE - under orders to be issued by G.O.C.10th Infantry Brigade.

   Route - ALLONVILLE - QUERRIEU - LA NEUVILLE.
   Head of column to reach QUERRIEU between 2 pm. and 3 pm.

   (c) 9th Field Company and Renfrew Field Company from present area to ALLONVILLE.
   Route via POULAINVILLE.

2. ACKNOWLEDGE.

Major for Lieut-Colonel,
General Staff, 4th Division.

Issued at 2pm.

Copies to 4th Div.Arty.
           4th Div.Engineers.
           10th Inf.Bde.
           4th Div."Q".
           A.D.M.S.
           4th Div.Signals.
           10th Corps.
           A.P.M.4th Division.

S E C R E T COPY NO...13...

4TH DIVISION OPERATION ORDER NO.62.

Reference Sheet 17.AMIENS.1/100,000.   24th September 1918.

1. Moves in accordance with the attached table will take place on the 25th and 26th September.

2. All troops moving East of CORBIE will march by tracks alongside road and not by main road.

3. All billeting parties will report to Town Majors of villages 6 hours before troops are due to arrive.

4. 4th Division Headquarters will close at VILLERS BOCAGE at 2 pm. on 25th inst. and will re-open at CORBIE at the same hour.

5. ACKNOWLEDGE.

Major,
General Staff, 4th Division.

Issued at 12 noon.

Copies to :-
10th.11th.12th.Inf.Bdes.
4th Div.Arty.
C.R.E.4th Division.
4th Div."Q".
A.D.M.S.4th Division.
A.P.M.4th Division.
4th Div.Signals.
21st.W.Yorks.(Pioneers)Regt.
14th Corps.

TO ACCOMPANY OPERATION ORDER NO. 42.

Date and Unit.	From.	To.		Route.	Remarks.
25th September.					
10TH INFANTRY BRIG.	CORBIE	Bde.H.Q.	SAILLY-le-SEC.		) To march under orders of G.O.C.
		H.G.Coy.	—do—		) 10th Infantry Brigade.
		T.M.Bty.	—do—		)
		2 Bns.	—do—		) To be clear of CORBIE by 2 pm.
Durham Field Coy.	"	2 "	MERICOURT.		
11th Field Ambce.	"	"	SAILLY-le-SEC.		
25th September.					
11TH INFANTRY BRIG.	GARDONETTE	Bde.H.Q.	CORBIE.	ALLONVILLE -	) To march under orders of G.O.C.
	ALLONVILLE.	T.M.Bty.	—do—	QUERRIEU -	) 11th Infantry Brigade.
		2 Bns.	—do—	LA NEUVILLE.	)
		M.G.Coy.	VAUX-sur-SOMME.		) Head of column to reach
		2 Bns.	—do—		) QUERRIEU between 2 and 3 pm.
9th Field Coy.	ALLONVILLE.		VAUX-sur-SOMME.		
1/2 12th Field Ambulance.	VAUX-sur-AMIENOIS.		—do—		
25th September.					
Divisional H.Q.	VILLERS BOCAGE.		CORBIE.	QUERRIEU -	)
21st W.Yorks.	—do—		—do—	LA NEUVILLE.	) To march at 2 pm.
(Pioneers) Regt.					)
25th September.					
12TH INFANTRY BRIG.	BERTANGLES Area.		GARDONETTE & ALLONVILLE.		Under orders of G.O.C.Bde - Billets available from 5 pm.
26th September.					
12TH INFANTRY BRIG.	GARDONETTE	Bde.H.Q.	LA NEUVILLE.	ALLONVILLE	) To march under orders of G.O.C.
	ALLONVILLE.	M.G.Coy.	—do—	-	) 12th Infantry Brigade.
		T.M.Bty.	—do—	QUERRIEU.	)
		2 Bns.	CORBIE.		) Head of column to reach
		2 "	—do—		) QUERRIEU by 10.30 am.
12th Field Ambulance.	VILLERS BOCAGE.		CORBIE.	LA NEUVILLE.	
Renfrew Field Coy.	ALLONVILLE.		CORBIE.		

SECRET   Copy No. 12

4th DIVISION OPERATION ORDER No. 63.

Ref. Sheet 17
AMIENS 1/100,000   28th September, 1916

1.   The following moves will take place on 29th instant:-

(a)   2nd Battn. R. Dublin Fusiliers, 10th M. G. Coy, 10th T. M. Battery, and section of 11th Field Ambulance will march from SAILLY-le-SEC to DAOURS under orders to be issued by G.O.C. 10th Inf. Bde.

ROUTE:-   CORBIE - LA NEUVILLE

Column will start at 2 pm.

(b)   1/1st Renfrew Field Company, R.E. will march at 12 noon from CORBIE to Camp on CORBIE-VAUX-sur-SOMME Road.

(c)   One battalion of 11th Infantry Brigade will march at 2 pm. from VAUX-sur-SOMME to CORBIE.

2.   ACKNOWLEDGE.

                                                Major,
Issued at 7 pm.   General Staff, 4th Division.

Copies to 10th, 11th & 12th Brigades
          C. R. E.
          4th Division "Q"
          A. P. M.
          A. D. M. S.
          4th Signal Company
          XIV Corps

* S E C R E T *

Copy No. 12

4TH DIVISION OPERATION ORDER NO. 64.

Reference Sheet 17 AMIENS 1/100,000.

29/9/16

1. The following moves will take place on 30th September and on 1st October.

   (a) SEPTEMBER 30TH.

   10th Infantry Brigade Headquarters, 1st Royal Warwick Regt. 1st Royal Irish Fusiliers, No.2 Company Train will move from MERICOURT L'ABBE to DAOURS under orders to be issued by G.O.C. 10th Infantry Brigade.

   Route - CORBIE - LA NEUVILLE.

   (b) OCTOBER 1ST.

   1st Bn. East Lancashire Regt. will move from VAUX-SUR-SOMME to MEAULTE and will furnish working parties at present found by 2nd Seaforth Highlanders.
   Hour of march will be notified later.

   (c) OCTOBER 1ST.

   2nd Bn. Seaforth Highlanders will move from MEAULTE to LA NEUVILLE.
   Hour of march will be notified later.

2. A C K N O W L E D G E.

Lieut-Colonel,
General Staff, 4th Division.

Issued at 10 am.

Copies to :-
10th 11th 12th Infantry Bdes.
4th Div. Engineers.
4th Div. Arty.
4th Div. "Q".
4th Div. Signal Coy.
A.P.M. 4th Division.
A.D.M.S.
14th Corps.

10th Infantry Brigade
11th Infantry Brigade
4th Division "Q"
XIV Corps "G")
XIV Corps "Q") For information.

Reference 4th Division Operation Order No. 64.

1.   1st E. Lancashire Regiment will move from VAUX-sur-SOMME on 1st October as follows:-

Headquarters and 3 companies to billets in MEAULTE

1 company to new camp at F.17.b.2.8.

The march to be arranged so as to reach above places by 5 p.m.

An officer will be sent on in advance to each place to ascertain full details of all working parties at present found by 2nd Seaforth Highlanders. These working parties will be found by the 1st Battn. E. Lancashire Regiment from 1st October inclusive.

2.   2nd Seaforth Highlanders, less parties actually working on 1st October, will march from their present billets in MEAULTE and F.17.b.2.8 to LA NEUVILLE on morning of 1st October.

Working parties, will on completion of work on evening of 1st October, move to LA NEUVILLE by train.

Details will be issued later.

3.   All units will move by cross country tracks as far as possible.

Major,
General Staff, 4th Division.

30/9/16.

CASUALTIES - 4th DIVISION - 1st - 30th SEPTEMBER 1916.

	Killed	Wounded	Missing
Officers	1	6	
Other Ranks	8	68	
Total	9	74	-

4th Division
War Diaries
General Staff
July 1916

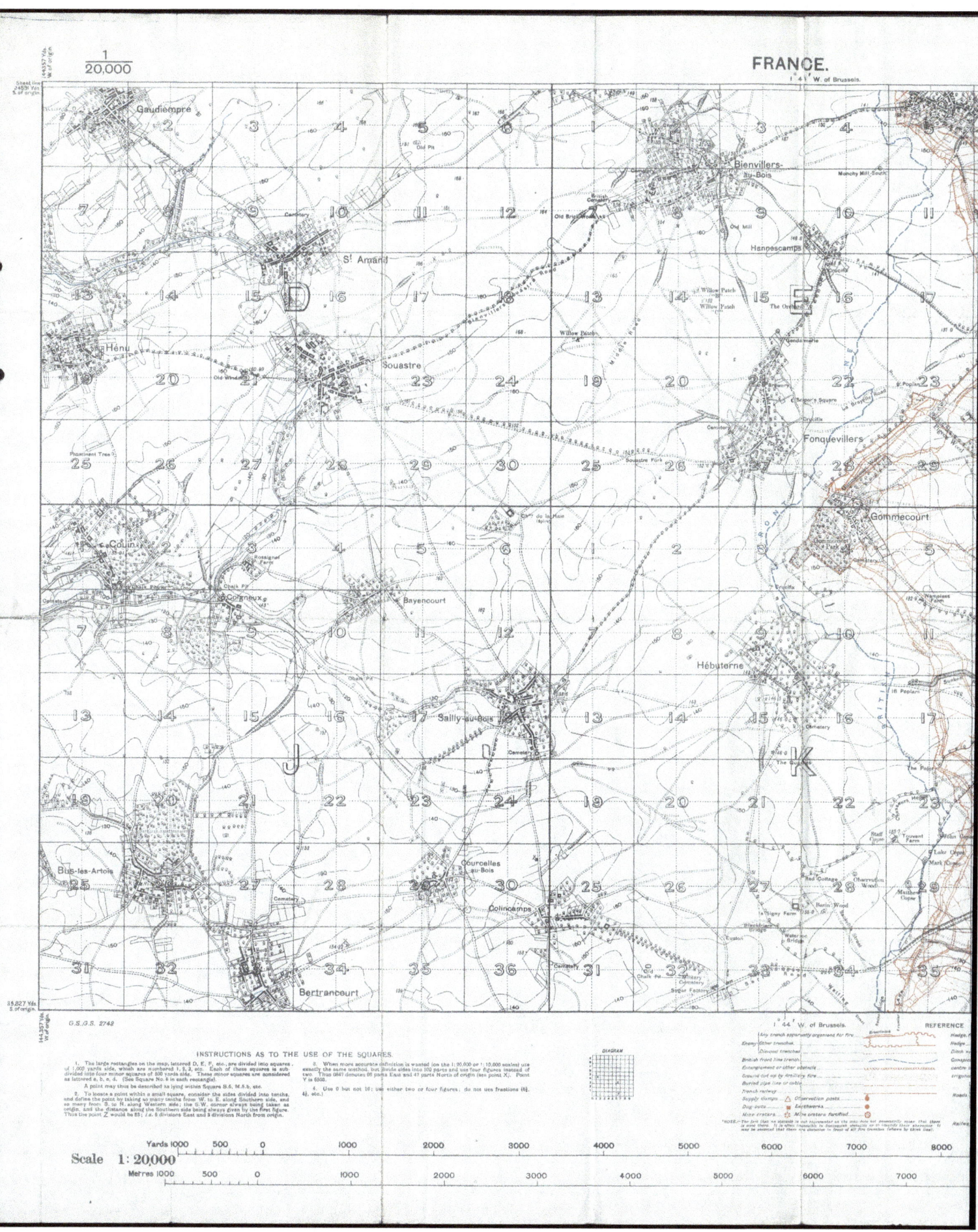

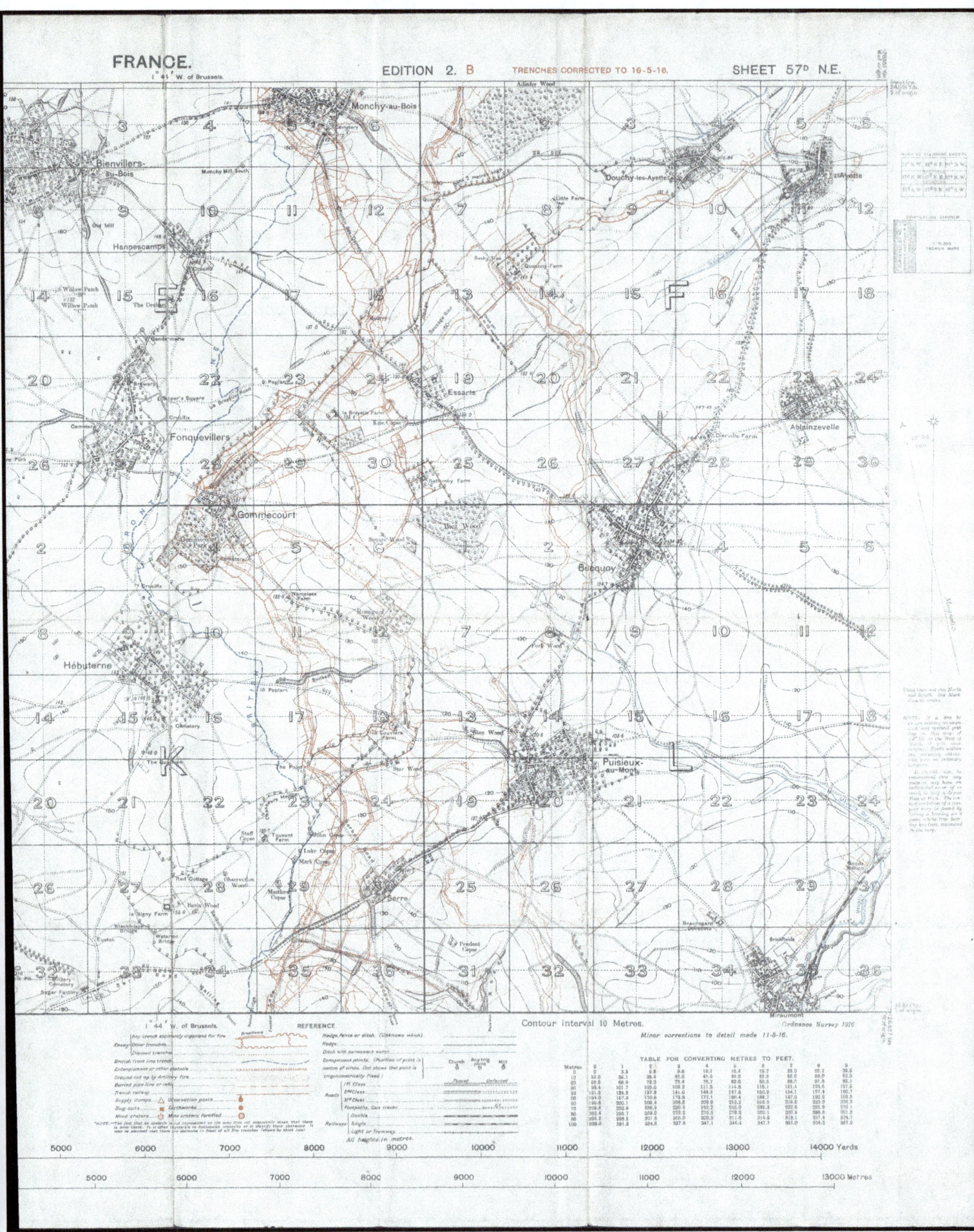

GLOSSARY.

Abbaye, Abbᵉ	Abbey.
Abreuvoir, Abʳ	Watering-place.
Abri de douaniers	Customs-shelter.
Aciérie	Steel works.
Aiguilles	Points (Ry.)
Allée	Alley, Narrow road.
Ancien -ne, Ancⁿ⁻ᵉ	Old.
Aqueduc	Aqueduct.
Arbre	Tree.
,, éventail	,, fan-shaped.
,, débarné	,, bare.
,, fourchu	,, forked.
,, isolé	,, isolated.
,, penché	,, leaning.
Arbrisseau	Small tree.
Arc	Arch.
Ardoisière, Ardʳᵉ	Slate quarry.
Arrêt	Halt.
Asile	Asylum.
,, des aliénés	Lunatic asylum.
,, d' ,,	
,, de charité	
,, des pauvres	Asylum.
,, de refuge	
Auberge, Aubᵉ	Inn.
Aune	Alder-tree.
Bac	Ferry.
,, à traille	
Bains	Baths.
Bains aux laius	Bathing place.
Balise	Booy, Beacon.
Banc de sable	Sand-bank.
,, vase	Mud-bank.
Baraque	Hut.
Barrage	Dam.
Barrière	Gate, Stile.
(Machine à) Bascule	Weigh-bridge.
Bassin	Dock, Pond.
,, d'échouage	Tidal dock.
Bassin de radoub	Dry dock.
Bateau phare	Light-ship.
Blanchisserie	Laundry.
B.M. (borne millière)	Mile stone.
Bᵉ (borne kilométrique)	
Boulonnerie	
Fabᵉ de boulons	Bolt Factory.
Bouée	Buoy.
Brasserie, Brasᵉ	Brewery.
Briqueterie, Briqᵉ	Brickfield.
Brise-lames	Breakwater.
Bureau de poste	Post office.
,, de douane	Custom house.
Butte	Butt, Mound.
Cabane	Hut.
Cabaret, Cabᵗ	Inn.
Câble sous-marin	Submarine cable.
Calvaire, Calᵛᵉ	Calvary.
Canal de dessèchement	Drainage canal.
Canal d'irrigation	Irrigation canal.
Fabᵉ de caoutchouc	Rubber factory.
Carrière, Carrᵉ	Quarry.
,, de gravier	Gravel-pit.
Caserne	Barracks.
Champ de courses	Race-course.
,, manoeuvres	Drill-ground.
,, tir	Rifle range.
Chantier	Building yard.
,,	Ship yard.
,,	Dock yard.
Chantier de construction	Slip-way.
Chapelle, Chᵉˡˡᵉ	Chapel.
Charbonnage	Colliery.
Château d'eau	Water tower.
Chaussée	Causeway, Highway.
Chemin de fer	Railway.
Cheminée, Chᵉᵉ	Chimney.
Chêne	Oak tree.
Cimetière, Cimᵉ	Cemetery.
Clocher	Belfry.
Clouterie	Nail factory.
Colombier	Dove-cot.
Coron	Workmen's dwellings.
Cour des marchandises	Goods yard.
Couvent	Convent.
Crassier	Slag heap.
Croix	Cross.
Darse	Inner dock.
Démoli -e	Destroyed.
Détruit -e, Détᵗ	
Déversoir	Weir.
Digue	Dyke, causeway.
Distillerie, Distᵉ	Distillery.
Douane	Custom-house.
Bureau de douane	
Entrepôt de douane	Custom-warehouse.
Dynamiterie, Dynamᵗᵉ	Dynamite magazine.
Dynamiterie	Dynamite factory.
Écluse	Sluice, Lock.
Écluzette, Eclᵗᵉ	Sluice.
École	School.
Écurie	Stable.
Église	Church.
Émaillerie	Enamel works.
Embarcadère, Embᵉ	Landing-place.
Estaminet, Estamᵗ	Inn.
Étang	Pond.
Fabrique, Fabᵉ	Factory.
Fabᵉ de produits chimiques	Chemical works.
Fabᵉ de faïence	Pottery.
Faïencerie	
Ferme, Fᵉ	Farm.
Filature, Filᵗ	Spinning mill.
Fonderie, Fondᵉ	Foundry.
Fontaine, Fontᵉ	Spring, fountain.
Forêt	Forest.
Forme de radoub	Dry dock.
Forge	Smithy.
Fosse	Mine, Pit.
Fossé	Moat, Ditch.
Four	Kiln.
,, à chaux	Lime-kiln.
Four à coke	Coke oven.
Ganterie	Glove Factory.
Gare	Station.
Garenne	Warren.
Garnison	Garrison.
Gazomètre	Gasometer.
Glacerie	
Fabᵉ de glaces	Mirror Factory.
Glacière	Ice factory.
Grue	Crane.
Gué	Ford.
Guérite	Sentry-box, Turret.
,, à signaux	Signal-box (Ry.)
Halte	Halt.
Hangar	Shed, Hangar.
Hôpital	Hospital.
Hôtel-de-Ville	Town hall.
Houillère	Colliery.
Huilerie	Oil factory.
Imprimerie, Impᵉ	Printing works.
Jetée	Pier.
Laminerie	Rolling mills.
Laisse de haute marée	High water mark.
Laisse de basse marée	Low ,,
Maison Forestière, Mᵒⁿ Fᵉʳᵉ	Forester's house.
Malterie	Malt-house.
Marbrerie	Marble works.
Marais	Marsh.
Marais salant	Saltern, Salt marsh.
Marché	Market.
Mare	Pool.
Meule	Rick.
Minière	Mine.
Monastère	Monastery.
Moulin, Mⁱⁿ	Mill.
,, à vapeur	Steam mill.
Mur	Wall.
,, crénelé	Loop-hold wall.
Nacelle	Ferry.
Orme	Elm.
Orphelinat	Orphanage.
Oseraies	Osier-beds.
Ouvrage	Fort.
Ouvrages hydrauliques	Water works.
Papeterie	Paper-mill.
Parc	Park, yard.
,, aérostatique	Aviation yard.
,, à charbon	Coal yard.
,, à pétrole	Petrol store.
Passage à niveau P.N.	Level-crossing.
Passerelle, Passᵉ	Foot-bridge.
Pépinière	Nursery-garden.
Peuplier	Poplar tree.
Phare	Light-house.
Pilier, Pilᵉ	Post.
Plaine d'exercice	Drill ground.
Pompe	Pump.
Ponceau	Culvert.
Pont	Bridge.
,, levis	Drawbridge.
Poste de garde	Coast-guard station.
Station côte	
Posteᵘ Pᵗᵉ	Post.
Poterie	Pottery.
Poudrière, Poudᵉ	Powder magazine.
Magasin à poudre	
Prise d'eau	Water supply.
Puits	Pit-head, Shaft, Well.
,, artésien	Artesian well.
,, ventilateur	Ventilating shaft.
,, de sondage	Boring.
Quai	Quay, Platform.
,, aux bestiaux	Cattle platform.
,, aux marchandises	Goods platform.
Raccordement	Junction.
Raffinerie	Refinery.
,, de sucre	Sugar refinery.
Râperie	Beet-root factory.

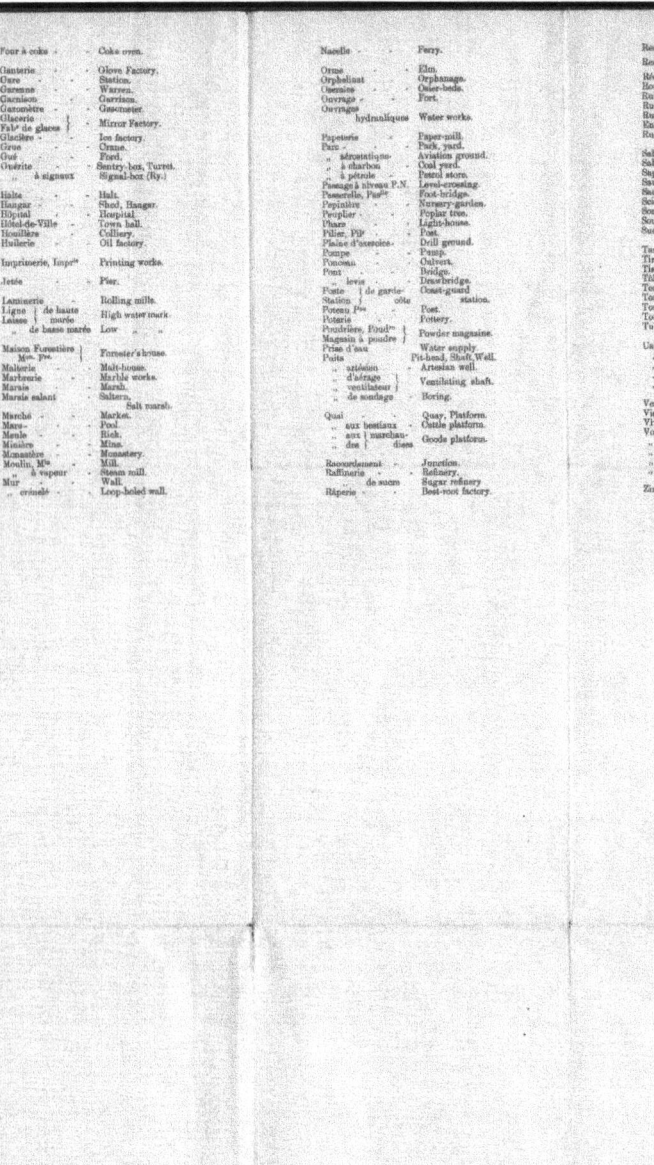

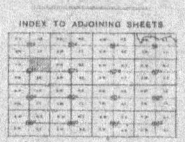

TRENCH MAP.

FRANCE.
SHEET 57D N.E.
EDITION 2. B

INDEX TO ADJOINING SHEETS

SCALE 20,000.

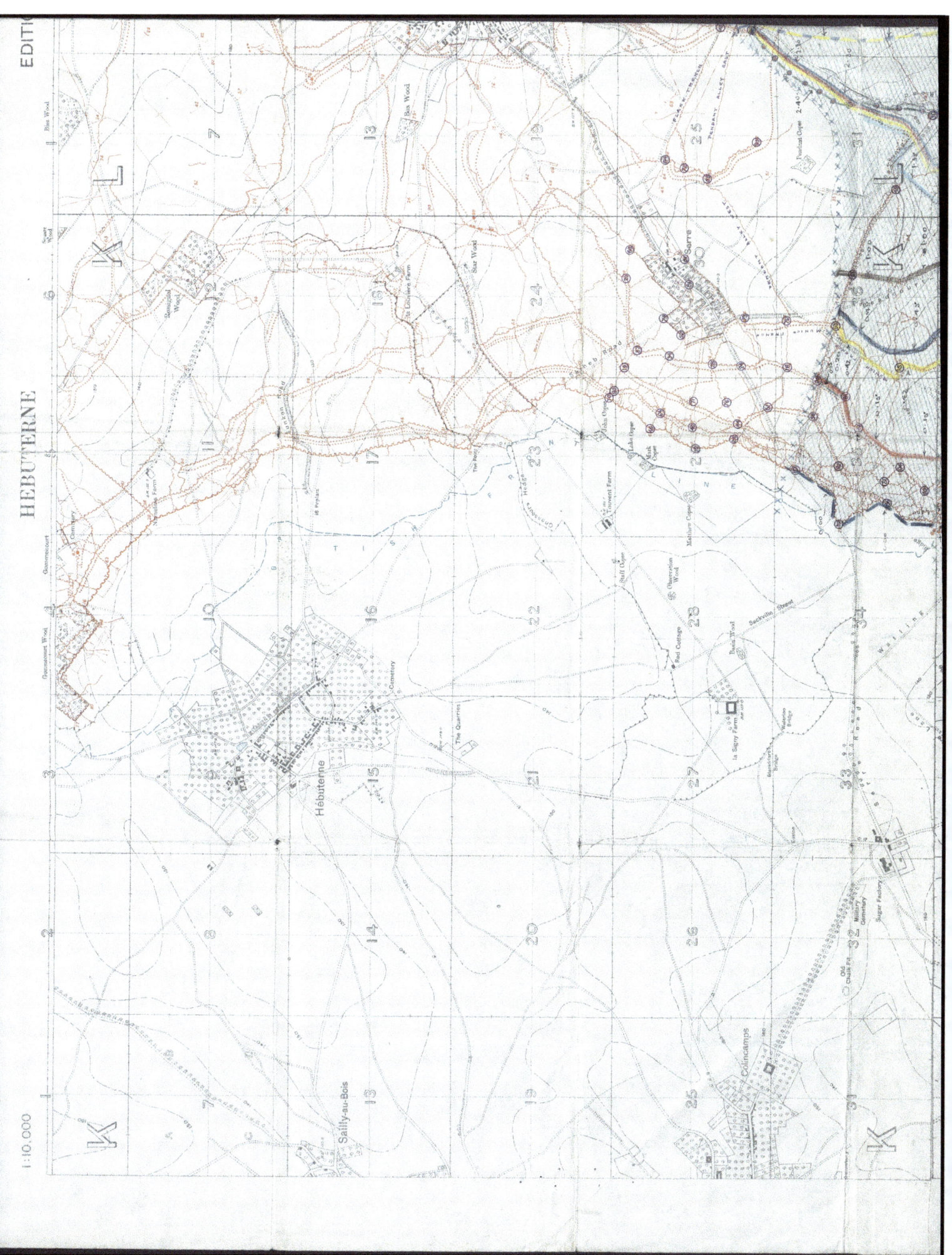

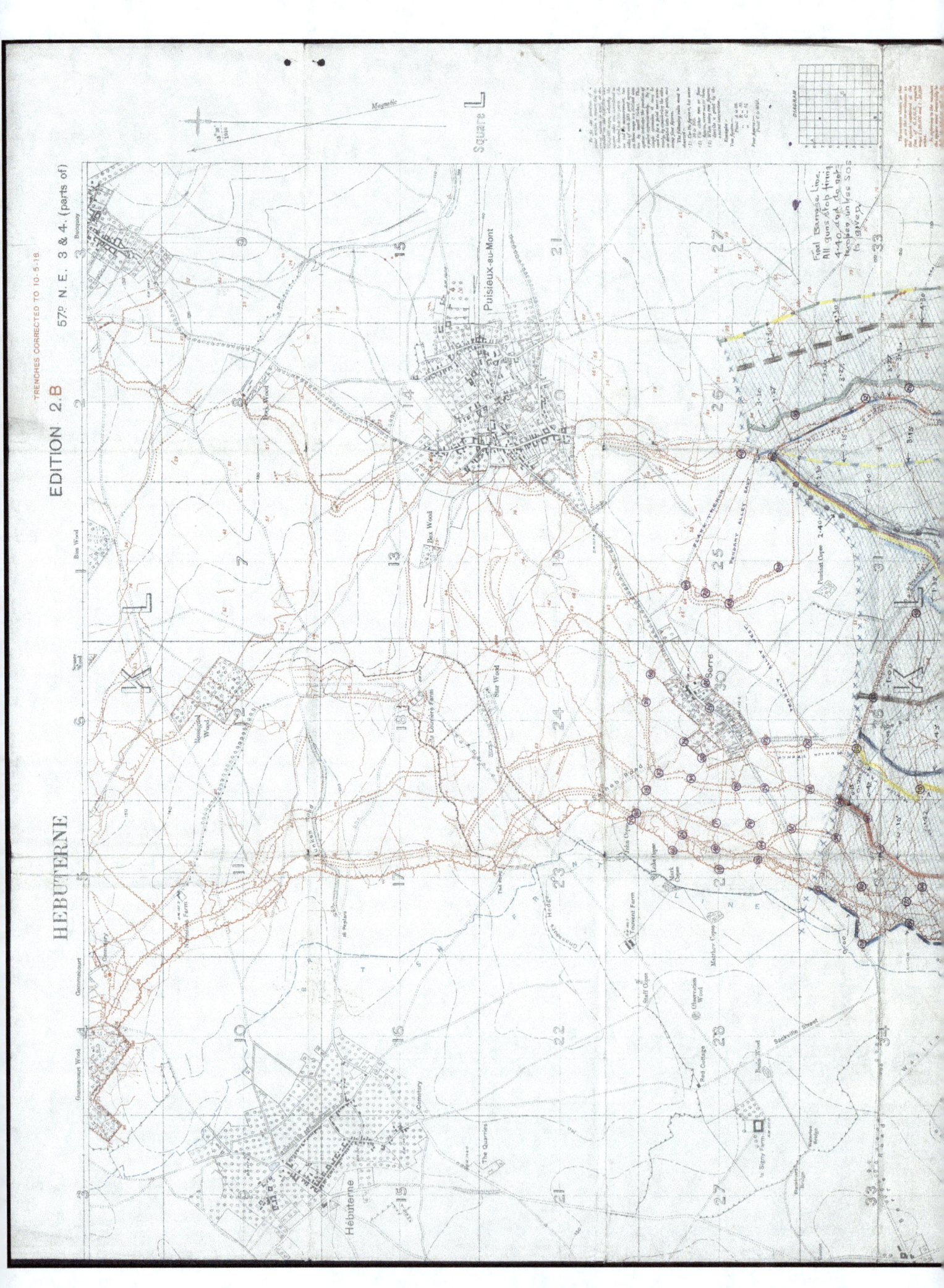

GLOSSARY.

Abbaye, Abbie	Abbey
Abreuvoir, Abr	Watering place
Abri de douaniers	Customs-shelter
Aciérie	Steel works
Aiguilles	Points (Ry.)
Allée	Alley, Narrow road
Ancien⁻ⁿᵉ, Anc⁻ⁿ	Old.
Aqueduc	Aqueduct.
Arbre	Tree.
" éventail	fan-shaped.
" déchaussé	bare.
" fourche	forked.
" isolé	isolated.
" penché	leaning.
Arrizeaux	Small tree.
Arc	Arch.
Ardoisière, Ard⁻ⁿᵉ	Slate quarry.
Ark	Ark.
Asile	Asylum.
" d'aliénés	Lunatic asylum.
" de charité	
" des pauvres	
" de refuge	
Auberge, Aub⁻ᵍᵉ	Asylum.
Aune	Alder-tree.
Bac	Ferry.
Bac à traille	
Bains	Baths.
Bains sur table	Bathing place.
Banc de sable	Sand-bank.
Baraque	Hut.
Barrage	Dam.
Barrière	Gate. Stile.
(Barrière à) Bascule	Weigh bridge.
Bassin	Dock. Pond.
d'échange	Tidal dock.

Blanchisserie	Laundry.
B.M. (borne milliaire)	Mile stone.
B⁻ⁿᵉ (borne kilométrique)	
Boulonnerie	Bolt Factory.
Fab⁻ᵉ de boulons	
Bouée	Buoy.
Brasserie, Brass⁻ᵉ	Brewery.
Briqueterie, Briq⁻ᵉ	Brickfield.
Brise-lames	Breakwater
Bureau de poste	Post office.
" de douane	Custom house. Post. Manuel
Butte	
Cabane	Hut.
Cabaret, Cab⁻ᵗ	Inn.
Câble sous-marin	Submarine cable.
Calvaire, Calv⁻ᵉ	Calvary.
Canal de dessèchement	Drainage canal.
Canal d'irrigation	Irrigation canal.
Fab⁻ᵉ de caoutchouc	Rubber factory.
Carrière, Carr⁻ᵉ	Quarry.
Champ de courses	Race course.
" " manœuvres	drill-ground.
" " de tir	Rifle range.
Chantier	Building yard. Ship yard. Dock yard.
Chantier de construction	
Chapelle, Ch⁻ᵉˡ	Chapel.
Charbonnage	Colliery.
Château d'eau	Water tower.
Chaussée	Highway.
Chemin de fer	Railway.
Cheminée, Ch⁻ᵉᵉ	Chimney.
Chêne	Oak tree.
Cimetière, Cim⁻ᵉ	Cemetery.
Cidrerie	Cidery.
Clouterie	Nail factory.
Colombier	Dove-cot.

Cour des marchandises	Goods yard.
Couvent	Convent.
Crassier	Slag heap.
Creux	Creek.
Darse	Inner dock.
Démoli ₋ e, Dét	Destroyed.
Détruit ₋ e, Dét	
Déversoir	Weir.
Digue	Dyke, causeway.
Distillerie, Dist⁻ᵉ	Distillery.
Douane	Custom-house.
Bureau de douane	
Entrepôt de douane	
Dynamitière, Dynam⁻ᵉ	Dynamite magazine. Dynamite factory.
Dynamiterie	
Écluse	Sluice, Lock.
Échauette, Éch⁻ᵉ	
Ècole	School.
Écurie	Stable.
Église	Church.
Émaillerie	Enamel works.
Embarcadère, Emb⁻ᵉ	Landing place.
Établissem, Estam⁻ᵗ	Inn.
Étang	Pond.
Fabrique, Fab⁻ᵉ	Factory.
Fab⁻ᵉ de produits chimiques	Chemical works.
Faïencerie	Pottery.
Fab⁻ᵉ de faïence	
Ferme, F⁻ᵐᵉ	Farm.
Filature, F⁻ʳᵉ	Spinning mill.
Fonderie, Fond⁻ᵉ	Foundry.
Fontaine, Font⁻ᵉ	Spring, fountain.
Forêt	Forest.
Forme de radoub	Dry dock.
Forge	Smithy.
Fort, F⁻ᵗ	Fort.
Four	Oven.
Four à chaux	Lime-kiln.

Ganterie	Glove Factory.
Gare	Station.
Garenne	Warren.
Garnison	Garrison.
Gazomètre	Gasometer.
Glacerie	
Fab⁻ᵉ de glaces	Mirror Factory.
Glacière	Ice factory.
Grue	Crane.
Guérite à signaux	Sentry-box. Turret, Signal-box (Ry.)
Halle	Hall.
Hangar	Shed, Hangar.
Hôpital	Hospital.
Hôtel-de-Ville	Town hall.
Houillère	Colliery.
Huilerie	Oil factory.
Imprimerie, Impr⁻ᵉ	Printing works.
Jetée	Pier.
Laminurie	Rolling mills.
Ligne de haute mer	High water mark.
Laisse de basse marée	Low
Maison Forestière, M⁻ⁿ f⁻ᵉ	Forester's house.
Malterie	Malt-house.
Marbrerie	Marble works.
Marais	Marsh.
Marais salant	Salt marsh.
Marché	Market.
Mare	Pool.
Meule	Rick.
Minières	Mine.
Monastère	Monastery.
Moulin, M⁻ⁿ	Mill.
Mⁿ à vapeur	Steam mill.
Mur crénelé	Wall. Loop-holed wall.

TRENCH MAP
HEBUTERNE.
57d N.E. 3 & 4 (parts of).
EDITION 2. B
Scale 1:10,000.

INDEX TO ADJOINING SHEETS.

GLOSSARY.

Abbaye, Abb^e	Abbey.
Abreuvoir, Abr^r	Watering-place.
Abri de douaniers	Customs-shelter.
Aciérie	Steel works.
Aiguilles	Points (Ry.)
Allée	Alley, Narrow road
Ancien - ne, Anc^{ne}	Old.
Aqueduc	Aqueduct.
Arbre	Tree.
,, éventail	,, fan-shaped.
,, décharné	,, bare.
,, fourchu	,, forked.
,, isolé	,, isolated.
,, penché	,, leaning.
Arbrisseau	Small tree.
Arc	Arch.
Ardoisière, Ard^{re}	Slate quarry.
Arrêt	Halt.
Asile	Asylum.
,, des aliénés	Lunatic asylum.
,, de charité	
,, des pauvres	Asylum.
,, de refuge	
Auberge, Aub^{ge}	Inn.
Aune	Alder-tree.
Bac	Ferry.
,, à traille	
Bains	Baths.
Place aux bains	Bathing place.
Balise	Boom, Beacon.
Banc de sable	Sand-bank.
,, vase	Mud-bank.
Baraque	Hut.
Barrage	Dam.
Barrière	Gate, Stile.
(Machine à Bascule)	Weigh-bridge.
Bassin	Dock, Pond.
,, d'échouage	Tidal dock.
Bassin de radoub	Dry dock.
Bateau phare	Light-ship.
Blanchisserie	Laundry.
B.M. (borne milliaire)	Mile stone.
B.^K (borne kilométrique)	
Boulonnerie, Fab^e de boulons	Bolt Factory.
Bouée	Buoy.
Brasserie, Brass^{ie}	Brewery.
Briqueterie, Briq^{ie}	Brickfield.
Brise-lames	Breakwater.
Bureau de poste	Post office.
,, de douane	Custom house.
Butte	Butt, Mound.
Cabane	Hut.
Cabaret, Cab^t	Inn.
Câble sous-marin	Submarine cable.
Calvaire, Cal^{re}	Calvary.
Canal de dessèchement	Drainage canal.
Canal d'irrigation	Irrigation canal.
Fab^e de caoutchouc	Rubber factory.
Carrière, Carr^{re}	Quarry.
,, de gravier	Gravel-pit.
Caserne	Barracks.
Champ de courses	Race-course.
,, manœuvres	Drill-ground.
,, tir	Rifle range.
	Building yard.
Chantier	Ship yard.
	Dock yard.
Chantier de construction	Slip-way.
Chapelle, Ch^{lle}	Chapel.
Charbonnage	Colliery.
Château d'eau	Water tower.
Chaussée	Causeway. Highway.
Chemin de fer	Railway.
Cheminée, Ch^{ée}	Chimney.
Chêne	Oak tree.
Cimetière, Cim^{re}	Cemetery.
Clocher	Belfry.
Clouterie	Nail factory.
Colombier	Dove-cot.
Coron	Workmen's dwellings.
Cour des marchandises	Goods yard.
,, aux dises	
Couvent	Convent.
Crassier	Slag heap.
Croix	Cross.
Darse	Inner dock.
Démoli - e	Destroyed.
Détruit - e, Dét^t	
Déversoir	Weir.
Digue	Dyke, causeway.
Distillerie, Dist^{ie}	Distillery.
Douane	Custom-house.
Bureau de douane	
Entrepôt de douane	Custom warehouse.
Dynamitière, Dynam^{re}	Dynamite magazine.
Dynamiterie	Dynamite factory.
Ecluse, Ecl^{se}	Sluice, Lock.
Ecluzette, Ecl^{te}	Sluice.
Ecole	School.
Ecurie	Stable.
Eglise	Church.
Emaillerie	Enamel works.
Embarcadère, Emb^{re}	Landing-place.
Estaminet, Estam^t	Inn.
Etang	Pond.
Fabrique, Fab^e	Factory.
Fab^e de produits chimiques	Chemical works.
Fab^e de faïences	Pottery.
Faïencerie	
Ferme, F^{me}	Farm.
Filature, Fil^{re}	Spinning mill.
Fonderie, Fond^{ie}	Foundry.
Fontaine, Font^{ne}	Spring, fountain.
Forêt	Forest.
Forme de radoub	Dry dock.
Forge	Smithy.
Fosse	Mine, Pit.
Fossé	Moat, Ditch.
Four	Kiln.
,, à chaux	Lime-kiln.
Four à coke	Coke oven.
Ganterie	Glove Factory.
Gare	Station.
Garenne	Warren.
Garnison	Garrison.
Gazomètre	Gasometer.
Glacerie, Fab^e de glaces	Mirror Factory.
Glacière	Ice factory.
Grue	Crane.
Gué	Ford.
Guérite	Sentry-box, Turret.
,, à signaux	Signal-box (Ry.)
Halte	Halt.
Hangar	Shed, Hangar.
Hôpital	Hospital.
Hôtel-de-Ville	Town hall.
Houillère	Colliery.
Huilerie	Oil factory.
Imprimerie, Impr^{ie}	Printing works.
Jetée	Pier.
Laminerie	Rolling mills.
Ligne de haute laisse marée	High water mark.
,, de basse marée	Low ,,
Maison Forestière, M^{on} F^{re}	Forester's house.
Malterie	Malt-house.
Marbrerie	Marble works.
Marais	Marsh.
Marais salant	Saltern, Salt marsh.
Marché	Market.
Mare	Pool.
Meule	Rick.
Minière	Mine.
Monastère	Monastery.
Moulin, M^{lin}	Mill.
,, à vapeur	Steam mill.
Mur	Wall.
,, crénelé	Loop-holed wall.

Nacelle	Ferry.
Orme	Elm.
Orphelinat	Orphanage.
Oseraies	Osier-beds.
Ouvrage	Fort.
Ouvrages hydrauliques	Water works.
Papeterie	Paper-mill.
Parc	Park, yard.
" aérostatique	Aviation ground.
" à charbon	Coal yard.
" à petrole	Petrol store.
Passage à niveau P.N.	Level-crossing.
Passerelle, Pas^{lle}	Foot-bridge.
Pepinières	Nursery-garden.
Peuplier	Poplar tree.
Phare	Light-house.
Pilier, Pil^r	Post.
Plaine d'exercice	Drill ground.
Pompe	Pump.
Ponceau	Culvert.
Pont	Bridge.
" levis	Drawbridge.
Poste de garde	Coast-guard station.
Station côte	
Poteau P^u	Post.
Poterie	Pottery.
Poudrière, Poud^re / Magasin à poudre	Powder magazine.
Prise d'eau	Water supply.
Puits	Pit-head, Shaft, Well.
" artésien	Artesian well.
" d'aérage / " ventilateur	Ventilating shaft.
" de sondage	Boring.
Quai	Quay, Platform.
" aux bestiaux	Cattle platform.
" aux marchandises	Goods platform.
Raccordement	Junction.
Raffinerie	Refinery.
" de sucre	Sugar refinery.
Râperie	Beet-root factory.

Remblai	Embankment.
Remise des Machines	Engine-shed.
Réservoir, Rés^r	Reservoir.
Route cavalière	Bridle road.
Rubanerie	Ribbon Factory.
Ruine / Ruines / En ruine / Ruiné-e	Ruin.
Sablière	Sand-pit.
Sablonnière, Sablon^re	
Sapin	Fir tree.
Saule	Willow tree.
Saunerie	Salt-works.
Scierie, Sc^ie	Saw-mill.
Sondage	Boring.
Source	Spring.
Sucrerie, Suc^ie	Sugar factory.
Tannerie	Tannery.
Tir à la cible	Rifle range.
Tissage	Weaving mill.
Tôlerie	Rolling mill.
Tombeau	Tomb.
Tour	Tower.
Tourbière	Peat-bog, Peat-bed.
Tourelle	Small tower.
Tuilerie	Tile works.
Usine à gaz	Gas works.
" électrique / " d'électricité	Electricity works.
" métallurgique	Metal works.
" à agglomérés	Briquette factory.
Verrerie, Verr^ie	Glass works.
Viaduc	Viaduct.
Vivier	Fish Pond.
Voie de chargement / " déchargement / " d'évitement / " formation / " manœuvre	Siding.
Zinguerie	Zinc works.

TRENCH MAP.
BEAUMONT.
57d S.E. 1 & 2 (parts of).
EDITION 2. B
Scale 1:10,000.

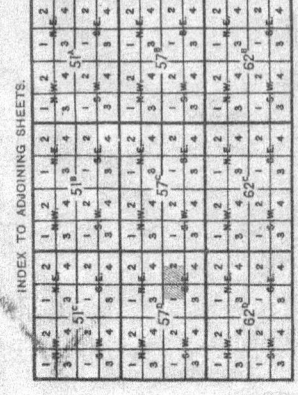

INDEX TO ADJOINING SHEETS.

APPENDIX "H"

APPENDIX "H"

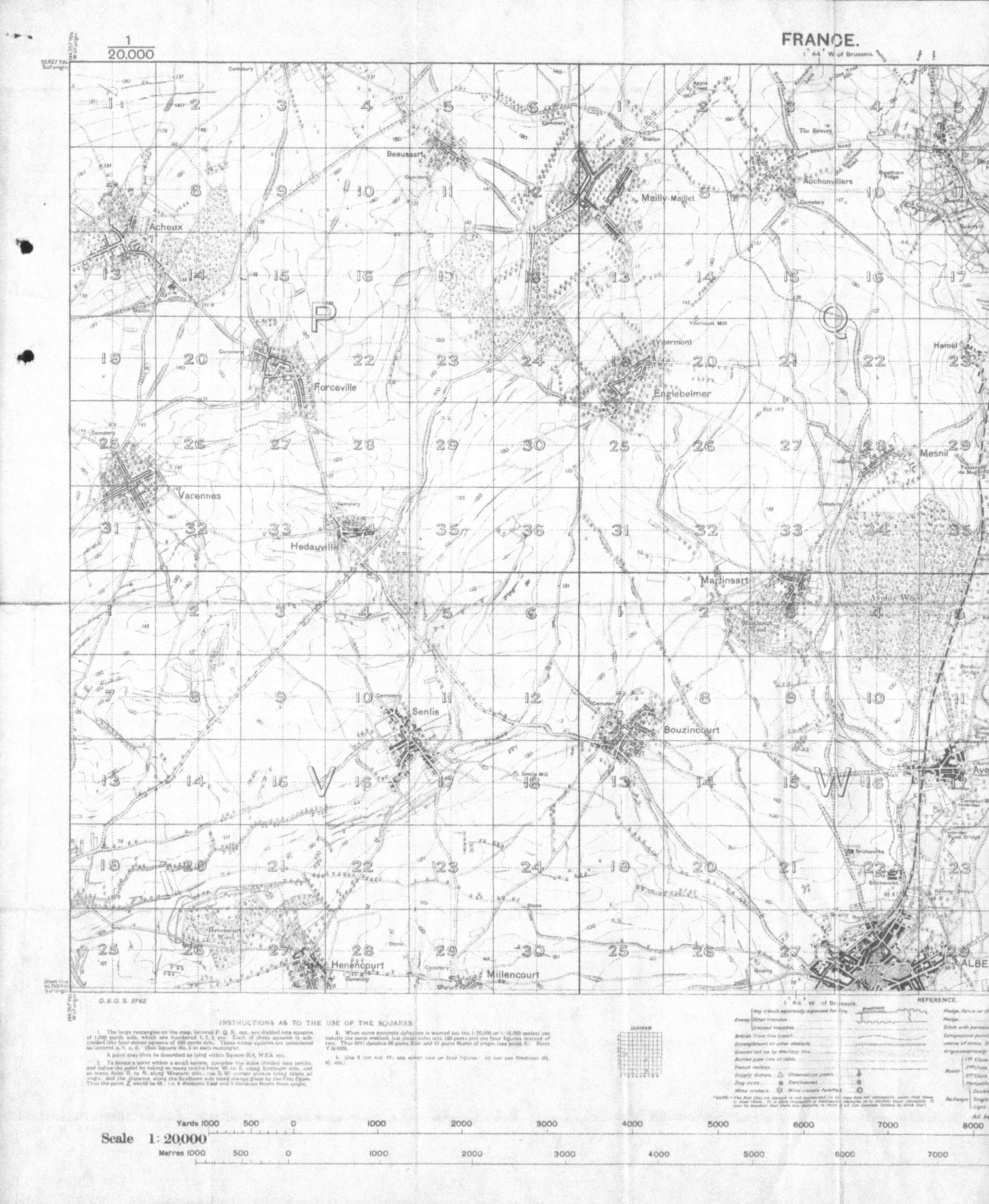

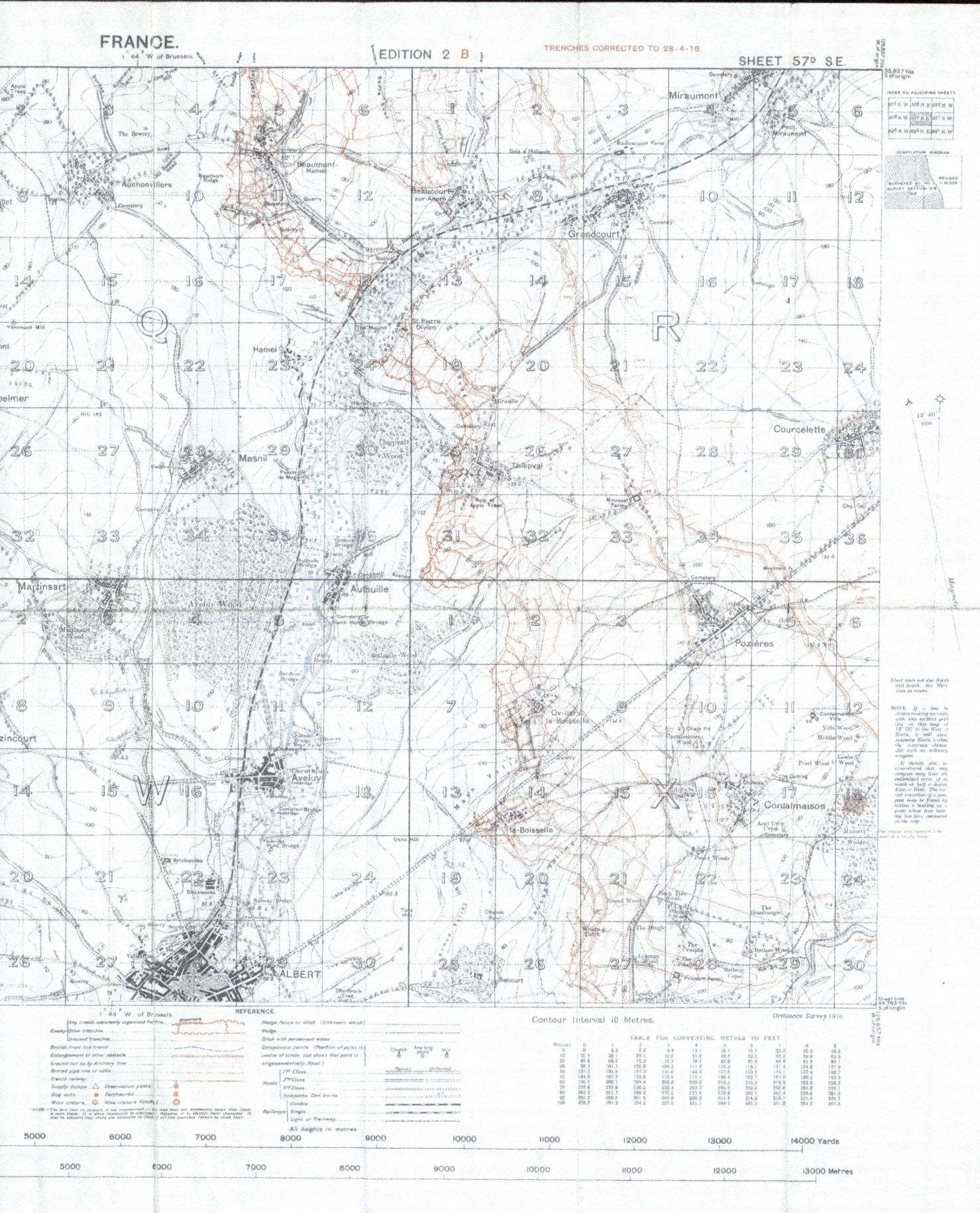

GLOSSARY.

Abbaye, Abb⁶	Abbey.
Abreuvoir, Ab⁶	Watering-place.
Aciérie	Steel works.
Abri de douaniers	Custom-shelter.
Aiguilles	Points (Rly.)
Allée	Alley, Narrow road.
Ancien ... anc⁶	Old.
Aqueduc	Aqueduct.
Arbre	Tree.
" éventail	" fan-shaped.
" déchiré	" torn.
" fourchu	" forked.
" isolé	" isolated.
" penché	" leaning.
Arbrisseau	Small tree.
Arc	Arch.
Ardoisière, Ard⁶⁶	Slate quarry.
Asile	Asylum.
" d'aliénés	Lunatic asylum.
" de charité	Asylum.
" des pauvres	"
" de refuge	"
Auberge, Aub⁶⁶	Inn.
Aune	Alder-tree.
Bac	Ferry.
Balise	Buoy.
Bain	Baths.
Place aux bains	Bathing-place.
Balise	Boom, Beacon.
Banc de sable	Sand-bank.
" de vase	Mud-bank.
Baraque	Hut.
Barrage	Dam.
Barrière	Gate, Sluice.
Bascule (Machine à)	Weigh-bridge.
Bassin d'échouage	Dock, Pond.
	Tidal dock.
Bassin de radoub	Dry dock.
Bateau phare	Light-ship.
Blanchisserie	Laundry.
B.M. (borne militaire)	Mile stone.
B⁶ (borne kilométrique)	
Boulonnerie, Fab⁶ de boulons	Bolt Factory.
Bouée	Buoy.
Brasserie, Brass⁶⁶	Brewery.
Briqueterie, Briq⁶⁶	Brickfield.
Brise-lames	Breakwater.
Bureau de poste	Post office.
" de douane	Custom house.
Butte	Butt, Mound.
Cabane	Hut.
Cabaret, Cab⁶	Inn.
Câble sous-marin	Submarine cable.
Calvaire, Calv⁶⁶	Calvary.
Canal d'irrigation	Drainage canal.
" de dessèchement	Irrigation canal.
Fab⁶ de caoutchouc	Rubber factory.
Carrière, Carr⁶⁶	Quarry.
Caserne	Barracks.
" de gravier	Gravel-pit.
Champ de courses	Race course.
" de manœuvres	Drill-ground.
" de tir	Rifle range.
Chantier	Building yard.
	Ship yard.
	Dock yard.
Chantier de construction	
Chapelle, Ch⁶⁶	Chapel.
Charbonnage	Colliery.
Château d'eau	Water tower.
Chaussée	Causeway.
Chemin de fer	Highway.
	Railway.
Cheminée, Ch⁶⁶	Chimney.
Chêne	Oak tree.
Cimetière, Cim⁶⁶	Cemetery.
Clocher	Belfry.
Clouterie	Nail factory.
Colombier	Dovecot.
Coton	Cotton.
Cour des marchandises	Goods yard.
" aux	
Couvent	Convent.
Crassier	Slag-heap.
Croix	Cross.
Danse	Inner dock.
Démoli-e	Destroyed.
Déversoir	Weir.
Digue	dyke, causeway.
Distillerie, Dist⁶⁶	Distillery.
Douane	Custom-house.
Bureau de douane	
Entrepôt de douane	Custom warehouse.
Dynamitière, Dynam⁶⁶	Dynamite magazine.
Dynamiterie	Dynamite factory.
Écluse	Sluice, Lock.
Éclusette, Ecl⁶⁶	Sluice.
École	School.
Écurie	Stable.
Église	Church.
Émaillerie	Enamel works.
Embarcadère, Emb⁶⁶	Landing-place.
Estaminet, Estam⁶	Inn.
Étang	Pond.
Fabrique, Fab⁶⁶	Factory.
Fab⁶ de produits chimiques	Chemical works.
Faïencerie	Pottery.
Fab⁶ de faïence	
Ferme, F⁶⁶	Farm.
Filature, T⁶⁶	Spinning mill.
Fonderie, Fond⁶⁶	Foundry.
Fontaine, Font⁶⁶	Spring, fountain.
Forêt	Forest.
Ferme de radoub	Dry dock.
Forge	Smithy.
Fosse	Mine, Pit.
Fossé	Moat, Ditch.
Four	Kiln.
" à chaux	Lime-kiln.
Four à coke	Coke oven.
Ganterie	Glove Factory.
Gare	Station.
Garenne	Warren.
Garnison	Garrison.
Gazomètre	Gasometer.
Glacerie	Mirror Factory.
Fab⁶ de glaces	
Glacière	Ice factory.
Grue	Crane.
Gué	Ford.
Guérite, à signaux	Sentry-box, Turret, Signal-box (Rly.)
Halte	Halt.
Hangar	Shed, Hangar.
Hôpital	Hospital.
Hôtel-de-Ville	Town hall.
Houillère	Colliery.
Huilerie	Oil factory.
Imprimerie, Impr⁶⁶	Printing works.
Jetée	Pier.
Laminerie, de haute	Rolling mills.
Ligne	
Laisse de basse marée	High water mark.
	Low
Maison Forestière, M⁶⁶ F⁶⁶	Forester's house.
Malterie	Malt-house.
Marbrerie	Marble works.
Marais	Marsh.
Marais salant	Salt marsh.
Marché	Market.
Mare	Pond.
Meule	Rick.
Minière	Mine.
Monastère	Monastery.
Moulin, M⁶⁶	Mill.
" à vapeur	Steam mill.
Mur	Wall.
" crénelé	Loop-holed wall.
Nacelle	Ferry.
Orme	Elm.
Orphelinat	Orphanage.
Ossuaire	Osser-beds.
Ouvrage	Fort.
Ouvrages hydrauliques	Water works.
Papeterie	Paper-mill.
Parc	Park, yard.
" aérostatique	Aviation ground.
" à charbon	Coal yard.
" à pétrole	Petrol store.
Passage à niveau P.N.	Level-crossing.
Passerelle, Pass⁶⁶	Foot-bridge.
Peuplier	Poplar tree.
Pépinière	Nursery-garden.
Phare, Pᵉ	Light-house.
Pilier, Pil⁶	Post.
Plaine d'exercice	Drill ground.
Pompe	Pump.
Ponceau	Culvert.
Pont	Bridge.
" levis	Drawbridge.
Poste (de garde côté)	Coast-guard station.
Station P⁶⁶	
Poterie	Pottery.
Poudrière, Poudᵉ	Powder magazine.
Magasin à poudre	
Prise d'eau	Water supply
Puits	Pit-head, Shaft Well.
" artésien	Artesian well.
" d'aérage ventilation	Ventilating shaft.
" de sondage	Boring.
Quai	Quay, Platform.
" aux bestiaux	Cattle platform.
" aux marchandises	Goods platform.
Raccordement	Junction.
Raffinerie	Refinery.
" de sucre	Sugar refinery.
Râperie	Beet-root factory.

TRENCH MAP.

FRANCE.
SHEET 57D S.E.
EDITION 2 B.

SCALE 20,000

INDEX TO ADJOINING SHEETS

Pont à coke	Coke oven
Ganterie	Glove Factory
Gare	Station
Garenne	Warren
Garnison	Garrison
Gazomètre	Gasometer
Glacerie	
Fab^e de glaces	Mirror Factory
Glacière	Ice factory
Gué	Ford
Guérite	Sentry-box, Turret
,, à signaux	Signal-box (Ry.)
Halte	Halt
Hangar	Shed, Hangar
Hôpital	Hospital
Hôtel-de-Ville	Town hall
Houillère	Colliery
Huilerie	Oil factory
Imprimerie, Imp^{ie}	Printing works
Jetée	Pier
Laminerie	Rolling mills
Ligne de haute	High water mark
Laisse marée	
,, de basse marée	Low ,, ,,
Maison Forestière	Forester's house
M^{on} for^{re}	
Malterie	Malt-house
Marbrerie	Marble works
Marais	Marsh
Marais salant	Salt marsh
Marché	Market
Mare	Pond
Meule	Rick
Minière	Mine
Monastère	Monastery
Moulin, Mⁱⁿ	Mill
,, à vapeur	Steam mill
Mur	Wall
,, crénelé	Loop-holed wall

Nacelle	Ferry
Orme	Elm
Orphelinat	Orphanage
Ossuaires	Ossar-beds
Ouvrage	Fort
Ouvrages hydrauliques	Water works
Papeterie	Paper-mill
Parc	Park, yard
,, aérostatique	Aviation ground
,, à charbon	Coal yard
,, à pétrole	Petrol store
Passage à niveau P.N.	Level-crossing
Passerelle, Pas^{lle}	Foot-bridge
Pépinière	Nursery-garden
Peuplier	Poplar tree
Phare	Light-house
Pilier, Pil^r	Post
Plaine d'exercices	Drill ground
Pompe	Pump
Ponceau	Culvert
Pont	Bridge
,, levis de garde	Drawbridge
Poste de côte	Coast-guard station
Station P^{ssn}	Post
Poterie	Pottery
Poudrière, Poud^{re}	Powder magazine
Magasin à poudre	
Prise d'eau	Water supply
Puits artésien	Pit-head, Shaft, Well
,, d'aérage	Artesian well
,, ventilateur	Ventilating shaft
,, de sondage	Boring
Quai aux bestiaux	Quay, Platform
,, aux marchandises	Cattle platform
,, dises	Goods platform
Raccordement	Junction
Raffinerie	Refinery
Râperie de sucre	Sugar refinery, Beet-root factory

Remblai	Embankment
Remise des Machines	Engine-shed
,, aux	
Réservoir, Rés^r	Reservoir
Route cavalière	Bridle road
Rubanerie	Ribbon Factory
Ruine	
Ruines	Ruin
En ruine	
Ruiné · s	
Sablière	Sand-pit
Sablonnière, Sablon^{re}	
Sapin	Fir tree
Saule	Willow tree
Saunerie	Salt-works
Scierie, S^{le}	Saw-mill
Sondage	Boring
Source	Spring
Sucrerie, Suc^{ie}	Sugar factory
Tannerie	Tannery
Tir à la cible	Rifle range
Tissage	Weaving mill
Tôlerie	Rolling mill
Tombeau	Tomb
Tour	Tower
Tourbière	Peat-bog, Peat-bed
Tournille	Small tower
Tuilerie	Tile works
Usine à gaz	Gas works
,, électrique d'électricité	Electricity works
,, métallurgique	Metal works
,, à agglomérés	Briquette factory
Verrerie, Verr^{ie}	Glass works
Viaduc	Viaduct
Vivier	Fish Pond
Voie de chargement	
,, de déchargement	Siding
,, d'évitement	
,, de formation	
,, de manœuvre	
Zinguerie	Zinc works

4TH DIV. G.S.
July 1916

GENERAL STAFF

4th DIVISION

JULY 1916

APPENDICES ARE SEPARATE

WAR DIARY - GENERAL STAFF., 4th DIVISION.

BERTRANCOURT.   **1st JULY 1916.**

The action of the 4th Division in the attack on July 1st 1916, is described in the following appendices, which are attached.

- A. Narrative of operations on July 1st 1916.
- B. (1) Copy of telephone conversations at General Staff Office, 4th Division, July 1st.
  (2) Telegrams received and despatched.
- C. Division Operation Order No: 38, Copy No: 1.
- D. (1) Orders for march to positions of assembly.
  (2) Map showing routes to positions of assembly.
- E. Map showing assembly positions and objectives.
- F. Diagram showing formations of Brigades in the advance.
- G. Report on action of Artillery, July 1st.
- H. Map showing artillery lifts.
- I. Report on communications.
- J. Map showing positions of dumps, etc, in the trenches.
- K. Casualty report. July 1st. 1916.
- L. Instructions as to the provision of Rations, Water, Grenades, S.A.A. Gun & T.M. Amm. R.E. Stores.
- M. Casualties for month of July
- N. Operation Orders 40-47 inc.

WAR DIARY - GENERAL STAFF., 4th DIVISION.

BERTRANCOURT   2nd JULY 1916.

12-15 am. Situation unchanged.

1-35 am. Situation unchanged.

2-40 am. Situation unchanged.

3-0 am. 31st Divn report sets of five red rockets sent up south of PENDANT COPSE. Rifle and Machine Gun fire also heard from that direction.

4-0 am. Situation unchanged. Enemy's artillery fire slight and intermittent. Patrol from 10 Brigade attempted to approach German front line between Pts 27 and 45 but was unable to do so owing to heavy rifle and Machine gun fire.

6-0 am. Situation unchanged. Enemy used Trench mortars to bombard our trenches on 10th Bde front.

7-55 am. Situation unchanged. Very little hostile shelling now.

9-0 am. Situation unchanged.

10-0 am. Situation unchanged.

10-38 am. 135th Battery reported at, 10.10 a.m. considerable traffic, either lorries or considerable bodies of troops moving from GREVILLERS to IRLES.

11-5 am. "D" Coy. R. Irish Fusiliers now clear of QUADRILATERAL and in our own lines, all wounded except one safe. He can be brought in later. Two prisoners brought in - one wounded. ~~Lewis Gun and Casualty coming across.~~

12 noon. Situation unchanged. Divisional Arty report that all this morning small parties of Germans have been dribbling over from Pt 81 (K.35.b.) to Pt 92 (K.35.a.). They came out as though communication trench broken down. They are in lightish blue uniform, have packs on their backs and appear fresh and clean..

3 p.m. Our artillery bombarded German trenches till 3-30 p.m.

3-20 pm. Situation unchanged. G.O.'s.C. 10th & 12th Inf.Bdes convinced none of our troops remain in QUADRILATERAL. G.O.C. 10th Bde reports that last few men crawled out this morning. Aeroplane may have seen some of these, remainder were probably our own dead with steel helmets on of which there are a large number. Wounded from QUADRILATERAL collected in an old dug-out 20 yards outside our line ; these will be brought in to-night. There are others in "NO MAN'S LAND" in front of QUADRILATERAL, these will be removed to-night.

4-40 pm. Situation unchanged. Enemy artillery slightly more active. Work of collecting dead and wounded still continues.

6-30 pm. Our artillery bombarded German trenches till & 7 p.m.

10-26 pm. Div Artillery report that there is considerable movement in the German lines. Movement especially visible at Pt

Q.5.a.26.55. Troops have helmets and fresh new uniforms.
They are carrying large tins which might possible be
FLAMMENWERFER.

31st Division on our left reported hourly that situation
on their front remained unchanged.

29th Division on our right reported situation unchanged also
that at about 2.30 p.m. a party of about 40 unarmed Germans
came out of their trenches immediately north of BEAUMONT HAMEL
and assisted our wounded back to our lines, other Germans
watched from their own trenches. Some of our stretcher bearers
were out in the same sector at the same time.

Dispositions of 12th Inf. Brigade 10.45 a.m.

ESSEX REGT. (280 men) hold from CAT ST to SERRE ROAD (inclusive)
and as far back as VALLADE (inclusive).

WEST RIDING RGT (320 men) from SERRE ROAD (exclusive) to
DELAUNEY AVENUE (inclusive) and as far back as LEGEND (inclusive)

KING'S OWN. in reserve at LYCEUM.
  The O.C. West Riding Regt commands the whole of the above
sector.

LANCS FUSRS (300) in Brigade Reserve at ELLES SQUARE.

Bde Machine Guns & T.M.Battery at FORT HOYSTED.

Pioneer Battn. STIRLING STREET.

3rd JULY 1916.

BERTRANCOURT

12-30 am. 31st Divn on our ~~right~~ left report situation unchanged (also at
           2.15 a.m., 3.10 a.m. 4-15 a.m., 5.4 a.m., 6 a.m., 7 a.m.,
           8 a.m., and hourly afterwards till 11 when discontinued.

8-0 am.   Situation unchanged. 10th Bde reported that 5 men of the 11th
           Inf. Bde came in from enemy's lines at 1 a.m. and stated
           they had been lying in shell holes and enemy front line having
           been buried there with shells during the attack. Enemy machine
           guns and rifle fire very active between 10 p.m. and 2 a.m.
           opposite 12th Brigade.

11.30 am. 31st Divn reported that at 10-55 a.m. 3 columns of Infantry
           each about 200 strong preceeded by mounted men and followed
           by the same and by transport wagons moving S.E. along
           ABLAINZEVILLE - ACHIET Road - all warned.

5-0 pm.   Evening report. Situation unchanged.

5-30 pm.   29th Divn on our right report situation unchanged.; artillery
           are destroying wire.

8-30 pm.   8th Corps wired during course of afternoon a number of Germans
           seen moving up into their front line trenches. Units warned
           of possibility of an attack.

8-55 pm.   31st Division reported large bodies of enemy Infantry
           proceeded across open towards PUISIEUX. Cylinders being
           carried into SERRE. ROSSIGNOL WOOD full of men.

Movements. Portions of 48th Division now at MAILLY ordered to return to COUIN area.

BERTRANCOURT.   4th JULY 1916.

5-0 a.m.   Morning report. Situation normal. Enemy very quiet during night. No transport heard. At 4 a.m. several red flares fired by enemy accompanied by heavy machine gun fire which traversed our parapets. At 4.20 a.m. enemy artillery bombarded our front and support trenches. Wind. S.W.

6-0 a.m.   Further report. Generally speaking during night enemy seemed very nervous; whenever our artillery fired he sent up many ~~red rockets~~ flares. About 4 a.m. enemy threw several bombs about the QUADRILATERAL. They also opened rifle fire.

5-30 a.m. 31st Divn on our left reported situation quiet.

1.30 p.m. 10th Inf. Bde wired 1st R.Warwick Regt report about 10 p.m. and 12 midnight and 9 a.m. and 11 a.m. TENDERLOIN and vicinity was shelled with H.E. shrapnel, and 4.2" Howitzers shells. About 120 shells were fired. During night an enemy machine gun was active from BEAUMONT HAMEL. All night through the enemy sent up VERY Lights and Red flares.

5-10 p.m. Situation normal.

6 p.m.   29th Divn on our right reported situation normal. Some hostile shelling in the neighbourhood of HAMEL - WHITE CITY and junction of CARLISLE and FETHARD STREETS.
Weather very heavy rain in afternoon and night. Trenches very wet.
MOVES. The 12th Infantry Bde took over portion of the 10th Inf. Bde. line and the 10th Inf. Bde took over portion of the 86th Inf. Bde line down to BLOOMFIELD AVENUE.
48th Division relief of the 31st Division on the sector north of 4th Division front was carried out and G.O.C. 48th Divn reported at 12.55 a.m. that he had taken over command.

                                5th JULY 1916.
BERTRANCOURT

3 a.m.   Reliefs of 10th and 12th Inf. Brigades reported complete at 2.30 a.m.

5.15 am.   Morning report - situation normal, wind westerly, enemy dropped a few shells in 10th Bde. area, right sector.

5.30 am.   29th Division on our right reported situation normal, heavy firing during night reported to S. of River ANCRE. Working parties observed all yesterday working on earthworks at points 06, 20 and 38.
48th Division on our left reported nothing to report.

1.30 pm.   Situation unchanged, wind NNW

5.15 pm.   Evening report - situation normal. Some hostile shelling with 4.5" shells about ROMAN Road ~~reported.~~ ~~Quiet day.~~ FREDDIE St & TOURNAI during afternoon

6 pm.   48th Division on our left reported quiet day.
29th Division on our right reported situation unchanged, artillery active in afternoon towards MESNIL.

9.35 pm.   Disposition of units of Division. 10th Bde. H.Q. Cafe Jourdain,
          1st R. Irish Fus.   -   Q.10,11 to Q.4.7)   MAILLY
          1st R. Warwicks   Q.4,8 to Q.4,18)
          2nd R. Dublin Fus.   MAILLY   )
          2nd Seaforth Highrs.   in bivouacs P.17.b)

          12th Inf. Brigade at BRASSERIE - MAILLY
          1st R. Lancs. Regt.   ELLES SQUARE   )
          2nd Essex Regt.   MAILLY   )
          2nd Lancs. Fus.   K.34.6 to Q.4.19)
          2nd W. Riding Regt.   K.35.4 to K.34.6)

          11th Inf. Bde.   BERTRANCOURT
          1st Somerset L.I.   "
          1st E. Lancs. Regt.   "
          1st Hants. Regt.   "
          1st Rifle Brigade   "
          14th Bde. R.F.A.   AMPLIER
          29th Bde. R.F.A.   Q.6 central
          32nd Bde. R.F.A.   2.B.5.2
          9th Fd. Coy. R.E.   BEAUSSART
          1st Durham Fd. Coy.   BERTRANCOURT
          Renfrew Fd. Coy.   MAILLY
          10th Fd. Ambulance   BERTRANCOURT
          11th   "   VAUCHELLES
          12th   "   BERTRANCOURT
          Supply Column   BEAUVAL
          Train   VAUCHELLES

4.30 pm. A party from the 12th Field Ambulance went out under a Red
          Cross flag and picked up 8 wounded men who had been lying out
          since it 1st July.   The party was unmolested by the enemy.

6th JULY, 1916.

BERTRANCOURT.

4.40 a.m.   Situation normal, wind West.

8.30 a.m.   Situation unchanged reported by 29th Division on our right.
          48th Division reported situation normal. Patrols report no
          working a wiring and no work in enemy trenches, but trenches
          strongly held.

          Work during night. New trench 2½' deep 2' broad was dug
          during night from junction Q.4.11/12 To SUNKEN ROAD. Trench
          has been wired throughout its length.

4.30 pm.   Evening report - situation normal, wind SW
          Rain commenced about 5 p.m. moderately heavy shower.

6 p.m.   29th Division report no change. More shelling than usual from
          10.30 a.m. to present time along whole front. New trench from
          Q.17.a.50.05 to Q.24.a.8.3 being registered by enemy
          48th Division on our left report situation normal. Raiding pa
          party reported enemy's trenches in bad condition, but
          strongly held.

BERTRANCOURT.   ## 7th JULY, 1916.

5 a.m.   Morning report, situation normal.

7.30 a.m.   Smoke discharge postponed on account of unfavourable wind.

4.45 p.m.	Evening report - situation unchanged. Occasional shell bursts round front line and proximity of VALLADE Corner.
5.55 p.m.	48th Division report enemy fired a few tear shells into K.29.a and c.
10.4 p.m.	10th Brigade report relief of Warwicks and Irish Fusiliers by Dublins and Seaforths completed 8.45 p.m. VIII Corps informed.

BERTRANCOURT.   8th JULY, 1916.

4.50 a.m.	Situation normal. Enemy shelled front line trench NORTH of SERRE Road very heavily last night. Wind S.
7 a.m.	There was to have been a discharge of smoke but wind was unfavourable and it was postponed.
4.25 p.m.	With exception of slight hostile shelling of our front line about JACOB'S LADDER and our extreme left, situation normal. *Op. Order 41 issued - 11 Bde will relieve 12 Bde. on night 10/11 July in Left Sector.*

BERTRANCOURT   9th JULY, 1916.

4.55 a.m.	Morning report, hostile artillery shelled SUNKEN ROAD opposite JACOB'S LADDER with field guns between 11 p.m. and 2 a.m. Our extreme left was also occasionally shelled heavily during night.
12.20 p.m.	Situation unchanged, wind W.
5 p.m.	Situation normal. Enemy put down heavy barrage on our front line at 3.20 p.m. as soon as smoke cloud was perceived. This smoke cloud was discharged in error from Divisional front.

BERTRANCOURT   10th JULY, 1916.

1 a.m.	Enemy's line between Q.11.c 5.4 and Q.17.b.1.3 was bombarded intensely for 10 minutes commencing at 1 a.m.
4.10 a.m.	Situation normal. New trench deepened 9 inches and made a little broader. Raiding party of Lancashire Fusiliers failed to get into enemy's lines. They arrived at his wire having slightly lost direction and were fired on from the trench. 2nd Lieut. Waghorne ordered party to retire. He states enemy's line was held thickly. Party returned at 2.30 a.m. having left our lines at 1.30 a.m.
12.20 p.m.	Situation normal
4.15 p.m.	Situation normal. Wind changeable. The 11th Inf. Bde. relieved the 12th Inf. Bde. in the left sector on the afternoon of the 10th and night of 10th/11th. 4th Div. Op. Order No. 41 issued.

BERTRANCOURT   11th JULY, 1916.

1 a.m.	Relief of 12th Inf. Bde. by 11th Inf. Bde in left sector of Divisional front completed.
4.25 a.m.	Situation normal. Left sector working party unable to work on new trenchdf trench during night owing to it being too bright and enemy shelling party each time it attempted to go out.
1.35 p.m.	Situation unchanged, wind SW.
5 p.m.	Evening report - Between 11 a.m. and 1 p.m. hostile 7.7 cm.

guns searched South of KING STREET and CHATHAM and track leading from SUCRERIE to TENDERLOIN. There was practically no reply to our bombardment of enemy's trenches at 3.30 p.m. Wind SW.

BERTRANCOURT   12th JULY, 1916.

5.15 a.m.   Right Sector report hostile artillery very active. No work was possible on new trench in Q.4.d as it was too light. Wind SW.

12.45 p.m. Situation unchanged.

4.30 p.m.   Situation unchanged, Wind SW. Six 5.9 How. Shells were fired at DELAUNAY AVENUE this afternoon.

9.15 p.m.   200 cylinders of gas were delivered and carried up during night and installed in right sector.

BERTRANCOURT   13th JULY, 1916.

During night 200 cylinders were installed in 4th Div. front necessitating a carrying party of 832 men from 10th Brigade all in position by 5.30 a.m.

4.45 a.m.   Morning report, situation normal. 2nd Dublin Fusiliers report it was impossible to work in sap 9 during the night owing to artillery and machine gun fire.

Party of 650 men from 35th Inf. Bde. arrived for working parties. They were billeted in BERTRANCOURT.

2 p.m.   Situation unchanged, wind Westerly

4.59 p.m.   "   "   "   "

            Artillery programme carried out.

10 p.m.   Gas was discharged at 10 p.m. successfully until 10.15 p.m.

10.10 pm.   Artillery bombarded enemy's trench with intense fire from Q.11.c.0.3 to Q.10.b.7.7

11 p.m.   A raid on enemy's trenches was to take place, but owing to hostile artillery and M.G. fire party could not leave our trenches.

            Op. order No. 42 issued. 12 Bde. will relieve 10th Bde. on night 17/18th in the right sector. On relief 10th Bde. will become Divisional Reserve and will be billeted in BERTRANCOURT.

BERTRANCOURT.	14TH JULY.
2.25 am.	Our artillery subjected Q.11.c.03 to Q.4.d.8.0. to an intense bombardment till 3.30.
3.10 am.	Smoke was discharged from 4th Division front very successfully till 3.30 am.
3.15 am.	Our machine guns opened a heavy fire on whole of enemy front till 3.45 am.
4.20 am.	Morning report - situation unchanged. Smoke discharge caused enemy to barrage our second line. Barrage continues South of REDAN.
5.50 am.	29th Division report gas and smoke successfully discharged along their front. Enemy retaliated vigorously with heavy artillery and H.E.
12.45 pm.	Midday report - enemy's artillery active in left sub-sector.
4.30 pm.	Evening report - intermittent shelling of left sector. BEET STREET, VALLADE and MAXIM TRENCH blown in.
BERTRANCOURT.	15TH JULY.
4.40 am.	Morning report - situation unchanged. Reply of the enemy to our bombardments of the last few days has at times been heavy, but there is no evidence of a decrease in number of his guns firing on this front.
12.50 pm.	Midday report - no change.
4.25 pm.	Evening report - situation normal.
5.40 pm.	38th Division report between 11.30 am. and 1 pm. 20 - 15 cm. shells fell near junction of SERRE ROAD & CARENCY.
5.55 pm.	29th Division report - situation normal. Enemy retaliated slightly with H.E. on front trenches and HAMEL.
6.25 pm.	10th Brigade report relief of Dublin's in left sector by Warwick's completed at 5.30 pm.
BERTRANCOURT.	16TH JULY.
4.20 am.	Quiet night - nothing of interest occurred.
12.45 pm.	Midday report - a large column of enemy transport has just passed from IRLES to GREVILLERS only just visible.
4.25 pm.	Evening report - situation unchanged.
BERTRANCOURT.	17TH JULY.
4.15 am.	Morning report - situation normal.
12.55 pm.	Midday report - a few 5.9" shells were fired near EGG STREET about 10 am - no damage.
4.40 pm.	Evening report - slight shelling of right sector trenches of Right Brigade. Relief of 10th Brigade by 12th Brigade in Right sector completed.
BERTRANCOURT.	18TH JULY.
4.35 am.	Morning report - enemy's reply to our bombardment was very slight a few 77 mm. shells being fired into AUCHONVILLERS, and a few heavier shells on front line of right sector.

BERTRANCOURT.	18TH JULY. (Contd).
12.16 pm.	Midday situation unchanged.
5 pm.	Evening report - no change.
BERTRANCOURT.	19TH JULY.
4.45 am.	Quiet night.
12.5 pm.	Midday report - situation normal. New trenches dug last night from BRIDGEND to BEAUMONT Road, Q.4.d.4.3.
4.40 pm.	Evening report - situation normal.

Op. Order 43 issued - 4th Div (less Arty) will be relieved in its present line by the 12th Div. Further instructions to be issued later.

BERTRANCOURT.	20TH JULY.
4.30 am.	Morning report - situation normal. Enemy shelled front line between EGG STREET and the REDAN between 12.30 am. and 1.30 am. and put a large number of shells into MAILLY MAILLET.
12.30 pm.	Midday report - situation unchanged.
4.15 pm.	Evening report - no change.

Operation Order 44 issued. 4th Division (less Divisional Artillery) will be relieved in the present line by 12th Division and will move to the area at present occupied by 25th Division.
At 2 pm. 20th inst. 10th Brigade will move from BERTRANCOURT TO BEAUVAL.
On 20th 11th Brigade will be withdrawn from trenches and proceed to BUS.
On 21st inst. 11th Brigade will move from BUS to BEAUVAL.
12th Brigade will be withdrawn from trenches and move to LOUVENCOURT and VAUCHELLES.
On 22nd inst. 12th Brigade will move from LOUVENCOURT and VAUCHELLES and proceed to AMPLIER.
G.O.C. 12th Division will take over command of the line from G.O.C. 4th Division at 9 am. on 22nd inst.
4th Divisional Headquarters will close at BERTRANCOURT at 10 am. 22nd July and reopen at same hour at BEAUVAL.

BERTRANCOURT.	21ST JULY.

11th Brigade moved from BUS to BEAUVAL.
12th Brigade were withdrawn from the trenches in right sector and proceeded to LOUVENCOURT and VAUCHELLES.
Operation Order No.45 issued.
On 22nd July 12th Brigade will move from LOUVENCOURT and VAUCHELLES to AUTHIEULE.

BERTRANCOURT. BEAUVAL.	22ND JULY.
10 am.	4th Div.H.Q. closed at BERTRANCOURT and reopened at BEAUVAL, command of the line passing to G.O.C. 12th Division.

Orders issued for move of 4th Division (by train) to XIV Corps area in the YPRES district. Entrainment commenced on 22nd inst. Copy of order attached.

	23RD JULY.
CHATEAU COUTHOVE.	Divisional Headquarters established at Chateau Couthove on the POPERINGHE-PROVEN Road.

CHATEAU COUTHOVE.   23RD JULY. (Continued).

H.Q.10th Brigade established at PROVEN.
"   11th   "   "   " WORMHOUDT.
"   12th   "   "   " HOUTKERQUE.

Operation Order 46 issued - 4th Division will take
over the line of trenches at present held by the
Guards Division.

10th Brigade will relieve 1st Gds.Bde in Right Sector
11th   "   "   " 3rd   "   "   " Left   "
12th   "   "   " 2nd   "   "   " Div. Reserve.

On 26th inst. 11th Brigade will move from WORMHOUDT
to Camp in A.30.
On 27th inst. 11th Brigade will move from Camp in A.30
to the CANAL BANK, and 10th Brigade will move from
PROVEN to CANAL BANK.
On 28th inst. 12th Brigade will move from
HOUTKERQUE to Camp in A.30.
Relief of artillery will be arranged between G.Os.C.
R.A. of 4th and Guards Divisions and will commence
on night 28/29th. Relief will be completed on
night 29/30th.
G.O.C.4th Division will take over command of the line
at 4 pm. on July 27th.

CHATEAU COUTHOVE.   24TH JULY.

Operation Order No.47 issued.

G.O.C.10th and 11th.Brigades will take over command
of their sectors from relieved Brigades of Guards
Division on night 27/28th July.
To effect this relief units of the Division will
move up into positions as under :-

On 25th July.
    A Battan.11th Bde. from WORMHOUDT to Camp E.
                                        in A.30.

    B.Battn. 11th Bde. from WORMHOUDT to Camp P.
                                        in A.15.d.

    11th Bde M.G.Coy. from WORMHOUDT to Camp in
                                        A.22.d.

On 26th July :-

11th Bde H.Q. from WORMHOUDT to Camp in A.30.
C & D Bns.11th Bde from WORMHOUDT to Camps O and D
                                        in A.30.
A & B Bns.11th Bde from Camps E and P to CANAL BANK.
11th Bde M.G.Coy. from A.22.d.to CANAL BANK and trench
                    -es left sector.
A & B Bns.10th Bde from K and M Camps to CANAL BANK.
10th Bde M.G.Coy. from E.12.b.to CANAL BANK and
                    trenches right sector.

On 27th July :-

H.Q.11th Bde from Camp in A.30 to CANAL BANK.
A & B Bns.11th Bde from CANAL BANK to trenches left
                                        sector.
C & D "   "   " from Camps O & D to CANAL BANK.
10th Bde H.Q. from PROVEN to CANAL BANK.
A & B Bns.10th Bde from CANAL BANK to trenches Right
                                        Sector.
C & D Bns. "   " from Camps L & N to CANAL BANK.

CHATEAU COUTHOVE.	24TH JULY (Continued).

On 27th July (continued).

A & B Bns.12th Bde from HOUTKERQUE - HERZEELE Area to K. and M. Camps.
C & D "   "   " from HOUTKERQUE - HERZEELE Area to E and P Camps.
12th Bde M.G.Coy. from HOUTKERQUE - HERZEELE Area to A.22.d.(Camp).

On July 28th :-

A & B Bns.12th Bde from K and M Camps to Camp in A.30.
12th Bde H.Q. from HOUTKERQUE to Camp in A.30.

Divisional Headquarters will close at CHATEAU COUTHOVE at 4 pm. 27th July and re-open at same hour at SAINTE SIXTE.

CHATEAU COUTHOVE.	25TH JULY.

Moves carried out in accordance with Operation Order 47 of 24th July.

CHATEAU COUTHOVE.	26TH JULY.

Moves carried out in accordance with Operation Order 47 of 24th July.

CHATEAU COUTHOVE. SAINTE SIXTE.	27TH JULY.

Moves carried out in accordance with Operation Order No.47 of 24th July.
H.Q.4th Division moved to SAINTE SIXTE at 4 pm. and command of the line passes to G.O.C.4th Division.

4.55 pm.   Evening report - about 3 am. hostile patrol approached trench at C.15.c.18, threw 2 bombs and ran when fired on. Hostile machine guns active. Small minenwerfer fired on ESSEX TRENCH.

SAINTE SIXTE.	28TH JULY.

4.45 am.   G.O.C.10th and 11th Brigades assumed command of their respective sectors in accordance with Operation Order 47 of 25th July. XIV Corps informed.

5 am.   Morning report - quiet night.

11.45 am.   Midday report - situation unchanged.

4.48 pm.   Evening report - nothing of interest to record.

A & B Bns. moved to Camp in A.30.

H.Q.12th Brigade established at Camp in A.30.

29TH JULY.

SAINTE SIXTE.

5.15 am.   Morning report - quiet night.

10.30 am.   Two Germans were shot last night opposite Right Sector belonging to 235th Regiment.

11.55 am.   Nothing to report at midday.

SAINTE SIXTE.

    5.5 pm.   Evening report - situation unchanged.

    5.10 pm.   6th Division (on right of 4th Division) report a few heavy shells on S.21 and SUNKEN ROAD about 3.30 pm.

    6.50 pm.   Command of XIV Corps line handed over to VIII Corps.

SAINTE SIXTE.   30TH JULY.

Quiet day - situation unchanged.

Relief of Guards Divisional Artillery by 4th Divisional Artillery completed.

SAINTE SIXTE.   31ST JULY.

Situation unchanged.

****

G.S. 4th Division
July 1916

Appendix "A"

The following Appendices are attached.

A. Equipment carried by men.
B. Map I showing routes to Assembly Trenches.
   Map II showing Assembly Trenches.
C. Report on Communications.
D. Report on action of Artillery.
E. Diagrams of formations :-
   (i) 11th Brigade.
   (ii) 10th Brigade.
   (iii) 12th Brigade.

APPENDIX "A"

OPERATIONS ON 1st JULY, 1916.

During the preparatory bombardment, Brigades were stationed as follows :-

10th Brigade holding the Divisional front, with two battalions in billets in MAILLY MAILLET.

11th Brigade in billets and bivouacs in MAILLY MAILLET, BEAUSSART and VAUCHELLES.

12th Brigade in billets at BERTRANCOURT.

On the 27th, three battalions of the 11th Brigade took over the Divisional front, relieving the 10th Brigade, which returned to billets in BEAUSSART and BERTRANCOURT.

On the night of 30th June, Brigades marched to their Assembly places by specially prepared routes (see App."B"). Advance parties from each battalion, including machine guns and Stokes mortars, were sent forward by communication trenches during the afternoon. The march of the main bodies of the Brigades was carried out without hitch or serious interference by hostile artillery, and all units were reported to be safely assembled in their allotted places before daylight.

1st JULY.

During the final stages of our preliminary bombardment, the enemy's reply was not intense. It was mostly directed at the trenches between our front line and east of the line VALLADE -TENDERLOIN. This barrage, however, became intense when our Heavy Artillery lifted at 7.25 a.m., and was accompanied by a violent machine gun fire from the front line trenches and from positions in the second and third German lines, the fire being directed on our front line trenches, on "NO MAN'S LAND" and on the area behind our own lines. The machine gun fire was particularly intense from the RIDGE REDOUBT and BEAUMONT-HAMEL, while further to the North the artillery fire of both heavy and field guns was

concentrated

concentrated on our front line trenches and increased in severity towards the northern boundary of the Division. At 7.30 a.m. our Divisional Artillery lifted, and the three assaulting battalions of the 11th Brigade advanced -

East Lancs on the right at 7.26 a.m.

Rifle Brig. in the centre at 7.29 a.m.

6th Royal Warwicks on the left at 7.30 a.m.

The East Lancs at once came under a heavy machine gun fire from BEAUMONT-HAMEL and RIDGE REDOUBT, and rifle fire from the front German parapet, and, with the exception of three platoons of the left company, was unable to cross the German wire, which was, in some places, uncut. Portions of the platoons which succeeded in entering the trenches are reported to have gained their objective. At 7.40 the Hamps. Regt. advancing in support of the East Lancs at once came under a very heavy machine gun fire and rifle fire and none of the battalion were able to cross "NO MAN'S LAND" where they took cover in shell holes.

The right company of the Rifle Brigade, under heavy machine gun fire, was unable to reach the German lines. North of Pt.K.35.c 4.5 the left and supporting companies broke through and gained trench 77 - 92 and a small semi-circular trench to the East of those points. Later on, when reinforced by the Som.L.I. small parties occupied for a short time trench 94 - 49 until driven out by strong bombing parties which advanced from RIDGE REDOUBT and down communication trenches leading to Points 62, 94 and 77.

The right companies of the 8th Royal Warwicks succeeded in entering the German trenches and advanced to Pt. 92 without much loss, where they joined hands with the Rifle Brigade. When reinforced by the 6th Royal Warwicks a further advance was made and trench 49 to 05 occupied by small parties of both battalions. The left companies

of

3.

of these battalions suffered heavy losses from machine gun fire from the direction of SERRE, and few were able to penetrate the front line. The general situation at this time (about 10 a.m.) appears to be as follows :-

The line Points 94 - 49 - 05 was held by small parties of the Som. L.I., Rif. Brig., and 6th and 8th Warwicks.

Further back, the same units were holding more strongly the line 56 - 77 - 92 - 55.

South of the line Points 56 - 94, the two right battns. namely, Hants and East Lancs, had failed to penetrate the German lines, with the exception of the small party of the East Lancs referred to above. From this time onwards, the parties holding the forward line, Points 94 - 05, were subjected to heavy bombing attacks on both flanks and down communication trenches leading from MUNICH trench.

At 9 a.m. the leading battalions of the 10th and 12th Brigades advanced in the following order from right to left -

    2nd Dublin Fusiliers)
)   10th Inf. Brigade.
    2nd Seaforth Highrs.)

    2nd Essex Regt.   )
)   12th Inf. Brigade.
    1st King's Own.   )

The Dublins and Seaforths immediately came under heavy machine gun and rifle fire from BEAUMONT-HAMEL and the front line trenches. The Dublins especially suffered severely, and were ordered to halt and take cover in our own trenches, the front being already occupied by the East Lancs and Hants battalions. Orders to the Seaforths to halt until the situation became clearer were not received and the battalion, inclining to the North to avoid the machine gun fire from BEAUMONT-HAMEL and neighbourhood, pushed forward to Points 62 and 94 and to the trenches already occupied by units of the 11th Brigade. Orders sent to the battalion to bomb southward from Points 77 and 62, in order to relieve pressure

on

on our right, never reached the battalion. The King's Own and Essex advanced in rear of the left company of the Rifle Brigade and the 6th and 8th Royal Warwicks and though suffering considerably from artillery fire, entered the German line and pushed up supports to the line held by the 11th Brigade, and small parties are reported to have gained MUNICH trench and even to the western edge of PENDANT COPSE.

From 11 a.m. onwards, communications from the front were uncertain and information vague. Mixed units of the 11th and 12th Brigades were gradually driven back from MUNICH trench to the line 94 - 05 by bombers, and by 12 noon the majority of these parties had been pushed back to the line 77 - 92. The heavy casualties among carriers who attempted to cross the barrage prevented an adequate supply of bombs or mortars being sent forward.

Meanwhile, soon after 11 a.m., the Lancashire Fusiliers and one company of the Duke of Wellingtons had reinforced the companies holding the line 56 - 92 - 85 and the QUADRILATERAL. Fighting continued in this area during the whole afternoon, and, though there was some disorganisation owing to the heavy losses in officers and platoon commanders in this sector, units were organised by Colonels HOPKINSON and FREETH and continued to hold the line mentioned.

The general situation between noon and 1 p.m. was as follows :-

On the right the attack by the 29th Division had failed.

In the centre the 4th Division was holding the line 56 - 77 - 92 and the QUADRILATERAL.

On the left the attack of the 31st Division had failed, although parties were reported at this time to be in SERRE.

As

As it now became evident that the objective of the VIIIth Corps could not be obtained without fressh artillery preparation, at 1.40 p.m. I ordered the G.O's.C. 10th and 12th Brigades to organise the defence of our own line, allotting the right sector to the 10th Bde and the left to the 12th Bde, the dividing line being an East and West line through Pt 56. The G.O.C. 12th Bde was entrusted with the defence of the German trenches held by us, with orders to consolidate and hold them. The scattered units of the 11th Brigade were to be collected within our own lines and to be reformed as a Divisional Reserve.

From 2 p.m. till midnight, the Lancs Fus, Seaforths and parties of 11th Brigade continued in occupation of the German trenches West of the line 56 - 77 - 92. These parties though reinforced by two companies of the Irish Fusiliers and supplied with bombs which it was found possible to push over on the low ground to the North of the QUADRILATERAL were gradually driven back and from 5 p.m. onwards we were holding the line Points 56 - 92 across the base of the QUADRILATERAL. This line was held till about midnight, by which time the evacuation of all troops in occupation was successfully accomplished with the exception of one company of the Irish Fusiliers under Captain BAREFOOT. It was impossible to communicate with this Company which remained in its position until 11.30 a.m. on the 2nd, when it returned, bringing in all its wounded, three German prisoners and some material.

G.S. 4th Division
July 1916.

Appendix "B" (1).

APPENDIX "B"(1)

1st JULY 1916.

Messages received on the Telephone.

Time	From	
7-33 am	Bde Maj. 11th Bde.	Rifle Brigade on line 92 - 77. Machine gun fire v.heavy. ~~Above message was probably misunderstood.~~ to exact position gained. This message delivered by runner probably inaccurate as
7-42	Div.O.P.	Troops reported over front line and moving towards second line. The German barrage in on our front line. There is very little M.G. fire as far as can be heard. Rather ragged rifle fire.
8-3	11th Bde.	German barrage has gone a long way back. M.G. fire has considerably slackened.
8-6	Div O.P.	German barrage seems to be on their own front line, " NO MAN'S LAND " and our own front line. It is heaviest about the REDAN. There is very little rifle or M.G. fire.
8-12	Div O.P.	German barrage very heavy on the REDAN and West of SERRE. Their heavy guns are firing. No barrage at all from Pt 35 southwards for some distance. Germans have opened fire with 4.2" Hows air bursts (high explosives). Rifle fire has started again. German barrage has been lifted off REDAN and is further back in the German lines.
8-20	Div O.P.	German Artillery fire has slackened a lot. There is no rifle fire now.
8-38	Div O.P.	The 12th Bde are now visible advancing in Artillery formation. 10th Bde are just leaving SUNKEN road. The Lancs Fus ha just past the POMMIER Hedge.
8-35	Div H.Q.	Bde Major told that 12th Bde was not to move to the assault until the situation was clear.
8-50	Div O.P.	12th Bde leading troops have nearly reached our front line, still in Artillery formation. 10th Brigade are rather bunching and are not quite so far as 12th Brigade.
9 a.m.		Communication with 11th Brigade severed.
9-1	Div O.P.	Germans putting on barrage again. Capt Fellowes thinks three Very lights that were fired came from the first objective.
9-7	29th Divn	The attack of 29th Divn on the BEAUMONT-BEAUCOURT road is postponed till 1.50 from ZERO (i.e - 9.20am) The attack may possibly not be made then.
9-8	Div.O.P.	Rifle fire has started heavily as if from MUNICH Trench . The 10th Bde are losing direction badly and moving as if to the REDAN.
9-20	12th Bde	Two leading Battns of 12th Bde are now in "NO MAN'S LAND " and they are holding back their two rear battalions.

Time	From	
10-7	10th Bde	Dublin patrols are now past the old German front line and are under heavy fire. The leading battalions of the Dublins have two leading lines in the ~~enemy front line~~ 10th Brigade were ordered not to send leading battalions to assist in the attack on the 11th Brigade final objective. 10th Brigade say this order has been conveyed to battalions. heavier than against the left.
10.20	Div. O.P.	Captain Fellowes has had a message from the 11th Brigade that General PROWSE has been badly wounded. Two VERY lights seen North of REDAN, point at which discharged unknown.
10.24	12th Bde.	93rd Brigade on our left have not left their front line trenches. Message from 93rd Brigade states two of their battalions have been cut up. King's Own are in 4th Division front line and have asked 93rd Brigade for reinforcements as the enemy are attacking them. Left of King's Own is at Point 97.
11.10	12th Bde. (General Crosbie)	Captain Milne of the ~~Suk's~~ Duke's has just come back wounded from German 2nd line. He says 11th Brigade in front of him had got objective and that King's Own and Essex are going forward steadily supported by Lancashire Fuslrs. I have no information from King's Own or Essex since operation began. From Lancashire Fusiliers I heard that advance was steady. I have in my own hand about 3 companies Duke's, leading company probably in front line trench. Battalion H.Q. Duke's with small reserve in TAUPIN.
11.25	Bde. Major 11th Bde.	Some of Somersets and some of 12th Brigade reached 11th Brigade first objective neighbourhood of Points 81 and 49. Rifle Brigade about 77 trench. Germans still in front line trench opposite REDAN. E. Lancs. and Hants. in German 2nd line S. of REDAN. Bde. Major is at 11th Bde. H.Q.
12 noon	Essex thro' 12th Brigade.	Essex are in MUNICH Trench probably at 63 and Germans bombing towards them. Barrage wanted 200 yards in front. ~~Essex will~~ Essex not in touch with anyone on their right. Lancs. Fusiliers have detachments in QUADRILATERAL. General Crosbie says 31st Division are back in our front line.
	Div. H.Q.	12th Brigade informed 11th Brigade hold line 81 - 49 - 77 and further South. E. Lancs. are in trench between Pt. 62 and Pt. 59.
12.45 pm.	12th Bde.	93rd Brigade retiring from their own front line, being heavily counter-attacked from direction of SERRE. General Crosbie doubtful whether Essex are in MUNICH Trench. Detachments Essex and King's Own in German 2nd Trench. Lancs. Fus. in QUADRILATERAL. All holding their own but being heavily counter-attacked and have suffered heavy casualties. 12th Brigade have

Time	From	
10-7	10th Bde	Dublin patrols are now past the old German front line and are under heavy fire. The leading battalions of the Dublins have two leading lines in the German front line.
10th Brigade are not quite certain where the Seaforths are, but they have definite orders not to go forward.
The rifle fire against the right is considerably heavier than against the left.
10.20	Div. O.P.	Captain Fellowes has had a message from the 11th Brigade that General PROWSE has been badly wounded. Two VERY lights seen North of REDAN, point at which discharged unknown.
10.24	12th Bde.	93rd Brigade on our left have not left their front line trenches. Message from 93rd Brigade states two of their battalions have been cut up.
King's Own are in 4th Division front line and have asked 93rd Brigade for reinforcements as the enemy are attacking them. Left of King's Own is at Point 97.
11.10	12th Bde. (General Crosbie)	Captain Milne of the Duke's has just come back wounded from German 2nd line. He says 11th Brigade in front of him had got objective and that King's Own and Essex are going forward steadily supported by Lancashire Fuslrs. I have no information from King's Own or Essex since operation began. From Lancashire Fusiliers I heard that advance was steady. I have in my own hand about 3 companies Duke's, leading company probably in front line trench. Battalion H.Q. Duke's with small reserve in TAUPIN.
11.25	Bde. Major 11th Bde.	Some of Somersets and some of 12th Brigade reached 11th Brigade first objective neighbourhood of Points 81 and 49. Rifle Brigade about 77 trench. Germans still in front line trench opposite REDAN.
E. Lancs. and Hants. in German 2nd line S. of REDAN. Bde. Major is at 11th Bde. H.Q.
12 noon	Essex thro' 12th Brigade.	Essex are in MUNICH Trench probably at 63 and Germans bombing towards them. Barrage wanted 200 yards in front. Essex not in touch with anyone on their right.
Lancs. Fusiliers have detachments in QUADRILATERAL. General Crosbie says 31st Division are back in our front line.
	Div. H.Q.	12th Brigade informed 11th Brigade hold line 81 - 49 - 77 and further South. E. Lancs. are in trench between Pt. 62 and Pt. 59.
12.45 pm.	12th Bde.	93rd Brigade retiring from their own front line, being heavily counter-attacked from direction of SERRE. General Crosbie doubtful whether Essex are in MUNICH Trench.
Detachments Essex and King's Own in German 2nd Trench. Lancs. Fus. in QUADRILATERAL. All holding their own but being heavily counter-attacked and have suffered heavy casualties. 12th Brigade have

Time p.m.	From	
		have only 500 men in hand including carriers, Duke's in LEGEND and BURROW had heavy casualties. In reply General Crosbie ordered to keep all troops he can lay his hand on in hand.
12.55	From 31st Division	First four waves of 31st in possession of SERRE and PENDANT COPSE line. 93rd Brigade being counter-attacked by small detachments only. Probably fallen back because of bad state of our trenches - very little fear of Germans getting round 4th Division left.
	Div. H.Q.	In reply. 31st Division informed of possibility of Essex being in MUNICH Trench and 31st asked to bomb southwards to meet them.
1.0	Div. H.Q.	General Crosbie informed 94th Brigade hold line SERRE - PENDANT COPSE and little chance of Germans getting round our left.
1.6	11th Bde.	Report that that our men can be seen retiring from Point 63 being counter-attacked.
1.4	11th Bde.	Essex from Point 63 send message "For goodness sake send reinforcements."
1.25	29th Div.	Whole of 86th Brigade expended. 29th Division trying to organise another attack on line Pt. 89 - Pt. 83, attack timed for 12.45 p.m. had to be postponed owing to trenches being blocked.
1.30	8th Corps O.P.	Our men are in German front line N. of BEAUMONT HAMEL. Germans, probably prisoners, can also be seen.
1.40	11th Bde.	Rifle Brigade and Somersets reported back in our own front line. 8th Warwicks and portions of 12th Brigade units who had pushed through are almost back in our front line. G.O.C. 12th Brigade to take charge of line North of an East and West line through Pt. 56. G.O.C. 10th Brigade to take charge South of this line.
1.45	10th Bde.	Germans who ru entered BEET St. ejected. Pt. 56 held by about 50 men under Col. Hopkinson who asked urgently for reinforcements. General Wilding sent 1 Company Irish Fusiliers and bombs. Whole length Pt. 56 - Pt. 26 - 38 still held by Germans.
2.15	12th Bde.	A very few men holding QUADRILATERAL, barrage wanted on Eastern side of line Pt. 92 - 87 77. O.C. Lancs. Fus. organising line of defence in our front line. A second line being organised in VALLADE by 11th Bde. where there are a good many men. 12th Bde. only 2 machine guns left.

Time	From	
2.35	10th Bde.	South of Pt. 56 a few of 11th Brigade are believed to be in trenches East of German front line opposite REDAN and a few other small detachments are believed to be in German 2nd line trenches farther South. O.C. Seaforths is in point 56 with about 50 men. Our front line is held by 10th and 11th Bde.
2.45	29th Div. (Gen. de Lisle)	The 29th Division is going to stop in its present position and is not going to attack.
3.23	12th Bde.	12th Bde. still has a few men in the German front line N. of QUADRILATERAL.
3.43	10th Bde.	The front and support lines are held by scattered bodies of all units of the division. The state of battalions of 10th Bde. is as follows:- Warwicks. They started on the attack but were met by very heavy machine gun fire from BEAUMONT HAMEL and several places in the German front line also by artillery barrage. They have 1 company in our front line about opposite Pt. 35 and 3 other companies are between our front line and TENDERLOIN. Dublins. Have withdrawn what is left of their men (under 200) and they are now in YOUNG STREET. Seaforths There are a few in Pt. 56 and a good many others back in our front line. These are distributed along front line N. of REDAN. Irish Fusiliers. 1 company is in REDAN, 1 Company believed to be in QUADRILATERAL. 2 companies still in MOUNTJOY. The Seaforths and Dublins suffered heavily; the other battalions did not. T.M.Batteries. 1 in REDAN 　　　　　　　　　2 in TENDERLOIN Machine Guns. 4 machine guns hold front line South of REDAN, 4 in reserve, 8 are unaccounted for. There is nobody in front line South of QUADRILATERAL
4.15	11th Bde.	11th Brigade has a party in the QUADRILATERAL; the 10th Brigade has sent a party to reinforce them. An orderly has come in from 8th Warwicks, who says that the 8th Warwicks at 3.35 p.m. are still in the 3rd German line. They got to their objective in the 4th German line but had to come back. They have nearly exhausted their bombs and ammunition. Details of other units are in a similar condition. 8th Warwicks ask for reinforcements. Some of the Rifle Brigade are in the German line opposite ROX Street, there they are consolidating. There is a party of Hampshires numbering about 30, who are dug

Time	From	
p.m.		in between BEAUMONT HAMEL and the REDAN, just our side of the German front line. The 11th Bde. has heard nothing of the E. Lancs.
5.35	31st Div.	170 Bde. F.O.O. reports from bits of information that are coming in to battalion headquarters that a junction has been effected in SERRE between our troops and the 4th Division.
5.40	11th Bde.	A party of the 8th Warwicks is in the apex of the QUADRILATERAL, the Germans are in the base, and are bombing towards them. They have asked for a barrage to be put on the base.
6.0	14th Bde. R.F.A.	14th Bde. R.F.A. can see Germans crawling up to the German front line between Pt. 35 and their trenches opposite the REDAN and they think that they may possibly be going to attack.
6.2	~~10th~~ Div. H.Q.	Above message repeated to 10th Bde.
6.20	10th Bde.	The Staff Captain, 10th Bde. has been to the QUADRILATERAL and seen Col. Hopkinson, who is in German trench just South of the QUADRILATERAL. There are a party of a 100 men of different regiments with Col. Hopkinson, who are holding out well. They have plenty of bombs. They are being attacked but are holding out. As far as Col. Hopkinson knows, there are no other troops of the 4th Division in that vicinity. He will withdraw after dark.
6.40	Div. O.P.	The Germans are still shelling their front line near the REDAN. Signalling from BIEFVILLERS church can be seen. Some of our men are digging themselves in in front of the German trenches.
7.10	11th Bde.	Bde. Major has heard that there are some of the Rifle Brigade in the German line between the QUADRILATERAL and REDAN (but nearer the QUADRILATERAL). This is not confirmed. He has heard a rumour (also unconfirmed) that there are some of the Rifle Brigade in the German trenches South of the REDAN. The Rifle Brigade report that they have 120 men exclusive of carriers. They have orders to go to ELLES SQUARE. There are 50 stragglers of the Hants. and E. Lancs. in TENDERLOIN. He has heard nothing of E. Lancs. beyond this. There are also about 80 or 90 of the Somersets, 6th and 8th Warwicks in the support trenches but General Crosbie has not yet told them where to go to. He can see a mixed party of nearly all units in the division in the apex of the QUADRILATERAL; they are walking about in the shell holes, etc. and fighting. He can also see Germans near this point.
~~9.48~~ 9.54	8th Corps.	The heavy artillery have orders to put their night lines on the German second trench Pt. 62 - Pt. 77 - Pt. 92

4th Divn. G.S.
July 1916

Appendix "D"(1)

SECRET-
~~~~~~~~

4th Divn Q.R.1150/5

22/7/16

The 4th Division with S.A.A & Grenade Portion of D.A.C less R.A. and motor vehicles will entrain in accordance with the attached Time Tables.
MARCHE indicates the official train number.
Time - continental - e.g

Date	Hour of departure	
21/7	21/19	= 9.19 p.m. 21st July.

(1) The R.A will proceed by march route under instructions that will be issued later.

(2) Motor vehicles except cars with Staff Officers will move as convoys on July 22nd and 23rd via BEAUVAL-DOULLENS-ST POL - LILLERS - HAZEBROUCK - WORMHOUDT.

(3) The Divisional Supply Column will move under instructions to be issued by the D.D.S & T. Reserve Army.

(4) The D.A.A & Q.M.G. will proceed on the 21st instant with Captain Hewitt.1st R.War. Regt. to H.Qrs, 14th Corps -

Staff Officer attached to A.D.R.T. II Army.
HAZEBROUCK - Captain Hewitt. 1st R.War.Regt.

Staff Officer attached to A.D.R.T. III Army.
DOULLENS - 2/Lieut: Wallace. R.E.Signal Coy.

These Officers will report to the A.D.R.T's at 6 p.m. on 22nd and will remain attached until completion of the move.

(5) The O.C. 21st West Yorkshire Regt will detail three parties consisting of 2 Officers and 100 other ranks to report to the R.T.O's at CANDAS, DOULLENS N. & S. stations at 19-17-18 hours respectively on 22nd instant,rationed for 23rd and 24th instants inclusive. These parties will assist in loading the trains under the directions of Brigade Transport Officers and will proceed by the last train leaving these stations on the 23rd instant to rejoin their units.

(6) Rendezvous for troops entraining at -

DOULLENS N. will be the MOAT of CITADELLE.
DOULLENS S. will be BOULEVARDE A.17 (a)
CANDAS Short of the village on the BEAUVAL road.

All transport will reach the entraining point 3 clear hours and the personnel of units 1½ clear hours before the train is due to depart.

(7) Infantry Brigades will detail their Brigade Transport Offrs to act as Entraining Officers at their respective stations.These Officers will be responsible for superintending the entrainment of all troops leaving and will proceed on the last train with the parties mentioned in para. (5).

(8) Supplies. All troops will entrain with the current days rations for the 23rd on the man and Supply Wagons loaded with rations for the 24th. Rations for 25th will be delivered on arrival in the new area.

The O.C. Train will arrange to hand over baggage and Supply wagons to R.A.Units, the Supply Wagons will be loaded with rations for consumption 24th.

O.C. Supply Column will arrange for the necessary lorries and accompany these units by roads.

(9) Water Carts and water bottles will be filled before leaving – horses will be watered before being trucked.

(10). Units will provide breast ropes for all trucks carrying horses.

(11) Detraining.

The following officers will proceed by the 1st trains from Stations as follows:-

DOULLENS N.   Lieut. Gandy. R.F.A.

DOULLENS.S.   Capt. Ravenscroft. Lancs. Fuslrs.

CANDAS.   2/Lieut. Carver. R.Dub. Fuslrs.

They will act as detraining officers on arrival under instructions which will be given them by D.A.A.& Q.M.G. and will remain on duty until the detrainment is completed.

(12). The O.C. Signal Coy. will detail two motor cyclist orderlies to report to H.Qrs. Q.14th Corps by 9 a.m. on 22nd to await the arrival of Captain Koster D.A.A.&.Q.M.G.

W.P.H.Hill; Lt.Colonel.
A.A. & Q.M.G., 4th Division.

10th.Bde.Group continued.   TABLE OF MOVES BY UNITS.

UNIT.	Serial No.	Entraining Station.	Hour of departure.	Date.	Marche.	Detraining Station.	Hour of arrival-	Remarks.
2nd.R.Dublin Fusiliers.	414	CANDAS.		July. 23rd.			Approx: 23rd.	
10th.Bde.M.G. Coy: 1 Sect: Billeting party of T.9.	416		11.06	23rd.	T.3		17.54	
9th.Fld.Coy. "Res:Coy: Billeting party T.12.	484 408	CANDAS.	13.51	23rd.	T.6		20.34	
H.Q. & H.Q. Coy. Div.Train. Sa Sanitary Sect: No.4 Mob:Vet: Section. 2/3 Res.Coy.	487 404 495 408	CANDAS.	16.51	23rd.	T.9		23.34	
10th.Fld.Amb: Dismt.Portion. 10th.Fld.Amb: T.4 & Personnel Heavy T.M.Bty.	491 491A. 499 A & 499 B	CANDAS	19.51	23rd.	T.12		24th. 2.34	
1/3rd S.A.A. Section D.A.C.	481	CANDAS.	23.06	23rd.	T.15		5.54	

10th.Brigade.Group.   TABLE OF MOVES BY UNITS.   Station:- CANDAS.   4th.Div.Q.R.1150/4/A.

UNIT.	Serial No.	Entraining Station.	Hour of departure.	Date.	Marche.	Detraining Station.	Hour of arrival	Remarks.
Bde. H.Q. No.2 Sect:Sig: Company. No.2.Coy:Train. Billeting parties of Trains T.18. T.21.	410 415 488 —	CANDAS.	23.06	July, 22nd.	T.15.		Approx: 23rd. 5.54	
1st.R.Warwicks. 10th.Bde.M.G. Company. 1 Sect: 1/3 10th.T.M.Bty. Billeting parties of Train T.24.	411 416 417 —	CANDAS.	1.51	23rd.	T.18		8.34	
2nd. Seaforth Highlanders. 10th.Bde.M.G. Coy: 1 Sect: 1/3rd 10th. T.M.Bty. Billeting party of Train. T.3.	412 416 417 —	CANDAS	5.06	23rd.	T.21		11.54	
1st.R.Irish Fus. 10th.Bde.M.G. Coy: 1 Sect: 1/3rd.10th.T.M. Bty. Billeting party of Train T.6.	413 416 417 —	CANDAS.	7.36	23rd.	T.24		14.34	

P.T.O.

4th.Div.Q.R.1150/4/B.

11th.Brigade group.   TABLE OF MOVES BY UNITS.   Station DOULLENS N.

Unit.	Serial No.	Entraining Station.	Hour of departure.	Date.	Marche.	Detraining Station.	Hour of arrival. Approx: 23rd.	Remarks.
Bde.H.Q.	420	DOULLENS North.	21.19	July. 22nd.	T.13		3.34	
3 Sect. Sig. Company.	425							
3 Coy Train.	489							
Billeting parties of Trains T.16. T.19.	"							
1st.Som.L.I.	421	DOULLENS North.	0.19	23rd.	T.16		6.34	
1 Sect. M.G.								
Bde.M.G.Coy.	426							
1/3rd.Lon. T.M.Bty.	427							
Billeting parties of Trains T.22. T.1.	"							
1st.East Lancs.	422	DOULLENS North.	3.19	23rd.	T.19		9.34	
1 Sect. 11th Bde.M.G.Coy.	426							
1/3rd.Lon. T.M.Bty.	427							
Billeting parties of Trains T.4 T.7.	"							

P.T.O.

11th.Bde. group continued — TABLE OF MOVES BY UNITS.

Entraining Station: DOULLENS N.
Detraining Station: DOULLENS N.

UNIT.	Serial No.	Entraining Station.	Hour of departure.	Date.	Marche.	Detraining Station.	Hour of arrival.	REMARKS.
1st.Hants. 1 Sect. 11th Bde.M.G.Coy. 1/3rd.11th T.M.Bty. Billeting parties for Train.T.10 T.12.	425 426 427 1	DOULLENS North.	6.19	23rd.	T.22		12.34	Approx 23rd.
1st.Rifle Brigade. 1 Sect. 11th.Bde. M.G.Coy.	424 426	DOULLENS North.	9.04	23rd.	T.1		15.24	
H.Q.Div. R.E. 1/1 Fen-row Fld Company.	483 486	DOULLENS North.	12.19	23rd.	T.4		18.34	
Div.H.Q. H.Q. & 1 Sect.Div. Signals. H.Q. Div Artillery. W.S.Cable Section.	401 405 402 1	DOULLENS North.	15.34	23rd.	T.7		21.54	
11th.Fld. Ambulance. Dismt port: X.4 & Y.4. T.M.Btys.	492 492A 496 & 427	DOULLENS North.	18.19	23rd.	T.10		24th. 0.34	
1/3rd.S.A.A. Sect.D.A.C.	481	DOULLENS North.	21.19	23rd.	T.13		3.34	

4th.Div.Q.R.1150/4/0.

12th.Bde.Group.   TABLE OF MOVES BY UNITS.   Station DOULLENS South.

UNIT.	Serial No.	Entraining Station.	Hour of departure.	Date.	March.	Detraining Station.	Hour of arrival. Approx: 23rd.	REMARKS.
Bde.H.Q. 4 Sec: Sigs. No.4 Coy Div Train. Billeting parties of Trains.T.17. T.20.	450 435 490 -	DOULLENS South.	22.19	July. 22nd.	T.14		4.34	
1st.Kings Own R.L. 1 Sect.12th M.G.Coy. 1/2 12th.T.M. Battery. Billeting parties of Trains.T.23 T.3.	431 436 437 -	DOULLENS South.	1.19	23rd.	T.17		7.34	
2nd.Lancs Fusiliers. 1 Sect. 12th Bde.M.G.Coy. 1/2 12th.T.M. Battery.	432 436 437	DOULLENS South.	4.34	23rd.	T.20		10..	
2nd.Essex. 1 Sect. 12th Bde.M.G.Coy. Billeting parties of Trains.T.5.	434 436 -	DOULLENS South.	7.34	23rd.	T.23		13.54	

P.T.O.

12th.Bde.Group continued.   TABLE – MOVES BY UNITS.   Station DOULLENS South.

UNIT.	Serial No.	Entraining Station.	Hour of departure.	Date.	Marche.	Detraining Station.	Hour of arrival. Approx. 3rd.	REMARKS.
2nd. West. Ridings. 1 Sect. 12th. Bde. M.G.Coy. Billeting Party/N.S.	435 } 436 } — }	DOULLENS South.	10.04	July 23rd.	T.2.		16.34	
1/1st Durham Fld.Coy.R.E. Billeting parties of Train T.11. T.14.	485 } — }	DOULLENS South.	13.19	23rd.	T.5.		19.34	
21st West Yorks. M.M.P.	404 }	DOULLENS South.	16.19	23rd.	T.8.		22.34	
12th.Fld.Amb: Dismt portion. 2.4 & S.4. T.M.Bty.	493 } 493A. } 498 & } 499 }	DOULLENS South.	19.34	23rd.	T.11.		24th. 1.54	
1/3rd.S.A.A. Sect. D.A.C.	481 }	DOULLENS South.	22.19	23rd.	T.14.		4.34	

G.S. 4th Division
July 1916

Appendix "F"

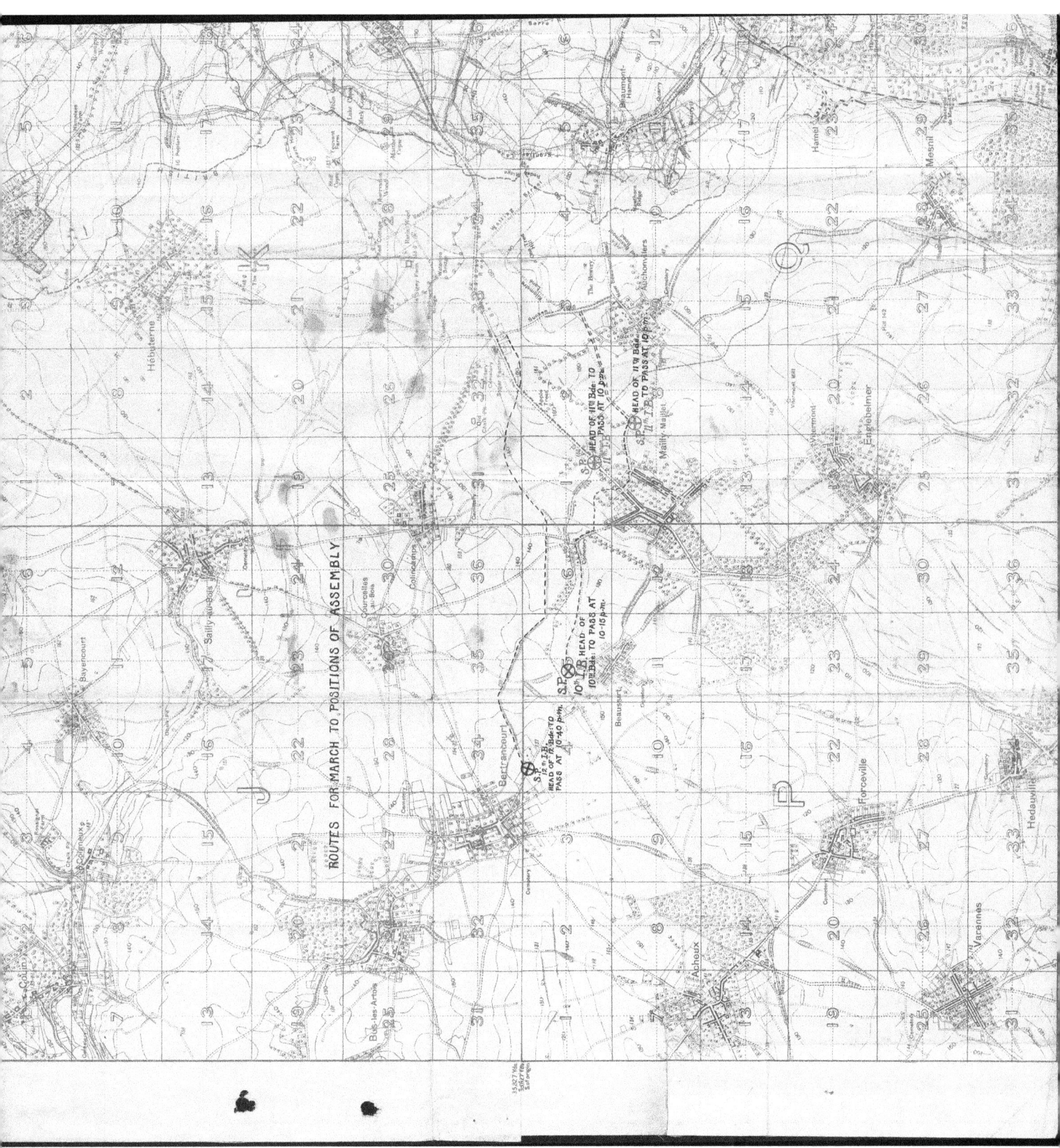

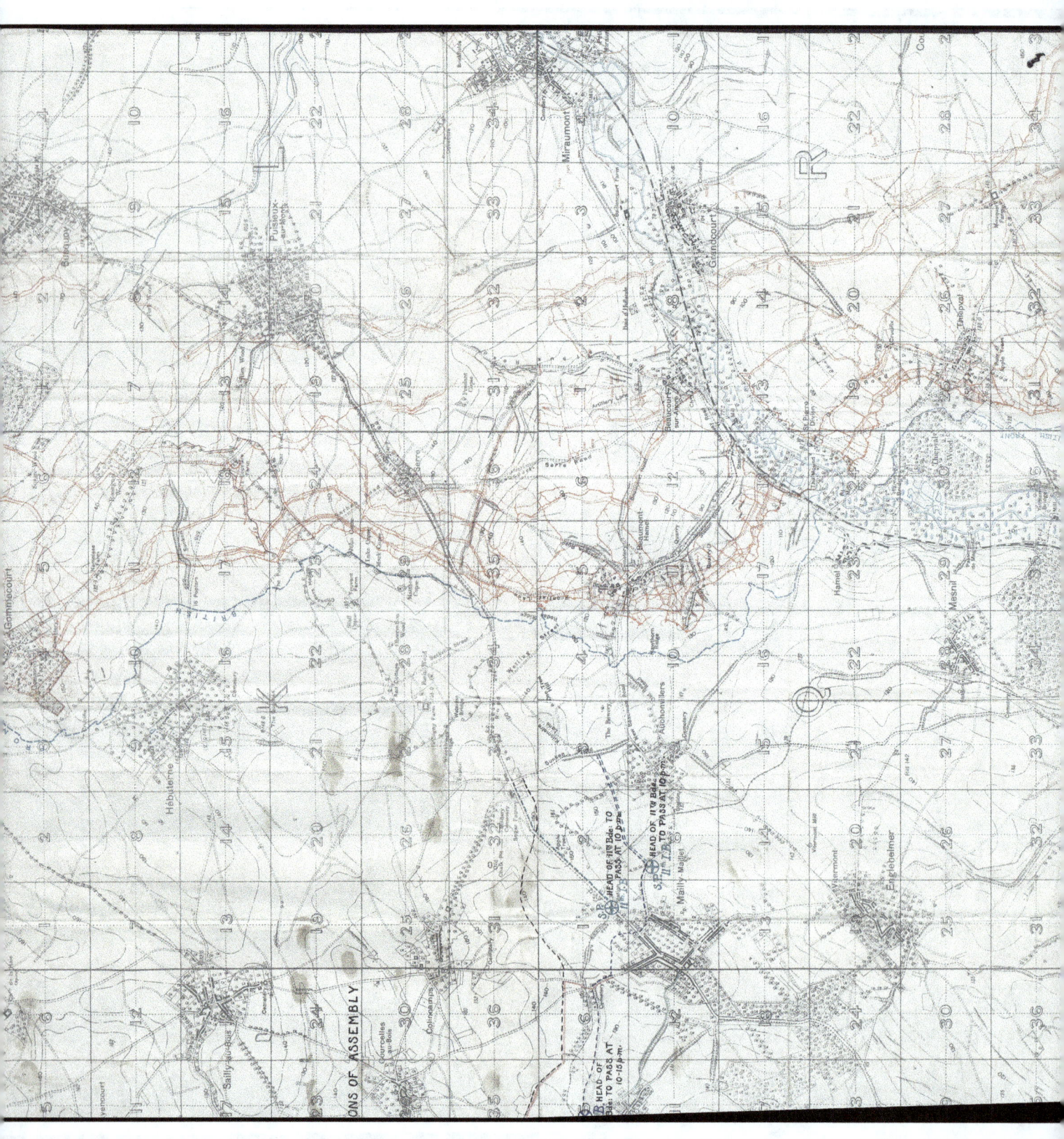

APPENDIX D2

APPENDIX D(2)

Bassin de radoub	Dry dock.
Bateau phare	Light-ship.
Blanchisserie	Laundry.
B.M. (borne milliaire)	Mile stone.
Bk (borne kilométrique)	
Boulonnerie / Fabr de boulons	Bolt Factory.
Bouée	Buoy.
Brasserie, Brassie	Brewery.
Briqueterie, Briqie	Brickfield.
Brise-lames	Breakwater.
Bureau de poste	Post office.
,, de douane	Custom house.
Butte	Butt, Mound.
Cabane	Hut.
Cabaret, Cabt	Inn.
Câble sous-marin	Submarine cable.
Calvaire, Calve	Calvary.
Canal de dessèchement	Drainage canal.
Canal d'irrigation	Irrigation canal.
Fabr de caoutchouc	Rubber factory.
Carrière, Carre	Quarry.
,, de gravier	Gravel-pit.
Caserne	Barracks.
Champ de courses	Race course.
,, ,, manœuvres	Drill ground.
,, ,, tir	Rifle range.
Chantier	Building yard. / Ship yard. / Dock yard.
Chantier de construction	Slip-way.
Chapelle, Chle	Chapel.
Charbonnage	Colliery.
Château d'eau	Water tower.
Chaussée	Causeway. / Highway.
Chemin de fer	Railway.
Cheminée, Chée	Chimney.
Chêne	Oak tree.
Cimetière, Cimre	Cemetery.
Clocher	Belfry.
Clouterie	Nail factory.
Colombier	Dovecot.
Coron	Workmen's dwellings.
Cour des / aux marchandises	Goods yard.
Couvent	Convent.
Crassier	Slag heap.
Croix	Cross.
Darse	Inner dock.
Démoli - e	Destroyed.
Détruit - e, Détt - e	,,
Déversoir	Weir.
Digue	Dyke, causeway.
Distillerie, Distie	Distillery.
Douane / Bureau de douane	Custom-house.
Entrepôt de douane	Custom warehouse.
Dynamitière, Dynamre	Dynamite magazine.
Dynamiterie	Dynamite factory.
Ecluse	Sluice, Lock.
Eclusette, Eclte	Sluice.
Ecole	School.
Ecurie	Stable.
Eglise	Church.
Emaillerie	Enamel works.
Embarcadère, Embre	Landing-place.
Estaminet, Estamt	Inn.
Etang	Pond.
Fabrique, Fabe	Factory.
Fabe de produits chimiques	Chemical works.
Fabe de faïence / Faïencerie	Pottery.
Ferme, Fme	Farm.
Filature, Filre	Spinning mill.
Fonderie, Fondie	Foundry.
Fontaine, Fontne	Spring, fountain.
Forêt	Forest.
Forme de radoub	Dry dock.
Forge	Smithy.
Fosse	Mine, Pit.
Fossé	Moat, Ditch.
Four	Kiln.
,, à chaux	Lime-kiln.
Four à coke	Coke oven.
Ganterie	Glove Factory.
Gare	Station.
Garenne	Warren.
Garnison	Garrison.
Gazomètre	Gasometer.
Glacerie / Fabr de glaces	Mirror Factory.
Glacière	Ice factory.
Grue	Crane.
Gué	Ford.
Guérite	Sentry-box, Turret.
,, à signaux	Signal-box (Ry.)
Halte	Halt.
Hangar	Shed, Hangar.
Hôpital	Hospital.
Hôtel-de-Ville	Town hall.
Houillère	Colliery.
Huilerie	Oil factory.
Imprimerie, Imprie	Printing works.
Jetée	Pier.
Laminerie	Rolling mills.
Ligne / Laisse de haute marée	High water mark.
,, de basse marée	Low ,, ,,
Maison Forestière / Mon Fre	Forester's house.
Malterie	Malt-house.
Marbrerie	Marble works.
Marais	Marsh.
Marais salant	Saltern, Salt marsh.
Marché	Market.
Mare	Pool.
Meule	Rick.
Minière	Mine.
Monastère	Monastery.
Moulin, Min	Mill.
,, à vapeur	Steam mill.
Mur	Wall.
,, crénelé	Loop-holed wall.
Nacelle	Ferry.
Orme	Elm.
Orphelinat	Orphanage.
Oseraie	Osier-beds.
Ouvrage	Fort.
Ouvrages hydrauliques	Water works.
Papeterie	Paper-mill.
Parc	Park, yard.
,, aérostatique	Aviation ground.
,, à charbon	Coal yard.
,, à pétrole	Petrol store.
Passage à niveau P.N.	Level-crossing.
Passerelle, Passlle	Foot-bridge.
Pepinière	Nursery-garden.
Peuplier	Poplar tree.
Phare	Light-house.
Pilier, Pilr	Post.
Plaine d'exercice	Drill ground.
Pompe	Pump.
Ponceau	Culvert.
Pont	Bridge.
,, levis	Drawbridge.
Poste / Station de garde-côte	Coast-guard station.
Poteau Pau	Post.
Poterie	Pottery.
Poudrière, Poudre / Magasin à poudre	Powder magazine.
Prise d'eau	Water supply.
Puits	Pit-head, Shaft, Well.
,, artésien	Artesian well.
,, d'aérage / ,, ventilateur	Ventilating shaft.
,, de sondage	Boring.
Quai	Quay, Platform.
,, aux bestiaux	Cattle platform.
,, aux / ,, des marchandises	Goods platform.
Raccordement	Junction.
Raffinerie	Refinery.
,, de sucre	Sugar refinery.
Râperie	Beet-root factory.
Remblai	Embankment.
Remise des / aux Machines	Engine-shed.
Réservoir, Résr	Reservoir.
Route cavalière	Bridle road.
Rubanerie	Ribbon Factory.
Ruine / Ruines / En ruine / Ruiné - e	Ruin.
Sablière	Sand-pit.
Sablonnière, Sablonre	,,
Sapin	Fir tree.
Saule	Willow tree.
Saunerie	Salt-works.
Scierie, Scie	Saw-mill.
Sondage	Boring.
Source	Spring.
Sucrerie, Sucie	Sugar factory.
Tannerie	Tannery.
Tir à la cible	Rifle range.
Tissage	Weaving mill.
Tôlerie	Rolling mill.
Tombeau	Tomb.
Tour	Tower.
Tourbière	Peat-bog, Peat-bed.
Tourelle	Small tower.
Tuilerie	Tile works.
Usine à gaz	Gas works.
,, électrique / ,, d'électricité	Electricity works.
,, métallurgique	Metal works.
,, à agglomérés	Briquette factory.
Verrerie, Verrie	Glass works.
Viaduc	Viaduct.
Vivier	Fish Pond.
Voie de chargement / ,, ,, déchargement / ,, ,, d'évitement / ,, ,, formation / ,, ,, manœuvre	Siding.
Zinguerie	Zinc works.

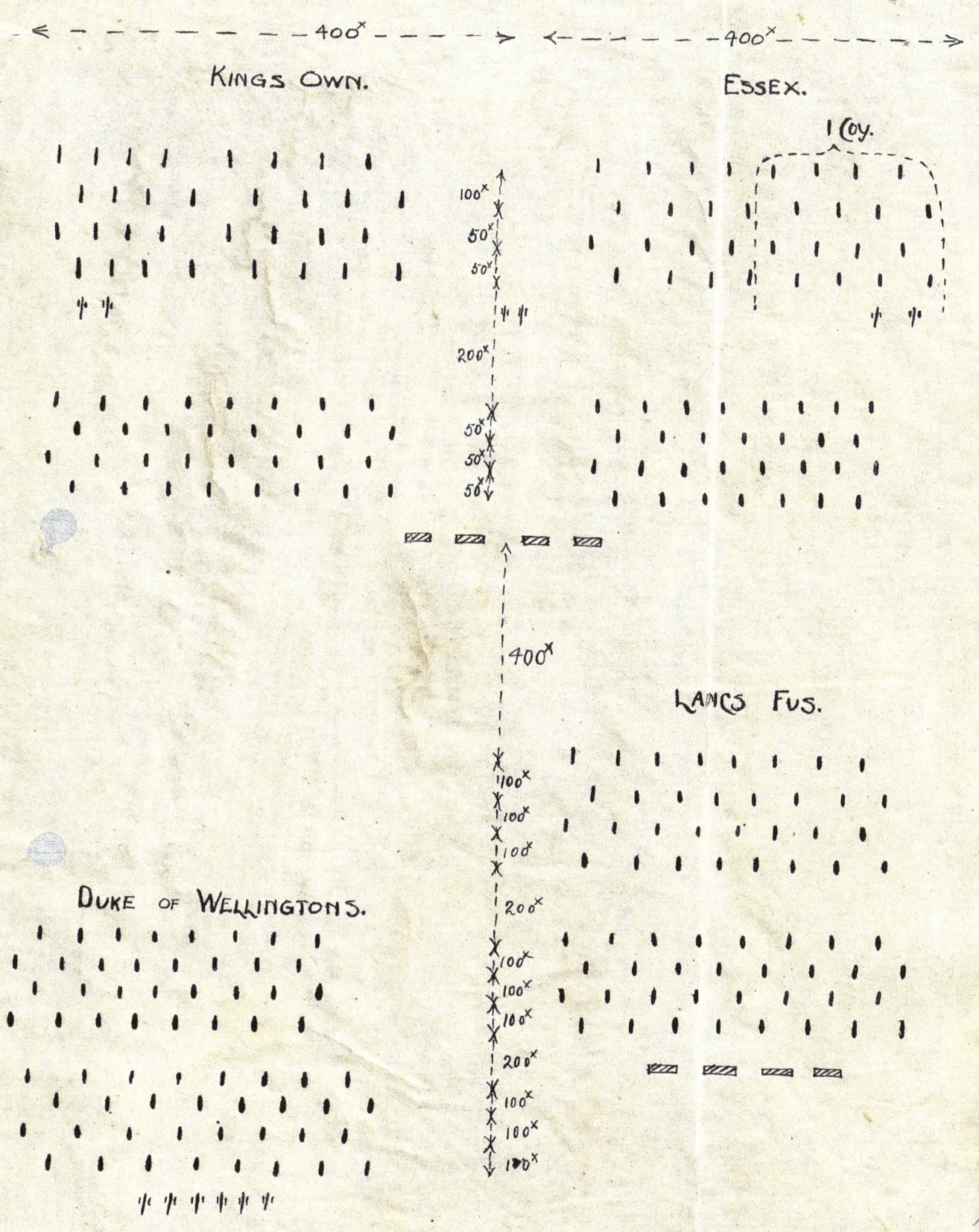

10th Brigade

2nd Seaforth Hgrs.   2nd Dublin Fus.

1 Coy.   1 Coy.   1 Coy.   1 Coy.   1 Coy.   1 Coy.

100 yds.
100 yds.
100 yds.

←——— 375 Yds. ———→

200x
200x
200x

←——— 1 Coy. ———→   ←——— 1 Coy. ———→

1st R. Irish Fus.   1st R. Warwick. Regt.

←— 90x —→

1 Coy.   1 Coy.   1 Coy.

80 yds.
80 yds.
80 yds.
200 yds.

←——— 1 Coy. ———→

200 yds.

←——— 1 Coy. ———→

11TH BRIGADE. — 2ND OBJECTIVE.

1/ HAMPSHIRE R.

A Coy. | B Coy. | C Coy. 2 platoons.

2 platoons. C. Coy.

D. Coy.

Hd. Qrs. Sect.

1/ SOMERSET. L.I.

1 Coy. | 1 Coy.
1 Coy. | 1 Coy.

100 yds. — 25 yds. — 100 yds. — 100 yds.

30x

Lewis gun carriers & Platoon bombing squads

6TH WARWICKS

1 Coy. | 1 Coy.
1 Coy. | 1 Coy.

▨ = Stokes Gun.
╬ = Lewis Gun.

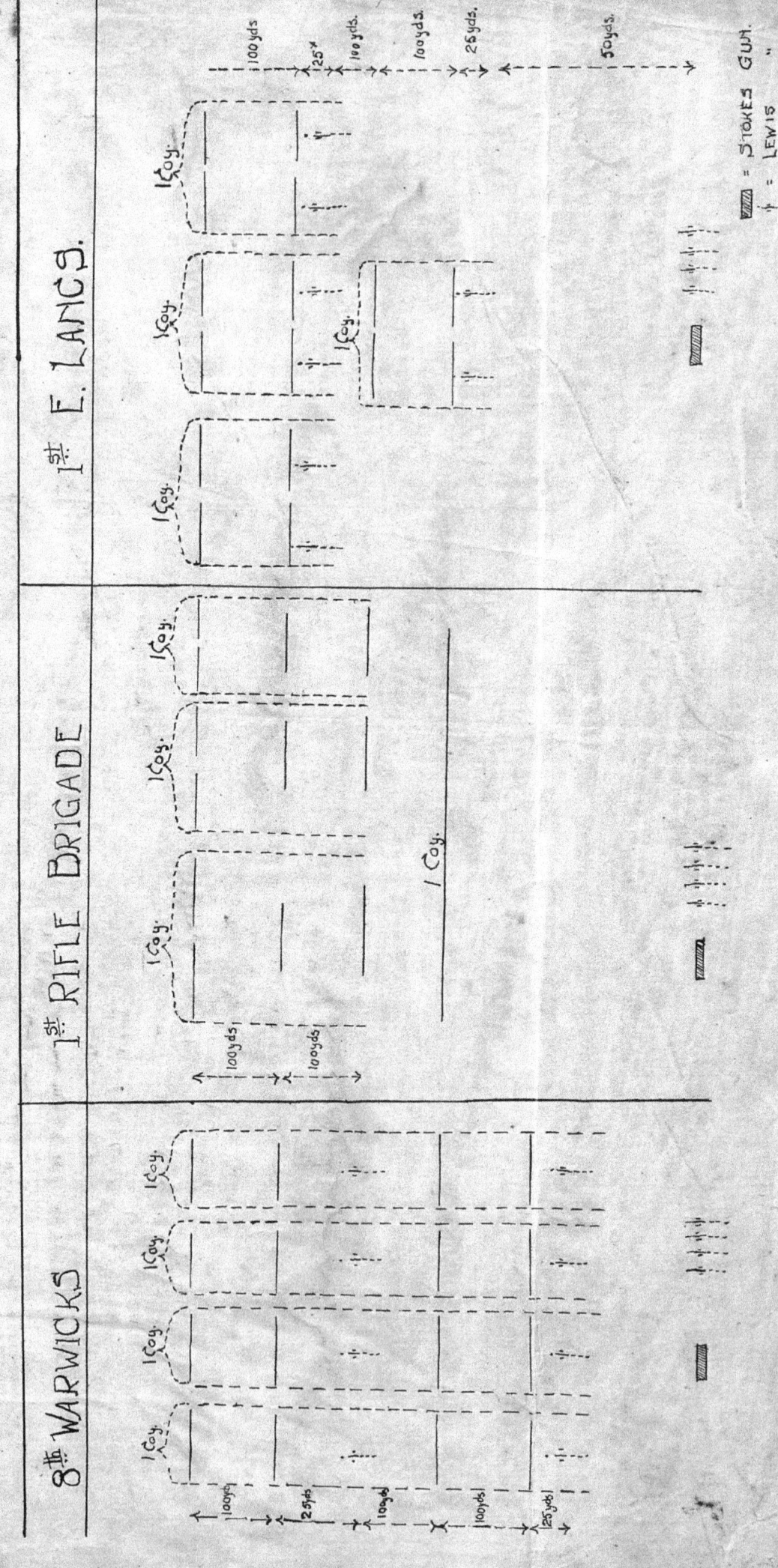

4th Division G.S.
July 1916

Appendix "G"

SECRET.

~~APPENDIX "D"~~   4th Div.Arty B.17.

APPENDIX "F6"

4th Div. G.

Reference 4th Div. GGG/766/71 -

The following is a short narrative of the dispositions and action of Div. Artillery during the operations leading up to and culminating in the assault on July 1st.

Grouping.

The Artillery of the Division was organized in 3 Groups - Left, Centre and Right.

These corresponded to the 3 Artillery Brigades belonging to the Division, with exception that 2 batteries were lent by 48th Div. Artillery and grouped with the left group - O.C.29th Brig. R.F.A.

To each group certain frontages on the German Line were allotted with the areas due East of these. The O.C's Groups were responsible for allotting definite and permanent barrage lines within these areas, and any special bombardments were directed on to these lines.

This method of grouping facilitated the dispositions for an advance, had this taken place, in that Artillery Brigade Commanders were throughout in charge of their own batteries and these only, with exception of the two 48th Div. batteries mentioned.

Forward Batteries.

These latter 2 48th Div. Batteries were dug in in a forward position 500 yards behind our own front line and were only to be used during the attack on, and to form a barrage, about the third objective, as the range to this from the other batteries was very great.

As things went these batteries were not used.

Besides these two batteries another belonging to the 14th Brig. R.F.A. was dug in about 1200 yards behind our front trenches for the purpose of cutting some of the more distant wire. It only commenced firing on 'V' day.

Tasks.

The 18 pdrs of the Left and Centre Groups with one battery of the Right Group were specially detailed for wire-cutting during the day and forming barrages at night to block communications.

The Right Group (less 1 battery) was specially detailed for keeping all cut wire open and for bringing periodical concentrations of fire on selected points during the night.

O's.C. Left and Centre Groups reported every evening to O.C. Right Group what wire had been cut during the day, so that Right Group might attend to this during the night. One of the latter's batteries was an enfilade battery.

4.5" Hows. were used -

(i) to bombard selected points
(ii) to assist in forming barrages.

2.

Tasks. (cont'd).

2" Trench Mortars cut all wire and bombarded front trenches within their reach. Their action was ~~not~~ most effective.

Heavy Trench Mortars bombarded the N. end of BEAUMONT HAMEL and trenches immediately N. of it.

Disposition for Advance.

At 10 pm. on the night preceding the assault two batteries of 32nd Brigade (134 and 135), which were at the greatest range from German front line came out of action and spent the night at BEAUSSART, the intention being to have these batteries in hand and ready to move forward immediately should circumstances permit.

The remainder of this Brigade was to be brought out of action, if, and as soon, as the course of the action permitted.

The 29th Brigade was to be the next to move and positions for this were to be reconnoitred, as soon as the 3rd Objective was taken.

Liaison with Infantry.

This was provided for by detailing an Artillery Officer to accompany each Infantry Brigade Hd. Qrs and N.C.Os. with Signallers to accompany Infantry Battalions.

On the actual day no information was obtained, either from Officers or N.C.Os., as no Brig. Hd.Qrs proceeded beyond our front trench, and the N.C.Os. lost touch with Battalion Hd.Qrs as soon as they got into the German Lines.

F.O.O's.

In addition to the above, F.O.O's were detailed to move forward as soon as 2nd Objective was taken, to establish O.P's for future work and primarily to act as Intelligence Officers.
They were to be accompanied by visualling signal parties.

Communications

A good system was designed, but owing to lack of wire it could not be finished in time, and in the end it had to be made up as well as cable would allow.
Luckily communications held throughout.

Action on Day of Assault.

The Artillery Programme was adhered to up to a certain hour and lifts carried out strictly according to Time Table. For a long time the situation was so confused, that it was impossible to vary the tasks, and time table, laid down for the artillery, but as soon as reports became clearer the barrage was dropped from time to time on to different parts of the front, to try and cover our own Infantry as well as possible. All the guns were controlled by Hd.Qrs Div.Arty throughout, as it was only at Hd. Qrs that any judgment of the situation could be formed by comparing the various reports coming in from time to time. This system worked satisfactorily as communication was good throughout.

                    Sd. D.C.SPENCER SMITH. Major R.A. for
                              Brigadier General,

18/7/16.   Commanding 4th Divisional Artillery

****

G.S. 4th Division
July 1916.

Appendix "I"

REPORT.

APPENDIX. I

Communications during the action of July 1st '16.

The following system was adopted during the action of July 1st.

Lines were buried from Divisional Headquarters by three routes to a report centre, and thence on to Infantry and R.F.A. Brigades and the front line trenches.

One route was used for telephone circuits and the other two for Morse.

At the Divisional Observation Post a telephone exchange was used and a commutator for the Morse circuits.

Each Infantry and Artillery Brigade had a magneto telephone and a Diii telephone for Morse signals installed.

All circuits were controlled from Report Centre.

Morse messages from Headquarters were plugged through the report centre on the call being received on the instrument there. This system was found to answer very well.

Lines were buried forward to the front line trenches and barrow parties were in waiting to carry these lines forward with the Brigade Headquarters as they advanced.

One of these spurs was manned in the front line trenches so that battalions or runners from the front could make use of it.

Two Divisional visual stations were established, one of which proved useful, in, that it picked up messages from a party who had fought its way well forward and was asking for more bombs.

WIRELESS. Two wireless sets were in waiting at 12th Brigade Headquarters. The intention was, that when the Brigade moved forward one set should be erected at old brigade Headquarters and the other at the proposed new H.Qrs and be used in the interval, that would have occurred whilst wires were being laid forward.

This brigade did not attempt to establish an Advanced Report Centre in the German lines.

One wireless set went with this party, but on reaching the point arranged, near Point 62, the set was damaged by machine gun fire before the station could begin working.

/Visual

Visual communication was opened from here to the old Brigade H.Q.

The order then came for the proposed Advanced Brigade H.Q. to withdraw.

BATTALIONS. When battalions moved forward messages were sent back to Bdes by visual and by runners.

Had the advance been maintained lines would have been carried forward to battalions as they moved forward. In one case a line was carried forward and maintained for about an hour.

PIGEONS. Each Brigade had eight pigeons distributed amongst its battalions, but these do not seem to have been used, as only one pigeon came back and that carried no message of any value.

All pigeons have returned to the loft with the exception of four birds.

All the lines buried in the 6' trenches held. Communication to Infantry and Artillery Brigades was maintained throughout without interruption.

Runners were held in waiting at the Divisional Report Centre, to take forward any letter correspondence that might have come from the Division.

Two motor despatch riders were also kept there to take back any letter correspondence that might come from Brigades to Division.

I consider that if an advance had been made, the two Divisional Visual Stations would have been of great value; as affairs turned out the wires were sufficient.

Captain,

8/7/16.   O.C., Signals, 4th Division.

4th Division G.S.
July 1916

Appendix "J"

Reference

- ▲ = Grenades.
- ▬ = S.A.A.
- ● = R.E. Depôt.
- ▲ = T.M. Ammunition
- ● = Rations
- ▬ = Water (tins)
- ●〜 = " (tanks & pipe line)
- → = Forward Road
- ← = Return Road
- ▬ = Div. Dump
- ⊢┼┼⊣ = Trench Railway

<u>Note.</u> Positions only approximate.

G.S. 4th Division
July 1914.

Appendix "K"

CASUALTIES 1/7/16.

APPENDIX "K"

10th Brigade.

Officers.

	Killed.	Wounded.	Missing.	Wounded and Missing.	Missing believed Killed.	Total.
1st R. Warwicks.	-	2	-	-	-	2.
2nd Seaforths.	12	10	-	2	-	24.
1st R. I. Fus.	-	5	-	-	-	5.
2nd R. Dub. Fus.	2	12	-	-	-	14.
10th Bde. M.G.Coy.	1	1	1	-	1	4.
10th T.M. Btty.	-	-	-	-	-	-

49

Other Ranks.

	Killed.	Wounded.	Missing.	Wounded and Missing.	Missing believed Killed.	Total.
1st R. Warwicks.	15	57	-	-	3.	75.
2nd Seaforths.	56	218	100.	-	-	374.
1st R. I. Fus.	14	111	11	-	-	136.
2nd R. Dub. Fus.	52	222	40.	-	-	314.
10th Bde M.G.Coy.	2	15	7	-	-	24.
10th T.M. Btty.	-	2	-	-	-	2.

925

11th Brigade.

Officers.

	Killed.	Wounded.	Missing.	Wounded and Missing.	Missing believed Killed.	Total.
Somerset L.I.	4	9	5	1	7	26.
1st East Lancs.	3	6	1	4	3	17.
1st Hants.	10	16*	-	-	-	26.
1st Rifle Bde.	7	7*	1	2	3	20.
1/6th R.Warwicks.	5	11	3	3	-	22.
1/8th R.Warwicks.	6	16	-	3	-	25.
11th Bde M.G.Coy.	1	2*	-	-	1	4.
11th T.M. Btty.	1	4	-	-	-	5.

145

Other Ranks.

	Killed.	Wounded.	Missing.	Wounded and Missing.	Missing believed Killed.	Total.
Somerset L.I.	47.	171.	232.	-	-	450.
1st East Lancs.	65	251.	169.	-	-	485.
1st Hants.	113.	249.	197.	-	-	559.
1st Rifle Bde.	52	239	163	-	-	454.
1/6th R.Warwicks.	43	173	234.	-	-	450.
1/8th R.Warwicks.	52	238	273.	-	-	563.
11th Bde M.G.Coy.	3	54	8	-	-	65.
11th T.M. Btty.	5	17	12.	-	-	34.

3060

12th Brigade.

Officers.

	Killed.	Wounded.	Missing.	Wounded and Missing.	Missing believed Killed.	Total.
1st Kings Own.	6	13	3	-	-	22.
2nd Lancs Fus.	5	12	1	1	-	19.
2nd Essex.	5	13*	1	3.	-	22.
2nd W. Ridings.	3	17	-	-	-	20.
12th Bde M.G.Coy.	1	3	-	-	-	4.
12th T.M. Btty.	-	2	-	-	-	2.

89

Other Ranks.

	Killed.	Wounded.	Missing.	Wounded and Missing.	Missing believed Killed.	Total.
1st Kings Own.	37	209	177.	-	-	423.
2nd Lancs.Fus.	21	241	101	-	-	363.
2nd Essex.	43	167	205.	-	-	415.
2nd W. Ridings.	21	292	61.	-	-	374.
12th Bde M.G.Coy.	8	47	6	-	-	61.
12th T.M. Btty.	3	21	26.	-	-	50.

1686

* Includes 1 Died of Wounds in each case.

4th Division G.S.
July 1916

Appendix "L"

SECRET

Q.O.S./785/A.
D.D.O.S. No.H.O./16/3/3.
VIII Corps No.308/Q.S.

Fourth Army.

It is considered necessary to bring to notice that the stock of spare gun parts, especially for the heavier natures of ordnance, is extremely short, and in many cases no stock exists.

Many heavy and siege batteries have recently come out to this country with spares deficient, and so long as the number of complete artillery units that are sent out from home continues to be so numerous, the home authorities state that it is not possible to maintain the supply of spare parts.

When heavy fighting is in progress, it may therefore happen that guns will be out of action through want of spares, which it is not at the moment possible to provide.

The attention of the War Office is being drawn to this scarcity in supply, but it is considered that Armies should realize the position and be prepared to make the best arrangements possible to meet the difficulties that may arise.

(Sd) R.C.MAXWELL,

G.H.Q.,
    4th July 1916.

Lieut-General,
Quartermaster General.

2.

4th Division.
29th Division.
31st Division.
35th Division.
48th Division.
G.S.
G.O.C., R.A.
B.G.R.A., C.H.A.
A.D.O.S.

For information.

B.J. Lang

VIII Corps H.Q.,
6-7-16.

Lieut-Colonel,
A.Q.M.G.

4th Division Q. Thro' DADOS

Noted and returned.

7.7.16.   [signature] Capt.
                                           S.C., 4th Div. Arty.

AA & QMG 4 Div

Noted & returned
[signature] McKirdy Capt
DADOS 4 Div

(PA)

SECRET

4Dv QC /177

VIIIth. Corps. G.S. 15/3/A.

4th. Division.	G.S.
29th. Division.	G.O.C.R.A.
~~48th. Division.~~	B.G.R.A.G.H.A.
48th. Division.	Corps Park.
Corps Siege Park.	

HEADQUARTERS,
8th CORPS.
ADMINISTRATIVE STAFF.

No..........
Date..........

1.   The following instructions were given by the Reserve Army today.

(a) Dumps of ammunition whether at the guns or in Divisional gun dumps are to be reduced to the following:-

		Remarks.
18 pdr.	400 rounds per gun.	Including 150 rounds to be kept in divisional dumps.
4.5" How.	300 " " "	-ditto-
4.7	150 " " ")	No reserve for these
60 pdr.	40 " " ")	natures will be kept
6" How. (30 cwt).	100 " " ")	in divisional
6" How. (25 cwt).	100 " " ")	dumps.
6" Gun.	10 " " "	
8" How.	16 " " "	
9.2" How.	10 " " "	
12" How.	30 " " "	
15" How.	Nil.	~~As the only howitzer is out of action.~~ left

(b) Steps will be taken as soon as possible to take all surplus ammunition away from all guns (except Field Guns) and after retaining sufficient to fill echelons including Parks the remainder will be returned to PUCHEVILLERS railhead and placed in Reserve Army Reserve.

(c) No more field gun ammunition will be sent up to Divisions until the dumps in front of Park have been reduced to the figures mentioned in paragraph (a) above.

(d) Immediate steps will be taken to fill all battery wagons and D.A.C's to their authorised establishment.

2.   It will be noted that the above instructions aim at reducing the amount of ammunition locked up in forward positions where it is not fluid, while the maximum amount possible is kept on wheels or in Army reserve where it is fluid and available for switching off in any direction as required.

3.   Guns and Howitzers transferred to another Corps will immediately be struck off strength, their ammunition vehicles transferred full and surplus dumped ammunition returned to railhead.

4. An account

4.   An account will be kept by VIIIth. Corps "Q" shewing the amount in hand in front of Corps and Siege Parks with each Heavy and Siege Battery and indents for ammunition will only be rendered to retain the dumps at the strength now authorised. The battery wagons and Battery Ammunition Columns of 4.7 and 60 pounder batteries will only be drawn on in emergency.

5.   Ammunition will not be issued by Corps or Siege Parks without reference to VIIIth. Corps "Q".

B. J. Lang

7th. July, 1916.

Lieutenant Colonel,
A. Q. M. G., VIIIth. Corps.

Secret

4th.Div. No. Q.C.179

A.D.M.S.
4th.Div. Supply Column.
4th.Div. Train.
A.D.V.S.
D.A.D.O.S.

An Allied Airship may be expected to be cruising in this area during the ensuing 3 weeks.

The type of the ship is as depicted below.

It is painted black and has no national markings.

Copy

10th July 1918.

Major,
D. for A.A. & Q.M.G., 4th Division.

- S E C R E T -
****

4th Divn GGG/
VIII Corps No. G.1906

4th Division.

With reference to my G.1766 of the 30th June.
An Allied Airship may be expected to be cruising in the Third, Fourth and Reserve Army areas during the ensuing 3 weeks.
The type of the ship is as depicted on the silhouette attached herewith. The ship is painted black and has no national markings.

8th Corps.H.Qrs.
9th July 1916.

Sd/ W. RUTHVEN. B.G.
General Staff., VIII Corps.

(2)

~~10th.11th.12th Inf.Bde.~~
~~4th Div Arty.~~
~~O.R.E.~~
~~" Q "~~
~~21st West.Yorks.Regt.~~

For information. 1 Copy is forwarded herewith.
Every unit should be informed of the contents of the above letter. Please inform all administrative units.

Captain.
General Staff., 4th Division.

10th July 1916.

Small British Airship.
Dirigeable Anglais Petit.

SECRET.

Headquarters,
    4th Division.

I

      The recent readjustment of boundaries between the 4th and 29th Divisions involved the handing over of the following rations :-

	Iron Rations.	Jam & Oxo.
"F" Street Forward Dump	3325	3325
AUCHONVILLERS (Defense Scheme)	2240	-

      Will you kindly acknowledge the receipt of these quantities, which I understand, have been verified by your S.S.O.

J. C. Bell Capt.
for
Major General,
Commanding 29th Division.

20th July, 1916.

II

TRAIN

Can you verify, if not send direct to 10th Bde.

21/7/16

C H Martin Major
D A Q M G

III

10 H. Bde.

Passed to you, please. These have not been verified as nothing was known of this.

21/7/16

R P Edwards
Major

P.T.O. SSO 4th Division

4th Div. Q

AUCHONVILLERS. 2000 boxed iron rations were taken over by this bde. from 86" bde.. All except 400 rations were sent to train by us before handing over to 12" bde.. Your office was advised of this by wire.

F. Street   The 86" bde did not hand over their rations then to this bde..

23/7/16.

McCracken Capt &c
f. Brig. Gen.
cmdg. 10" Inf. bde.

4th.Div. Q.C. 185.

Headquarters,

 29th Division.

   Reference your S.A. 800/12, re rations handed over.

   The 2000 rations handed over by the 86th Brigade to the 10th Brigade in AUCHONVILLERS is the only transaction that can be traced.

25/7/16.

           Major,
       D. for A.A. & Q.M.G., 4th Division.

29th Divn.

Reference your
S.A. 800/12.
fra rations handed
over.

The 2000 rations
handed over by
the 86 E Bde to
the 10th Bde in
Auchonvillers is
the only transaction
that can be traced.

~~2000~~
give receipt for 2000
iron Rations —

S E C R E T.   4th. Div. Q.C. 182.

Headquarters,

    VIIIth Corps.

        Reference VIII Corps Q.S. 60 dated 12/6/16.
        I have the honour to report as follows :-

(a).	10th.Field Amb: at LOUVENCOURT. (rations)	11th.Field Amb: at VAUCHELLES. (rations)	12th.Field Amb: at BERTRANCOURT. (rations)
Biscuits.	2345	2000	2000
Presd Meat.	2068	1650	1984
Jam.	1600	1866	1867
Tea.	2688	1920	450
Sugar.	2133	2133	427
Butter.	320	640	640
M & V (in lieu of Bacon)	1728	2016	2016

(b).   The total numbers consumed are approximately 400 meat rations and in addition 400 tea rations.

(c).   The rations have been handed over to the 12th Division.

(d).   The rations are in good condition.

    The surpluses in 10th Field Ambulance are accounted for by the fact that in the course of operations the 10th Field Ambulance took over a dressing station that had previously been rationed by the 12th Field Ambulance.

                                            Major-General.,

20th July 1916.   Commanding 4th Division.

VIIIth. Corps, Q.S. 60.

SECRET

4th. Division. ✓
29th. Division.
48th. Division.

===========================

2,000 reserve rations and certain extras were issued to each Field Ambulance prior to the commencement of operations, will you please state :-

(a) Present location of these rations and the amount at each place.
(b) Number (if any) consumed.
(c) Unit in whose charge rations now are.
(d) Any general remarks regarding the condition of the rations remaining.

B.J. Lang
Lieutenant Colonel,
A. Q. M. G., VIIIth. Corps.

12th. July, 1916.

TRAIN (thro ADMS).

The train to prepare a statement in conjunction with the OC Field Ambulances and return to Q thro ADMS for his remarks.

G.W. Mackin, Major
D.A.Q.M.G.

R 12/7/16.

4th Division. (A.D.M.S.)
List of Rations herewith. All are in good condition.
R.P. Steward, Major, R.A.M.C.
SSO 4th Division

10/7/16

SECRET.　　　　　　4th DIVISION - BILLETING LIST.　　　4th Div.Q/268.

Ref. map sheet 27 1/40,000.

Divisional Head-Quarters,	COUTHOVE Chateau, F.21.a.
H.Q. Divisional Artillery,	" " "
R.A. units, including Div.Amm.Col.,	On the move.
Heavy and Medium Trench Mortar Batteries,	OUDEZEELE.
H.Q. Divisional Engineers,	COUTHOVE Chateau, F.21.a.
4th Div. Signal Coy.,	" " "
9th Field Coy. R.E.,	E.17.b 2.9.
1/1st Renfrew Field Coy. R.E.,	D.7.c 5.2.
1/1st Durham Field Coy. R.E.,	HOUTKERQUE.
10th Inf. Bde. H.Q.,	PROVEN, F.7.
" " " Machine Gun Coy.,	E.12.b 2.2.
1st R. Warwick Regt.,	'K' Camp, L.3.d.
2nd Seaforth Highlanders,	'L' Camp, L.3.d.
1st R. Irish Fusiliers,	'M' Camp, F.27.c.
2nd R. Dublin Fusiliers,	'N' Camp, F.27.a.
Trench Mortar Battery,	Farm E.12.d 8.6.
11th Inf. Bde. H.Q.,	Chateau WORMHOUDT, C.16.
" " " Machine Gun Coy.,	ROOSENDAEL, I.5.d.
1st Somerset Light Inf.,	WORMHOUDT, C.16.
1st East Lancs.,	" " "
1st Hants,	" " "
1st Rifle Brigade,	" " "
Trench Mortar Battery,	ROOSENDAEL, I.5.d.
12th Inf. Bde. H.Q.,	HOUTKERQUE.
" " " M.G.Coy.,	Farm D.18.b 3.7.
1st King's Own R.L. Regt.,	HERZEELE.
2nd Lancs. Fusiliers,	"
2nd Essex Regt.,	HOUTKERQUE.
2nd West Riding Regt.,	"
Trench Mortar Battery,	Farm E.13.b 6.6.
H.Q. 4th Divisional Train,	ST.JEAN-TER-BIEZEN.
H.Q. Coy.,	F.25.a.
No. 2 Coy.,	F.25.a 2.9.
No. 3 Coy.,	WORMHOUDT.
No. 4 Coy.,	HOUTKERQUE.
A.D.M.S.,	COUTHOVE Chateau, F.21.a.
10th Field Ambulance,	WATOU, K.4.b.
11th " "	WORMHOUDT.
12th " "	HERZEELE.
3a Sanitary Section,	WATOU, K.4.b.
A.D.V.S.,	COUTHOVE Chateau, F.21.a.
Mobile Vet. Section,	Farm E.12.d 5.8.
A.P.M.,	COUTHOVE Chateau, F.21.a.
Div. Supply Column,	HERZEELE.
D.A.D.O.S.,	COUTHOVE Chateau, F.21.a.
21st West Yorks (Pioneers),	WINNEZEELE, J.17.a.
Reserve Coy.,	Farms, F.13.a and E.18.b.

24/7/16.

W.P.H.HILL, Lt.Col.,
A.A. & Q.M.G., 4th Division.

SECRET.   XIV Corps No. Q.Z./101.

Guards Division.

      Attention is drawn to Second Army Routine Order No. 310.

      All stores in your possession other than those mentioned in paragraphs (1), (2) and (3) of that order will be handed over to the 4th Division.

2.   The three motor cycles for Field Companies and the Thresh Disinfector on Foden Lorry now in your possession will be handed over to the 4th Divisional Supply Column.

3.   Files of Second Army Routine Orders and all documents affecting the area only, such as the scheme drawn up by you for the collection of stores in the event of an advance, should likewise be handed over to the 4th Division.

24-7-16.

Lieutenant-Colonel.,
A.Q.M.G., XIV Corps.

Copy to 4th Division.

Second Army Routine Order

No. 310   -   Special Stores.

---------*---------

Para. 3 of Army Routine Order No. 277 is cancelled.

The only stores to accompany formations or units on transfer are:-

(1) Those authorised by Mobilisation Store Tables (Army Form G.1098).

(2) Those authorised on a definite scale per unit by General Routine Orders.

(3) Lamps or lanterns specially issued for billets and horse-lines (those issued for tents and huts will not be taken).

All other stores will be handed over by formations or units on transfer under arrangements to be made by Corps Headquarters.

(PA)

Held in readiness for incoming division

1. List of troops to be rationed in the week
2. List of troops in area for accommodation.
× 3. Billetting list of the division
4. Sketch map showing Ammunition Supply and R.E. Dumps.
5. ditto traffic routes.
× 6. Baths short statement.
× 7. Canteens
× 8. Theatres etc.
× 9. List of employments —

× Should be sent to the division before hand if possible.

Required from New Area.

1. Billetting list of division.
2. List of Employments
3. Canteens etc to be taken over.
4. Watering Scheme —

A.A.Q.M.G. 4th Division.

As requested I beg to make some remarks about recent entraining and detraining for future consideration.

1. Generally all units of this bde. consider that arrangements made were most excellent.

2. Instead of 3 hours for horses and wagons and 1½ hours for troops being at entraining station previous to departure of train 2 hours and ¾ hours would be ample time.

3. If units have to march to entrain more than 3 miles officers chargers should be allowed to entrain ½ an hour before departure of train.

4. All billeting parties going in advance should consist of 4 C.Q.M. sergts. 4 cyclist orderlies and 1 officer (preferably the 2nd in command); 8 bicycles should be taken and officers horse, or 9 bicycles.

5. One unit in this bde. managed to supply dinner to men cooked on cooks wagon and also at end of journey had hot water ready for tea immediately after detraining. This cooking was done on the train. Perhaps French railway authorities would not allow this to be done generally however, but it can be done if journey necessitates it.

6.   It seems unnecessary for such small units as T.M. battery to be divided into 4 teams. There is plenty of room on 1st team for them. Especially so, would this be more convenient as usually bde H.Q. wagons are T.M. batt. transport and their rations can go with bde H.Q. During last move rations for T.M. batt. had to be divided into 4 lots equal proportions being carried by each of 4 infantry units.

26/7/16.

W. McCracken Capt s.c.
10" Inf. bde.

SECRET-

4th Divn Q.R.1150/5

The 4th Division with S.A.A & Grenade Portion of D.A.C less R.A. and motor vehicles will entrain in accordance with the attached Time Tables.
MARCHE indicates the official train number.
Time - continental - e.g

Date   Hour of departure
21/7   21/19   = 9.19 p.m. 21st July.

(1) The R.A will proceed by march route under instructions that will be issued later.

(2) Motor vehicles except cars with Staff Officers will move as convoys on July 22nd and 23rd via BEAUVAL-DOULLENS-ST POL - LILLERS - HAZEBROUCK - WORMHOUDT.

(3) The Divisional Supply Column will move under instructions to be issued by the D.D.S & T. Reserve Army.

(4) The D.A.A & Q.M.G. will proceed on the 21st instant with Captain Hewitt.1st R.War. Regt. to H.Qrs, 14th Corps -

    Staff Officer attached to A.D.R.T. II Army.
    HAZEBROUCK - Captain Hewitt. 1st R.War.Regt.

    Staff Officer attached to A.D.R.T. III Army.
    DOULLENS - 2/Lieut: Wallace. R.E.Signal Coy.

These Officers will report to the A.D.R.T's at 6 p.m. on 22nd and will remain attached until completion of the move.

(5) The O.C. 21st West Yorkshire Regt will detail three parties consisting of 2 Officers and 100 other ranks to report to the R.T.O's at CANDAS, DOULLENS N. & S. stations at 19-17-18 hours respectively on 22nd instant, rationed for 23rd and 24th instants inclusive. These parties will assist in loading the trains under the directions of Brigade Transport Officers and will proceed by the last train leaving these stations on the 23rd instant to rejoin their units.

(6) Rendezvous for troops entraining at -

    DOULLENS N. will be the MOAT of CITADELLE.
    DOULLENS S. will be BOULEVARDE A.17 (a)
    CANDAS Short of the village on the BEAUVAL road.

All transport will reach the entraining point 3 clear hours and the personnel of units 1½ clear hours before the train is due to depart.

(7) Infantry Brigades will detail their Brigade Transport Offrs to act as Entraining Officers at their respective stations. These Officers will be responsible for superintending the entrainment of all troops leaving and will proceed on the last train with the parties mentioned in para. (5).

(8) Supplies. All troops will entrain with the current day's rations for the 23rd on the man and Supply Wagons loaded with rations for the 24th. Rations for 25th will be delivered on arrival in the new area.

The O.C. Train will arrange to hand over baggage and Supply wagons to R.A. Units, the Supply Wagons will be loaded with rations for consumption 24th.

O.C. Supply Column will arrange for the necessary lorries and accompany these units by roads.

(9) Water Carts and water bottles will be filled before leaving - horses will be watered before being trucked.

(10). Units will provide breast ropes for all trucks carrying horses.

(11) Detraining.

The following officers will proceed by the 1st trains from Stations as follows:-

DOULLENS N.   Lieut. Gandy. R.F.A.

DOULLENS.S.   Capt. Ravenscroft. Lancs. Fuslrs.

CANDAS.   2/Lieut. Carver. R.Dub. Fuslrs.

They will act as detraining officers on arrival under instructions which will be given them by D.A.A.& Q.M.G. and will remain on duty until the detrainment is completed.

(12). The O.C. Signal Coy. will detail two motor cyclist orderlies to report to H.Qrs. Q.14th Corps by 9 a.m. on 22nd to await the arrival of Captain Koster D.A.A.&.Q.M.G.

          W.P.H.Hill: Lt.Colonel.
          A.A. & Q.M.G., 4th Division.

Table shewing allocation of Units to trains and Hours of Departure.   Ref. Sheet 27. 1/40,000

Place of Entrainment   GODEWAERSVELDE.

Train No / Number No	Date	Time of Departure	Name of Unit	Rendezvous prior to entrainment	Remarks
No.1 W.B.2	21/4	9.33 ✓	12th Bde H.Q., No.4 Coy Sig. Co., No.4 Co Train, Cable Secn.	Q.11.d 3.1	arr 4.30 pm
No.2 W.B.4	21/4	14.45	1st Kings Own	Q.14.b N.W	arr 9.45 pm
No.3 W.B.6	21/4	14.33	2nd Lancs Fus, Bde Reserve Co.	Q.14.b S.E.	arr 12.30 am
No.4 W.B.8	21/4	21.33	2nd Essex Regt.	Q.18 Central	arr 4.30 am
No.5 W.B.10	22/4	2.33	2nd R. Irish Regt.	Q.11.d 3.1	arr 9.30 am
No.6 W.B.12	22/4	6.33 ✓	5th S. Lancs	Q.14.b N.W.	arr 1.30 pm
No.7 W.B.14	22/4	9.33	Div HQ, 10th Bde H.Q., No.2 Secn. Sig. Co., No.2 Co Train	Q.14.b S.E.	arr 4.30 pm
No.8 W.B.16	22/4	14.45 ✓	1st R. Warwicks	Q.18 Central	arr 9.45 pm
No.9 W.B.18	22/4	14.33 ✓	2nd Seaforth Hghrs	Q.11.d 3.1	arr 12.30 am
No.10 W.B.20	22/4	21.33 ✓	1st R. Irish Fus	Q.14.b N.W	arr 4.30 am
No.11 W.B.22	23/4	2.33 ✓	2nd R. Dublin Fus	Q.14.b S.E	arr 9.30 am
No.12 W.B.24	23/4	6.33 ✓	A & S. Hghrs	Q.18 Central	arr 1.30 pm
No.13 W.B.26	23/4	9.33 ✓	1st Som. L.I.	Q.11.d 3.1	arr 4.30 pm
No.14 W.B.28	23/4	14.45	1st E. Lancs Regt.	Q.14.b N.W	arr 9.45 pm
No.15 W.B.30	23/4	14.33	1st Hants Regt.	Q.14.b S.E.	arr 12.30 am
No.16 W.B.32	23/4	21.33	1st Rifle Brig.	Q.18 Central	arr 4.30 am
No.17 W.B.34	24/4	2.35	11th Field Arty, 128th How. Amm. Col.	Q.11.d 3.1	9.30 am 2nd
No.18 W.B.36	24/4	6.33	10th Fd Arty, 66th How. Ammn. Col.	Q.14.b N.W	arr 1.30 pm
No.19 W.B.38	24/4	9.33	3/4 5th Secn. Div. Ammn. Col.	Q.14.b S.E	arr 4.30 pm
No.20 W.B.40	24/4	14.45	3/4 6th Secn. Div. Ammn Col	Q.18 Central	arr 9.45 pm
No.21 W.B.41	24/4	14.33	4th Div. Ammn Col & 5th + 6th. Sections.	Q.11.d 3.1	arr 12.30 am 25th
W.B.42	24/7	21.33	2 Monmouths		

Table shewing allocation of units to trains and Hours of Departure   Ry sheet 27 40,000

Place of Entrainment   CASSEL

Train No & marche No	Date	Time of Departure	Name of Unit	Rendezvous prior to Entrainment	Remarks
No. 1 W.B. 1	21/7	8.31 ✓	12th Field Ambce	O.22.c.5.8	arr 3.30 pm
No 2 W.B. 3	21/7	13.51 ✓	Div. Sqn. H.Q. & No 1 Sec Sig. Co.	O.15.c.7.5	arr 8.50 pm
No. 3 W.B. 5	21/7	16.31 ✓	Cyclist Coy. H.Q. & No 1 Coy Div Train	O.15.c.7.5	arr 11.30 pm 5 haywagons belonging to Div Train, to go with No. 134, 135, 126, 127 & 128 Btties.
No 4 W.B. 7	21/7	19.11 ✓	W. Lancs Fd. Coy. San. Sec. Mob. Vet. Sec.	O.15.c.7.5	arr 2.11 am
No. 5 W.B. 9	22/7	0.31 ✓	H.Q. 14 F.A.B. 68th Bty R.F.A.	— " —	arr 7.30 am
No. 6 W.B. 11	22/7	4.31 ✓	88th Bty. R.F.A.	— " —	arr 11.30 am
No. 7 W.B. 13	22/7	8.31 ✓	86th	— " —	arr 3.30 pm
No. 8 W.B. 15	22/7	13.51 ✓	H.Q. 29 F.A.B. 125 Bty R.F.A.	— " —	arr 8.50 pm
No. 9 W.B. 17	22/7	16.31 ✓	126 Bty RFA	— " —	arr 11.30 pm
No. 10 W.B. 19	22/7	19.11 ✓	Div. Arty. H.Q. H.Q. 11th Bde No. 3 Sig. Sec. No 3 Coy. Train	— " —	arr 2.11 am
No. 11 W.B. 21	23/7	0.31 ✓	127 Bty R.F.A.	— " —	arr 7.30 am
No. 12 W.B. 23	23/7	4.31 ✓	128 Bty. R.F.A.	— " —	arr 11.30 am
No. 13 W.B. 25	23/7	8.31	H.Q. 32 F.A.B. 27 Bty R.F.A.	— " —	arr 3.30 pm
No. 14 W.B. 27	23/7	13.51	134 Bty. R.F.A.	— " —	arr 8.50 pm
No. 15 W.B. 29	23/7	16.31	135 — " —	— " —	arr 11.30 pm
No. 16 W.B. 31	23/7	19.11	Div. Eng. H.Q. 9th Fd Co R.E.	— " —	arr 2.11 am
No. 17 W.B. 33	24/7	0.31	3/4 14 Bde Am Col.	— " —	arr 7.30 am
No. 18 W.B. 35	24/7	4.31	3/4 29 — " —	— " —	arr 11.30 am
No. 19 W.B. 37	24/7	8.31	3/4 32 — " —	— " —	arr 3.30 pm
No. 20 W.B. 39	24/7	13.51	1/4 14 Bde Am Col 1/4 29 1/4 32		arr 8.50 pm

TIMETABLE OF MARCHES FOR 4th and 48th DIVISIONS.

Station																		
LA GORGUE	19.48	21.18	22.48	0.18	1.03	2.33	4.03	5.33	7.03	7.48	9.18	13.03	14.33	16.03	17.33	19.03		
MERVILLE	20.08	21.38	23.08	0.38	1.23	2.53	4.23	5.53	7.23	8.08	9.38	13.23	14.53	16.23	17.53	19.23		
BERGUETTI	20.47	22.17	23.47	1.17	2.02	3.32	5.02	6.32	8.02	8.47	10.17	14.02	15.32	17.02	18.32	20.02		
POPERINGE	19.23	20.51	21.51	23.23	0.51	1.51	2.51	4.51	5.50	7.08	8.59	12.31	13.58	15.25	16.50	18.19		
ABEELE	19.54	21.14	22.14	23.54	1.14	2.14	3.54	5.14	6.14	7.34	9.14	12.54	14.25	15.54	17.14	18.34		
GODEWAERKVELDE	20.13	21.33	22.33	0.13	1.33	2.33	4.13	5.33	6.33	7.53	9.33	13.13	14.45	16.13	17.33	18.53		
CAESTRE	20.33	21.53	22.53	0.33	1.53	2.53	4.33	5.53	6.53	8.13	9.53	13.33	15.13	16.33	17.53	19.13		
CASSEL	20.31	21.51	23.11	0.31	1.51	3.11	4.31	5.51	7.11	8.31	9.51	13.51	15.11	16.31	17.51	19.11		
HAZEBROUCK (arr	20.48	22.08	23.08	0.48	2.08	3.08	4.48	6.08	7.08	8.28	10.08	13.48	15.28	16.43	18.08	19.28		
(dep	20.59	22.19	23.39	0.59	2.19	3.39	4.59	6.19	7.39	8.59	10.19	14.19	15.39	16.59	18.19	19.39		
BERGUETTE	21.31	22.51	0.11	1.31	2.51	4.11	5.31	6.51	8.11	9.31	10.51	14.51	16.11	17.31	18.51	20.11		
LILIERS	21.41	23.01	0.21	1.41	3.01	4.21	5.41	7.01	8.21	9.41	11.01	15.01	16.21	17.41	19.01	20.21		
FOUQUEREUIL (arr	21.59	23.19	0.39	1.59	3.19	4.39	5.59	7.19	8.39	9.59	11.19	15.19	16.39	17.59	19.19	20.39		
(dep	22.09	23.29	0.49	2.09	3.29	4.49	6.09	7.29	8.49	10.09	11.29	15.29	16.49	18.09	19.29	20.49		
RAC^t de (arr	0.42	2.12	3.27	4.42	6.12	7.27	8.42	10.12	11.27	12.42	14.12	18.12	19.27	20.42	22.09	23.27		
FREVENT (dep	0.57	2.17	3.37	4.57	6.17	7.37	8.57	10.17	11.37	12.57	14.17	18.17	19.37	20.57	22.10	23.37		
DOULLENS (arr	2.13	3.33	4.53	6.13	7.33	8.53	10.13	11.33	12.53	14.13	15.29	19.32	20.53	21.53	23.33	0.52		
(dep	2.23	4.23	5.23	6.23	8.23	9.23	10.23	12.23	13.23	14.23	16.23	20.23	21.23	22.23	0.23	1.23		
MONDICOURT	2.55	4.55	5.55	6.55	8.55	9.55	10.55	12.55	13.55	14.55	16.55	20.55	21.55	22.55	0.53	1.55		

4th Division.

UNITS	NO.	DESCRIPTION	Off	O.R.	Horses H.D	Horses L.D	Vehicles 4W	Vehicles 2W	Bicycles
Divisional Units.	401	Divl H.Q.	15	70	8	54	3	2	2
	402	H.Q. Divl Artillery	4	20	2	18	1	1	6
	403	Divl Cavalry	6	155	6	165	5		
	404	Divl Cyclist Coy	9	197	4	2	3		203
	405	H.Q. & 1 Sec Signal Coy	2	86	2	62	8	2	8
10th Infantry Bde.	410	Bde H.Q.	4	25	4	23	4	1	9
	411	1st Royal Warwicks	30	981	17	48	11	9	9
	412	2nd Seaforths	30	981	17	48	11	9	9
	413	1st Irish Fusiliers	30	981	17	48	11	9	9
	414	2nd Royal Dublin Fus	30	981	17	48	11	9	8
	415	2 Sec Signal Coy	1	24		6	1		
	416	1/7 L. & S. Highldrs) 1/9 " ")	14	680	42	28	22	4	10
11th Infantry Brigade	420	Bde H.Q.	4	25	4	23	4	1	9
	421	1st Somerset L. I.	30	981	17	48	11	9	9
	422	1st E. Lancs	30	981	17	48	11	9	9
	423	1st Hants	30	981	17	48	11	9	9
	424	1st Rifle Brigade	30	981	17	48	11	9	8
	425	3 Sec Signal Coy	1	24		6	1		

4th Division.

UNITS	NO	DESCRIPTION	Off	O.R	Horses H.D.	Horses L.D.	Vehicles 4w	Vehicles 2w	Bicycles
12th Infantry Bde.	430	Bde H.Q.	4	25	4	23	4	1	
	431	1st Royal Lancs	30	981	17	48	11	9	9
	432	2nd Lancs Fus.	30	981	17	48	11	9	9
	433	2nd Essex	30	981	17	48	11	9	9
	434	2nd R. Irish	30	981	17	48	11	9	9
	435	4 Sec Signal Coy	1	24		6	1		8
	436	1/5 S Lancs	17	595	42	28	22	4	10
14th Bde R.F.A.	440	Bde H.Q.	5	38	4	34	2	1	1
	441	68th Battery	5	195	4	172	20 & 6 guns	1	1
	442	88th Battery	5	195	4	172	20	1	1
	443								
	444								
	445	Bde Amnm Col.	2	104	2	130	16	6	1
29th Bde R.F.A.	450	Bde H.Q.	5	38	4	34	2	1	1
	451	125th Battery	5	195	4	172	20	1	1
	452	126th "	5	195	4	172	20	1	1
	453	127th "	5	195	4	172	20	1	1
	454								
	455	Bde Amnm Col.	3	157	4	196	27	8	1
32nd Bde R.F.A.	460	Bde H.Q.	5	38	4	34	2	1	1
	461	27th Battery	5	195	4	172	20	1	1
	462	134th "	5	125	4	172	20	1	1
	463	135th "	5	125	4	172	20	1	1
	464								
	465	Bde Amnm Col.	3	157	4	196	27	8	1

4th Division.

UNITS	NO.	DESCRIPTION.	Off	O.R.	Horses H.D.	Horses L.D.	Vehicles 4w	Vehicles 2w	Bicycles
12th Bde R.F.A. (How)	470	86th Battery	5	194	4	172	20x	1	1 x 6 guns.
30th Bde R.F.A.	471	128th "	5	194	4	172	20x	1	1
	472								
	473								
	474	Ammn Col.	2	80	3	96	14	1	1
	475	Heavy Battery	5	163	90	32	18	1	1
	476	" Ammn Col.	1	29	23	3	4	1	1
	477								
Divl Ammn Col.	478	H.Q. Divl Ammn Col.	4	25	4		3	3	2
	479	No 1 Sectn.	2	111		144	21		
	479a	" 5 "	1	37		50	8		
	480	" 2 "	2	111		144	21		
	480a	" 5 "	1	37		50	8		
	481	" 3 "	2	111		144	21		
	481a	" 5 "	1	37		50	8		
	482	No 4 Section	2	87	30	87	20		
Divl Engineers.	483	H.Q. Divl Engineers.	3	10	2	10	1	3	1
	484	9th F. Coy.	6	212	4	74	6	13	33
	485	1/1 West Lancs F Coy TF	6	218	55	21	18	1	33
	486								
Divl Train (less transport with troops)	487	H.Q. & H.Q. Coy.	9	28	30	22	5	3	9
	488	No 2 Coy	4	59	12	18	4	2	7
	489	" 3 "	4	59	12	18	4	2	7
	490	" 4 "	4	59	12	18	4	2	7
Medical Units.	491	10th Fld Ambulance	10	225	39	29	18	6	1
	492	11th " "	10	225	39	29	18	6	1
	493	12th " "	10	225	39	29	18	6	1
	494	Divl Sanitary Sect	1	27	1		1		
	495	Divl Vet Sect	1	13	2	13			

Table shewing allocation of units to trains
and
Hours of Departure.   Ref. sheet 27, 1/40,000

Place of Entrainment   -   CASSEL.

Train No. & Marche No.	Date.	Time of Departure.	Name of unit.	Rendezvous prior to Entrainment.	Remarks.
No. 1 W.B.1	21/7	8.31	12th Field Ambulance	0.22.c 5.8	
No. 2 W.B.3	21/7	13.51	Div. Sqn., H.Q. and No. 1 Sec. Sig. Coy.	0.15.c 7.5	
No. 3 W.B.5	21/7	16.31	Cyclist Coy., H.Q. and No. 1 Coy. Div. Train	"	5 hay wagons belonging to Div. Train to go with No.134,135,126,127 & 128 Batteries.
No. 4 W.B.7	21/7	19.11	W.Lancs.Fd.Coy., San. Sec., Mob. Vet. Sec.	"	Contents of Div Store on this train
No. 5 W.B.9	22/7	0.31	H.Q. 14 F.A.B. 68 Bty. R.F.A.	"	
No. 6 W.B.11	22/7	4.31	88th Battery R.F.A.	"	
No. 7 W.B.13	22/7	8.31	86 th Battery R.F.A.	"	
No. 8 W.B.15	22/7	13.51	H.Q. 29 F.A.B. 125 Bty. R.F.A.	"	
No. 9 W.B.17	22/7	16.31	126 Bty. R.F.A.	"	
No.10 W.B.19	22/7	19.11	Div.Arty H.Q. H.Q., 11th I.B. No.3 Sec. Sig. Coy., No.3 Coy. Train.	"	
No.11 W.B.21	23/7	0.31	127th Bty. R.F.A.	"	
No.12 W.B.23	23/7	4.31	128th Bty. R.F.A.	"	
No.13 W.B.25	23/7	8.31	H.Q. 32 F.A.B. 27 Bty. R.F.A.	"	
No.14 W.B.27	23/7	13.51	134 Bty. R.F.A.	"	
No.15 W.B.29	23/7	16.31	135 Bty. R.F.A.	"	
No.16 W.B.31	23/7	19.11	Div.Engrs.H.Q. 9th Fd. Co. R.E.	"	
No.17 W.B.33	24/7	0.31	¾ 14 Bde.Am.Col.	"	
No.18 W.B.35	24/7	4.31	¾ 29 Bde.Am.Col.	"	
No.19 W.B.37	24/7	8.31	¾ 32 Bde.Am.Col.	"	
No.20 W.B.39	24/7	13.51	¼ 14 Bde.Am.Col. ¼ 29 " ¼ 32 "	"	

Train No.	Unit	Officers	O.R.	Horses H.D.	Horses L.D.	Vehicles 4 W.	Vehicles 2 W.	Bicycles	Godowaersvelde. Remarks.
1.	12th Bde.H.Q.	4	124	7	59	4	1		Nos. 1-16.
	No. 4 Sec.Sig.Co.	1	24		6	1	1	8	Type, Combatant
	4 Coy.Train	5	60	27	15	5	2	7	1 coach, 34 covered
	Cable Sec.Sig.Co.		35		30	4			and 13 flat.
	Total	10	243	34	110	14	4	15	
2.	1/Kings Own	23	914	12	62	22	4	9	Nos. 17-20. Type
3.	2/Lancs. Fus.	11	586	12	54	22	4	9	Parque. 1 coach
	Div.Res.Coy.	1	88						24 covered, 23 flat.
	Total	12	674	12	54	22	4	9	
4.	2/Essex	23	792	14	58	22	4	9	
5.	5/S. Lancs.	20	591	17	53	22	4	9	
6.	Div. H.Q.	8	83	6	90	3	2		
	10th Bde.H.Q.	4	74	6	36	4	1		
	2 Sec.Sig.Coy.	1	24	6			1		
	2 Coy. Train	5	64	19	15	5	2		
	Total.	18	245	37	141	13	5		
7.	1/R.Warwicks	20	874	16	55	22	4	9	
8.	2/Sea.Highrs.	22	862	16	58	22	4	9	
9.	1/R.Irish Fus.	26	852	15	60	22	4	9	
10.	2/R.Dub.Fus.	23	901	14	56	22	4	9	
11.	A.& S.Highrs.	15	688	17	57	22	4	9	
12.	Div.Arty.H.Q.	4	20	2	18	2		6	
	11th Bde.H.Q.	4	104	6	38	4	1		
	3 Sec.Sig.Coy.	1	24		6	1			
	3 Coy.Train	5	62	19	17	5	2	7	
	Total	14	210	27	79	12	3	13	
13.	1/Som.L.I.	17	835	28	43	22	4	9	
14.	1/East Lancs.	14	715	17	54	22	4	9	
15.	1/Hants.	23	853	19	50	22	4	9	
16.	1/Rifle Bde.	15	608	18	55	22	4	9	
17.	12th Fd.Ambce.	10	230	7	59	11	6		
18.	½ 5th Sec.D.A.C.	1	102	13	125	24			
19.	½ 6th Sec.D.A.C.	1	97	4	116	20			
20.	H.Q. and remainder Nos.5 & 6	3	76	4	31	4	4		
		1	34	6	40	5		1	
	Secs. D.A.C.	1	34		40	5		1	
	Total	5	144	10	111	14	4	2	

Cassel.

Train No	Unit	Officers	O.R.	Horses H.D.	Horses L.D.	Vehicles 4 W.	Vehicles 2 W.	Bicycles	Remarks
1.	10th Fd.Amb.	12	273	50	14	11	6		Any surplus vehicles in No. 3 train.
	86 How.Am.Col.	1	36	2	43	7			
	Total	13	309	52	57	18	6		
2.	11th Fd.Amb.	10	330	41	20	11	6		Any surplus vehicles in No. 3 train.
	128 How.Am.Col.	1	33		46	7			
	Total	11	363	41	66	18	6		
3.	Div. Sqadron	6	124		150	5			
	H.Q.& No. 1 Sec. Sig.Coy.	2	86	4	62	9	2	8	
	Total	8	210	4	212	14	2	8	
4.	Cyclist Coy.	3	102	4	2	2	1	105	The 5 hay wagons belonging to "Train" to go with 134, 135, 126, 127 and 128 Btys. respectively.
	H.Q.& No.1 Coy. Train	11	155	57	25	10	5	7	
	Total	14	257	61	27	12	6	112	
5.	Div.Eng.H.Q.	3	13	2	11	1	3	2	
	9th Fd. Co.	5	233	7	83	12	5		
	Total	8	246	9	94	13	8	2	
6.	H.Q.14 F.A.B.	5	38	3	33	2	2	1	
	68th Batty.	5	195	4	167	20	2		
	Total	10	233	7	200	22	4	1	
7.	88th Batty.	5	191	4	167	21	1	1	
8.	86th Batty.	6	197	6	167	22	2	2	
9.	H.Q.29 F.A.B.	5	44	4	34	3	1	1	
	125th Batty.	5	199	4	165	21	1	1	
	Total	10	243	8	199	24	2	2	
10.	126th Batty.	5	204	4	171	21	1	1	
11.	127th Batty.	5	195	4	172	21	1	1	
12.	128th Batty.	5	201		178	21	1	1	
13.	H.Q.32 F.A.B.	5	38	4	39	4	1	1	
	27th Batty.	5	195	4	172	20	2	1	
	Total	10	233	8	211	24	3	2	
14.	134th Batty.	5	197	4	172	20	2	1	
15.	135th Batty.	5	197	4	172	20	2	1	
16.	J.Lancs.Fd.Co.	7	160	67	13	12	6		
	Sanitary Sec.	1	28		1				
	Mob.Vet.Sec.	2	28		70	2	1		
	Total	10	216	67	84	14	7		
17.	½ 14 Bde.A.C.	1	99		124	17	5		Trains 1-16 Type Combatant, 1 carriage, 34 covered and 13 flat.
18.	½ 29 Bde.A.C.	2	116		151	22	6	1	
19.	½ 32 Bde.A.C.	2	118		148	20	7		
20.	¼ 14 Bde.A.C.	1	33	4	40	6	2		17-20 Type Parque 1 carriage, 24 covered and 23 flat.
	¼ 29 Bde.A.C.	1	38	4	48	7	2		
	¼ 32 Bde.A.C.	1	39	4	48	7	2		
	Total	3	110	12	136	20	6		

A covered truck holds either (a) 40 men
or (b) H.D horses
or (c) L.D horses

A flat holds three pairs of wheels easily and some long flats are on every train and hold five pairs of wheels.

4th Division.

UNITS	NO.	DESCRIPTION	Off	O.R.	Horses H.D	Horses L.D	Vehicles 4w	Vehicles 2w	Bicycles
Divisional Units.	401	Divl H.Q.	15	70	8	54	3	2	2
	402	H.Q. Divl Artillery	4	20	2	18	1	1	6
	403	Divl Cavalry	6	155	6	165	5		
	404	Divl Cyclist Coy	9	197	4	2	3		203
	405	H.Q. & 1 Sec Signal Coy	2	86	2	62	8	2	8
10th Infantry Bde.	410	Bde H.Q.	4	25	4	23	4	1	9
	411	1st Royal Warwicks	30	981	17	48	11	9	9
	412	2nd Seaforths	30	981	17	48	11	9	9
	413	1st Irish Fusiliers	30	981	17	48	11	9	9
	414	2nd Royal Dublin Fus	30	981	17	48	11	9	8
	415	2 Sec Signal Coy	1	24		6	1		
	416	1/9 L. & S. Highldrs) 1/9 " ")	14	680	42	28	22	4	10
11th Infantry Brigade	420	Bde H.Q.	4	25	4	23	4	1	9
	421	1st Somerset L. I.	30	981	17	48	11	9	9
	422	1st E. Lancs	30	981	17	48	11	9	9
	423	1st Hants	30	981	17	48	11	9	9
	424	1st Rifle Brigade	30	981	17	48	11	9	9
	425	3 Sec Signal Coy	1	24		6	1		8

4th Division.

UNITS	NO	DESCRIPTION	Off	O.R	Horses H.D.	Horses L.D.	Vehicles 4w	Vehicles 2w	Bicycles
12th Infantry Bde.	430	Bde H.Q.	4	25	4	23	4	1	
	431	1st Royal Lancs	30	981	17	48	11	9	9
	432	2nd Lancs Fus.	30	981	17	48	11	9	9
	433	2nd Essex	30	981	17	48	11	9	9
	434	2nd R. Irish	30	981	17	48	11	9	8
	435	4 Sec Signal Coy	1	24		6	1		
	436	1/5 S Roncs	17	593	42	28	22	4	10
14th Bde R.F.A.	440	Bde H.Q.	5	38	4	34	2	1	1
	441	68th Battery	5	195	4	172	20*	1	1 –6 gpns
	442	88th Battery	5	195	4	172	20*	1	1
	443								
	444								
	445	Bde Amnn Col.	2	104	2	130	16	6	1
29th Bde R.F.A.	450	Bde H.Q.	5	38	4	34	2	1	1
	451	125th Battery	5	195	4	172	20*	1	1
	452	126th "	5	195	4	172	20*	1	1
	453	127th "	5	195	4	172	20*	1	1
	454								
	455	Bde Amnn Col.	3	157	4	196	27	8	1
32nd Bde R.F.A.	460	Bde H.Q.	5	38	4	34	2	1	1
	461	27th Battery	5	195	4	172	20*	1	1
	462	134th "	5	195	4	172	20*	1	1
	463	135th "	5	195	4	172	20*	1	1
	464								
	465	Bde Amnn Col.	3	157	4	196	27	8	1

4th Division.

UNITS	NO.	DESCRIPTION.	Off	O.R.	Horses H.D.	Horses L.D.	Vehicles 4w	Vehicles 2w	Bicycles.
12th Bde R.F.A. (How)	470	86th Battery	5	194	4	172	20ˣ	1	1 x 6 guns.
30th Bde R.F.A.	471	"	5	194	4	172	20ˣ	1	1
	472								
	473								
	474	Ammn Col.	2	80	3	96	14	1	1
	475	Heavy Battery	5	163	90	32	18	1	1
	476	" Ammn Col.	1	29	23	3	4	1	1
	477								
Divl Ammn Col.	478	H.Q. Divl Ammn Col.	4	25	4	24	3	3	2
	479	No 1 Sectn.	2	111		144	21		
	479a	"	1	37		50	8		
	480	" 2 "	2	111		144	21		
	480a	"	1	37		50	8		
	481	" 3 "	2	111		144	21		
	481a	"	1	37		50	8		
	482	No 4 Section	2	87	30	87	20		
Divl Engineers.	483	H.Q. Divl. Engineers.	3	10	2	10	1	1	1
	484	9th F. Coy.	6	212	4	74	6	3	33
	485	1/1 West Lancs F Coy TF	6	218	55	21	18	13	33
	486							1	
Divl Train (less transport with troops)	487	H.Q. & H.Q. Coy.	9	28	30	22	5	3	9
	488	No 2 Coy	4	59	12	18	4	2	7
	489	" 3 "	4	59	12	18	4	2	7
	490	" 4 "	4	59	12	18	4	2	7
Medical Units.	491	10th Fld Ambulance	10	225	39	29	18	6	1
	492	11th "	10	225	39	29	18	6	1
	493	12th "	10	225	39	29	18	6	1
	494	Divl Sanitary Sect	1	27	1		1		
	495	Divl Vet Sect	1	13	2	13			

TIMETABLE OF MARCHES FOR 4th and 48th DIVISIONS.

Station																			
LA GORGUE		19.48	21.18	22.48	0.18	1.03	2.33	4.03	5.33	7.03	7.48	9.18	13.03	14.33	16.03	17.33	19.03
MERVILLE		20.08	21.38	23.08	0.38	1.23	2.53	4.23	5.53	7.23	8.08	9.38	13.23	14.53	16.23	17.53	19.23
BERGUETTI		20.47	22.17	23.47	1.17	2.02	3.32	5.02	6.32	8.02	8.47	10.17	14.02	15.32	17.02	18.32	20.02
POPERINGHE		19.23	20.51	21.51	23.23	0.51	1.51	2.51	4.51	5.50	7.08	8.59	12.31	13.58	15.25	16.50	18.19
ABEELE		19.54	21.14	22.14	23.54	1.14	2.14	3.54	5.14	6.14	7.34	9.14	12.54	14.25	15.54	17.14	18.34
GODEWAERSVELDE		20.13	21.33	22.33	0.13	1.33	2.33	4.13	5.33	6.33	7.53	9.33	13.13	14.45	16.13	17.33	18.53
CAESTRE		20.33	21.53	22.53	0.33	1.53	2.53	4.33	5.53	6.53	8.15	9.53	13.33	15.13	16.33	17.53	19.13
CASSEL		20.31	21.51	23.11	0.31	1.51	3.11	4.31	5.51	7.11	8.31	9.51	13.51	15.11	16.31	17.51	19.11
HAZEBROUCK	arr	20.48	22.08	23.08	0.48	2.08	3.08	4.48	6.08	7.08	8.28	10.08	13.48	15.28	16.43	18.08	19.28
	dep	20.59	22.19	23.39	0.59	2.19	3.39	4.59	6.19	7.39	8.59	10.19	14.19	15.39	16.59	18.19	19.39
BERGUETTE		21.31	22.51	0.11	1.31	2.51	4.11	5.31	6.51	8.11	9.31	10.51	14.51	16.11	17.31	18.51	20.11
LILLERS		21.41	23.01	0.21	1.41	3.01	4.21	5.41	7.01	8.21	9.41	11.01	15.01	16.21	17.41	19.01	20.21
FOUQUEREUIL	arr	21.59	23.19	0.39	1.59	3.19	4.39	5.59	7.19	8.39	9.59	11.19	15.19	16.39	17.59	19.19	20.39
	dep	22.09	23.29	0.49	2.09	3.29	4.49	6.09	7.29	8.49	10.09	11.29	15.29	16.49	18.09	19.29	20.49
RAGᵗ de	arr	0.42	2.12	3.27	4.42	6.12	7.27	8.42	10.12	11.27	12.42	14.12	18.12	19.27	20.42	22.09	23.27
FREVENT	dep	0.57	2.17	3.37	4.57	6.17	7.37	8.57	10.17	11.37	12.57	14.17	18.17	19.37	20.57	22.10	23.37
DOULLENS	arr	2.13	3.33	4.53	6.13	7.33	8.53	10.13	11.33	12.53	14.13	15.29	19.32	20.53	21.53	23.33	0.52
	dep	2.23	4.23	5.23	6.23	8.23	9.23	10.23	12.23	13.23	14.23	16.23	20.23	21.23	22.23	0.23	1.23
MONDICOURT		2.55	4.55	5.55	6.55	8.55	9.55	10.55	12.55	13.55	14.55	16.55	20.55	21.55	22.55	0.55	1.55

SECRET.   4th Div. Q.C.95/1.

INSTRUCTIONS AS REGARDS TRANSPORT, ROADS, ROCKETS, GRENADE CARRIERS, PACKS, TENTS, VERY LIGHTS, S.A.A.

The reference numbers shown in the margin refer to 4th Div. Q.C.95 dated 9/6/16 and 4th Div. Operation Order No.58, para. 1, which will be modified accordingly.

VII.   1.   Rations will be delivered to the 1st Line Transport at BERTRANCOURT at such an hour as will allow of their being loaded on the cookers by 8 p.m. on Z day.

VIII & IX.   2.   The 11th Brigade will reconnoitre the MAILLY MAILLET - SERRE road as far as point K.35.b 2.9. The 10th Brigade will reconnoitre the forward track which is being laid out and runs South of SIXTH AVENUE crossing the MOUNTJOY trench at its junction with ROMAN ROAD and North of the REDAN. The 10th and 11th Brigades will report to the Division by 4 p.m. as to their practicability for transport.

An officer, with guides, will be sent by each unit to their Brigade Ration Dumps, where they will report to the Brigade Supply Officers. These guides will be prepared to lead the ration carriers forward if the Transport cannot proceed or to lead the Transport forward if the situation admits. The General Staff will decide this, and Staff Captains will be notified of the result of the decision and which of the two forward roads have been selected. On receipt of this information, the guides will be sent to the point where the route selected crosses the VALLADE trench or MOUNTJOY trench respectively.

3.   The forward tracks from BERTRANCOURT as far as the MAILLY MAILLET - SERRE road are allotted as follows. They will be taken into use, if weather permits, on and after Z day.

<u>Infantry.</u> By the track BERTRANCOURT - COURCELLES road Pt. J.33.d 8.3 - P.6.b 7.3 - J.31.c 8, by marked track to MAILLY MAILLET - SERRE road and return by the same route.

                                                                          <u>Artillery.</u>

2.

Artillery. P.4.b 5.4 – P.5.central to cemetery, then by track to J.31.c 8 to MAILLY MAILLET road and return by the same route.

Should tracks be impracticable, the main BERTRANCOURT – MAILLY MAILLET – SERRE road will be used.

The forward roads beyond MAILLY MAILLET – SERRE road are shewn in para. 2 and will be notified to units later.

_{XVI and 4th Div. Op. Order No. 38, para.}

4. Carriers.

The detail of carriers, and distribution, will be as follows. Instructions in Operation Orders referred to in the margin will be modified accordingly. Each Battalion will detail 2 officers, sergeant major, and 125 other ranks as permanent carriers. These will be distributed as follows:-

At 10th and 12th Brigade Dumps – Per Brigade, Brigade Dump Supply Officer and assistant. Per Battalion, 1 officer, 12 other ranks. Total, 6 officers, 48 other ranks (per Brigade).

At 11th Brigade Dump – Per Brigade, Brigade Dump Supply Officer and assistant. Per Battalion, 1 officer, sergeant major, and 75 other ranks. Total, 8 officers, 6 sergeant majors, 450 other ranks, per Brigade.

In Reserve, in trenches Q.1.d 4, Q.7.b 4.8.

10th and 12th Brigades – Per Battalion, 1 officer, sergeant major, and 113 other ranks. Total, 4 officers, 4 sergeant majors, 452 other ranks, per Brigade.

11th Brigade – Per Battalion, 1 officer, 50 other ranks. Total, 6 officers, 300 other ranks, per Brigade.

5. Hour of Assembly.

Brigades will arrange for their Brigade Dump carrying parties to be in their assembly trenches by 8 p.m. on Y/Z night. The Reserve carrying parties to be in their positions in trenches Q.1.d 4, Q.7.b 4.8 at the same hour. These Reserve carrying parties will move forward at 2.0 hours on Z morning in rear of 10th and 12th Brigades. Routes – 12th Brigade party by CHEEROI trench.

11th

3.

11th Brigade party by ROMAN ROAD.   10th Brigade party by FOURTH AVENUE.   Routes will be reconnoitred beforehand and the main MAILLY MAILLET - SERRE road will be avoided.

6.   Red rockets.

Distribution, 4 cases of 48 rockets with sticks, placed in Brigade Dumps.   Brigades will arrange to draw from D.A.C. up to the scale of one box or 12 rockets for each Battalion, for use in accordance with VIII Corps Operation Order No.3, para.6, dated 15/6/16.

7.   Very Lights.

Brigades will arrange to draw one box of one-inch Very pistol ammunition per Battalion for distribution.   Brigades will arrange to have the Very Light ammunition already placed in their dumps marked clearly with a red cross to facilitate distribution.

8.   S.A.A.

Brigades will draw direct from the D.A.C. sufficient S.A.A. to supply each man of assaulting troops up to a total of 170 rounds required.   The Lewis gun limbers will be complete up to the number of rounds laid down to be carried by them.

9.   Grenade Carriers.

1000 Sandbag carriers to carry 12 grenades each to be drawn by Brigades from D.A.D.O.S.   These will be placed in the Brigade grenade dugouts.

10.   Packs.

In the case of units requiring their packs, it will be impossible to select them.   Men, therefore, should be warned not to pack articles of personal value in them.   Such articles should be tied in bundles and marked with the labels issued by

D.A.D.O.S.

4.

D.A.D.O.S.   These bundles can then be placed in sandbags and stored under unit arrangements.   Packs will be filled in accordance with Field Service Manual, Infantry.

11. Tents.

These will be left standing.   Town Majors will indent on O.C. Reserve Coy. for sufficient men to take charge of the camps.

21/6/16.

W. P. H. HILL, Lt.Col.,
A.A. & Q.M.G., 4th Division.

S E C R E T.   4th Div. O.O. 129.

TRANSPORT OF AMMUNITION, STORES, etc.

Date.	Party. O.O.R.	Rendezvous.	Hour.	Work.	Route.	Destination.
13/14 to 19/20 incl.	1 84 1 84 1 30	EUSTON. TENDERLOIN. QUARRY.	9 p.m. 9.30 p.m. 9 p.m.	Carrying 2" Ammn. " " Dumping 2" Ammn.	EUSTON Trolly line. SUNKEN ROAD —	Div. T.M.Officer responsible for officers to meet and direct parties. Gun Positions. Quarry.
13/14	10th B.S.O. Permt. Party.	TENDERLOIN	9.30 p.m.	Dump 246 boxes S.A.A.	SUNKEN ROAD	6 G.S. wagons to be found by Div. Arty. TENDERLOIN.
14th	E.D. Permt. Party.	Div. Ration Dump.	9 a.m.	Dump {12000 rations {1000 poles {3000 sand- { bags.		Div. Dump S.O. responsible for organising dump. Train will find necessary wagons for this duty. Divisional DUMP.
14/15	10th B.S.O. Permt. Party.	TENDERLOIN.	9.30 p.m.	" 500 tins. 550 sandbags 550 poles.	SUNKEN ROAD	TENDERLOIN. Train will arrange for necessary wagons; 10th Bde. Dump S.O. for unloading party on arrival. Those tins will be placed in shelters. (at TENDERLOIN.)
15th	S.O. Permt. Party.	Div.Ration Dump.	3 a.m.	" 1000 tins 1300 poles 1300 sandbags		4 lorries to be detailed by O.C. Supply Col. to report Ration Dump at BERTRANCOURT by 6 p.m. 14th. To Div. Ration Dump.
15/16	O. O.R. 1 80	SUCRERIE.	9 p.m.	Carry 160 boxes S.A.A.	OHEROI TRENCH return 6th AVENUE.	VALLADE DUMP. The 160 boxes will be drawn from the reserve handed over by the 51st Division and stored in the SUCRERIE. Two trips are allowed for.
15/16	Permt. Party.	TENDERLOIN.	9.30 p.m.	Dump 720 boxes grenades.	SUNKEN ROAD	TENDERLOIN. These will be drawn by 7 wagons to be detailed by D.A.C. These grenades will be loaded at 6 p.m. by Div. Grenade party. The wagons to report to Lieut. FLINT at the Railway Crossing N. of MAILLY MAILLET at this hour.

(contd.)

Date.	Party.	O.O.R.	Rendezvous.	Hour.	Work.	Route.	Destination.
15/16	3	300	SUCRERIE.	9 p.m.	Carry 6800 rations 600 sandbags	CHEROI TRENCH return 6th AVENUE.	HYDE PARK CORNER, where they will be taken over by B.D.S.O. 12th Bde. This officer will detail a guide to conduct this party from the SUCRERIE to the Brigade Dump.
16/17	5	250	QUARRY	9 p.m.	" 247 boxes S.A.A.	SUNKEN ROAD	VALLADE DUMP. The B.D.S.O. 11th Bde. will meet this party and be responsible for the dumping in the Brigade Dump.
16/17	Permt. Party.		TENDERLOIN	9.30 p.m.	Dump 6800 rations 600 sandbags		TENDERLOIN. The B.D.S.O. 10th Bde. will be responsible for the dumping of these rations in selected shelters, Train for delivery at TENDERLOIN.
17/18	5	250	QUARRY	9 p.m.	Carry 247 boxes S.A.A.	CHEROI TRENCH return ROHAN ROAD.	HYDE PARK CORNER. The Bde.D.S.O. 12th Brigade will be responsible for a guide from QUARRY to Dump and for storing in Brigade Dump.
17/18	5	300	SUCRERIE	9 p.m.	" 6800 rations 600 sandbags	ROHAN ROAD return 6th AVENUE.	VALLADE DUMP. B.D.S.O. 11th Bde. will be responsible for a guide to meet and conduct this party and for the storing of these rations in the Brigade Dump. Train will be responsible for the delivery at the SUCRERIE.
18/19	4	200	SUCRERIE	9 p.m.	" 720 boxes grenades	ROHAN ROAD 6th AVENUE.	VALLADE DUMP. The Bde.D.S.O. 11th Bde. will be responsible for a guide to meet the party and conduct them to the Brigade Dump, and for storing in the Dump.
18/19	6	600	SUCRERIE	9.30 p.m.	" 500 sandbags 500 water tins 500 poles	CHEROI TRENCH ROHAN ROAD	HYDE PARK CORNER. The B.D.S.O. 12th Bde. will be responsible for a guide to meet and conduct these parties and for the storing of the water in the Dumps. The Train for loading up these stores from Divisional Dump during the day and sending them forward.
19/20	6	600	SUCRERIE	9 p.m.	" 500 sandbags 500 water tins 500 poles.	ROHAN ROAD 6th AVENUE	VALLADE DUMP. The B.D.S.O. 11th Bde. Dump will be responsible for the guide to conduct this party and for the storing in the trenches. The Train for loading up these stores at the Divisional Dump /- during the day and sending forward.

(contd.)

Date.	Party.	O.O.R.	Rendezvous.	Hour.	Work.	Route.	Destination.
19/20	4	200	SUCRERIE.	9.30 p.m.	Carry 720 boxes grenades.	CHEROI TRENCH ROMAN ROAD.	HYDE PARK CORNER. The B.D.S.O. 12th Bde. Dump will be responsible for a guide to meet this party and the D.A.C. for loading on the wagons. These wagons will report to Lieut. FLINT at the Railway Crossing N. of MAILLY MAILLET Station at 6 p.m. where the Divisional Grenade Party will load them.

Lieut.Col.,

A.A. & Q.M.G., 4th Division.

13th June 1916.

SECRET.   4th Div.Q.C./157.

APPENDIX E

4th Div. Train.
4th Div. Artillery.
10th Brigade.
11th Brigade.
12th Brigade.
C.R.E.
A.D.M.S.
Divisional Trench Mortar Officer.
Divisional Trench Railway Officer.
────────────────

The management of the trench tramways has been taken over by Lieut. CARVER, Royal Dublin Fusiliers. This officer will be known as the officer in charge of Divisional tramways. 17 trucks are now available on the track. Tramways will be known as -

a. MAILLY - SUCRERIE Sector. This sector starts at the Divisional Dump and runs South of the SERRE road to SUCRERIE. 5 trucks are kept at the Dump terminus.

b. The ROMAN ROAD Sector. This sector runs from the SUCRERIE up the ROMAN ROAD to VALLADE Trench.

c. SERRE ROAD Sector. This sector runs from the SUCRERIE South of the SERRE ROAD to within a short
distance of the VALLADE trench.

11 trucks are allotted to the ROMAN ROAD and SERRE road sectors, which are now connected with a switch.

There is, therefore, direct communication from the Divisional Dump to VALLADE Trench.

Units wishing to use these tramways will apply direct to Lieut. Carver, Officer in charge of Divisional Tramways, Town Commandant's Office, MAILLY MAILLET, 24 hours before the time the trucks will be required. Units will provide their own trolly men, and the Officer in charge Divisional Tramways will detail a member of his staff who will be responsible for the running of the line. All trucks must be returned to the siding from which they are taken.

When indenting for the tramways, units will state the hour and place the trucks are required, destination, and the probable hour of completion. The hours allotted to units

must

2.

not be exceeded.   Ammunition will have preference to other stores.   On Z day the line has been placed at the disposal of the A.D.M.S. until 8 p.m. and after if not required for stores.

These regulations come into force from 12 noon June 24th.

[signature]

Lieut.Colonel,
A.A. & Q.M.G., 4th Division.

24/6/16.

APPENDIX F

4th. Div. Q.C. 166/2.

10th Brigade.
11th Brigade.
12th Brigade.
4th Div. Artillery.
4th Div. Engineers.
A.D.M.S.
4th Div. Train.
A.D.V.S.
21st West Yorks.

WATER.

Reference to C.E. No. W.T./774 dated 7/6/16, issued on 27/6/16 to all units.

Para. 3. The proposed situation of the 3 sets of 3 2,000 gallon tanks therein mentioned will be as follows :-

 (a) BEAUMONT - HAMEL VALLEY.

Map reference.

Pt. Q.5.c.2.8.
" Q.11.b.3.3.
" Q.19.c.3.3.

 (b) GRANDCOURT VALLEY.

Pt. K.35.b.2.9.
" K.36.a.9.4.
" L.31.c.5.7.

All water carts should be provided with canvas buckets for filling purposes in the case of the pumps failing.

These points should be marked on maps carried by all Officers.

W.P.H.HILL, Lieut-Col:
A.A. & Q.M.G., 4th Division.

28/6/16.

4th DW Q C 166

VIII Corps No. Q.S.44

The following to be substituted for entry on page 3

WATER SUPPLY REPORT VIII CORPS.

Locality.	Sources from which Water is obtained.	State of work.	Supply in Gallons per diem.	Stand pipes.	Horse troughs.	Remarks.
LOUVENCOURT.	1 power pump on new well.	to be completed 28-6-16.	16,000	-	800	Horse trough on track (O.5.a.4.2.

COPY.

C.E. No.W.T./774.

FORWARD PUMPING SCHEME

This consists of two Advanced Pumping Stations:-

    (a) At HEBUTERNE.

    (b) At SUCRERIE (MAILLY) K.33.c.0.5. which pump to tanks near the ROMAN ROAD trench:-

    (a) Near the junction with WATLING STREET.

    (b) At ELLES SQUARE.

2. The SUCRERIE scheme is to be reinforced by a pumping station at the DELL (J.16.b.38) with a pipe line to the ELLES SQUARE TANKS.

3. From these tanks the water runs by gravitation to two main forward pipe lines:-

    (a) BEAUMONT-HAMEL VALLEY.

    (b) GRANDCOURT VALLEY.

There are to be three sets of canvas tanks on each line, each set to consist of 3 2,000 gallon tanks (6,000 gallons). Water Carts are to pump out direct from these tanks. Officer in charge of Advanced Water Supply, Fourth Army, is considering whether small motor pumps should also be placed at these.

The attached sketch shows the pipe lines and proposed positions of these tanks.

The 2nd (Royal Anglesey) Siege Coy., R.E. are detailed for the work of carrying the line forward.

The necessary stores are dumped at BERTRANCOURT, and 4 trestle wagons at a time will be employed to carry pipes etc. forward as required.

(Sd) S.H.J.
for Lieut.,
Chief Engineer, VIIIth Corps.

7/6/16.

WATER SUPPLY REPORT. VIII CORPS AREA.

6-6-16.

Locality.	Sources from which water is obtained.	State of work.	Supply in Gallons per day.	Stand pipes for lorries and carts.	Horse Troughs or Watering places.	REMARKS.
HEBUTERNE.	Wells. 2 power pumps.	Existing.	24,000	1 (carts only)	-	Advanced Pumping Station
SUCRERIE (MAILLY).	Wells. 2 power pumps.	Existing.	30,000	-	-	" " "
MAILLY-COLINCAMPS. Road (P.6.b.7.1.)	SUCRERIE (above)	Existing.	20,000	4	-	Initial Water Point.
MAILLY-MAILLET.	8 Wells. 2 power pumps.	Existing.	30,000	10	To water 1,000 horses an hour.	2 Initial Water Points (4 stand pipes each.)
THE DELL (a) (J.16.b.3.8.)	New well and power pump.	Existing.	20,000	4	-	Initial Water Point.
(b)	New well and power pump.	Existing.	20,000	-	-	Advanced pumping Station.
COLINCAMPS.	Wells.	Existing.	4,000	1 (carts only)	-	Supply supplemented by 2 inch pipe from SUCRERIE (MAILLY) and 2" branch from pipe line (b) THE DELL.
ENGLEBELMER.	4 Wells.	Existing.	3,000	-	-	
SAILLY.	12 Wells.	Existing.	10,000	-	-	
COURCELLES.	6 Wells.	Existing.	3,000 + 8,000*	-	-	* A branch from pipe line (b) The DELL fills canvas tank (8,000 galls) N. corner COURCELLES.
BERTRANCOURT.	9 Wells 2 power pumps.	In hand.	9,000	-	-	(R) = Horses can be watered direct from River AUTHIE at those places.
BEAUSSART.	2 Wells		2,000	-	-	

WATER SUPPLY REPORT. VIII CORPS AREA.

Locality.	Sources from which water is obtained.	State of work.	Supply in Gallons per day.	Stand pipes for lorries and carts.	Horse Troughs or Watering places.	REMARKS.
COIGNEUX.	16 Wells. 1 Power pump.	Existing.	20,000	1	For 200 horses an hour. (R).	
BUS.	10 Wells. 2 Power Pumps.	In hand.	8,000	2 (carts only)	—	
Between COUIN-ST-LEGER (1.12.b.f.4.) with pipe line to BUS-COIGNEUX Road. (J.20.d.5.5.)	New Well and power pump.	Existing.	20,000	8 * Carts. 1 Lorry.	For 1-500 horses an hour.	(* 5 exist - 3 more to be added (across road.
1.31.a.6.9. Pipe line to Cross Roads N.E. of RAINCHEVAL. (O.1.b.0.2.)	New Well and power pump.	Existing	16,000	(carts &) 4 (light lorries)	For 800 horses an hour.	For supplying water carts and horses in ARQUEVES & RAINCHEVAL.
AUTHIE.	Wells (good)	Existing.	30,000			(R)
MARIEUX.	Wells. 2 L & F Pumps.	Existing.	12,000	2	For 800 horses an hour. (R).	
RAINCHEVAL.	Wells.	Existing.	4,000	—	—	
THIEVRES.	Wells.	Existing.	20,000	—	—	(R)

WATER SUPPLY REPORT. VIII CORPS AREA.

Locality.	Sources from which water is obtained.	State of work.	Supply in Gallons per day.	Stand pipes for lorries and carts.	Horse troughs. capacity in horses per hour.	REMARKS.
SARTON.	Wells (good) Hand pumps.	Existing.	10,000	-	800	
BEAUQUESNE.	Wells.	Existing.	5,000	-	-	
ORVILLE.	Wells. 2 power pumps.	Existing.	50,000	3	1,000	
ACHEUX.	Wells. 1 power pump at SUCRERIE.	Existing.	60,000	6	1,500	Approch road to stand-pipes not suitable for lorries, but if necessary 2 lorries can fill at one time.
LOUVENCOURT	Wells. 2 power pumps 1 Persian Wheel) 1 power pump.)	Existing.	14,000	2 (carts only)	250	
COUIN.	Well. 1 power pump.	Existing.	26,000	2	500 (R).	
WARNIMONT.WOOD.	2 Wells. 2 L & F Pumps.	Existing.	4,000	-	-	
VAUCHELLES.	12 Wells. 1 Persian Wheel.	Existing.	15,000	1 (carts only)	500	
AUTHEUVES.	5 Wells. 1 Persian Wheel.	Existing.	4,800	-	-	

4.

WATER SUPPLY REPORT. VIII CORPS AREA.

Locality.	Sources from which water is obtained.	State of work.	Supply in Gallons per day.	Stand Pipes for lorries and carts.	Horse Troughs. Capacity in horses per hour.	REMARKS
AMPLIER.	Wells. 1 Power pump. 1 " "	Existing.) In hand.)	20,000	3	400.	
BEAUVAL.	1 Power pump.	Existing.	5,000	2 (carts only)	300.	
CANDAS.	9 Wells.	Existing.	4,800	"	"	
TERRAMESNIL.	4 Wells.	Existing.	3,000	"	"	
FAMECHON.	Wells. Hand pumps.	Existing.	2,000	"	500.	

14th Division G.S.
July 1916

Appendix "M"

CASUALTIES - 4th DIVISION - 1st to 31st JULY 1916.

	Officers	Other Ranks
Killed	63	652
Wounded	179	3538
Missing	61	2397
Total	303	6587

G.S. 4th Division
July 1916

Appendix "N"   O.O's. 40-47 Inc.

APPENDIX G

SECRET & URGENT.   4th Div.Q.C.189.

ALTERATION IN ADMINISTRATIVE ARRANGEMENTS.

Owing to zero hour being postponed until 48 hours later than was originally intended, the following alterations will be made:-

Rations. 1. The two days' rations issued to troops in the line will be consumed today, 28th, and tomorrow, 29th. Tomorrow, 29th, a further issue of 2 days' rations will be made to units concerned for the numbers required, viz: 2 companies of 3 battalions 11th Brigade and the Artillery with the guns. This will give a complete day's rations in hand for the 1st July, and save the necessity of sending up transport on the night 30th/1st.

2. The rations deducted for reinforcements for consumption on the original Z day, 29th, will be distributed by the Train direct to units this afternoon. No deduction will be made for carrying parties on 29th for consumption on 30th, but this deduction will be made on 1st for consumption 2nd.

3. The extra bread issued by the Division today for breakfast tomorrow will be consumed, but the ration bread issued tomorrow must be saved to make up the equivalent ¼ lb. for breakfast on 1st July.

Assembly. 4. The arrangements for the assembly of carriers and reserves will now be postponed until night 30th/1st.

Storing of Kits. 5. The storing of packs, spare kit, etc., will be postponed at the discretion of units.

Road Control. 6. Traffic Control orders issued will hold good for night 30th/1st.

W.P.H.HILL, Lt.Col.,

28/6/16.   A.A. & Q.M.G., 4th Division.

Distribution:-

10th Brigade.	Lieut. Flint.
11th Brigade.	Lieut. Carver.
12th Brigade.	Town Commdt. BERTRANCOURT.
R.A.	Town Commdt. MAILLY.
R.E.	Town Commdt. BEAUSSART.
A.D.M.S.	D.A.D.O.S.
Train.	A.D.V.S.
21st West Yorks.	Camp Commdt.
G.	A.P.M.

SECRET ~~DIARY~~   Copy No. 15

4th DIVISION - OPERATION ORDER No. 40.

Ref. 1/10,000 Map.   4th July, 1916.

1.   The 31st Division will be relieved tonight (4/5th July) by the 48th Division.

2.   The 4th Division will relieve the 29th Division tonight (4/5th July) in that portion of the line between Q.10.b.2.2 (BLOOMFIELD AVENUE exclusive) and Q.4.d.3.9 (present right of the 4th Division).

3.   10th Infantry Brigade will take over the above portion of the line. Arrangements to be made by G.O.C. 10th Infantry Brigade direct with G.O.C. 86th Brigade (29th Division). 10th Brigade Headquarters will remain in MAILLY-MAILLET.

4.   12th Infantry Brigade will extend its right to the junction of WATLING STREET with our front line. Arrangements for the relief to be made by G.O's C. 10th and 12th Infantry Brigades.

5.   On completion of reliefs boundaries will be as follows:-
Between 29th Division and 10th Brigade.

    Q.10.b.2.2 - BLOOMFIELD AVENUE (exclusive) - BROADWAY (exclusive) - road junction Q.13.b.2.2.

Between 10th and 12th Infantry Brigades.

    Junction of WATLING Street with front line - Q.4.a.9.6 - 5th AVENUE (inclusive to 10th Brigade.)

Between 12th Brigade and 48th Division.

    As at present between 4th Division and ~~29th~~ 31st Division.

6.   All reliefs to be completed tonight by 12 midnight and to be reported to Divisional H.Q.

7.   Artillery arrangements for covering the new portion of the front will be notified later.

                                            W. Matthew
                                            Lieut.-Colonel,
                                    General Staff, 4th Division.

Issued at 4 pm

Copy No. 12

4TH DIVISION OPERATION ORDER NO. 41.

1. 11th Infantry Brigade will relieve 12th Infantry Brigade on night 10/11th July in the Left Sector.

2. On relief, 12th Infantry Brigade will become Divisional Reserve and will be billeted at BERTRANCOURT.

3. Times and routes of reliefs will be arranged between 11th and 12th Infantry Brigades.

    Relief may begin in daylight provided battalions move in small parties.

4. Completion of relief to be reported to Divisional Headquarters.

[signature]

Lieut-Colonel,
General Staff, 4th Division.

8/7/16.

Issued at ....

To :- 10th, 11th and 12th Infantry Brigades.
       4th Division "Q".
       4th Divisional Artillery.
       4th Divisional Engineers.
       A.D.M.S. 4th Division.
       4th Divisional Signal Company.
       48th Division.
       VIIIth Corps.

S E C R E T   COPY No. 13

4th DIVISION - OPERATION ORDER No. 42.

1.   The 12 Infantry Brigade will relieve the 10th Infantry Brigade on the night 17/18th July in the Right Sector.

2.   On relief the 10th Infantry Brigade will become Divisional Reserve and will be billeted at BERTRANCOURT.

3.   Times and routes of reliefs will be arranged between 10th and 12th Infantry Brigades.

        Relief may begin in daylight provided Battalions move in small parties.

4.   Completion of relief to be reported to Divisional Headquarters.

                                            Lieut.-Colonel,
13/7/16.   General Staff, 4th Division.

Issued at 15 pm

Copies to 10th)
          11th) Infantry Brigade
          12th)
          4th Division "Q"
          4th Divisional Artillery
          4th Divisional Engineers
          A.P.M.
          A.D.M.S.
          4th Signal Coy.
          29th Division
          VIII Corps.

SECRET.  Copy No. 15

4th DIVISION - OPERATION ORDER No. 45.

Reference Sheet 57 D 1/40000.   19th July, 1916.

1. 4th Division (less Div. Arty.) will be relieved in its present line by the 12th Division.

2. 4th Div. Arty. will remain in the line for the present.

3. Infantry Brigades of the 4th Division holding trenches will be relieved as follows :-

   11th Inf. Brigade by 36th Inf. Brigade.
   12th Inf. Brigade by 35th Inf. Brigade.

4. 4th Divnl. Hd. Qrs. will remain at BERTRANCOURT.

5. Moves will be carried out in accordance with the attached March Table. A supplementary March Table for remaining units will be issued later.
   Necessary arrangements for relief of battalions in the trenches and in Divnl. Reserve will be made direct between G.Os.C. Brigades concerned.
   Completion of reliefs will be reported to Divnl. Hd.Qrs.

6. All dumped S.A.A. grenades and reserve rations and trench stores will be handed over to 12th Division, receipts being obtained.
   Special instructions will be issued regarding Vermorel Sprayers on charge of 4th Division.
   The mobile reserve of grenades will accompany units.

7. ACKNOWLEDGE.

                                              Lieut.Colonel,
Issued at 11-30 p   General Staff, 4th Divn.

Copies to 10th, 11th, 12th Inf. Brigs.
          4th Div. Arty.
          4th Div. Engrs.
          4th Div. Q.
          4th Div. Sig. Coy.
          A.D.M.S.
          A.P.M.
          12th Division.
          29th Division.
          38th Division.
          8th Corps.

MARCH TABLE TO ACCOMPANY OPERATION ORDER NO.43.

Unit and Date.	From.	To.	Remarks.
20th MAY. 11th Infantry Brigade.	Trenches Left Sector and MAILLY MAILLET.	BUS.	(Relief will take place in daylight under arrangements to be made direct between G.Os.C.Brigades concerned.
36th Infantry Brigade.	BUS.	Trenches Left Sector and MAILLY MAILLET.	
10th Infantry Brigade.	BERTRANCOURT.	Brigade H.Q. AUTHIE. BOIS de WARNIMONT.	ditto
35th Infantry Brigade.	BOIS de WARNIMONT.	BERTRANCOURT.	
21st MAY. 12th Infantry Brigade.	Trenches Right Sector and WOOD P.17. H.Q.MAILLY MAILLET.	Brigade H.Q. & 2 Bns. VAUCHELLES. 2 Bns. LOUVENCOURT.	ditto
35th Infantry Brigade.	BERTRANCOURT.	Brigade H.Q.MAILLY MAILLET. Trenches Right Sector and WOOD P.17.	
37th Infantry Brigade.	VAUCHELLES & LOUVENCOURT.	BERTRANCOURT.	

SECRET.   Copy No. 15.

4th DIVISION - OPERATION ORDER NO.44.

20th July, 16.

1. 4th Division Operation Order No. 43 is cancelled.

2. The 4th Division (less 4th Divnl. Arty.) will be relieved in its present line by 12th Division and will move back to the area at present occupied by the 25th Division.

3. Moves will take place as shown on the attached table.

4. Orders regarding the move of remaining units will be issued later.

G.O.C. 12th Division will take over command of the line from G.O.C. 4th Division at 9 a.m. on the 22nd instant.

5. H.Q. 4th Div. will close at BERTRANCOURT at 10 a.m. 22nd July, and will reopen at BEAUVAL at the same hour.

Issued at 11 a.m.   Sgd. W.H.Bartholomew. Lt.Col.

                                 General Staff, 4th Division.

Copies to 10th, 11th, 12th Inf. Brigs.
          4th Div. Arty.
          4th Div. Engrs.
          4th Div. Q.
          4th Sig. Co.
          A.D.M.S.
          A.P.M.
          12th Divn.
          29th Divn.
          38th Divn.
          8th Corps.
          War Diary.

MARCH TABLE TO ACCOMPANY 4th DIVISION OPERATION ORDER NO. 44.

UNIT AND DATE.	FROM	TO	Time of starting	ROUTE
20th July.				
10th Inf. Brig.	BERTRANCOURT	BEAUVAL	2 p.m.	LOUVENCOURT–MARIEUX–BEAUQUESNE.
35th Brigade.	WARNIMONT WOOD	BERTRANCOURT	2.45 p.m.	BUS.
7th Brigade.	BEAUVAL	WARNIMONT WOOD	2 p.m.	HULEUX–TERRAMESNIL–SARTON–THIEVRES–AUTHIE.
36th Brigade.	BUS	Trenches Left Sector.		Will take place during daylight under arrangements to be made direct between G.Os.C. Brigades
11th Brigade.	Trenches Left Sector.	BUS		
11th Fd. Ambce.	VAUCHELLES	BEAUVAL		
21st July.				
10th Brigade.	BUS	BEAUVAL	10 a.m.	LOUVENCOURT–MARIEUX–BEAUQUESNE.
74th Brigade.	BEAUVAL	BUS	10 a.m.	HULEUX–TERRAMESNIL–SARTON–THIEVRES–AUTHIE.
35th Brigade.	BERTRANCOURT	Trenches Right Sector.		Will take place during daylight under arrangements to be made direct between G.Os.C. Brigades.
12th Brigade.	Trenches Right Sector.	LOUVENCOURT–VAUCHELLES.		
37th Brigade.	LOUVENCOURT & VAUCHELLES.	BERTRANCOURT.		
22nd July.				
75th Brigade.	AMPLIER	LOUVENCOURT & VAUCHELLES	10 a.m.	ORVILLE–THIEVRES–AUTHIE.
12th Brigade.	LOUVENCOURT & VAUCHELLES.	AMPLIER	10 a.m.	SARTON.

ADDEMDUM to 4th DIVISION OPERATION ORDER NO: 44

Reference 4th Divn Operation Order No: 44, the following moves additional to those shewn in the table issued with the above order will take place.

<u>21st W.Yorks.Regt</u> (Pioneers.

From BEAUSSART to BUS starting 10.30 a.m. 21st July.

<u>10th Fd Amb.</u>

LOUVENCOURT to BEAUVAL 8.30 a.m. via VAUCHELLES, - " -
MARIEUX, BEAUQUESNE, TERRAMESNIL.

<u>12th Fd Amb.</u>

BERTRANCOURT to BUS. Not to move before 11 a.m. - " -

<u>1/Renfrew Fd Coy.R.E.</u>

P.6.a.3.2 to BERTRANCOURT starting at 7.30 a.m. - " -

<u>1/Durham Fd Coy.R.E.</u>

J.32.central to BUS, starting at 8.30 a.m. - " -

Lieut: Colonel.
General Staff., 4th Divn.

Copies to :-

10th.11th.12th Inf. Bde.
4th Div Arty.
  -:- Engineers.
  -:- " Q "
  -:- Signal Coy.
A.D.M.S.
A.P.M.
12th Divn.
29th Divn.
38th Divn.
8th Corps.
21 West Yorks.

SECRET.   Copy No. 15.

4th DIVISION - OPERATION ORDER NO. 45.

21st July, 1916.

Ref. Sheet 11 LENS 1/100000.

    Moves will be carried out in accordance with the attached March Table.

Issued at 12 noon.

Sgd. W.B.Somerville. Major,
General Staff, 4th Division.

Copies to 10th, 11th, 12th Brigades.
          4th Div. Arty.
          4th Div. Engrs.
          4th Div. Q.
          4th Div. Sig. Co.
          A.D.M.S.
          A.P.M.
          8th Corps.
          12th Division.
          29th Division.
          38th Division.
          War Diary.
          Train.

MARCH TABLE - TO ACCOMPANY 4th DIVISION OPERATION ORDER NO. 45.

UNIT AND DATE.	FROM	TO	HOUR OF START	ROUTE	REMARKS.
22nd July.					
12th Brigade.	LOUVENCOURT and VAUCHELLES.	AUTHIEULE&	7 a.m.	MARIEUX-SARTON-Road S. of river to cross roads 400 yds. S. of AUTHIEULE Church.	By battalions at 5 minutes interval.
9th Fd.Co. R.E.	BUS	BEAUVAL	7.45 a.m.	LOUVENCOURT-MARIEUX-BEAUQUESNE.	
Renfrew Fd.Co.	BERTRANCOURT	AMPLIER	8 a.m.	LOUVENCOURT-MARIEUX-SARTON- S. of river to road junction 400 yds. S. of R in AMPLIER.	
rham Fd. Co.	BUS	AMPLIER	8 a.m.	-- do --	
12th Fd.Ambce.	BUS	ORVILLE	9 a.m.	LOUVENCOURT-MARIEUX-SARTON.	
H.Q.4th Division.	BERTRANCOURT	BEAUVAL	9.30 a.m.	LOUVENCOURT-MARIEUX-BEAUQUESNE.	

Copy No: 15

4th DIVISION OPERATION ORDER N0: 46

Reference Sheet HAZEBROUCK 5A 1/100,000
Sheet 28.N.W. 1/20,000

23rd July 1916.

1.   The Division will take over the line of trenches at present held by the Guards Division.

2.   10th Infantry Brigade will relieve the 1st Guards Brigade in the Right sector.
        11th Infantry Brigade will relieve the 3rd Guards Brigade in the Left sector.
        12th Infantry Brigade will relieve the 2nd Guards Brigade in Divisional Reserve.
        Reliefs will be carried out as shewn in attached appendix.
        A table of movement giving routes and times will be issued later.

3.   Relief of Artillery will be arranged between G.O's.C. R.A. 4th Division and Guards Division and will commence on night 28/29th.
        The relief will be completed on night 29th/30th.

4.   Reliefs of Field Coys R.E and Pioneer Battalions will be arranged between U.R.E's 4th Division and Guards Division in accordance with Appendix 1.

5.   Reliefs of Field Ambulances will be arranged between A.D's.M.S. 4th Division and Guards Division.

6.   Arrangements for relief of units not mentioned in this order will be made between Administrative Staffs of 4th and Guards Division.

7.   Brigades will take over Defence Schemes and Secret Maps from Guards Brigades.

8.   All trench stores, dumped S.A.A and grenades will be taken over by relieving units.
        Lists will be sent to Divisional Headquarters.

9.   G.O.C. 4th Division will take over command of line at 4 p.m. on July 27th. Completion of reliefs to be reported to Divisional H.Qrs.

10.   ACKNOWLEDGE.

                      Sd/ W.H.B.BARTHOLOMEW. Lieut:Colonel

Issued at 10 p.m.   General Staff., 4th Division.

Copies to :-   10th.11th.12th Inf. Bdes.
                4th Div Arty.
                  -:- Engrs.
                  -:- "Q"
                A.D.M.S.
                A.P.M.
                Signals.
                XIVth Corps.
                Guards Division.
                6th Division.
                War Diary.
                File.

TO ACCOMPANY 4th DIVISION OPERATION ORDER NO: 46.

Date	Unit	From	Destination	Remarks.
25th July	A & B Bns 11th Bde) 11th Bde M.G.Coy.) 9th Field Coy. R.E. 1/1 Renfrew Fd Coy.RE 1/1 Durham Fd Coy.R.E	WORMHOUDT 10th Bde area 11th Bde area 12th Bde area	Camp in A.30 POPERINGHE. -:- -:-	Personnel by rail as far as POPERINGHE. advanced parties of 9th and 1/1 Renfrew Fd Coy R.E to CANAL BANK night 25/26th July.
	21st W.Yorks Regt (PIONEERS)	WINNIZEELE	POPERINGHE	Further movements will be notified.
26th July.	11th Bde H.Q.) C & D Bns 11th Bde.) Light T.M.Bty.)	WORMHOUDT	Camp in A.30	Personnel by rail as far as POPERINGHE.
	A & B Bns 11th Bde.	Camp in A.30	CANAL BANK	
	A & B Bns 10th Bde.) 10th Bde M.G.Coy.)	Camps K.L.M.N.	CANAL BANK	Personnel by rail as far as POPERINGHE.
27th July	H.Q. 11th Bde.) A & B Bns 11th Bde.) C & D Bns 11th Bde.)	Camp in A.30 CANAL BANK Camp in A.30	CANAL BANK Trenches Left Sect. CANAL BANK.	
	A & B Bns 10th Bde.) 10th Bde M.G.Coy.) C & D Bns 10th Bde.)	CANAL BANK	Trenches Right Sector.	
	Light T.M.Bty.) 10th Bde H.Qrs.) & B Bns 12th Bde	Camps K.L.M.N. PROVEN HOUTKERQUE HERZEELE area.	CANAL BANK. CANAL BANK. Camps K.L.M.N.	Personnel by rail as far as POPERINGHE. By march route.
	C.& D Bns 12th Bde) 12th Bde M.G.Cy)	- ditto -	Camp in A.30	Personnel by rail as far as POPERINGHE.
28th July	A & B Bns 12th Bde 12th Bde H.Qrs.	Camps K.L.M.N. HOUTKERQUE	Camp in A.30 - ditto -	

-SECRET-

Copy No: 17

4th DIVISION OPERATION ORDER NO: 47.

25th JULY 1916.

1. Reference 4th Division Operation Order No: 46 of July 23rd, Tables of movement are attached.

2. G.O's.C. 10th and 11th Inf. Bdes will take over command of their Sectors from relieved Brigades of Guards Division on the night 27th/28th July.

3. During the relief, the Brigade Commander at PROVEN will command troops of Guards & 4th Division at Camps K L M N, and the Brigade Commander in Camp in A.30 will command troops of Guards & 4th Division in Camps E D O & P.

4. Artillery programme of reliefs, movements of D.A.C and Field Ambulances will be arranged later.

5. Divisional Headquarters will close at COUTHOVE CHATEAU at 4 p.m. on July 27th and re-open at the same hour at SAINT SIXTE.

6. ACKNOWLEDGE.

W.H. Bartholomew
Lieut:Colonel.

Issued to Signals at 11 a.m.   General Staff., 4th Division.

Copies to :-
    10th.11th.12th Inf.Bde.   XIVth Corps.
    4th Div Arty.   Guards Divn.
    -:- Engrs.   6th Divn.
    -:- " Q "   29th Divn.
    -:- Signal Coy.
    A.D.M.S.
    A.P.M.

TO ACCOMPANY 4th DIVN OPERATION ORDER NO: 47.

Date	Unit	From	To	Remarks.
July 25th	A Battn, 11th Bde.	WORMHOUDT	Camp E in A.30. (Sheet 28)	By train to L.6.a.8.8 - thence via POPERINGHE - VLAMERTINGHE road to road junction in G.5.d. - Camp E. All vehicles by road. Transport Lines in G.5.
	B Battn, 11th Bde.	WORMHOUDT	Camp P in A.15.d.	By train to L.6.a.8.8 - thence by SWITCH road through L.5.d. - L.6.a. - G.1.b. - PESELHOEK - Camp P. All vehicles by road. Transport Lines in G.5.
	11th Bde M.G.Coy.	WORMHOUDT	Camp in A.22.d.	By train to L.6.a.3.8 - thence by march route via SWITCH Road - POPERINGHE - ELVERDINGHE Road to A.22.d. All vehicles by road. Transport Lines in G. 5.

Date	Unit	From	To	Remarks
July 26th	11th Bde H.Qrs.	WORMHOUDT	Camp in A.30.	Personnel by rail to L.6.a.8.8 and thence by march route via POPERINGHE
	C & D.Bns 11th Bde Light T.M.Bty.	WORMHOUDT	Camp C) in A.30. Camp D)	Road junction G.5.d.2.1. Transport to march via WATOU-ST JAN TER BIEZEN.

- ENTRAINMENT TABLE -

Train	Accommodation	Depart WORMHOUDT	Arrive L.6.a.8.8
1st Train.	400	7.48 a.m.	9.45 am
2nd Train.	400	7.58 a.m.	9.56 am
3rd Train.	200	8.8 a.m.	10.06 am
4th Train.	200	8.18 am	10.16 am
5th Train.	200	8.28 am	10.26 am
6th Train.	200	8.38 am	10.36 am

Date	Unit	From	To	Remarks
	A & B.Bns 11th Bde	Camp E & Camp P.	Canal Bank.	Move to take place after dark and to be arranged direct with G.O.C. 3rd Guards Brigade.
	11th Bde M.G.Coy.	A.22.d.	Canal Bank & Trenches.	Relieves M.G.Coy in Left Sector. Details to be arranged direct with G.O.C. 3rd Guards Brigade.

Date	Unit	From	To	Remarks
July 26th	A & B Coys 10th Bde.	K. Camp & M. Camp.	Canal Bank.	Personnel by rail to Asylum in H.12.b. Railway time table will be issued evening July 25th. Details of relief to be arranged direct with G.O.C. 1st Guards Brigade.
	10th Bde M.G.Coy	E.12.b.	Canal Bank & Trenches Right Sector.	March at 8 a.m. to Camp in A.30. Route - Main POPERINGHE road to junction with SWITCH road in L.5.d. - SWITCH road to junction with VLAMERTINGHE road in G.3.c. - VLAMERTINGHE road to road junction in G.5.d. - A.30. Company will bivouac in A.30 during day, and march in evening to Canal Bank and trenches. Details of relief to be arranged direct with 1st Guards Brigade.

Date	Unit	From	To	Remarks.
July 27th	H.Q.11th Bde.	Camp in A.30	Canal Bank.	
	A.& B. Bns 11th Bde	Canal Bank.	Trenches Left Sector.	Details of relief to be arranged direct with G.O.C. 3rd Guards Bde.
	C & D. Bns 11th Bde	Camps O & D.	Canal Bank	
	10th Bde H.Q.	PROVEN	Canal Bank	Details of relief to be arranged direct with G.O.C. 3rd Guards Bde.
	A & B. Bns.10th Bde	Canal Bank.	Trenches Right Sector.	
	C & D Bns.10th Bde Light T...Bty.	Camps L & N.	Canal Bank.	Personnel by rail to Asylum in H.12.b. Railway time table will be issued evening July 28th.
	A & B Bns 12th Bde	HOUTKERQUE-HERZEELE area	K & H Camps.	Head of column to pass Eastern end of HOUTKERQUE at 2 p.m. and march via WATOU & ST JAN TER BIZEN.
	C & D Bns.12th Bde	- ditto -	E & P. Camps.	To move by Bus - time to be notified.
	12th Bde M.G.Coy.	- ditto -	A.22.d.(camp)	By march route to follow A and B Bns. to ST. JAN TER BIZEN - thence via SWITCH Road to junction with POPERINGHE-ELVERDINGHE Road in G.3.a

Date	Unit	From	To	Remarks
July 28th	A & B.Bns 12th Bde.	K & M. Camps.	Camp in A.30	To be clear of Camps K and M by 9.30 a.m.
	12th Bde H.Qrs.	HOUTKERQUE	Camp in A.30	

Date	Unit	From	To	Remarks
July 28th	4th D.A.C01.	OUDERZEELE area.	A.16. A.31. A.28.	via STEENWOORDE – ABEELE – POPERINGHE SWITCH Road. To arrive Camp by 10 a.m. Column will march with 5 minutes interval between sections.
	1st ½ Batts.	-do-	Wagon Lines	Route as for D.A.C. To arrive at Wagon Lines not later than 3 p.m. 5 minutes interval between Batteries.
Night July 28/29th.	1st ½ Batts.	Wagon Lines.	Gun Positions	
July 29th	2nd ½ Batts.	OUDERZEELE area.	Wagon Lines.	Via STEENWOORDE – ABEELE – POPERINGHE SWITCH Road – to arrive at Wagon lines not later than 10 a.m.
Night July 29/30th	2nd ½ Batts.	Wagon Lines.	Gun Positions	

War Diary

-SECRET-

4th Division No. OGG/19/4

1. With reference to 4th Division Operation Order No: 47, para 4, Artillery relief will be carried out in accordance with the attached movement table.

2. G.O.C, 4th Divnl Arty will take over responsibility for Artillery defence of the Line at 9 a.m. on 30th instant.

27th July 1916. W.H.BARTHOLOMEW. Lieut:Colonel.
                                  General Staff., 4th Division.

Copies to :-

    10th.11th.12th Inf.Bde.
    4th Div Arty.
      -:-   Engrs.
      -:-   Q
      -:-   Signal Coy.
    A.D.M.S.
    A.P.M.
    Guards Division.
    6th Division.
    20th Division.
    XIVth Corps.

www.ingramcontent.com/pod-product-compliance
Lightning Source LLC
Chambersburg PA
CBHW081431300426
44108CB00016BA/2345